Northern Saskatchewan
CANOE
TRIPS

Northern Saskatchewan
CANOE
TRIPS

A Guide to Fifteen Wilderness Rivers

Laurel Archer

The BOSTON
MILLS PRESS

A BOSTON MILLS PRESS BOOK

Published by Boston Mills Press, 2003
Copyright © 2003 Laurel Archer

First printing, 2003

Cataloguing in Publication Data

Archer, Laurel, 1964-
Northern Saskatchewan canoe trips : a guide to fifteen
wilderness rivers / by Laurel Archer.

Includes index.
ISBN 1-55046-369-1

1. Canoes and canoeing—Saskatchewan, Northern.
2. Saskatchewan, Northern—Description and travel. I. Title.

GV783.A73 2003   797.1'22'097124   C2002-901688-6

Publisher Cataloging-in-Publication Data (U.S.) is available.

Published in 2003 by
BOSTON MILLS PRESS
132 Main Street
Erin, Ontario N0B 1T0
Tel 519-833-2407
Fax 519-833-2195
e-mail books@bostonmillspress.com
www.bostonmillspress.com

IN CANADA:
Distributed by Firefly Books Ltd.
3680 Victoria Park Avenue
Toronto, Ontario M2H 3K1

IN THE UNITED STATES:
Distributed by Firefly Books (U.S.) Inc.
P.O. Box 1338, Ellicott Station
Buffalo, New York 14205

Cover design by Gillian Stead
Interior design and map drawings by Mary Firth
Photographs by Laurel Archer
Photographs by Sheila Archer: Sheila Archer © CARCC. No repro-
duction by any means without the written permission of CARCC.
Printed and bound in Canada by Friesens, Altona, Manitoba

*The publisher acknowledges the financial support of the Government of Canada through the Book Publishing Industry
Development Program for its publishing efforts.*

CONTENTS

ACKNOWLEDGMENTS

I want to thank my sister, Sheila Archer, for without her help I might never have paddled in northern Saskatchewan at all, much less have written this book. She and her husband, Craig Nielsen, took me canoeing in the North for the first time. She also introduced me to Ric Driediger, who gave me a job at Churchill River Canoe Outfitters (CRCO). Without Sheila, I also probably wouldn't have met my husband, Brad Koop, to whom she traded me for a pair of warm boots on the Seal River in northern Manitoba long before I even knew he existed. And finally, not only has she always shared her extensive knowledge of canoeing and wilderness tripping with me, but in order to help me with this guidebook she shared her unbeatable trip notes and photos of some of the rivers in this book. I am forever grateful.

I also want to thank Brad, my partner of choice in the wilderness and the love of my life. He taught me how to make the northern wilderness my home, and he made it possible for me to write this book in many, many ways, including paddling thousands of kilometres with me and flying all over the North. I love you, Fuddle.

As well, thanks to Kevin Shultz for being my mentor when I was a novice canoe guide and instructor. He showed me how to make paddling and working with a group look easy.

A number of other people have also helped make this book possible, and in no particular order I want to acknowledge their assistance: Felicia Daunt; May Partridge; Craig Nielsen; Dave Koop; Ric Driediger; Kathryn Mulders; Sid Robinson; Alex Robertson; Bill Jeffrey; Dave Bober; Doug Chisholm; Adrian Johnston; Judy Studer; Denise D'Amour; Wayne Roach at CHRS; Bob Herbison, Wayne Schick, Gord Gray, and John Leonard at SERM; and the staff at Minor Bay Lodge and Camps on Wollaston Lake, the Map and Photo Distribution Centre in Regina, and the Comox Valley Library; Dalvin Euteneier at SaskWater and Karl Runion at Environment Alberta.

My gratitude to Saskatchewan Environmental Resource Management for giving me permission to use the "Ecoregions of Saskatchewan" map and to the Canadian Recreational Canoe Association for giving me permission to use their Canoeists Code of Ethics. Thank you to my companions on the Fond du Lac and Porcupine Rivers in 2001 for sharing your trips with me. Thank you to all the people who shared their lives and histories with me as I travelled through their homelands. I hope we meet again.

Last, but not least, I toast the Universe for the wild rivers, especially for the Churchill — the river that taught me what it means to be free.

INTRODUCTION

ABOUT THIS BOOK

This guidebook is the product of over 15 years of canoeing and kayaking on many rivers all over the world and countless days on the waterways of northern Saskatchewan. I lived in this region from 1988 to 2000, residing in Missinipe, Buffalo Narrows and La Ronge. I moved to the North to work as a canoe guide and instructor in this prime wilderness canoe-tripping country, and met my life's partner there. Brad and I spent an average of 50 days each summer paddling, camping and fishing during those years.

I will never forget how magical it was. But sometimes things happen that make you decide to move on. In late May 1999, we lost our log home and all our belongings in a forest fire that burned out of control just north of La Ronge. So in the summer of 2000 we moved to Vancouver Island to experience the adventures the West Coast had to offer. I started writing full-time, and it was then that I decided to spend another summer in what I still consider the most amazing place on Earth. So in 2001, I spent 68 days on the river, paddling the waterways that had changed the course of my life so many years before and gathering the information I needed to finish this comprehensive guidebook.

I wrote this book because I love to write about the North and canoeing, and I believe that we will lose our wild places if they are not part of people's lives. It is our experience of the wilderness that will encourage us to work to preserve it. I also think some wild places are overused and travelled in inappropriate ways and that others are best left unvisited. These places should be protected too. That is an understanding that comes with living in the true wilderness, even if just for a few days. It is my hope that this book will not only assist canoeists on their river travels and foster appreciation for northern Saskatchewan's wilderness and waterways, but it will also translate into better care for them.

I haven't included all the navigable rivers in northern Saskatchewan by any means. The reason I chose the canoe trips I did was because of my familiarity with them, the quality or uniqueness of the experience available, their popularity with wilderness canoe trippers, or the fact that they are less commonly travelled. A good cross-section of the types of rivers that are found in northern Saskatchewan is represented in the selections.

Finally, this is not a "how to" book; it is a guidebook for paddlers. There are many other resources available to help canoeists develop their paddling and tripping skills, including courses, books and videos. Canoe tripping in northern Saskatchewan definitely requires a certain level of bushcraft and paddling skill, and a lot of good judgment, but this book is not about how to develop those skills. It is designed to provide canoeists with the information they require in order to choose a river trip appropriate to their skill level and special interests. Canoeists can measure their skill level and the kind of river they wish to paddle against the information provided in the book, instead of measuring it against the river when it is too late to make another choice. The detailed Trip Notes are designed only to provide information about what is around the next corner, not to help canoeists wanting to run rivers they do not have the skill to run.

∗∗ DISCLAIMER ∗∗

The information in this guidebook is intended only to assist canoeists in choosing and navigating a river suitable to their skill and fitness level and their interests; I assume no responsibility for the use of this guidebook. Water levels vary and rivers are not static entities. Adverse weather and local conditions can alter a canoe trip dramatically, making it more physically challenging, longer than expected, or demanding of a higher level of paddling and wilderness skills. Canoeists are responsible for their own safety and use of good judgment, and I encourage you to err on the side of caution and be constantly on the lookout for hazards.

ABOUT CANOEING IN NORTHERN SASKATCHEWAN

Northern Saskatchewan is an international wilderness canoe-tripping destination, and it is a completely different land than the one people often associate with Saskatchewan — the wide-ranging prairie of the south. Saskatchewan means "the river that flows swiftly," It is an apt name for this province, especially the northern region, which was travelled by canoe for thousands of years, long before the fur trade. Vast lakes, streams rushing through rocky banks, forests of black spruce with feather moss carpets, tamarack bogs and granite cliffs made overland travel difficult in many places. The canoe was the most efficient way to move north, south, east or west.

Northern Saskatchewan is a rugged, remote, sparsely populated area. The northern regions referred to in this book account for 40 percent of the total area of Saskatchewan, yet its people are only 1 percent of the total population of the province. That's one person per 23 square kilometres! Solitude, scenery, whitewater thrills, culture, history, and tourist services can all be found in northern Saskatchewan — it has the best of everything under the sun (or the Northern Lights) that anyone could want in wilderness canoeing.

The First People

Northern Saskatchewan is a wilderness with a rich history. It has been home to First Nations people for thousands of years; Dene, Woods Cree and Metis people live in the communities that dot the major lakes and rivers. They once travelled these bodies of water to move to their seasonal settlements and foraging and hunting grounds, and they are still the living highways that provide sustenance.

Each culture has its own language, history and unique adaptations to the northern environment. Traditionally, the Dene people's main source of food and materials was the barren ground caribou. Dene life was centred on the caribou migrations, and they moved north and south seasonally to their hunting camps. They often travelled overland, as birch for making canoes was scarce in their Far North home. During the fur-trading era, they predominantly used the waterways running north and south that took them to and from the barren grounds or the Churchill River. Trappers also used the east-west routes in between the Cree and Wollaston Lake regions. The Dene First Nations' current homelands are in the far northern areas of Saskatchewan around Lake Athabasca and Black Lake, the western part of the Upper Churchill and north and south of there, and the Wollaston Lake area.

The Cree also moved seasonally, relying on the resources of the boreal forest. The canoe was their primary means of travel, and the routes they paddled were extensive. The Cree were the authors of the pictographs found throughout the North, and the sites indicate important canoe routes in prehistory. Prior to contact between the Native people and the Europeans, Cree territory is thought to have extended as far north as Lake Athabasca in the west, Cree Lake in the central region, and the north end of Reindeer Lake in the east. The Cree First Nations' current homelands are generally south of the Churchill in the west, and in the areas north and south of the Churchill beginning around Pinehouse Lake to the mid-Reindeer Lake region.

The extent of change the fur trade had on traditional Dene and Cree lifestyles and territories was significant. With the smallpox epidemic of 1781 decimating the Cree population in northern Saskatchewan and the adaptation of a significant number of Dene to the fur-trading economy, traditional travelling patterns changed. Areas with high yields of furs and viable canoe routes gained importance. And although the two cultures usually gave each other wide berth, they both gathered in Ile-à-la-Crosse, the most important trading centre in fur-trade history.

Communities grew at the trading posts, with more and more traders and voyageurs coming to the Northwest, and the Metis population became a strong force in northern Saskatchewan. These children of "country marriages" became the backbone of the fur trade, working as traders, trappers and guides. Where major fur-trading houses such as Cumberland House, Ile-à-la-Crosse, and Stony Rapids existed, there are still thriving Metis communities.

Many of the canoe trips outlined in this book follow traditional First Nations' travel routes, and rock paintings signal the way. Some follow the voyageur and explorer routes, and some pass through areas more lightly travelled by all.

Early Exploration and Fur Trade

Louis Primeau, the Frobishers, the Henrys, Samuel Hearne, Peter Pond, Alexander Mackenzie, David Thompson, Simon Fraser, John Franklin — all the famous fur traders and explorers travelled northern Saskatchewan's rivers in their journeys. The Sturgeon-weir joins the Saskatchewan River to the Churchill River and was key to the fur traders accessing the rich furs of the Athabasca Basin. At its outflow, Cumberland House, established in 1774, was the first non-First Nations settlement in Saskatchewan, and it boasts the oldest schoolhouse in the province. Over a short portage at the headwaters of the Weir, the Churchill River, the great highway of northern Saskatchewan, opened up huge possibilities for travel to the Northwest. The Methy Portage, a famous 20-km (12 mi) portage, linked the Churchill and Clearwater Rivers on the northern fur-trading route to the Mackenzie Basin. First Nations groups and trappers travelled these and many other lesser-known rivers on their way to the trading posts that began to spring up all over.

The fur traders and explorers came, fast and furious, to northern Saskatchewan, followed by the missionaries. The oldest church in Saskatchewan is found on the Churchill at Stanley Mission, and is still used by that First Nations community today.

The Environment

In northern Saskatchewan there are shallow technical rivers with granite or sandstone ledges, big-water rivers with huge green waves, tiny tributaries hosting Arctic grayling, and vast, cold, clear lakes. There aren't many places in the world where it is safe to drink the water from the source without boiling, filtering or treating it, but in northern Saskatchewan you often can, unless you are in the vicinity of a community. The boreal forest predominates in northern Saskatchewan, and a large part of it can be found on the Precambrian Shield, the oldest land mass on Earth. The Shield is an incredibly resource-rich environment. Lichen-covered outcroppings and deep lakes accent the forested landscape. The sandy soils host black spruce and jack pine, while the clay soils in the eastern region support spruce and aspen. There are many low-lying peatlands scattered with tamarack trees. Almost 40 percent of this region is water, and flying in a floatplane above it you may not recognize the Earth below you; it appears instead to be a vast surface of blue, with green islands and yellow muskegs joining together here and there.

Farther north, the work of the glaciers is the dominant art form. The Athabasca Sand Dunes — the most northerly active sand dunes in the world — are home to plant life found nowhere else on the planet. Some of the dunes reach up to 35 m in height, and others come right to the shores of Lake Athabasca, the largest lake in the province. A provincial park was created to protect this unique area. It is a photographer's dream.

In the Far North, beyond Lake Athabasca, the taiga begins. The taiga is a transitional subarctic area between the boreal forest and the tundra. In the west you find a rocky, almost mountainous region where the trees are small and sparse. Farther east there is more sand and glacial till covering the bedrock, giving it a somewhat gentler appearance.

In every ecoregion of northern Saskatchewan, canoeists can observe a variety of wildlife. Most areas are home to moose, black bears, timber wolves, otters and beavers, and fish-eating birds such as eagles and osprey. In some places, mule and white-tailed deer, elk, caribou and Arctic foxes are found. Fish are plentiful, the most common species being the northern pike, walleye, whitefish, Arctic grayling and lake trout.

Forest fires are a common occurrence in northern Saskatchewan. They are a natural part of the regeneration process. Areas of old burn provide excellent habitat for wildlife, but they can sometimes change a river trip dramatically. Familiar portages and campsites can be lost, as well as features of natural beauty.

The long days and short nights of these high latitudes make for many extra hours of enjoyment off the river, swimming, fishing, exploring, hiking and sitting around camp telling stories. Observing the Northern Lights is more difficult, though. They are not as frequently seen in the summer, and by the time it is dark enough and they really get going it might be 1 A.M.! But the stars that you will see on a clear night while you are waiting will keep you company and boggle your mind. Bring a star chart. There is no better place to find the northern hemisphere's heavenly bodies and constellations.

Climate

Though it is very cold in the winter and the ice does not usually leave the bigger lakes until late May to June in the Far North, summer temperatures are comfortable. The average daytime temperature for June, July and August in the Churchill region is 16°C (61°F). The nighttime average temperature for this period is 9°C (49°F), and it can often be much warmer than that. However, in the Far North, especially in the extreme northeast corner of the province, these temperatures are lower on average by several degrees.

Generally, the summer months are very pleasant, but the thing to remember is that the temperature can fluctuate greatly, and you must be fully prepared for extreme heat or cold and rain. The ecoregions in northern Saskatchewan get most of their precipitation in June, July and August — July having the most rain on average. Now that's not saying much at an average of 7 cm (3 in) per month, but it can pour and get socked in at times. Sometimes the wind can be more of a factor on your trip than temperature or rain. Expect the prevailing winds to be from the west and northwest. My motto is to plan and pack for the worst possible weather and enjoy what you get.

Insects

Given a warm summer and plenty of water around, the insects can be voracious. The North is a silent place where you can hear the rapids you are approaching for several kilometres. Every sound is amplified, so you sometimes will actually hear the insect life all around you. However, don't let the bugs scare you off. Some areas are worse than others. You can't completely escape the blackflies, mosquitoes, no-see-ums (or midges and sandflies), horse and deer flies, or biting houseflies, but you can deal with them. The blackflies are usually at their worst in the early summer, late May to late June. In the Boreal Shield ecozone, where you find the Churchill and its tributaries, once the dragonflies come out in mid-June the population of blackflies begins to go down remarkably. Farther north, the blackflies are around longer. The key is protecting those places where blood is close to surface of your skin. The beggars love to crawl into your clothing and bite there, at your wrists and ankles, and around your hairline, neck and ears. So protecting those areas with a bug net or jacket — clothing that restricts the flies from crawling into it — or using repellent is key.

The mosquitoes can be a real nuisance or not, depending on the year. Their peak season is usually early June to late July, and they are active in the morning and evening and anywhere there is shade, like on the portage trail and under your canoe when it's on your head! Repellent or a bug jacket works well. So does wearing light-coloured clothing and staying away from strong-smelling soaps. They also like heat, as do no-see-ums, the midges and sandflies that take little bites that really get your attention. Their season is about the same as the mosquitoes, and clothing and repellent are the best protection.

When it gets really hot in July you have the deer and horse flies and biting house flies. They are a pain, and take out big chunks, but usually only in the heat of the day. I just hate when they bite the top of my head where my hair parts! A hat and repellent help, but not much else does, except swatting them — hard.

Generally, the later in the season you go on a trip the less the bugs are a problem, and by August the insects really settle down. However, insect repellent is a must on your list no matter which river you choose at what time, and I recommend purchasing a head net or preferably a bug jacket with a hood for trips in the Far North.

Bears

I've spent so much time in the wilderness camping, people often ask me if I'm afraid of bears. Yes, I'm afraid of grizzly and polar bears, but not black bears. I certainly respect them, but normally black bears in northern Saskatchewan will not harm you if you do not threaten them by surprising them or coming between them and their cubs or food cache. However, the more you know about black bears, the better off you will be if you do end up having a bear encounter. *Bear Attacks: Their Causes and Avoidance*, by Steven Herrero, is an excellent resource for learning about bear behaviour.

The goal is to avoid encounters. Key is being alert, paying attention to your surroundings, and taking precautions. Make lots of noise if approaching rapids where a bear can't hear you coming. Keep your distance if you spot a bear, and leave the area. Don't camp near a bear trail or where there is bear sign (droppings, tracks), or where food or garbage has been left (like a shore lunch spot). In camp, pitch your tent away from the cooking area. Keep the area clean of food scraps and throw fish guts and carcasses in deep water away from your camp. Hang your food or store it in bear-proof containers, away from your tents.

WHAT YOU NEED TO KNOW TO GO

The minimum you need to know to attempt even the easiest of these river trips is how to paddle a canoe in a straight line and in current. These are river trips and therefore involve moving water. You must also have a solid understanding of how to read moving water and how rapids are classified. Competency in bushcraft is required, and you must know how to pack for canoe travel and an extended stay in the wilderness. You should also have wilderness survival and emergency first-aid skills. You must be able to read a topographical map, understand the basics of using the Universal Transverse Mercator (UTM) grid system the required 1:50,000 maps are based on, and be competent using a compass to navigate.

To preserve the wilderness values of the rivers, you must know how to practise no-trace camping. Tread lightly: the wilderness is a non-renewable resource. Once it's gone, it's gone. Recognize that you will often be travelling through lands that provide sustenance to the indigenous people of that area. Use the resources of the wilderness as sparingly as possible. Bring what you need with you. If you are going to fish, you must have a valid Saskatchewan angling licence and obey the regulations that are applicable to the region you are travelling in. Be aware that all prehistoric and historic period sites and artifacts in Saskatchewan are protected by a law, the Heritage Property Act, and should not be collected or in any way disturbed.

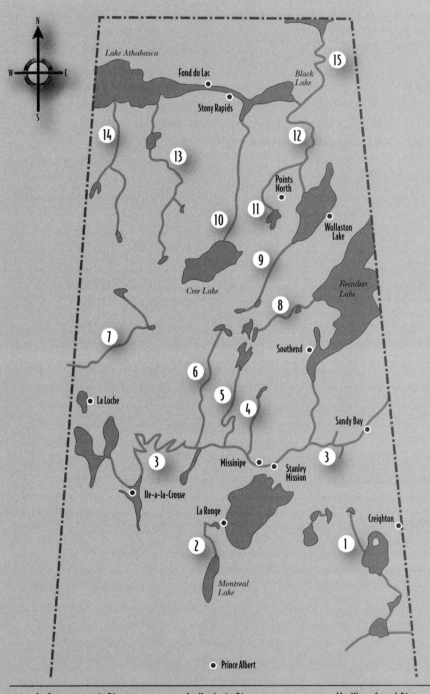

1 Sturgeon-weir River	6 Haultain River	11 Waterfound River
2 Montreal River	7 Clearwater River	12 Fond du Lac River
3 Churchill River	8 Wathaman River	13 MacFarlane River
4 Paull River	9 Geikie River	14 William River
5 Foster River	10 Cree River	15 Porcupine River

HOW TO USE THIS GUIDEBOOK

FINDING THE RIVER FOR YOU

This guidebook is meant to provide you with enough information so that you can choose a wilderness river trip that will suit your skill level and your interests. Each chapter introduces a river with a short summary of its attractions and a map of its location. Then each trip is described with reference to the following: length, required topographic maps, travel and shuttle arrangements, when to go, difficulty level, character of the river and region, historical importance of the river, level of solitude to expect, wildlife-viewing potential, fishing, special equipment considerations, and finally, map coordinates of the location and nature of rapids, hazards, campsites and special attractions.

This guidebook is not meant to be anything more that a paddler's guide to the river trips. It is not a historical, anthropological, geological or zoological treatise, and references for interesting reading and resources for finding out more about the river and the region are provided throughout each trip description.

LOCATING THE RIVERS

Each river trip is outlined on a locator map showing the major landmarks of the region. Use the map on page 12 to see the rivers described in this guidebook.

THE LOGISTICS: LENGTH, MAPS, ACCESS AND WHEN TO GO

The length of the trip in kilometres is given, and in most cases options for shortening or extending the trip are also described. Except for the most difficult trips — ones with many rapids that must be scouted, waded, lined or portaged — you can estimate travelling 20 km a day and having a pretty relaxing time of it. That is, unless you encounter big winds. Where deemed necessary, the minimum number of days for a particular trip will be indicated.

In this section you will also find the required 1:50,000 scale topographical maps for each trip. Maps required for the optional routes are also provided. All 1:50,000 scale maps are listed by index numbers and letter, for example, 74K/10, and all the maps and aerial photographs can be mail ordered from:

Information Services Corporation of Saskatchewan
200, 10 Research Place
Regina, Saskatchewan, Canada
S4P 3V7
Phone: 306-787-2799   Toll free in Canada: 1-866-275-4721
Fax: 306-787-3335
saskmaps@isc-online.ca
www.isc-online.ca

If you don't have a credit card, try one of the Centre for Topographical Information of Natural Resources Canada Regional Distribution Centres (for a list, see http://maps. nrcan. gc.ca/cmo/dealers.html), or try your local map store.

Beware! Many of the rapids and falls (a drop of 1 m, or 3 ft or more) are not marked on these maps, or are improperly marked. I suggest you use the Trip Notes in this book to mark in the features missing from the originals. Beyond helping you plan your paddling days, marking your map beforehand makes it easier to prepare for what's coming up while you are on the river.

Recommendations on the best time to paddle each of the rivers are provided, but they are only recommendations. Water levels may fluctuate significantly month by month and year by year, depending on precipitation. In northern Saskatchewan, water levels usually reach their peak with spring runoff. Only some of the rivers described in this guidebook have active water-gauging stations on them. For those rivers (which are indicated in the trip descriptions), current and average yearly and monthly mean water flows can be obtained by contacting SaskWater at 306-694-3966, or by fax at 306-694-3944. Forecasts for water flows are limited to the Reindeer and Churchill Rivers. For limited online information see the SaskWater website at www.saskwater.com.

In 1995, many of the province's data-collection stations were closed down due to federal cuts. However, the Canoe Saskatchewan website, www.lights.com/waterways/, can provide you with average yearly and monthly mean water flows for various rivers from before 1995. At the least, checking out this site will give you some idea of how much and when the water levels fluctuate in some of the rivers. For the rivers without historical or current water-flow data, you will have to rely on information collected from local sources. Contacts for checking local water levels are given for all rivers, for example, Saskatchewan Environment and Resource Management (SERM) field offices, local outfitters or aviation companies located in the area. I suggest you check with a local body before setting out on any river, regardless of what the monthly mean charts show or the forecasts say. You will want to check forest-fire conditions as well as water levels.

Be prepared to change your plans. If the water level is very high or very low, you may want to choose a different trip. Some rivers become unnavigable at low water or very dangerous at high water, or you may have to plan for more time on the river to deal with the unusual conditions. Current water-flow information can be helpful for making equipment choices. You may need to take a Royalex canoe if the water is low. If it is high, you may want to take a spray cover — if you have the skill to run rapids that require the use of spray covers.

Transportation options for the canoe trip's start and end points are given. Some trips can be accessed by road, while some require chartering a floatplane. Contacts for information on transportation and canoe and equipment rentals are listed in the Directory of Services.

I seriously advise you not to leave your vehicle(s) unattended while you are out on a trip. If left in picnic areas, parks, unserviced campgrounds, or on the roadside overnight, they are targets for vandalism and theft. The communities you fly out from or put in at will have fenced compounds or parking areas for tourists, especially at aviation companies, outfitters, hotels and the like. For remote road-accessible put-ins you may want to make special shuttle arrangements with long-distance taxi services in the area. These are also listed in the Directory of Services.

DIFFICULTY RATINGS: IS THIS TRIP FOR YOU?

The trips are rated according to their comparative level of difficulty, much like ski runs are graded so that skiers can choose the run that best matches their skill levels and terrain preferences. The rating system is based on the level of whitewater that canoeists will encounter, that is, what class of rapids to expect (see the International Scale of Rapid Classification at page 236); the amount of whitewater to expect (the quantity of rapids and their nature — a few, sporadic rapids versus continuous sections); the number of mandatory portages; the existence and condition of portages; and the number and type of special hazards, including large lake crossings, sweepers and undercuts. The length and isolation of the river trip is also factored in.

The ratings are generalizations, but details on the difficulty of the river are given following the star rating. The rating system can give you a fair idea of what to expect; however, not all factors may be relevant to each river and at all times, as high water or low water can significantly increase or decrease the difficulty of some river trips. Skills levels are recommended so that you are aware of what skill and knowledge base is required to navigate the river in a reasonable amount of time and with a reasonable amount of safety. However, safety is your responsibility, and it is up to each canoeist to judge his or her own ability to deal with what a particular trip requires in terms of skill and physical stamina.

The following skill-level definitions are used in rating the difficulty of the rivers:

Beginner
- can run Class 1 with another beginner
- runs Class 2 only with an intermediate partner
- scouts everything
- has very little or no river tripping experience, but has done lake tripping

Intermediate
- can read and run Class 2
- scouts some Class 2+ and all Class 3
- may run short Class 3s empty, but usually walks around them
- has taken a whitewater course and has several seasons of tripping experience

Advanced
- can read and run Class 2+
- runs Class 3 with gear
- has taken certification courses in tandem and solo whitewater paddling
- has about five seasons of tripping experience
- extensive whitewater experience, plus whitewater rescue skills

Exceptional
- can read and run Class 3 and perform precision manoeuvres in this level of water, including surfing, jet ferries, back ferries and eddy turns
- paddles Class 4 comfortably with a skirt when tandem or in a solo playboat
- has Instructor certification in moving water, plus extensive tripping experience

The following comparative rating system is applied to the rivers:

* **Easiest**
- few rapids
- primarily Class 1, with some Class 2
- no or few mandatory portages
- portages around rapids are in good condition
- some lining or wading may be required
- few hazards, easily avoided with few or no large lake crossings
- suitable for the beginner river-tripping canoeist who is comfortable in moving water and has some experience lining

** **Average**
- rapids every day
- primarily Class 1 and 2, with some Class 3
- few mandatory portages
- portages in fair to good condition

- lining and wading may be required
- few hazards with few large lake crossings
- suitable for the intermediate canoeist comfortable in Class 1 and 2 rapids, who is able to front ferry and eddy in and out of current, and has lining experience
- suitable for guided beginners

✷✷✷ Difficult
- steady rapids throughout the day and or sections of continuous rapids
- primarily Class 1 to 2+, including rapids that must be read on the run
- some Class 3 rapids
- lining and wading are required
- mandatory portages in good to poor condition, with some non-existent, so bushwhacking is required
- a number of hazards, either undercuts, sweepers, or open lake crossings
- often a remote fly-in, fly-out river without road access or sources from emergency help
- suitable for the advanced canoeist comfortable in Class 2 and 3 rapids with strong front- and back-ferrying skills and good river-reading skills, including the ability to read rapids while running them
- suitable for guided intermediates
- physical stamina is required

✷✷✷✷ Most Difficult
- sections of continuous and steady rapids throughout the day, mostly Class 2 to 3, possibly Class 4, which often must be read on the run as there are no portage trails or easy scouting opportunities
- mandatory portages often not marked or non-existent — if there are trails they may be in very poor condition or bushwhacking is required
- usually an isolated fly-in, fly-out river without road access or sources for emergency help
- suitable for advanced and exceptional canoeists with strong front- and back-ferrying skills who are comfortable reading Class 2 and 3 rapids while on the run and have advanced lining and portaging skills
- physical stamina is required

The final piece of information in the difficulty section is the gradient of the river. The elevation drop of the river is shown in metres per kilometre and feet per mile, for example the river drops 1.05 m/km (5.5 ft/m). Also given are details on the reasons for the drop in elevation, so you will know if you are facing numerous rapids or a few large waterfalls. This information will give you a better idea of the nature of the whitewater to expect.

CHARACTER OF THE RIVER AND REGION: RAPIDS, ROCKS AND TREES

The rivers are also described according to type, for example, a shallow, fanning river in the Athabasca Sand Dunes, such as the William, compared to a deep, drop-pool river in the Precambrian Shield, such as the Churchill. The characteristics of the riverbed and environment are also described. You will find out whether a particular river you have been dreaming about is a big-volume, haystack experience in the Shield or a shallow wind through the Athabasca sandstone. For instance, the Clearwater is famous for a variety of different river characteristics, from sandy bottom and swampy shorelines to shallow, small rock rapids, to falls threading through granite gorges. The rivers are also located in the ecozones and

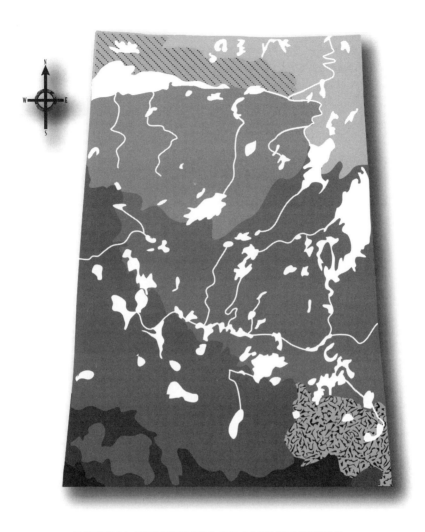

NATURAL ECOREGIONS OF SASKATCHEWAN

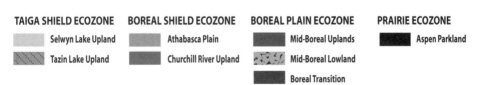

TAIGA SHIELD ECOZONE	BOREAL SHIELD ECOZONE	BOREAL PLAIN ECOZONE	PRAIRIE ECOZONE
Selwyn Lake Upland	Athabasca Plain	Mid-Boreal Uplands	Aspen Parkland
Tazin Lake Upland	Churchill River Upland	Mid-Boreal Lowland	
		Boreal Transition	

ecoregions of northern Saskatchewan they flow through, so you can visualize what the scenery and flora is like along the route.

Three ecozones predominate in northern Saskatchewan, and each one is made up of ecoregions. The following ecozones and ecoregions are the most relevant to describing the environment of the rivers in this guidebook and are listed in order from south to north.

ECOREGION CHART

ECOZONE	ECOREGION	CHARACTERISTICS
BOREAL PLAIN	Mid-Boreal Lowland	◆ flat, low-lying area in east of province ◆ dominated by wetlands and aspen ◆ in northern areas some sandy glacial till deposits and limestone outcrops ◆ peatlands with tamarack, black spruce
	Mid-Boreal Upland	◆ area of western and central Saskatchewan just south of the Precambrian Shield ◆ steeply sloping escarpments ◆ soil is often sandy and poorly drained in northern areas ◆ hilly, glacial till plains with level, plateau-type tops with large, sparsely treed peatlands in between ◆ where moisture, the forest is taller than in the Shield with aspen predominant, some white spruce, black spruce, and tamarack in low-lying peatlands
BOREAL SHIELD	Churchill River Upland	◆ typical Precambrian Shield with a mix of bedrock outcrops and rugged country ◆ lakes account for 40 percent of the area and are often linked by stretches of fast-flowing rivers ◆ soils are sandy and support black spruce and jack pine
	Athabasca Plain	◆ less rugged than Shield, with flat-lying sandstone bedrock and continuous cover of sandy glacial deposits ◆ lakes and wetlands less numerous ◆ spectacular sand dunes south of Lake Athabasca most outstanding feature ◆ sandy, droughty soils with young stands of jack pine ◆ birch and black spruce found in lower areas ◆ unique plant life
TAIGA SHIELD	Selwyn Lake Upland	◆ occurs within the subarctic zone of Canada, considered transitional to the boreal forest to the south and the tundra to the north ◆ perenially frozen soils with short trees and open forest ◆ Precambrian rocks forming broad sloping uplands together with numerous lakes and prominent sandy ridges ◆ rugged bedrock exposures are common, but most bedrock is covered by sandy glacial deposits ◆ black spruce with a conspicuous lichen under-storey is typical

A fine map showing these regions and more, called "Ecoregions of Saskatchewan," by G. A. Padbury and D. F. Acton, can be purchased by mail order from the Information Services Corporation at 306-787-2799. References for further research on the ecology and geology of the different regions and rivers are suggested where applicable.

Consider the impact you are making when you camp. Leave campsites cleaner and more natural than you found them. Many campsites that were once naturally beautiful — especially ones on the Churchill and Clearwater Rivers — have been ruined by people chopping down live trees and building benches and huge fire pits all over the place. For more information on no-trace camping, see page 237.

We are all custodians of the wilderness. Leave its beauty natural for others to enjoy. Never disturb natural features of the river or the forest. Throwing rocks into the river or altering the natural landscape in other inappropriate ways is unnecessary and destroys the beauty of a place. Pulling up moss from the forest floor and cutting live branches from trees is also unnecessary and disturbs the ecosystem.

LOCAL HISTORY

Often the trade-off for bumping into more people on the river is that the history of the river is more varied and richer. The voyageur routes were originally the highways of the First Nations, and they still are. Some of the rivers, like the upper Wathaman, too shallow and remote for convenient travel, are without the same extensive oral or written history, but they often have a natural history of interest.

It is important to remember that when travelling in the northern wilderness you are probably in what has been someone's backyard for thousands of years. Leave everything you find as it was, including antlers, rocks and other natural features. All prehistoric and historic period sites and artifacts are protected by law and should not be collected or in any way disturbed. Some trips will pass through provincial parks, where there may be regulations to preserve fragile environments (like the Athabasca Sand Dunes).

In the guidebook, the rivers are comparatively graded in terms of their First Nations', exploration, and fur-trade history values by the following star system:

*	Low	✦ this route was not used by First Nations regularly or used in exploration or for the fur trade
**	Average	✦ this route has an oral and or written history with First Nations but was not a major waterway — used by trappers but not traders
***	High	✦ this route was a regular travel route for the First Nations and trappers, and was of interest to fur traders and explorers
****	Very High	✦ this route was one of the most important waterways for First Nations communities, famous explorers passed this way, and it was a major link in the fur-trade routes

Where possible, references for further reading about a river or area with significant prehistorical and historical values will be supplied at the end of each short summary of a river's local history.

If you like, you can obtain a Saskatchewan Voyageur Certificate when you have completed your canoe trip. They are available from any of the SERM field offices listed in the Directory of Services in the back of the guidebook, the Visitor Information Centre at La Ronge, or Churchill River Canoe Outfitters. I got one in La Ronge after my first canoe trip on the Churchill in 1985, and was I thrilled!

SOLITUDE

Each river trip's level of solitude is also rated comparatively, and details about the trip follow the rating. A few routes have fallen from favour or have never seen many canoeists, while other canoe routes once paddled by only a few have become quite popular, and it would be usual to see at least one other group on a week-long trip in June or July. There are also routes that have fishing lodges and local motorboat traffic on them. On some rivers, a number of reserves, towns and hamlets are scattered along the shores, as in the case of the Churchill. The star rating indicates the level of solitude one can expect on a trip in peak season, as indicated in the When to Go section. The rating system is as follows:

*	Low	◆ expect to see local motorboat traffic, fishing parties, and canoeists frequently
**	Average	◆ expect to see local motorboat traffic, fishing parties and canoeists, but infrequently
***	High	◆ expect to see one other party of canoeists and possibly some local traffic or a fishing party
****	Very High	◆ expect to see no one, with the outside chance of meeting up with one other group of canoeists

WILDLIFE

Many people go on wilderness trips in hopes of seeing wildlife. Moose, black bears and timber wolves live in all the ecoregions in northern Saskatchewan. Smaller fur-bearing animals such as beavers, otters, muskrats, mink and foxes are also common. In some areas there are woodland caribou, mule and white-tailed deer, wolverines and lynx. Bald eagles are particularly plentiful, especially along the Churchill. Ospreys, loons and mergansers are other common fish-eating birds. Owl and golden eagle sightings are also possible. I have seen all these critters on northern Saskatchewan rivers, particularly bears, moose and the fish-eating birds. Each trip has been assigned a comparative rating based on the potential of seeing the common fauna of the region the river runs through.

*	Low	◆ very slight chance of seeing any large animals
**	Average	◆ you will probably see a variety of species indigenous to the area
***	High	◆ chances are good you will see a variety of large and small animals and birds
****	Very High	◆ you have the best chance of observing wildlife on this trip

Sources for further reading on the flora and fauna of particular regions are listed in the References section.

FISHING

Each river's fishing potential is comparatively rated on the star system from poor to excellent, much like a movie is. The ratings are generalizations, subject to natural cycles and fluctuations in the fish populations, so don't count on fish for supper because of what you read! However, some rivers are better than others for some species.

The most common species angled for in northern Saskatchewan waters are northern pike, walleye, lake trout and Arctic grayling. For each river in the book, the species of fish most commonly caught are listed, and the rivers are assigned a comparative rating based on the ease of catching whatever species are found in its waters. Specific fishing holes and their best times are indicated, and suggestions for tackle are noted where important.

*	**Poor**	◆ few fishing spots, luck and a lot of time fishing is involved, but you will probably catch a couple of northern pike here and there
**	**Average**	◆ you are bound to catch northern pike anywhere along the river if you try, and you may also have some luck with other common species, including walleye, trout or grayling
***	**Good**	◆ this river is known for its good fishing in two or more species, and you will catch a number of them
****	**Excellent**	◆ in certain spots you will have a great time catching one big one after another and throwing them back

Be aware that there are regulations you must comply with, and you will need a Saskatchewan fishing licence. De-barb your hooks and practice good catch-and-release techniques, keeping only what you can eat.

For more information on angling regulations, licences, and species of fish contact:

Saskatchewan Environment and Resource Management (SERM)
Box 5000
La Ronge, Saskatchewan, Canada, S0J 1L0
Phone: 306-425-4288
Fax: 306-425-2580

Or call the SERM Inquiry Centre at 306-787-2700, or 1-800-667-2757 within Saskatchewan. The following websites are excellent sources of information on angling in Saskatchewan: www.gov.sk.ca/govt/environ/ and www.serm.gov.sk.ca/fishwild/anglersguide/.

SPECIAL EQUIPMENT RECOMMENDATIONS

In most of the trip descriptions, equipment recommendations will be made. For example, for rivers such as the William that are shallow and rocky, you should have a Royalex canoe. In the Far North, you should seriously consider a bug head net and bug jacket with hood. For some rivers, like the Clearwater in a high-water year, great fun can be had by advanced and exceptional paddlers who take along a spray cover for their canoe, and for travel on the large lakes (as on the Churchill), you will need a compass.

TRIP NOTES:
YOUR DETAILED GUIDE TO THE RIVER'S FEATURES

In the Trip Notes section you will find a list of map coordinates and descriptions of notable features on the river. The coordinates used in the notes are derived from the Universal Transverse Mercator (UTM) grid system, and are shorthand versions of UTM coordinates. Each listed coordinate is a simplification and conglomeration of the easting (longitude) point and northing (latitude) point required to pinpoint a spot on the UTM grid. A full UTM coordinate consists of two numbers, one indicating the easting point, the other the northing point. The derivative coordinate form used in the notes is made up of one number of six digits, with the first three digits representing the easting (longitude) point and the last three numbers representing the northing (latitude) point. The third digit in both cases represents the closest tenth of a kilometre, or 100 m.

For example, according to the Trip Notes, rapids occur at coordinate 045329. This means the rapids are 500 m east of grid line 04 and 900 m north of line 32. To find these rapids on the 1:50,000 map, you would put your finger on east grid line 04 (east numbers are on the top and bottom of your map) and go halfway over to the next grid line to the right, and then put your other finger on north grid line 32 (north numbers are on the sides of your map) and go up to the nine-tenths of the square. This is the approximate location of the rapids as described in the Trip Notes.

This is not meant to be a lesson in reading UTM maps, just an explanation of the derivative used in the guidebook notes. For more information on UTM and reading maps based on UTM, see the US Geological Survey website at mac.usgs.gov/mac/isb/pubs/fact-sheets/fs15799.html. For a simple and practical example, look at the side of any 1:50,000 scale map, and you will see an example of how to determine a grid reference coordinate on a UTM map.

In the Trip Notes, the numbers and letters identifying the map referred to are found in the far left column. Then a six-digit coordinate from that map is given in the Grid Reference column, indicating a feature of the river that is of importance or interest. A brief description of the feature is given in the far right-hand column. If it is a rapid, a difficulty classification is provided as well as a brief description, and where appropriate the length in metres is estimated. See the example below:

MAP NO	GRID REF	FEATURE	DESCRIPTION
74K/15	042589	**Rapids**	**Class 2**. A straightforward chute at the top, with a boulder
	042590		fan at the end. The **portage (275 m)** is on RL starting at an
			opening in the willows just above the fast water.

I use a number of standard abbreviations in describing the river's features: RL means river left — what is on your left as you head downstream; RC means river centre — what is in the middle of the river; and RR means river right — what is on your right as you head downstream. Other common paddling terms are also used, such as chute, pillow, boulder fan and apron, rock garden. If you are not familiar with them, ask your paddling mentor, but I believe the meaning will become evident as you become familiar with the guidebook.

Do not expect the notes on the rapids and their classifications to help you to run harder rapids than you would attempt normally. That is not their purpose. They are meant to provide you with information about what is around the next corner, to assist you in assessing the difficulty of the rapids, and in particular cases to outline some of the options available to you.

Various hazards, campsites, natural attractions, sites of historic interest and fishing holes are also located using coordinates and are briefly described. Not every feature on the river is pinpointed, however, as the river is not a static entity and will change from year to year. You must always be on the lookout for hazards; it is your responsibility to take care of yourself. An attempt has been made to cover most features of interest, except in the case of historic sites, where it would not be possible to pinpoint and describe all of them for each of the 15 rivers. I would need several volumes! However, I have supplied you with references for finding this kind of information.

My suggestion for using the notes to assist you in navigating the river is to transfer the information from the notes to your 1:50,000 maps beforehand, so you can have them in front of you while you are paddling down the river. As I stated before, many of the rapids and falls are not marked on the maps, and you will probably want to know what class of rapids to expect around the next corner, where the portage is, or how far the next campsite is.

THE RIVERS AT A GLANCE: A COMPARATIVE CHART

The following chart summarizes some of the information provided in the guidebook, so that at a glance you can survey which trips may be suitable to your pocketbook and skill level and the time and interests you have. You can choose between a leisurely fishing and camping expedition, a more historical route or a whitewater adventure, or you can find a trip that will give you a taste of all three.

Km ◆ approximate trip length in kilometres
Difficulty ◆ rating the difficulty of the trip
In/Out ◆ the mode of transport required to reach the start and end points of the trip:
   DI drive in, **DO** drive out, **FI** fly in, **FO** fly out
When ◆ the best months to paddle the trip
Type ◆ the river's ecoregion(s) or type of environment:
   BL Mid-Boreal Lowland, **BU** Mid-Boreal Upland, **CU** Churchill River Upland, **AP** Athabasca Plain, **SU** Selwyn Lake Upland
History ◆ historical importance of the river
Solitude ◆ level of solitude one can expect to find
Wildlife ◆ potential for seeing wildlife
Fishing ◆ rating the fishing

River	Km	Difficulty	In/Out	When	Type	History	Solitude	Wildlife	Fishing
Sturgeon-weir	113	*/**	DI/DO	June–Sept	CU/BL	****	**	**	***
Montreal	66	*/**	DI/DO	May–June	BU	***	**	**	**
Churchill	608	*/**/***	DI/DO	June–Sept	BU/CU	****	**	**	***
Paull	105	**½	FI/DO	June–Aug	CU	**	***	***	****
Foster	260	***	FI/DO	May–July	CU	***	***	***	**
Haultain	150	***	DI/DO	May–Aug	CU	**	***	****	**
Clearwater	239	***	FI/FO DI/DO	May–July	CU/BU	****	***	**	***
Wathaman	162	****	FI/DO	May–Aug	CU	**	****	****	**
Geikie	85	***	FI/DO	May–July	CU	**½	***	***	***
Cree	200	**	FI/FO	June–Aug	AP	**½	***	****	***
Waterfound	105	**	FI/FO DI/FO	June–Aug	AP	**	**½	***½	****
Fond du Lac	222	***	FI/FO DI/FO	June–Sept	AP	***	**½	***	***
MacFarlane	210	**½/ ***½	FI/FO	June–Aug	AP	***	***½	***½	**½
Carswell-William	100	***	FI/FO DI/FO	June–July	AP	**	****	***	**
Porcupine	150	***	FI/FO FI/DO	June–Sept	SU	**½	***	***	***

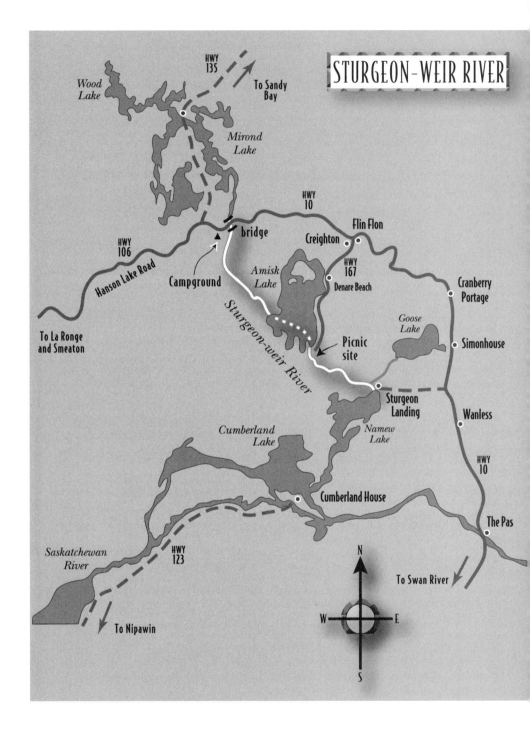

STURGEON-WEIR RIVER

The Sturgeon-weir River is a great trip for canoeists getting their "wilderness tripping legs." It has lots of smaller rapids, many historic sites and good fishing. The Weir is one of the easier and less remote trips in this guidebook. Don't let the voyageurs' name for it, Riviere Maligne, or "Wicked River," scare you. The Sturgeon-weir was the first canoe trip on which I captained my own ship, an aluminum Springbok named *Meredith*, compliments of Sheila and Craig, my sister and her husband. It was also my second real downriver trip in the North. Brad has been paddling it since the 1970s, as it's so close to his hometown of Flin Flon. So I have a soft spot for the Weir — it feels like home to me.

The Sturgeon-weir starts off as a Shield river and ends in the Hudson Lowlands. The major rapids of the upper section, or what the locals call the West Weir, are picturesque — pink granite shores up clear, green tumbling waves. Amisk Lake's red-and-yellow cliffs are spectacular, and its vast size is of note. The lower, South Weir has a quite different nature, however. The rapids are shallow and more numerous, running over rugged limestone, with grassy shores.

This river is one of the most historic in northern Saskatchewan, and will be fascinating to the canoeist with an interest in the history of the First Nations, early exploration and the fur trade. Pictographs on Amisk Lake are an indication of the area's importance in prehistory. The Weir was well travelled by the Cree long before the voyageurs. It is a tributary of the Saskatchewan River and is also connected to the Churchill River at its headwaters by the famous Frog Portage. Being a crossroads, the river became one of three major highways on the voyageur route through Saskatchewan. Many famous fur traders and explorers travelled from Montreal or Hudson Bay to the Mackenzie Basin and back between its banks.

Length

The trip described in the trip notes section is approximately 113 km, and will take around five or six days to complete, depending on the wind when you come to cross Amisk Lake.

It starts at Highway 106, the Hanson Lake Road (Kilometre 275), at the bridge across the narrows at Maligne Lake, and it ends at Sturgeon Landing. To shorten the trip, you could choose to paddle only the upper or lower section, as there is road access at Amisk Lake. To extend the upper section, the West Weir trip, canoeists can start at Pelican Narrows and paddle more of the historic fur-trade route passing through Mirond and Corneille Lakes and over Dog and Birch Portages. Or you could extend the South Weir portion of the trip by paddling all the way to Cumberland House and the confluence of the Sturgeon-weir and Saskatchewan Rivers.

Amisk Lake picnic site to Sturgeon Landing*	38 km
Maligne Lake to Amisk Lake picnic site*	75 km
Maligne Lake to Sturgeon Landing*	113 km
Pelican Narrows to Amisk Lake picnic site	129 km
Pelican Narrows to Sturgeon Landing	173 km
Pelican Narrows to Cumberland House	233 km

* These trips are described in detail in the Trip Notes section. For information on the extended trips, consult the Canoe Saskatchewan website for a SERM trip description, or contact SERM for the booklets. The trips described in this chapter are routes number 14 and 44.

Topographic Maps

I recommend 1:50,000. For the trip from Maligne Lake to Sturgeon Landing you will need 63L/15, 63L/10, 63L/9, 63L/8 and 63K/5. If you choose to put in at Pelican Narrows you will also need map 63M/2. For the Maligne Lake to Amisk Lake route you only need 63L/15, 63L/10, 63L/9 and 63L/8. From Amisk Lake to Sturgeon Landing you require only 63L/8 and 63K/5. If you choose to paddle all the way to Cumberland you will need 63K/4, 63L/1 and 63E/16 as well.

In order to make the best use of the information provided in this chapter, you should purchase the required maps in advance and use the grid reference coordinates in the Trip Notes section to mark in the large number of rapids missing on the maps. Note also that Crooked Rapids are not where they are marked on the map, but upstream of there. Crooked Rapids are the large rapids at grid reference 833332! You may want to note the classifications of the rapids and pencil in the portages. And it is important to note the camping opportunities, as there are stretches on the Sturgeon-weir where finding good campsites is difficult. You may also want to mark the historic sites of interest.

There are few visual clues for most historic sites on the trip, except, of course, you can view the pictographs and interesting geological features of natural history.

Getting There and Away

Getting to and from the Sturgeon-weir takes some time, as the trip is drive-in and drive-out. But the logistics are easy and much cheaper than flying. All you need to do is figure out your shuttle, and make sure you leave your vehicle(s) somewhere supervised.

Most groups put in either at Pelican Narrows on Mirond Lake or at the provincial campground on Maligne Lake at the Highway 106 bridge. The shuttle from the bridge is much shorter, as is taking out at Sturgeon Landing. If you paddle all the way to Cumberland House, you have a long drive back to Pelican or the 106 bridge via either Nipawin and Smeaton or a gravel stretch to The Pas and then through Flin Flon. The shuttle is approximately 500 km via Nipawin and approximately 440 km via the Manitoba route one way, compared to a 160-km shuttle one way from Sturgeon Landing via Highway 10 to Creighton. It's a big difference, but Cumberland is so historic, you might decide it's worth the extra time.

To get to either of the put-ins for the trips I describe in detail is easy. Pawistik Lodge sits on the north side of Highway 106, approximately 55 km west of Creighton/Flin Flon, where the 106 bridge crosses the river at Maligne Lake. You can rent canoes from the lodge. The second put-in, the picnic site at the top of the lower or South Weir, is 50 km south of Creighton on Highway 167. Denare Beach on Amisk Lake is approximately 19 km south of Creighton on Highway 167. You will want to arrange to park your vehicle(s) at Pawistik Lodge on Maligne Lake or in Denare Beach, perhaps at the marina, depending on where you decide to put in.

To reach the take-out at Sturgeon Landing, take Manitoba Highway 10 out of Creighton/ Flin Flon or from The Pas, depending on your direction of travel. Approximately 9 km south of Simonhouse Bible Camp, turn west on the gravel road (known locally as Atik Road) and drive 32 km to Sturgeon Landing. If you are coming from The Pas, turn west 10 km north of Wanless. To reach the river take-out, drive through Sturgeon Landing to the end of the road and turn right (south). The public launch is at the end of this street just before Namew Lake. To arrange for parking, call Sturgeon Landing Outfitters; they own the cabins and the store by the take-out.

You may want to hire a long-distance taxi to shuttle you back to your put-in spot, especially if you are going solo or are doing a one-canoe trip. Both Pawistik Lodge and Sturgeon Landing Outfitters do shuttles, and there is a taxi company in Flin Flon that will do long-distance trips if you book in advance. See the contact information for the Sturgeon-weir trip in the Directory of Services at the end of this guidebook.

When to Go

June to September. The upper Sturgeon-weir is one of the more accessible rivers in terms of its season. But the lower Weir can get too shallow in dry years. However, peak runoff isn't until early August, so in normal water years even a September trip can be good. You could begin paddling the upper Weir in late May, but don't go too early in May or the ice may still be on Amisk Lake, and the river may be low and difficult to navigate.

The Sturgeon-weir still has an operating water-gauging station on it, located at Leaf Rapids (the Amisk Lake station was closed in 1995), but it is not what is called a "real time" station, where flow data is available day by day. Water levels are only surveyed every few weeks at most, as a SaskWater employee must visit the station. So be warned, you can call SaskWater about the water level, but you may not be able to get up-to-date information. After you get the most recent flow reading, compare the cubic-metres-per-second rate with the monthly mean discharge chart on the Canoe Saskatchewan website to see if the river is at a high, low or normal water level before starting out. Make sure you look at the Leaf Rapids line, not the Amisk!

I've paddled the Sturgeon-weir twice at low water, around 35 cu m/sec, and once at relatively high water, 60 cu m/sec. Navigation is possible anywhere in that range. I wouldn't want to paddle the lower section at flows under 30 cu m/sec — you'd be dragging in spots. Extremely high water and flood conditions should be avoided as well, especially if you are a beginner.

Another way of checking the current water levels on the Weir is by contacting the SERM field office in Creighton or Pelican Narrows. Or you can call the outfitter at Sturgeon Landing.

Difficulty of the River * and **

Far from being what Alexander Mackenzie called "an almost continual rapid," the Weir drops over the 113 km described here at a rate of 0.35 m/km (2 ft/mi) — a pleasant gradient that keeps you moving and interested but not scrambling by any means. The upper section of the Weir drops at a rate of 0.20 m/km (1.1 ft/mi) and gets one star for difficulty because canoeists must make an exposed crossing of Amisk Lake to reach either the outlet of the lower Sturgeon-weir if they are carrying on to Sturgeon Landing or the take-out point at one of the picnic sites. You must cross Amisk Lake to get to any road access. Otherwise, there are only four rapids of note from Maligne Lake to Amisk Lake: Leaf Rapids, Class 2; Scoop Rapids, Class 4; Snake Rapids, Class 2; and Spruce Rapids, Class 3/3+. All the portages for those rapids are in good condition and easily accessible. There are no mandatory portages, but running Scoop is a very low-percentage move, even if you have a spray skirt. I personally don't enjoy the washing-machine action of a big hole! All in all, this part of the West Weir is not a difficult trip, and beginners who have basic moving-water skills and tripping experience should find the trip within their capabilities.

The second part of the trip, the South Weir from the Little Limestone Point or the Beaver City picnic sites on Amisk Lake down to Sturgeon Landing or Cumberland House, is more difficult. It is rated two stars out of four. This section drops much more steeply at 0.76 m/km (4 ft/mi), over twice the gradient of the entire trip and almost four times the upper section's gradient! There are really only two major rapids, Crooked Rapids and Rat Rapids (the set just before the Goose River confluence), meaning that the many, many smaller rapids, some of which are fairly continuous in this section, account for the steep drop. The average class of the rapids is 1+.

This section requires a higher level of moving-water skill. The biggest concern is that you may end up swimming in shallow, rocky rapids or wrapping your boat on the many boulders strewn here and there. If the water level is too low, navigation becomes much more difficult. On the other hand, if the river is in flood there are other hazards like tricky landings at portages, bigger waves, and less shoreline for lining. Additionally, for some easier rapids there are no portages, and the portages around the harder rapids are not as well used or marked as on the West Weir trip. All in all, intermediate canoeists will be comfortable making this trip, but less-skilled canoeists should be very cautious. If you are a beginner in moving water, evaluate your situation after paddling the West Weir before deciding on whether or not to paddle the South Weir.

Character of the River and Region

The moderate volume of the Sturgeon-weir never really alters until it becomes a chain of lakes at Namew, and it continues to be a relatively shallow river to the end. The riverbed changes as the river first flows through the Churchill River Uplands of the Boreal Shield ecozone, where it flows over Precambrian rock with occasional ledge formations of exposed shelves of granite. It then enters the Mid-Boreal Lowlands of the Boreal Plain ecozone, where it flows through limestone formations and clay banks; dolomite ledges are the identifying characteristic of this section. The Sturgeon-weir is the only river in this guidebook that reaches into the lowlands. Those with an interest in geology may be interested in visiting "the crevasses," a site at the southern end of Amisk Lake where the Precambrian rock meets the limestone, resulting in huge crevasses and sheer rock walls.

The rapids in each section of the river are different as a result of the changing geology. The four major rapids on the upper stretch are characteristic of the Precambrian Shield. The river drops over bedrock ledges or large boulders and then pools below the rapids. The increased current dropping through hard rock channels and narrows forms large compression or standing waves. The second, lower part of the river is characterized by rapids where there is fast water flowing over limestone slabs, and boulders and rocks to avoid. The shores are often dotted with dolomite ledges, but are mostly clay with lots of thick and low vegetation.

The rapids of the West Weir remind me of Churchill rapids — big waves and smoother rocks — while the shallow, rocky, continuous-type rapids of the South Weir remind me of some rapids on the Montreal and Clearwater Rivers. The limestone slab rapids in this lower section of the Weir remind me of the sandstone slab rapids of the Fond du Lac and Cree Rivers. Sometimes the slabs are so smooth, other times they are honeycombed and act like cheese graters on boats and feet!

In the Churchill Uplands ecoregion you have marvellous natural campsites due to the high bedrock outcroppings. Where the soil is sandy, there are low stands of black spruce and jack pine, and in the areas with more clay soils you will find more aspen and birch. Muskegs and tamarack swamps are common. Once you leave Amisk Lake, peatlands are the dominant feature, with some limestone outcropping and sandy glacial deposits. There are some great dolomite ledges for campsites on the lower Weir.

For more information about the two ecozones and ecoregions of the Sturgeon-weir consult the book, *The Ecoregions of Saskatchewan*, by Acton, Padbury and Stushnoff. It is simply the best source on the ecology and geology I have encountered yet. Another completely different kind of read is Sigurd Olson's *The Lonely Land*. It is the trip journal of six men in the 1960s who paddle from Ile-à-la-Crosse to Cumberland House. It describes the contrast between the Uplands and the Lowlands, with a marked bias on the part of the author towards the Shield country. It is interesting from a historic perspective as well.

Local History ✳✳✳✳

Amisk is Cree for "beaver," and long before the voyageurs, the First Nations people living to the north and south of the Weir and in the Amisk Lake area were harvesting the rich resources of the river. In fact, the name of the river comes from the Cree practice of trapping the once-plentiful sturgeon in pools created by stone weirs built across the shallow rapids of the lower Weir. *Namew* is Cree for "sturgeon," and this lake north of Cumberland Lake is considered the end of the Sturgeon-weir River.

There have been some archeological digs around Denare Beach. This area was one of the traditional summer gathering places of the Peter Ballentyne Cree Nation. This Woods

Cree Nation's traditional homelands range from as far south and east as Sturgeon Landing to as far north and west as the community of Southend, on Reindeer Lake. Their headquarters are in Pelican Narrows, located at the narrows between Pelican and Mirond Lake. In fact, this band was once part of the same nation as the Lac La Ronge First Nation, but split off in 1900 after the addition to Treaty 6 was signed.

The traditional Spruce Rapids Portage and the land from there to the outflow of the river on Amisk Lake is part of the Amisk Lake Reserve. There is a graveyard on river left after the portage that should be visited with respect; do not disturb the site in any way. There is a pictograph site in Warehouse Bay on Amisk Lake as well, a sign of the importance of the area to the First Nations.

The Sturgeon-weir was central in the exploration and fur-trade eras as a link between two major waterways. As a tributary of the Saskatchewan River it was important in itself, but then in 1774, when Joseph Frobisher crossed the height of land from the headwaters of the Sturgeon-weir to the Churchill River, via Frog Portage, everything changed once and for all. Not only did the discovery of the crossroads choke off the trade to Hudson's Bay Company (HBC) posts because the independent traders could buy the furs the Indians had for sale first, but finding that portage opened up the northwest, eventually all the way to the Arctic and Pacific Oceans. For more information on the history and importance of Frog Portage and the Churchill, see the Local History section of the chapter on the Churchill.

Cumberland House, where the Sturgeon-weir watershed ends, is the oldest post-European or continuous community in Saskatchewan and boasts its oldest schoolhouse. It was the HBC's first inland post, established by Samuel Hearne in 1774. All the other big names of the early northwest explorer days navigated the Sturgeon-weir: Joseph and Thomas Frobisher, Alexander Henry, Peter Pond, Alexander Mackenzie, David Thompson, Simon Fraser and John Franklin.

In 1775, Alexander Henry and the Frobisher brothers built the first trading post northwest of Cumberland House on Amisk Lake. It was located at the west end of the lake, south of the outflow of the Sturgeon-weir, in Moody Bay. The bay was named for Harry Moody, a Denare Beach resident who was integral in discovering important archaeological sites in the Amisk Lake area.

On June 26, 1822, John Franklin and his crew, returning from the first land expedition to the Arctic, were windbound on Amisk Lake, and they camped at the outflow of the Weir. In his journal, Franklin refers to the Sturgeon-weir by three different names. Historically, the upper, West Weir from Wood Lake to Pine (Les Pinettes) Portage was known as Grande (Great) River. The middle Sturgeon-weir was known as La Riviere Pente (Ridge River, for its portage over bare rock ridges). Franklin notes that the last section of the river, the South Weir, was called Riviere Maligne by Mackenzie in the late 1700s, but Franklin himself refers to the river below Amisk Lake as the Sturgeon-weir. This lower section is where the stone weirs were actually built by the Cree. Eventually, however, the name was applied to the entire route, all the way to Frog Portage.

A number of HBC trading posts were built in the 1800s and 1900s on the lake, and a detour to the northeast to Denare Beach may be of interest to history buffs, especially the Northern Gateway Museum. The southeast shore of Amisk, at the outflow of the Weir, was also home to trading posts at various times from the late 1700s to the early 1900s.

There is also an old gold rush community site called Beaver City, above the first rapids at the head of the South Weir. Gold was discovered on Amisk Lake in 1910, and by 1913 the peak of the gold rush was on, with more than 1,000 claims staked in the area. Beaver City was the community that developed to service the gold miners and the fishing industry that was growing rapidly from the rich waters of Amisk Lake. It was a boomtown until the First World War, when people began to leave to work at the mine at Namew Lake, and by 1918 it was a ghost town. You can see some rusted machinery on the site if you crash the bush on river right on the point where Amisk drains into the South Weir. At one time, a famous marathon canoe race, the Gold Rush Canoe Derby, was held in Flin Flon. World-famous racers like Solomon Carriere and Serge Corbin paddled in the gruelling 175-km race. So did my husband Brad, when he was a youngster of 19!

Consult both the chapter on the Churchill and the References section for sources on the prehistory and the fur-trade history of the area. For a far more detailed account of the Sturgeon-weir in the fur trade, consult Sid Robinson and Greg Marchildon's book, *Canoeing the Churchill: A Practical Guide to the Historic Voyageur Route.*

Solitude **

The Weir is not the best trip for wilderness solitude, but it is not a crowded river by any stretch. It gets two stars because it has several road-access points, an outfitter's lodge, and the communities of Denare Beach and Sturgeon Landing on its banks, and it is well-used for fishing at certain points, especially Spruce Rapids. You can expect to see local motorboat traffic as you near Amisk Lake and Sturgeon Landing, and expect to meet people fishing. However, I can say that the three times I've been on the Sturgeon-weir, I've never seen any other canoeists! The river is not as popular with recreational canoeists as it was 15 years ago. The two sections where you will find the most solitude are between Leaf and Scoop Rapids and after you leave Amisk Lake up until the Goose River confluence.

Wildlife **

The American white pelican, the most characteristic wildlife of the Sturgeon-weir, can almost always be sighted fishing below rapids or standing on shallow rocks in mid-river. On your trip you will also probably see eagles, beavers, muskrats, and maybe otters or a bear. If you are really lucky, you may see a moose on your trip.

The Churchill Uplands has the second-highest population of bald eagles next to Alaska, and the area around the Cumberland House delta is said to be home to the highest concentration of moose in the province. Woodland caribou are also at home in the lowlands. But the Sturgeon-weir watershed sees a lot of hunting, and therefore the populations are pretty shy, and are not what they would be if this were a more remote region.

One time when we were on our way to fish at Spruce Rapids in the motorboat, Brad and I came upon a mother black bear and her two cubs swimming across the Weir just below Spruce Rapids. And my first trip down the Weir, on our first night at the campground at Maligne Lake, a small bear came along for supper and wouldn't take no for an answer. Three people ate while one yelled and banged pots, and then that person would stop yelling and eat, and someone else would take over the dinner accompaniment, and so on until the food and dishes were put away in the vehicles. Then the pesky beast left, finally!

Fishing ***

Ironically, there are no more sturgeon in the Weir. They were fished out completely, as were the trout in Amisk Lake. However, the walleye fishing on the Sturgeon-weir can be great in the spring and fall. In the upper section, walleye are plentiful below the major rapids. Scoop Rapids, it is said, were so named because fish were so plentiful in the eddies below the huge pink granite shelf that you could scoop them out with your hands. I've had a lot of success jigging for walleye there in June. I've also seen the suckers running so thick that the water seemed to be writhing with black and silver snakes. About 20 pelicans were fishing below the rapids for them. It was surreal.

On the edges of these pools there are always lots of northern pike hoping to catch a hapless walleye out of the flow, so to speak. Spruce Rapids is another favourite fishing hole. When the walleye congregate in large numbers, you can expect to find many boats from the Flin Flon and Creighton area anchored below these rapids. On the South Weir there are a few rapids deep enough for fishing below for walleye, but you are more than likely to catch lots of northern pike, and that's why they call them slough sharks. Mud, weeds, stagnant bays with willows with the current running by the bay opening — they love it. That's where the monsters lurk. Supper? No problem, virtually anywhere.

Special Equipment

For the upper Sturgeon-weir any proper tripping canoe you are willing to portage and that can take the open crossing of Amisk Lake is probably all right. But if you are planning on doing the lower section of the river too, I would strongly recommend a Royalex hull. The best choice for a rocky river is a Royalex tripping canoe with Kevlar skid plates to protect it from the inevitable hard knocks. The South Weir can be very shallow in places and has limestone rock rapids that have slab bottoms that could be used for cheese graters, and there are lots of big boulders to wrap around. An ABS plastic canoe is ideal for this kind of river — it is a slippery toboggan when you run out of water, and if you do happen to wrap it around one of the countless big rocks, it will quite often regain its shape again (if you can get off the rock!), so you can carry on down the river. The worst choice of material for a canoe on this river is aluminum, unless the water levels are well up. It will stick to every rock you touch, and it is impossible to slide over rocks and ledges in the shallows. Kevlar and fibreglass also slide on rock, but are less able to withstand wrapping around boulders.

I would advise you to bring a small water filter or drops for treating your drinking water. Amisk Lake and the lower section of the Weir are too near communities for me to feel good about drinking the water straight out of the river. And bring a tarp — you may get lucky and have a chance to sail across Amisk Lake!

Bring insect repellent, especially for the blackflies in June. The Sturgeon-weir is swampy in places, especially as you approach Sturgeon Landing. In a normal year, August is the best month to travel on the Weir, as the bug populations have dwindled by then.

Trip Notes

MAP NO	GRID REF	FEATURE	DESCRIPTION
63 L/15	517797	Put-in point Campground	There is a provincial campground on the northwest shore of Maligne Lake across Highway 106 from Pawastik Lodge. Access to the lake is easy via the campsites on the water.
	519780	Leaf Rapids	At the extreme south end of Maligne Lake the current begins to quicken as you enter the river. A cable across the river with red markers on it indicates Leaf Rapids, a **Class 2 rapid** — standing waves are the only real feature of note. Scouting on RL is possible, and the **portage (200 m)** can be found on RL as well, about 50 m above the rapids. It's a good trail that starts on a sloping rock and ends in a cove below the rapids.
	519709	Scoop Rapids Campsite Fishing Hole	Scoop is a **Class 4** drop with a couple of ledges that make for nasty holes, the last one in particular. A good **portage (65 m)** exists on RL and starts about 20 m above the rapid. The flat, pink rocks at Scoop make for a great place to stop, eat lunch or fish. If the pelicans aren't hogging the eddies below, you, too, can try to scoop some fish. Once I was there in early June while the suckers where running, and the pelicans were in a frenzy. What with all the fish and the birds the place needed a good cleaning! Beware of bears if you camp around here during the fish spawns. The campsite is at the height of the portage trail and off to the left on a side trail.

MAP NO	GRID REF	FEATURE	DESCRIPTION
	515620	Campsite	On RL in a tiny bay with a rock landing.
	544588	Campsite	After big bend, at a rock ledge. The tent spots are in behind.
63 L/10	580572 589569	Snake Rapids Portage Campsite	If you want to scout or portage these longer rapids you must get out far above (500 m) where the rapids actually start. The **portage (950 m)** is on RR and begins in a break in the reeds and willows of the shoreline, where the river starts to turn to the left around the point of land Snake Rapids snakes around. The trail is well trodden, and camping is possible in a clearing at the trailhead and at the grassy landing at the end of the portage.
	582576 589569	Snake Rapids	A **Class 2** rapid approximately 625 m long with two basic parts. The top set is a chute with some waves and rocks, while the bottom is a shallower drop requiring rock dodging. Snake can be scouted from RR, but be sure to get out at the **portage (950 m)**, which is on RR, but starts way above the rapids. See the notes on the Snake Rapids portage above.
	597552	Rapids	**Class 1**, rapids and fast water at the narrows.
63 L/9	650514 650511	Spruce Rapids Campsite Fishing Hole	These **Class 3/3+** rapids are about 250 m long and, depending on the water level, it may be very difficult to navigate the rock apron at the bottom. An aluminum fishing boat was wrapped on the large rock in RC at the top of the rapids last time I was there and presented a serious hazard to those running the rapids. There is a good **portage (250 m)** on RL that starts in a cove on the left shore just above the start of the rapids. Approximately halfway down the trail there is a grassy spot to camp and view the rapids in their entirety. This high camp is a favourite of mine on the Sturgeon-weir, not least because fishing is great at the bottom of the rapids. Local people drive their boats up here to fish, it's that good.
	654505	Cemetery	On the Amisk Lake Reserve. The graves sit high on RL on a sand bank. Be respectful of this area.

CAUTION: Crossing Amisk Lake to carry on down the Sturgeon-weir or to take out at Denare Beach can be potentially dangerous in high winds, as there are few islands in the southern half of the lake. Be careful and cross in good weather. If you are crossing Amisk to the south, there are cliffs along the shoreline. Some of the points have camping potential (from 776407 to 779407), but in high winds, landing can be very difficult and the camps are exposed to north winds. If you are heading northeast to Denare Beach and the lake is rough, stay in the relative shelter of the islands along the shoreline. You could camp and wait out the wind at 733476, a rock camp on the northwest corner of a small island.

MAP NO	GRID REF	FEATURE	DESCRIPTION
	833608	Fort Henry/ Frobisher House	The site of the trading post built by Alexander Henry the elder and the two Frobisher brothers in 1775.
	855473	Crevasses	This natural history site is approximately 15 km south of Denare Beach.
63 L/8	835362	Little Limestone Point	Here you can have lunch at the same spot as the voyageurs before you. The ragged limestone ledges at this picnic site welcome you to the Mid-Boreal Lowlands ecoregion. Check out all the fossils in the rock slabs!

MAP NO	GRID REF	FEATURE	DESCRIPTION
	834357	**Put-in** **Picnic site** **Rapids**	This recreation site is a fine put-in for the southern Sturgeon-weir trip. A monument to a gold rush community called Beaver City, which was located at the head of the river on a point on RR directly across from Little Limestone Point, can be visited as well. A (350 m) **Class 2** rapid begins here. The rapid can be shallow and rocky, requiring the most manoeuvring in the shallows at the bottom. It can be lined by the cautious canoeist on RL. The far RR often has more water and is the route we ran at the beginning of August in lower water. To avoid the rapid altogether you can drive down the road off to the left just before you reach the recreation site, and put in there just downstream of the rapid.
	831339	**Rapids**	**Class 1**. Shallow, rocky and rather long (400 m).
	833332 836324	**Crooked Rapids Campsite**	**Class 2+**. This rapid has three parts. First there is a shallow riffle. Secondly there is a chute 100 m before you reach the difficult or "crooked" part of the rapids. The third and most difficult part of the rapid turns left then back right, with rocks, ledges and waves to contend with. We often run RR on the inside of the big turn, but you can also run far RL. Scouting and a **portage** around this 500-m-long section is possible via an old hauling road on RR. A short trail up to it can be found in a break in the shoreline vegetation about 125 m above the start of the set, but keep your eyes peeled, it's hard to find. It ends on a large limestone slab in a cove below the rapids. The dolomite ledges in this cove are a fine campsite. In lower water, there are a few sections of fast water and riffles for the next 3 km until you reach the rapids that are incorrectly labelled Crooked Rapids on the map.
	853317 849307	**Rapids Campsite**	**Class 2** rapids begin at a narrows and continue around a sharp turn to the right. After the main chute, rock dodging is required. In lower water the rapids carry on to above a small bay on RR where there are more great limestone ledges for camping on the downstream point. It isn't easy to scout or line these rapids, and there isn't really a portage. The old hauling road is set far back (600 m, it appears) in the bush on RR according to the old map, but we could not find it in August 2001. My suggestion is to stop on RR above the rapids, scout and make a plan for lining or running. The water level will dictate which shore or route is best. In lower water, the next 1.5 km after the limestone ledges have fast water and shallow, rocky rapids.
	857295	**Rapids**	**Class 1/1+**. A limestone slab ledge at 874286, a sharp bend to the left, followed by fast water and riffles for 1.5 km in lower water.
	915278	**Campsite**	A jack pine bench on RR runs along the shore almost to the point.
	933274	**Trapper cabin**	An old log cabin on RL.
63 K/5	059269	**Rapids**	**Class 1**. Where the river narrows significantly are shallow, rocky rapids. Expect fast water and more riffles for 2 km.
	065268	**Winter road Rapids**	An opening in the bush on both sides is a winter logging road. More **Class 1/1+** rock dodging carries on for 200 metres more.

sturgeon-weir river

33

| --- | --- | --- | --- |
	074255	**Winter road**	The winter road crosses for the second and final time above a turn
	076252	**Rapids**	to the right around a prominent point on RL. There, **Class 1+** rapids go around the corner to below the point. Watch for a rock apron at lower water levels. Some fast water sections follow for the next 6.5 km, but nothing over **Class 1** at any water level I've paddled.
	120233	**Rapids** **Campsite**	Approximately 100 m before a sharp turn to the right are **Class 1+** rapids with rock dodging required. There is a small camp for a couple of tents on RL on the limestone ledge at the top of the sharp turn.
	123228	**Rapids**	As the river turns back left, there are some **Class 1+** rapids to be negotiated among the islands. Rock dodging is required.
	161221	**Rat Rapids** **Rat Portage**	This is the most difficult rapid on the South Weir, a **Class 2+/3** rapid with some tricky ledges to be negotiated. The rapid starts at a sharp corner to the right above a small island and then the river turns sharply left. In lower water, we run the chute far RR and then quickly moved to RC for the final turn around the island. The portage is on RL, cutting across the point of land. The **portage (170 m)** starts just ahead of the rapids, and it's hard to distinguish the break in the willowy shoreline, so caution is recommended. Move to far RL early and carefully paddle down the left shore, stopping to walk at least 100 m before the rapids to assure that you will find the trail opening at **162222**.
	163221	**Campsite**	There is a great campsite at the end of the portage on a flat, grassy spot on top of a limestone slab in a little bay above the confluence of the Goose River.
	166222	**Cabin**	On the RL shore right at the confluence of the Goose and Sturgeon-weir Rivers. The Goose River is also a famous body of water, as it is part of the fur-trade route that connected the Grass(y) River system to the Saskatchewan.
	163206	**Rapids**	**Class 1+** rapids, formed by a slab of limestone, with standing waves.
	162202	**Rapids**	**Class 1+** rapids, formed by a slab of limestone, with standing waves.
	162197	**Rapids**	Fast water to **Class 1/1+** rapids, depending on the water level, occur pretty much continuously for the next 2 km. Either side of the river is accessible in most places to scout if you feel it is required for your skill level. Once you see the suspension footbridge you have reached Sturgeon Landing, but there are some small rapids to be negotiated yet.
	165176	**Take-out**	Join the line of boats on shore or use the public dock. You are at the end of the road.

MONTREAL RIVER

The Montreal River is the first river to run in the spring. If the water is high or at least normal in May or early June it's a "why not?" kind of trip. You can't beat the excitement of continuous rapids when you haven't paddled all winter. The Montreal is a fast-flowing, shallow river with lots of small rapids, and a good practice run for bigger or more technical water.

With all the road access to different sections of the Montreal, you can choose from day-trips, weekend trips or longer expeditions. I've paddled the picnic site to the Highway 165 bridge eight times in the past 13 years, and we used to paddle the Bigstone Rapids section every April. Sheila, Brad and I would run it in solo boats or kayaks and then drive back up and run it over again as many times as we could before it got too dark. In fact, the Montreal was the first river I ever paddled with Brad; we paddled it together the first day I met him. I made him paddle in the bow. It was one of the last times he listened so well up there.

The Montreal is not a remote river, but it is still a wilderness river. From Montreal Lake to Bigstone Lake you will not see very many people, and almost none of them will be tourists. The Montreal flows north to where the Shield begins at Lac La Ronge, and it is a rich environment with many deciduous trees that are just starting to leaf out in late May.

Length

The trip described in detail in the Trip Notes section of this chapter is 66 km long. It starts where the community of Molanosa used to be, at the northeast end of Montreal Lake, and it ends at the bridge on Highway 165, the gravel road to Besnard, Pinehouse and Key Lakes. There are two daytrip options in the described trip, one from Montreal Lake to the bridge on Highway 2, and the other (the most commonly paddled section) from the provincial picnic site off Highway 2 to Highway 165. You could extend the trip by carrying on past the Highway 165 bridge and paddling on to Bigstone Lake or down to Lac La Ronge. You could also make a two- or three-day trip on the Montreal and avoid most of the rapids by paddling from the Highway 165 bridge to Bigstone Lake. If you carry on to Lac La Ronge you could complete your trip at Stanley Mission via the Rapid River (also once known as the Montreal River) to the Churchill River. The 66-km trip can take as little as two days if you have good water levels, and if you have experience running shallow rapids. But they will not be short days, even though there is lots of current. The fact that there are so many rapids makes doing 30-some kilometres a day slower and more tiring than paddling straight flatwater, unless you have really high water levels and don't have to deal with the rocks. But why rush it anyway? Hit the river on a Friday afternoon, paddle a bit and camp, then paddle Saturday and Sunday and make the drive home Sunday afternoon.

Less-experienced paddlers should allow for two days to complete the first section and then reassess the situation at the Highway 2 bridge or the picnic site just downstream from there. The trip from Montreal Lake to Bigstone Lake or Lac La Ronge can take anywhere from three days to five depending on your skill, the wind and water levels.

Montreal Lake to Highway 2 bridge*	31 km
Picnic site off Highway 2 to Highway 165 bridge*	33 km
Highway 2 bridge to Highway 165 bridge*	35 km
Montreal Lake to Highway 165 bridge*	66 km
Highway 165 bridge to Bigstone Lake	80 km
Montreal Lake to Lac La Ronge	146 km

* These trip options are described in detail in the Trip Notes section.

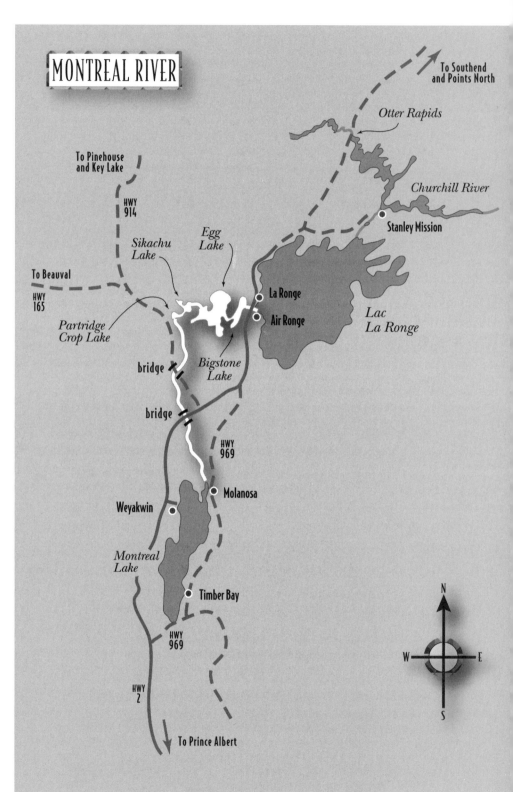

Topographic Maps

If you want to know where you are at all times, 1:50,000 scale maps are required. It's not as if you are going to make a wrong turn on the upper sections of the Montreal, and the bridges are not to be missed, but no other scale is going to show the detail you will need to figure out where you are in all those continuous rapids. For the trip described in detail you will need 73 I/5, 73 I/12 and 73 I/13. If you are paddling on from the Highway 165 bridge to Bigstone or Lac La Ronge you will also need 73 P/4 and 73 P/3.

In order to make the best use of the information provided in this chapter, canoeists should purchase the required maps in advance and use the grid reference coordinates in the Trip Notes section to mark in the large number of rapids missing on the maps. Classifications of the rapids and other notes about sites of interest can be added as well. Additionally, it is important to note the camping opportunities, as the Montreal has sections where finding good campsites is difficult.

Getting There and Away

The shuttles are short, but they require some organizing if you don't want to leave your vehicle unattended overnight. Finding someone to drive a shuttle for you from one of the outfitters, hotels or other tourist services in La Ronge shouldn't be too difficult. You can always hire a long-distance taxi as well. The canoe outfitter in Missinipe will shuttle people or vehicles for a fee. See the Directory of Services for contact information.

To reach the put-in at Molanosa on Montreal Lake you must first access Highway 2. There are two ways to the put-in from Highway 2. If you are coming from the south, turn right at Highway 969 to Timber Bay. It is a good gravel road. You will pass Timber Bay and drive for another 40 km until you see a medium-sized white sign for the Wapus Lake Elk Restoration Project. Turn left onto the two-track-only road at 641388. From points north, head south on Highway 2 and turn left at the Creighton turnoff and then right or south immediately onto Highway 969, which is a good gravel road. Drive 42 km and look for the white Elk Project sign on your right. Turn onto the track at the grid reference coordinates indicated above. Once you are on the track heading west you should end up at the shore of Montreal Lake after about 700 m or so, where there is a clearing to turn around in and an old dock to launch at.

The alternative launching site is at the community of Weyakwin on the west side of Montreal Lake. The problem with this put-in is the unprotected open-water crossing you must make to get to the northeast end of the lake. If you do choose another put-in option other than Molanosa, consider carefully the amount of time you will need to add on, including the possibility of being windbound or having to paddle the shoreline. On flatwater, without wind, a tandem river canoe loaded and paddled by two competent paddlers can make an average of 5 km/h.

Getting to the other put-ins on the river is straightforward. The Highway 2 bridge is about 178 km north of Prince Albert, and you can put in on the south and west side of the bridge. The Montreal River picnic site is another 2 km north on the west side of the highway. Drive as far west into the picnic site as you can to the parking spots closest to the river. There is a good path down to the put-in, a portage of about 150 m at most.

The Highway 165 bridge can be accessed from a junction on Highway 2. The junction is 183 km north of Prince Albert. Turn west and drive gravel Highway 165 for 20 km. The best place to park is on the south side of the bridge and the west side of the road. There is a good clearing.

The last two possible take-outs are at the end of the road to Bigstone Lake and the second Highway 2 bridge. If you are taking out at Bigstone Lake, turn west at Kathy's Corners, a store and gas station just north of the second Highway 2 bridge, which separates Air Ronge and La Ronge. The store structure is log — you can't miss it. Turn west and drive to the end of the road. You will pass the Bigstone Reserve and then a suburb and end up at a dead end at Bigstone Lake just above the beginning of the rapids.

To take out at the bridge at La Ronge, there is a good spot on the north side of the river and the east side of the road. You can park right by the bank on the gravel. Or you can take out at the campground upstream of the bridge on the southwest bank of the river. There is a sign for the campground immediately before the bridge. Follow the road to the river's edge.

When to Go

When the water is up in late May and June. Usually the best time to paddle this river is when the frozen groundwater is melting, at spring runoff. If it's been a wet spring or there was lots of snow in the winter, you should be fine. In really high water and rainy years you may be able to paddle it into July with no difficulty, but that is not normally the case.

One of the water survey stations is still operating on the Montreal. It is located at the river's outlet at Bigstone Lake, though it is not a "real time" station. This means that a SaskWater worker has to actually go to the water survey station and get a reading instead of reading it on a computer in an office. The reality is, you can call SaskWater to check the water level on the Montreal, but the data you get may be old and basically useless. It's worth a try, however. To put the reading into context, in mid-May of 2001, I paddled the Montreal solo. There was just enough water to run it without dragging. Though I eventually got a reading from SaskWater of 15.4 cu m/sec, I think the river was running at more like 20. I don't think you can run the river in a tandem boat at much less than 20 cu m/sec without having to wade.

The best alternative to getting a SaskWater reading of the river is to call the SERM office in La Ronge and ask if there is someone there who can tell you about the current water levels on the Montreal, and if it is a dry or wet spring.

Last, but not least, there is one final way to check water levels. Have an alternative route in mind when you plan to paddle the Montreal, and check the water levels yourself by going to the picnic site put-in off Highway 2. If you can barely paddle the first rapids, located where the path from the picnic site reaches the river, then do not attempt to paddle the Montreal. Go with the alternative route. You will never make it through the really shallow rapids to come much farther downstream. It is a fact that the Montreal cannot be run at all some years. In the early '90s you could barely fill a cup of water some places along the river. In 1991 and 1992 the river was flowing at an average of 7–9 cu m/sec for the entire spring and summer. The highest flows were in 1974 — May's average flow was 58.4!

Difficulty of the River * and **

Overall, the 66-km trip gets a one-and-one-half-star difficulty rating. The first section from Montreal Lake is suitable for those canoeists with basic skills in moving water, given that they have allowed enough time to spare for lining or wading the Montreal Rapids if necessary. Making a two-day trip to the Highway 2 bridge would accomplish this. It's a long daytrip at 31 km anyway, and shooting rapids when you are tired already, especially shallow ones as on the Montreal, is not a good idea. It takes more time and energy to negotiate them than flatwater, making for a very long day if you have to walk the majority of them.

The second section, from the bridge or picnic site on Highway 2 to the bridge on Highway 165, is the most difficult section of the trip. It requires you to paddle Class 1+/2 rapids. There is no way around the rapids, and if the water is at all low you will be bumping and grinding and wading because there are a zillion rocks to avoid. As well, the windy nature of the Montreal lends itself to startling corner and island rapids that require skill to negotiate. If the water is high, this section becomes much easier in terms of bump and grind, but the bigger water makes everything happen faster.

The third section, from Highway 165 to Bigstone Lake, is the easiest because there is only current and flatwater, except for the two sections of Class 1+ and 2 rapids. There is a little more water in these rapids, however. More rope to hang yourself with! But seriously, these sections can be waded or lined, it just takes time. Also, the crossings of Egg and Bigstone Lakes are potentially dangerous, as they are large lakes with few islands in your path. I was windbound for two days on Egg in May of 2001. Only advanced paddlers should consider paddling the section of the Montreal from Bigstone Lake to Lac La Ronge. This section of the Montreal is the most difficult of all. The rapids behind the residences at Bigstone are very fast and steep and require precision manoeuvring to get a loaded tandem boat down safely.

I've found only one portage on the Montreal — the trail around the dam on the first section of the river. This is the only mandatory portage. Keighley, in his book *Trader, Tripper, Trapper: The Life of a Bay Man*, indicates that when the Montreal was used for travel in the fur trade there were at least four portages along its length to Lac La Ronge. One was around the Montreal Rapids — 6 km (4 mi) long! There were also two short ones not referred to by location (I assume these are around the two sections of rapids below the Highway 165 bridge), and the last, "Mountain Portage," 1.6 km (1 mi) around the rapids between Bigstone and Lac La Ronge. In his day, those rapids were called Mountain Rapids and the lower ones behind Bigstone Reserve and just before you reach Lac La Ronge were called Kitsaki Rapids. So, though the Montreal is not big water, there are some serious rapids. Ask a couple of guys we know who trashed their wood-canvas freighter canoe while moose hunting on the Montreal and walked a couple of days to the road! We went down and picked up the pieces in our Royalex boat the next day.

The gradient of the first section from Montreal Lake to Highway 2 is 0.32 m/km (1.57 ft/mi), with most of the drop accounted for by the Montreal Rapids. The second section, from the picnic site to the Highway 165 bridge, is 2.61 m/km (13.63 ft/mi)! That's why there are all those continuous rapids. There are no really large drops, nor any lakes, so the shallow, windy rapids and swift current entirely account for the gradient. That is a very steep gradient for northern Saskatchewan. Good practice for the Cree or the William. The gradient of the third section is 0.17 m/km (0.92 ft/mi), indicating that the latter part of the river has lots of current, but there are few rapids and there's lots of lake area. The overall gradient of the Montreal River to Lac La Ronge is 0.87 m/km (4.56 ft/mi), lakes included.

Character of the River and Region

The volume of the Montreal increases slightly as it flows into the lakes to the north, but it continues to be a small-volume river to its end at Lac La Ronge. The rapids are almost all rock gardens with swift-flowing water. The rocks range in size from bread boxes to bears. There are some small, standing waves, but mostly it's all about finding the route through the rocks that has the most water. The rapids tend to go around corners, around islands, and are continuous in many places. The fast, shallow rapids on the Montreal remind me of many of the rapids on the Waterfound and Cree Rivers. The riverbed is either mucky or rocky, and not much in between. Beavers like to try and dam the river at the shallow rapids, and their handiwork makes for ledge-type rapids in places!

Because this is the Mid-Boreal Uplands, the landscape is less rugged than the Shield just to the north near Lac La Ronge. The soil is more loamy, though it can be sandy as well. The forest is made up of mixed stands of aspen and white and black spruce, with jack pine in the sandier areas. Beaver abound on the Montreal because of all the aspen to be had. In fact in some areas it's as if they have logged the place. Black spruce and tamarack flourish in the low-lying peatlands. The understory of the forest ranges from feather mosses and lichen in coniferous stands to shrubs, herbs and grasses in deciduous ones.

Open clearings for camping are often the result of beaver activity, and you will find some open jack pine benches on escarpments for camping, but you won't find rock camping like that in the Shield — there is virtually no outcropping to be seen. Though the uplands are obvious in the Thunder and Cub Hills, the Montreal is to the north of the higher elevations in the La Ronge Lowlands. The land around the river is flat and level for the most part. There are some signs of glacial till features here and there. Visually, the Montreal reminds me of places on the Clearwater, Haultain and lower Sturgeon-weir.

Local History ✱✱✱

The history of permanent settlement in the Montreal Lake region is fairly recent. Located between the Saskatchewan River system and the Churchill River system, the region does not contain any major river routes that were traditionally important for the establishment of human settlements. After initial contact between the European fur traders and the Native people, La Ronge was where most of the trading activity took place, as it had been an important post between the Churchill and points south since 1782, and was a traditional summer gathering place for the Cree. The La Lac Ronge First Nation has a number of reserves on the lower or northern section of the Montreal River, on Bigstone Lake, and around Lac La Ronge. These are traditional lands of Saskatchewan's largest Woods Cree Nation.

In 1820, the HBC abandoned its post at Lac La Ronge. To survive, some people moved into areas like the Montreal Lake region, where fur and game animals were still relatively abundant. Before 1889, the Woods Cree did not live year round at one place but instead followed a seasonal pattern of movement that took them to camping spots at Candle Lake, Bittern Lake, Red Deer or Waskesiu Lake and the north and south ends of Montreal Lake. Trapping areas were organized by individual extended families that established themselves at the various lakes.

Significant human occupation of Montreal Lake began in the middle of the 19th century with the arrival of a family of Woods Cree from Grand Rapids, at the northwest end of Lake Winnipeg. According to oral tradition, James Bird, his wife, two sons and a nephew followed an old fur-trade route that took them northwest along the Churchill River to Stanley Mission, across Lac La Ronge, and south towards Montreal Lake. Now the people of the Montreal Lake Cree Nation live on the southeast shore of Montreal Lake. This reserve was chosen during the addition to the Treaty 6 negotiations of 1889. An HBC trading post was eventually built at the northeast end of Montreal Lake, at Molanosa, and Montreal Lake became a freighting depot along the route from Prince Albert to La Ronge and other points north. Up until the 1920s teams of horses did most of the freighting in and out of Montreal Lake in the summer and winter. Canoes and York boats were also used in the spring and summer months. Often six or seven teams were seen coming and going each day, and occasionally up to fifteen teams were reported. Destinations included Big River and Stanley Mission.

Molanosa, which used to be at the northeast end of Montreal Lake, apparently got its name from its location, *Mo*ntreal *La*ke *No*rthern *Sa*skatchewan, and the post office in Weyakwin across the lake is still called that. According to a friend of mine, when the main highway was built on the west side of the lake, the government decided not to run power to Molanosa, and "moved" the community to Weyakwin. Apparently the files on this decision were closed to the public for a specified number of years. This led to speculation on the reasons for the community being moved. Some people living in Weyakwin reported seeing lights moving at night across the lake where Molanosa used to be. Rumour had it that the lights were from gold or diamond exploration taking place under the cover of night, and that the government had wanted to move the people so they could mine the wealth. The other interesting story that was shared with me about the Montreal River region is a Loch-Ness-monster-type legend about Montreal Lake. Because the lake is so deep, it is said that a large creature, like the Loch Ness monster or Ogopogo from Lake Okanagon, haunts its cold depths and shows itself every once in a while. Paddlers beware!

In the days when there was a horse-drawn freight run across the North in the winter, it was 65 miles from Montreal Lake to La Ronge over frozen muskeg. In the spring, the fur traders of the time paddled the Montreal as part of a route from Waskesui to La Ronge, when it was impossible to haul freight over the thawing muskeg. Keighley notes that in the spring they would paddle up the Deer River (*Waskesui*, or "Red Deer" in Cree, their word for elk) to reach Montreal Lake from the Prince Albert area. They would start at Waskesui Lake, go north down the Deer, paddle north across Montreal Lake and then down the Montreal River. Once reaching Lac La Ronge, all points north were accessible.

In fact, some people referred to the Rapid River, which drains Lac La Ronge into Iskwatikan Lake then Nistowiak Lake creating the well-known Nistowiak Falls, as the Montreal River. Tyrrell puts it this way in his *1986 Report on the Country Between Athabasca Lake and Churchill River*: the Montreal is a tributary of the Bigstone River, as it flows into Bigstone Lake. The Bigstone River flows from Bigstone Lake into Lac La Ronge. Then the Rapid River (or Forks River, as he also calls it!) is the last of the Montreal's flow from Lac La Ronge into Iskwatikan into the Churchill. Confusing! But essentially, the Montreal River does flow north into the Churchill, call it what you will. The Rapid River section was considered a very important link in the travel route from the Saskatchewan to the Churchill. Fidler suggests in his journal it was as important as the Upper Churchill in the fur trade.

It also had significance for the Cree people, as it was a major travel route, and the area was a seasonal home base. Additionally, Jones, in his book, *The Aboriginal Rock Paintings of the Churchill River*, indicates that a limestone cave along this northern section of the Montreal (on Hale Lake between Lac La Ronge and Iskwatikan) was thought to be the home of some *Memekwesiwak*, what he described as "a type of human being usually described as being small, often having no nose, possessing powerful medicine and knowledge of medicinal matters, whose homes are in rocks, water or other places." Elders used to go to the cave to obtain medicine.

Remarkably, although it is such a shallow, fast-flowing river, Sidney Keighley, a fur trader in the North for many years, and a companion ran the Montreal in the spring of 1921 with a 19-foot freighter canoe fully loaded. They were on their way from Montreal Lake to Stanley Post. Imagine portaging! Especially around the Montreal Rapids, well known for being a very long portage — 6 km (4 mi)! Keighley's book is an interesting source of information on the late days of the fur trade and on northern Saskatchewan.

In fact, the Montreal River was named for the "Montreal Men," as the Cree of the area called the North West Company (NWC) fur traders from Montreal when they first came to establish trade. For very good information on all aspects of the Montreal Lake region, consult the book, *The Montreal Lake Region: Its History and Geography*, by Peter Goode, Leslie Amudson and Joan Champ.

Level of Solitude **

The Montreal is not a remote river, but it is a wilderness river. From Montreal Lake to Bigstone Lake you will not see very many people, and they will generally not be tourists. Local trappers, hunters and fishing parties use the river, and there is some local sport and commercial fishing on Montreal and Bigstone Lakes. There are no communities along the river, though there are a number of cabins, seasonal camps and uninhabited reserves. You won't see any other canoeists, I'll bet. This is partly because you can only run the section with the all the rapids in spring runoff or into the summer in a high-water year, and partly because not many people know what a fun spring run it is. Personally, I do think the road access takes away from the feeling of being "out there," in the first two sections, but as you leave the Highway 165 bridge behind you, it seems wilder again. The swampy, twisty area through the willows for miles and miles is enough to leave you bushed if nothing else does! Don't say I didn't warn you.

Wildlife **

The Mid-Boreal Upland wildlife populations are high and diverse. Moose, woodland caribou, mule deer, white-tailed deer, elk, black bears, timber wolves and beavers are some of the large animals you might see. However, the river is in an area subject to hunting pressure. Populations are not as high as they might be in less accessible areas, and the wildlife makes itself as scarce as possible when humans are around. That said, I've seen lots of bears, a few moose, and three woodland caribou, and many, many beavers in the area north of Montreal Lake. Eagle sightings are also common.

An elk restoration project is underway in the northern Montreal Lake region. They were hunted out many years ago and are being reintroduced, thus the sign at the Montreal Lake put-in. Maybe you will be lucky enough to see one!

Fishing **

I wouldn't bother taking a rod if you are only doing one of the daytrips. You won't have time to fish, and the rapids are too shallow for walleye or anything else in most places. There are lots of walleye and northerns in the upper reaches of the river near Montreal Lake and in the lower reaches once you reach Sikachu Lake. Bigstone is a good walleye lake as well. Check the closures for fishing walleye in the area before starting out, and remember fishing season opens the May long weekend.

Special Equipment

If the water isn't high, you'll wish you'd brought a Royalex boat if you don't take one! You could get an aluminum canoe down the Montreal River in high water, but you don't want to try, believe me. If the water is low you will stick to every rock in the river, and there are zillions of them! If you paddle Kevlar, expect to repair your gel coat. The recommendation for an ABS boat is for ease and saving time, more than a big safety concern, as you are not too far away from a road most of the time. But that does not mean you should be cavalier about the Montreal. It requires solid moving-water skills to descend it intact. Your canoe could end up wrapped or really beaten up in those shallow rapids, and so could you.

If you go in May the bugs won't be an issue, but I never go anywhere in the bush without repellent. If you have high water in June you will have to deal with the blackflies.

Trip Notes

MAP NO	GRID REF	FEATURE	DESCRIPTION
73 I/5	637387	Put-in	At an old dock on the northeast shore of Montreal Lake at a clearing at the end of a rough road.
73 I/12	619410	Campsite	On RL in a small sandy bay on a high bank with birch trees.
	617433 616429	Camping	A nice jackpine bench on RR provides a number of campsites.
	605473	Campsite	On RL by a beaver lodge on an elevated bench. It's very open, but weedy to get to.
	595493	Campsite	On RR is an attractive bench.
	572523	Campsite	An old hunting camp, protected in the trees.
	565534	Dam	**CAUTION:** There is an old dam with a weir that must be portaged. It is easy to spot the wreckage on the sides of the river, but the drop is deceiving. The **portage (100 m)** is on RR over the hump of the old road. There is a landing spot at the steep, grassy slope just before the dam.

MAP NO	GRID REF	FEATURE	DESCRIPTION
	560567	Rapid	**Class 1+** This rapid is indicated by the first marked bar after the dam. It is rocky and shallow, a good indication of what you are in for during most of the next 8 km to the Highway 2 bridge, including the Montreal Rapids.
	559569	Riffle	The second marked bar is only a riffle.
	558570 558575	Rapids	**Class 1.** There are 500 m of shallow rapids starting at the third marked bar on the map and continuing to the sixth. The rapids split around an unmarked island. I ran RR of the island. RL is very shallow and rocky, and is probably unnavigable at lower water levels.
	558577 563584	Fastwater	The next five bars are only fastwater until you reach a weedy islet with old beaver dam wreckage.
	559585	Rapids	**Class 1/1+.** 500 m after the old beaver dam there is a rapid with rocks to avoid. This is the last rapid of any difficulty before the river narrows and the Montreal Rapids begin. These rapids consist of two sets of continuous rapids.
	556589	Montreal Rapids Part One	**Class 1/1+.** Continuous winding rapids with rocks to avoid for almost 2 km. The last rapid of note in this first section is at the sharp bend to the left between the "E" and "A" of MONTREAL, and it is the most difficult. It is **Class 2** in lower water where the rapid splits at the bottom. Rock dodging is required. It's steep at the corner.
	560605	Riffle	The marked bar is only a riffle.
	555608	Riffle	The marked bar is only a riffle again.
	555614	Potential campsite	On RR is a bench that appears suitable for camping. A steep scramble up.
	555615	Rapid	**Class 1+.** A beaver dam ledge to be negotiated! Located where marked bar is and the river widens.
	555618	Potential campsite	On RL on a bench there appears to be room for camping. A steep scramble up.
	553624 549632	Montreal Rapids Part Two	**Class 1+ to riffles.** The first rapid is the most difficult, requiring the most maneuvering. The rapids end just before the Highway 2 bridge.
	551632	Water survey station	High on the bank on RR. Old cable-car wreckage hangs where old road used to be.
	549632	Hwy 2 Bridge Take-out Put-in	RR just before or after the bridge is a good take-out for a daytrip from Montreal Lake. Approximately a seven-hour paddle, depending on skill and water level. It is also a possible put-in for the next section of the Montreal, though the parking is better in the picnic site just down the highway.
	547634 548636	Riffles	The three bars are fast water with the odd rock.

MAP NO	GRID REF	FEATURE	DESCRIPTION
	549637	Campsite	A flat open spot on RL on a grassy bank following the fast water and before creek coming in on RL.
	556645	Rapids Put-in	**Class 1+**. An unmarked rapid starts just above where the path from the picnic site comes down to the river. The rapid continues just around the bend to the left.
	556647 542670	Rapids	For the next 3 km there are many unmarked riffles and **Class 1** rapids. Rock dodging is required, less in higher water.
73 I/13	543670 541673	Riffles	The first three marked bars on the map are only riffles.
	539674 536676	Rapids	**Class 1 to Class 2.** This stretch is the most difficult you will encounter up to the Highway 165 bridge. As you go around the big S-turn the rapids become progressively harder. The tough Class 2 rapid comes at the end and is indicated by the last couple of marked bars. It ends with a steep and fast rock apron with a couple of larger boulders thrown in for fun.
	537676	Campsite	On RR high up on the sand bank. A nice open jack pine bench.
	536677	Cabin	There's an old trapper's cabin on RR on the shoulder of the sand bank just downstream of campsite noted above.
	525685	Campsite	On RL, in the clearing on the bench just after the beaver lodge.
	520697 520698 519703	Riffles	Three unmarked riffles occur in the places where the river narrows.
	519707	Rapids	**Class 1**. 150 m of unmarked rapids with waves where the river narrows. The rapids end 600 m upstream of next marked rapids.
	524709 523714	Rapids	**Class 1**. 550 m of marked rapids. Shallow and rocky.
	521716 520717	Riffles	For 250 m in between the marked rapids.
	519720	Rapids	**Class 1 to 1+**. 300 m of marked rapids, shallow and rocky with the last set the most difficult. I ran RC at the top and then RL in the middle and bottom sets, looking for the deepest water.
	520726 528739	Rapids	**Class 1 to 1+**. Unmarked shallow rapids for 1,650 m.
	528740	Campsite	On RR on a point of the bend, a nice high bench with birch trees.
	518742	Rapid	**Class 1**, with waves at narrows.
	513745	Riffle	At the sharp bend to the right.
	513748	Campsite	On RR on a point of the bend.
	511750 497777	Rapids	**Fastwater to Class 1+**. A windy, shallow section where you must find the deep-water route. All the marked rapids until the big bend are shallow. It's squint-as-you-run country — very difficult to see the rocks on a sunny day, so bring your sunnies!

MAP NO	GRID REF	FEATURE	DESCRIPTION
	525729	Trail Camping	The marked snowmobile trail meets the river here, and there is potential for camping in the clearing.
	496780 492785	Rapids	**Class 1+** around the big bend. This is probably as shallow as it gets, and if the water is low at all you will be fighting to keep from grounding out. Look for the deep-water route.
	492785 495795	Rapids	**Class 1+**, unmarked rapids in a burned area for 2 km. Very shallow and continuous.
	495796	Campsite	On RL at the bend. At the end of a very shallow set of rapids, up on the bench overlooking corner.
	491802	Campsite	On the other side of the bend on RL, same bench.
	495797 504807	Rapids	**Class 1/1+**. Another long stretch of basically continuous rapids. Approximately 3 km, no less! The rapids begin to braid around islands. Watch for fallen trees and sweepers. When you reach the low weedy islands there is only one short rapid left before the Highway 165 bridge. It comes after approximately 1 km of flatwater.
	510813	Rapid	**Class 1+**, standing waves around a corner where the river squeezes through a narrows. It looks like there was a trestle or bridge of some sort across here at one time. This is the last rapid before the bridge.
	512813	Cabin	On RR up high on a sand bank is a trapping and hunting cabin still in use. It's 1.25 km to bridge from here.
	520820	Hwy 165 Bridge	The path is on RL just before the bridge. It leads to a parking area down off road. Paddling from the picnic site on Highway 2 to this bridge (about 33 km) takes about $6^1/_2$ to 7 hours on average. Skill and water levels will make a big difference in how long it will take you. Plan to get on the river early and have the whole day to paddle this section.

montreal river

45

Note: If you paddle on to Bigstone Lake or Lac La Ronge, there are lots of sweepers in the river just after the bridge, and then a couple of sets of rapids to watch out for. Some approach Class 2. The marshy areas where the rivers winds non-stop do not have any good campsites. Plan on camping on one of the lakes where nice camping is easier to find, as there are rock outcroppings and jack pine benches. It is really a relief to get to Partridge Crop and Sikachu Lakes. Finally, if you are not an experienced whitewater boater, do not attempt to run the rapids between Bigstone Lake and Lac La Ronge. The rapids behind the residences at Bigstone are very fast and steep and require precision maneuvering to get a loaded tandem boat down safely. Take out at the end of Bigstone Road on RL instead.

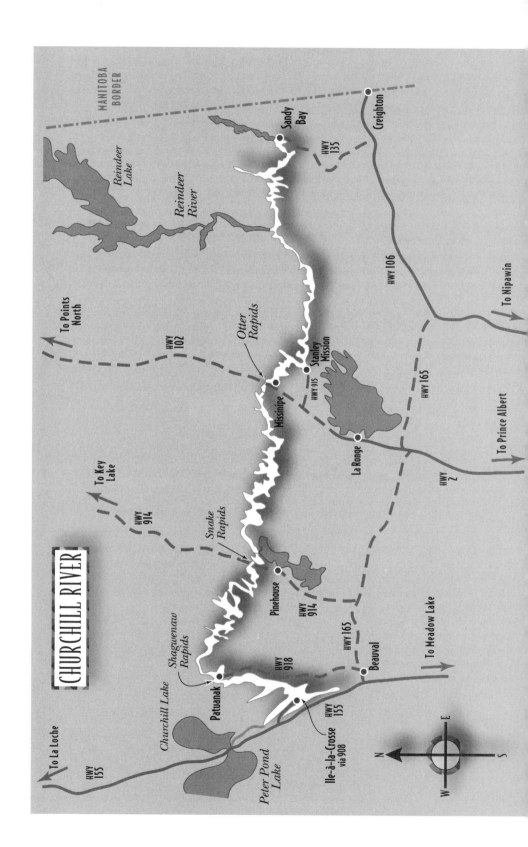

CHURCHILL RIVER

MANITOBA BORDER

Reindeer Lake

Reindeer River

Sandy Bay

Creighton

HWY 135

To Points North

HWY 102

Otter Rapids

Stanley Mission

HWY 915

Missinipe

HWY 106

HWY 165

To Prince Albert

La Ronge

To Key Lake

HWY 914

Snake Rapids

HWY 2

To Nipawin

Shagwenaw Rapids

Churchill Lake

Patuanak

HWY 918

Pinehouse

HWY 914

HWY 165

Beauval

To Meadow Lake

Peter Pond Lake

Ile-à-la-Crosse via 908

HWY 155

To La Loche

HWY 155

N
E
S
W

CHURCHILL RIVER

The Churchill is the mother river of northern Saskatchewan. Once you swim in her waters in the sunshine, smell the morning in the forest, and play in the rapids rushing to Hudson Bay, you will never be the same. The Churchill's green waves, rugged Precambrian outcropping, fine fens and bounty of fish and wildlife have won the heart of every canoeist I know.

The stories of the First Nations' way of life and travels and the coming of the fur traders and voyageurs have captured the imaginations of people all over the world. I've guided or met people from all over Europe and the United States, and even Mauritius and Mexico, on the Churchill. No other river in northern Saskatchewan is so well known, and for good reason.

The Churchill has many attractions. It is home to Cree, Metis and Dene people, and pictographs signal from rock faces along its length. Dotted with small communities, it flows through the entire width of northern Saskatchewan — a wilderness river crossed only twice by roads. It is home to the second-largest population of bald eagles in North America and is the richest ecoregion in the Precambrian Shield for moose, black bears and timber wolves. Angling can be excellent, especially in the eddies of the large rapids. There is luxurious camping on rock ledges and wooded islands, and all sorts of berries and herbs thrive in its forests.

Its Cree name, *Missinipi*, meaning "big water," couldn't be more apt. The Churchill is a large-volume river with big drops and huge haystacks that will make fire run in your veins. Massive lakes, narrow lakes, deep lakes and shallow weedy lakes span the width of Saskatchewan, with challenging rapids in between. It is the fifth-largest river in Canada, and runs free until Sandy Bay. It's one of my favourite rivers in the world.

Length

The trip described here is approximately 608 km long. It is a drive-in and drive-out trip, beginning at the community of Ile-à-la-Crosse and ending at the community of Sandy Bay.

To shorten the trip, you could fly in anywhere along the route or paddle in from one of the main tributaries, like the Mudjatik, Haultain, Foster or Paull, among others. You can also put in from any of the other canoe routes that link up to the Churchill, like the six-portages route from Nemeiben Lake. You could also paddle up the Sturgeon-weir and take Frog Portage in, and then carry on up to Sandy Bay. Or you could start at any road-accessible place and take out at another. For instance, you could paddle from Snake Rapids to Otter Rapids; there are many good choices.

To lengthen the trip, there are even more options. The Churchill is the major waterway of the North, and it is a crossroads. From the Churchill, you can go anywhere east, west, north or south. A couple of drive-in options include putting in at Churchill Lake at Buffalo Narrows, or driving a little farther to paddle more of the voyageur route by starting from Lac La Loche. Of course, if you really have the bug, you could start at Lloyd Lake and run most of the Clearwater River to the Methy Portage and make the famous trek into the Churchill. Or you could just paddle all the way to Hudson Bay. Imagine that.

In this chapter, because the trip is so long and most canoeists won't be able to paddle the entire trip in one shot, I break the trip into road-accessible segments. This is more appropriate for planning shorter excursions on the Churchill. I wouldn't want to do the entire 608-km trip in less than six weeks. That gives you some windbound/rest days if you paddle about 25 km a day. By the time you have paddled that many days, 25 km will seem like a walk in the park, even with a strong headwind!

Ile-à-la-Crosse to Patuanak	*	65 km
Patuanak to Snake Rapids	*½	150 km
Snake Rapids to Otter Rapids	**	164 km
Otter Rapids to Stanley Mission	*	33 km
Stanley Mission to Sandy Bay	**½	196 km
Ile-à-la Crosse to Sandy Bay	***	608 km

Difficulty Ratings: * Easiest   ** Average   *** Difficult   **** Very Difficult

Topographic Maps

I use the 1:50,000 scale topographic maps on the Churchill because of the numerous channels in some sections. It makes navigation easier, though it is harder on the budget! For the entire trip from Ile-à-la-Crosse to Sandy Bay you will need 22 maps: 73 O/5, 73 O/12, 73 O/13, 74 B/4, 74 B/3, 73 O/14, 73 O/15, 73 O/10, 73 O/9, 73 O/16, 73 P/12, 73 P/11, 73 P/10, 73 P/7, 73 P/8, 63 M/5, 63 M/6, 63 M/11, 63 M/10, 63 M/7, 63 M/8 and 63 M/9. You may want to lessen your expenses by borrowing maps, either from a friend or a university library that has a map department, and photocopying only those sections you need for the river trip. Don't forget that you will need to have the grid reference line numbers somewhere on the photocopies for the both north- and east-running lines in order to be able to use the Trip Notes!

If you are shortening your trip, look through the Trip Notes at the end of the chapter for the maps you will need. The features of the trip are described as you move downstream map by map, so it will be easy to determine which ones are required for the section of the river you want to paddle.

I suggest you purchase your maps ahead of time so you can mark in missing and interesting features on your maps before you start down the river. Using the Trip Notes, you can mark in the rapids that are missing, the rapids' classifications, the locations of the portages, where you might like to camp, and the historic sites you don't want to miss.

You may also want to consult three SERM booklets describing parts of the Churchill canoe trip detailed in the Trip Notes: *Route #1 Ile-à-la-Crosse to Otter Rapids*, *Route #29 Otter Lake to Sandy Bay*, and *Saskatchewan's Voyageur Highway: A Canoe Trip*. The two numbered routes can be obtained by printing an online version at the Canoe Saskatchewan website or by calling SERM. The Voyageur Route booklet must be ordered by phone from SERM.

Getting There and Away

The Churchill trip segments are all road accessible, making for a number of drive-in and drive-out opportunities. The fly in the ointment is that a long trip means a long shuttle on mostly gravel roads, and you simply don't want to leave your car or truck just anywhere. So, the cheapest thing to do is to call in all your favours with one or two friends, and have them come along for a ride. Then they can drive your vehicle(s) to a safe parking spot at the community you decide to take out at. If you want to take out at Snake Rapids, you might want to have a long-distance taxi pick you up and take you to your vehicle. Pinehouse would be an appropriate place to leave your vehicle. Besides being able to hire long-distance taxis in the North, you can take advantage of Churchill River Canoe Outfitters' long-distance shuttle service.

Sandy Bay can be reached via Highway 135, a decent gravel road. Highway 135 can be accessed via Highway 2 from La Ronge or Highway 106 from Prince Albert. Turn north on Highway 135, passing through Pelican Narrows. Carry on until you reach the end of the road. The air service in Sandy Bay let us park in their compound. To reach the air service, drive through Sandy Bay on the main road, keeping the lake on your left, until you reach the public dock. The floatplane base is just north of it.

To get to Ile-à-la-Crosse you must first access Highway 155 to Buffalo Narrows and La Loche. From 155, turn north on Highway 908 and drive to the end of the road. At Ile-à-la-Crosse you need to arrange for safe parking or a shuttle to your take-out of choice. Try contacting the SERM office or the RCMP. You can put in at the public beach on the north side of the peninsula by the Northern store or at the air service dock. There is an airstrip near the town, but there are no scheduled flights; you will have to charter if you want to fly in on wheels or floats.

For the other road access (put-in and take-out) points, including the picnic site on the South Bay of Lac Ile-à-la-Crosse, refer to a detailed map of Saskatchewan. For contact information for the services referred to above, canoe rentals, outfitting and guides, and for services near the other possible put-ins and take-outs, consult the Directory of Services under "Churchill" in the back of this guidebook.

If you are doing an extended trip on the Churchill you can plan on buying supplies at Ile-à-la-Crosse, Patuanak, Pinehouse (a round trip back to the river will be 45 km), Missinipe (on Otter Lake — a round trip adds only 7 km), and Stanley Mission. And some outfitters along the way have small stores where you can buy junk food! Sandy Bay has a good grocery store (across the street and up a bit from the air service) for buying treats of all kinds for the long drive home.

When to Go

Late May to the end of September. One of the great things about the Churchill is that is has so much volume you can paddle almost anywhere any time in the late spring, summer and fall. The large lakes are usually navigable by the third week of May. I've paddled around and through ice occasionally, but you can usually plan on heading out the May long weekend. Be careful if you head out early in the season: if the wind comes up, it can be very cold, and the water is like ice. The same goes for later in the season. A late September trip is beautiful when the leaves are changing, but the fall is also a windy season, and the water will be cold again. You must be very cautious about large lake crossings and running rapids in these conditions. The very best time for canoe tripping on the Churchill, in my opinion, is from early August to early September. There are few bugs, and the water is warm. Though the fishing isn't as good as in the spring, families from the communities along the river are out enjoying their summer camps, making for a happy atmosphere. In August of 2001, Dave Koop and I met an old friend, Sandy Ross, and his family on their way back from their summer camp below Drinking Falls. When we told him we were headed all the way to Sandy Bay, he laughed and said a motorboat would be faster. This from the guy who pulled me over the finish line first in a sprint event when the National Marathon Canoe Championships were held in Stanley Mission and La Ronge!

The water levels can vary extremely on the Churchill. Normally, maximum annual flows for the Otter Rapids area occur in July, and even later downstream on the eastern Churchill. There are two operating water-survey stations left on the Churchill, one at Otter Rapids and the other at Sandy Bay. To check current water levels you can call SaskWater. Comparing the readings you get to the chart on the Canoe Saskatchewan website will help you determine whether the current water level is high, normal or low. You can even check their website for water-level predictions for the next month, which may help you decide where on the Churchill you would like to paddle. The lower Churchill, after the Reindeer comes in, can get really gnarly at high water. It's very big water — 800 cu m/sec! Now compare that to the next biggest river in the guidebook, the Fond du Lac. At its outlet to Black Lake it flows around 400 cu m/sec on average in July — half the flow of the eastern Churchill.

Difficulty of the River * to **¹/₂ (*** for the entire trip)

The difficulty ratings, as shown for each segment in the Trip Length section, reflect the fact that some parts of the Churchill are good to learn to paddle whitewater on, and then there are some places where you just shouldn't be without lots of experience in moving water up to Class 2+. The volume of water is so big once the Reindeer flows into the eastern part of the Churchill that even just the current in the river becomes tricky to navigate. This is especially the case in narrows, below and above portages, and in the rapids. Boils, whirlpools and eddy fences get bigger and bigger as you move east.

I was amazed at the big-water experience Dave and I had in August of 2001. The water was rising all the way, and at one point after the Reindeer confluence, the water was only a few inches below the highest-ever water mark. Class 2 rapids became a standing wave dodge. The waves were so big that we could actually paddle between them and sideways through them! It reminded me of paddling on the Colorado River in the Grand Canyon.

Most of the rapids of the Churchill are chutes where the water drops over ledges or over a rocky bottom through narrows between the lakes. This type of rapids is dominated by big holes and large compression waves. The Churchill is a cartoon version of a drop-pool river. You generally have kilometres to pick up all your stuff if you wipe out. That is not to say that canoes don't wrap on the river, because I have seen numerous red, blue and green fortune cookies resting on rocks. There are some technical rapids, but usually swamping is the big issue. The average class of the rapids is Class 2/2+, generally because of the large standing waves. The sections rated the highest for difficulty are where there are the highest concentrations of rapids and falls.

Depending on the routes you choose, there are seven to ten mandatory portages around falls, and all the large, difficult rapids can be portaged on good trails. Most of the rapids along the entire length of the Churchill have portages around them. You will sometimes even have the luxury of using a rail car, log ramp, or ramp-and-roller system to push and pull your boat across the portage. Leaving half your gear in and carrying the rest on the second trip makes for easy portaging. There are exceptions; some rapids do not have proper portages, and cautious canoeists will have to bushwhack or line around them.

Rapids aside, the greatest hazards on the Churchill are the exposed distances of open water that canoeists must cross without shelter from wind. Paddling the massive lakes is potentially dangerous, and people have lost their lives when they swamped while paddling in rough water. Winds can come up very quickly, so if there is any doubt about the weather, stay close to shore at all times. Beginners should plan a route where they are never far from shore. Additionally, good map-reading and compass skills are required for navigating the large distances and many islands.

The trip can be strenuous, especially if it's windy. The trip is also long, exceptionally so if you do all the segments in the expedition, making experience with longer canoe trips important. If you have little experience, try one of the shorter trips that are so readily made on the Churchill to hone your tripping skills. For the 608-km trip, the planning and packing skill and level of bushcraft needed is higher than for a short trip with the same river features. It becomes much more important that you know how to stay warm and dry and generally take care of yourself.

Finally, beware of large jet boats speeding through the channels and rapids below Sluice Falls; move out of the way quickly. I've seen little regard for the canoeists from some of the jet-boat drivers. Watch for swamping waves, and if you tip below a rapids get out from below the drop quickly. At some of the larger drops the driver cannot see anything, and they go very fast through the rapids. Believe me, some of us have tried very hard to have these concerns addressed for years, but so far to no avail.

Beginners will enjoy the trips between Ile-à-la-Crosse and Patuanak and Otter Rapids and Stanley Mission. Guided beginners, or beginners paddling with more advanced whitewater and tripping canoeists, will find the trips downstream of these sections challenging. Intermediate canoeists with tripping and moving-water experience should be comfortable on most trips on the Churchill, and there are thrills for the advanced and exceptional paddlers in the big whitewater experience. The area upstream of Otter Rapids has lots of quality whitewater, as does the eastern section, which far fewer people frequent.

The gradient of the river is almost meaningless, as there are so many large lakes and some large drops. The gradient of the Churchill trip from Ile-à-la-Crosse to Sandy Bay is 0.20 m/km (1.03 ft/mi). The greatest drop in elevation and the greatest concentration of rapids occur between Trout and Mountain Lakes of the middle Churchill and Iskwatam and Pita Lakes of the Churchill's eastern reaches.

Character of the River and Region

To give you some idea of what is meant by calling the Churchill "large volume," at Patuanak in July the river runs, on a ten-year average, at 150 cu m/sec. At Otter Rapids, the flow is usually around 350 cu m/sec. Just above Wintego Rapids, downstream of the Reindeer's flow, the July flow is 600 cu m/sec. At Sandy Bay, we're talking 800! Now, compare that to the average flow of the next-biggest-volume rivers. The Fond du Lac reaches its peak flows in June, and on average discharges 415 cu m/sec into Black Lake. The Clearwater's highest flows occur in May, averaging 125 cu m/sec. The Porcupine peaks in June, averaging flows of 118 cu m/sec.

The riverbed changes as you move from west to east, and much like on the Clearwater trip, you experience a transition from glacial till to Shield landforms. The river shoreline changes from sand to gravel and rubble to Precambrian rock. At Sandy Bay you can see the flat, smooth channels of solid pink granite, where the water used to flow before the dam. It's really eerie, and calls up images of the satellite shots of the channels they found on Mars.

The rapids along the river are somewhat different as a result of the different riverbeds. In the west, where there are more alluvial deposits, the rapids are less likely to be steep falls; the river drops in a more gradual, consistent manner over glacial rubble. As you approach Black Bear Island Lake you really get into the polished bedrock outcropping, and here you find steep cataracts. Needle, Birch, Trout, Sluice, Robertson and Twin Falls are all characteristic of the Shield. Most of the falls have accompanying rapids in side channels. Ledges are common in the rapids, as are boulder beds. The eastern section of the river is dominated by deep-water rapids in smooth rock channels. Chutes and large standing waves are more often the flavour of the day.

Along the Churchill, you will find evidence of the Earth's geological history and the power of huge masses of ice upon the Earth's surface. At Ile-à-la-Crosse, in the Mid-Boreal ecoregion, undulating glacial till of sandy alluvial deposits and sand beaches are the predominant evidence of the Wisconsin Glaciers that covered the area 10,000 years ago. From there and through Dipper Lake the shores are often boulder-strewn, the rock originating from the glacial till left when the ice sheet receded.

Along the shores of the western reaches of the river, aspen, jack pine and black spruce dominate. The mixed stands have an understory of alder, blueberry, bearberry and reindeer moss. The lowlands and swamps are full of black spruce and tamarack with an understory of Labrador tea, cloud berry and peat moss. In areas with more moisture, and western alluvial areas near the mouth of the Mudjatik and nearby south-facing shores, stands of trembling aspen, balsam poplar, white spruce and white birch are predominant. A conspicuous shrub layer exists, and ground cover includes various herbs and feather mosses. In the wet alluvial terrain found near the mouth of the Haultain and other major streams in the area, white birch and black spruce dominate.

The Mudjatik, Haultain and Belanger Rivers were meltwater channels for the glaciers. The marsh areas at their mouths are unique, for nowhere else along the river are these types of areas found. There are also a number of esker-kame complexes in the western Churchill region. The Dene call the areas where there is sparse jack pine forest on sandy flats covered with lichen understory and little underbrush *taitl*, meaning "sandy blanket." It is the best forest for camping and travelling on foot, appreciated by the Dene, who used to do so through the North. You can see through the trees a long way, and walking is easy.

At Pinehouse Lake, the river runs through an area more typical of Precambrian Shield. Glacial deposits are thin and discontinuous, with areas of exposed bedrock. Granite and gneiss are predominant. The most common forests are black spruce and jack pine. In the black spruce forest, ground covers include feather mosses, Labrador tea, bog cranberry and various herbs, lichens and green alders, and small shrubs and herbs. Open jack pine forest can be found on the ridges of exposed bedrock. Birch, pin cherry and willow are also found in the jack pine forest. Lichen covers the rock, and the ground story is a dense carpet of lichen mosses, shrubs and herbs. Peatlands and wetlands are also characteristic of these uplands, with treed bogs to open bogs. Stunted black spruce and tamarack, willow and dwarf birch also occur.

Bedrock is the major influence on the landscape and drainage characteristics of the Churchill Uplands ecoregion. Local relief can reach as much as 90 m, but is generally less than 60 m. Clear lakes, fens and bogs fill the valleys and depressions between the ridges, hills and knolls. The Churchill Uplands is 40 percent water, and this shouldn't surprise anyone once they have paddled the great lakes of the Churchill River. You will also notice as you move east that low-lying Knee, Dreger, Sandy and Pinehouse Lakes are strongly oriented in a northeast-southwest direction. This reflects the direction of the folding and zones of weakness in the basement rock created in the Precambrian era and the direction of the ice movement during the Wisconsin Glaciation.

The bedrock outcroppings you encounter in earnest after Pinehouse Lake are the exhumed bases of the Precambrian Churchillian Mountains, after some 1.5 billion years of erosion. Common rock in this area includes granite, gneiss and schist. In fact, the composition of the rock changes as you move from west to east; there is more evidence of complex volcanic rock as you move downstream, and on the west side of Pikoos Island on Sandfly Lake there is a large quartz intrusion. Needle Falls is also interesting geologically because there is a fault in the bedrock that shows itself there. Tyrrell explains that it is called Needle Falls "because the surface of the rock has been weathered into rough sharp points and edges, over which the voyageurs were obliged to carry their heavy loads, usually walking with bare feet."

Approaching the mouth of the Foster, outcrops of Precambrian rock begin to dominate the landscape, and the mixed forest becomes more a black spruce and jack pine forest. Many granite cliffs surround Black Bear Island Lake, sometimes rising as high as 20 m above the lake. The rolling till terrain of the western Churchill has become elevations of rugged rock-knob complexes. There probably isn't any better rock camping than on Black Bear Island Lake. The Churchill runs through the Foster Upland until Otter Lake.

The eastern Churchill flows through the Sisipuk Plain, which extends from Mountain Lake to Sandy Bay and beyond. It is also a predominantly bedrock and black spruce area, but there is some mixed-wood forest. The berries and herbs are especially rich in this section. However, the spruce budworm has seriously damaged the old-growth spruce along the eastern Churchill. And camping is harder to find in the eastern reaches at times due to the large forest fires in the region in the past six years. Forest fires in the past twenty years have changed the Churchill, primarily on the river west of Knee Lake, at Mountain and Drinking Lakes, east of Trade Lake and Wapumon, Wintego and Pita Lakes.

For more reading on the geological history of the Churchill River, try the article by Walter Kupsch published in *The Muskox*, by the Institute for Northern Studies, which is online at the Canoe Saskatchewan website, at www.lights.com/waterways/geology/kupsch.htm. The *Atlas of Saskatchewan* and the *Geological History of Saskatchewan* also provide in-depth information on the geology of the Churchill region.

Local History ★★★★

Part of the Churchill, the 487-km stretch from Ile-à-la-Crosse to Frog Portage, has been nominated for Heritage River status due its outstanding heritage values, not to mention its natural and recreational values. The trip described in this guidebook is not the historic voyageur route of the NWC and HBC, although it follows a large part of it. It doesn't include the headwaters of the Churchill, but starts at Ile-à-la-Crosse, the most important trading post and fur depot in Saskatchewan's fur-trade history. Also, instead of leaving the Churchill at Frog Portage, the river's most famous portage, as the Montreal men did, this trip takes the canoeist through to Sandy Bay.

The eastern Saskatchewan section of the Churchill is often forgotten in all the hype about the opening up of the west by the independent fur traders via the Sturgeon-weir. However, if you carried on past Sandy Bay you could paddle the Churchill to Hudson Bay, taking some detours around the dams in Manitoba, mind you. First Nations people travelled this section, and the three rock-painting sites on the section downstream of Frog Portage signify its importance. There are more after Sandy Bay as well. A culture camp, Kitchi-Miskanow Outfitters, owned and operated by the Highway family from Pelican Narrows, is located on Iskwatam Lake, and offers educational packages for people wanting to learn about traditional Cree life. That's pretty neat, and historic.

The first evidence of people living along the Churchill dates back to somewhere around 5,000 to 6,000 years ago, the artifacts recovered indicating a Plains culture. Shortly after 3,000 years ago, the Taltheilei culture appeared in northern Saskatchewan. Evidence of this group is especially prominent in the western reaches of the Churchill, and these people are considered the ancestors of the contemporary Dene.

On the eastern Churchill, an upper Great Lakes Forest culture took form and spread throughout the boreal forest. A distinct Woods Cree culture developed sometime around AD 1000, and they were the predominant group on the Churchill from west to east when the European fur traders arrived. In the 1600s, Cree territory extended north far beyond the Churchill. It is said to have reached up to Lake Athabasca in the northwest, to just north of Cree Lake, to just south of Wollaston Lake in the northeast.

The Cree are believed to be the authors of all the pictographs, except perhaps one on the Clearwater. Their travel routes were obviously extensive. The Churchill was the most important waterway in northern Saskatchewan, by far, and there are seventeen pictograph sites that you can visit on this trip, from Pinehouse Lake to Wintego Rapids. All of the territory where the rock paintings are found on the Churchill is predominantly occupied by Cree people.

The Cree had a seasonal cycle that coincided with various food-getting activities and social events. They did not have permanent settlements in prehistory. In the summer, members of regional bands would congregate on the shores of lakes that could provide enough food for a concentrated population for two or three months. It was a time for socializing, reinforcing social ties, realigning families, and planning for wintering grounds and activities. After the influx of the Europeans, Cree families became increasingly reliant on the fur-trade economy, and there were three seasonal moves. In the autumn, families would travel to their wintering places, where they hunted and trapped. In the spring, they moved to a place near fast water where the ice would go out early and fish were plentiful. At breakup, the journey to the trading post and summer gathering place was made. Eventually, it was where the large trading posts were located that permanent settlements occurred. However, these posts were often located in the places that the First Nations had frequented for gatherings before trade with the Europeans began.

There are many Metis and Cree people in Ile-à-la-Crosse and Pinehouse. Grandmother's Bay, Stanley Mission and Sandy Bay are Cree communities on the Churchill. The Lac La Ronge Cree Nation and the Peter Ballentyne Cree Nation have a strong presence on the middle and eastern sections of the Churchill respectively.

In the very early days of the fur trade, the Dene would often carry their furs to the coastal forts on Hudson Bay and inland posts such as Ile-à-la-Crosse by foot. They made birchbark canoes when they reached the southern forest, which was more flush with birch, and then returned North with their trade goods. There was a Dene overland route that Mackenzie mentions in his journals that reached the Churchill River near Snake Rapids.

With peaceful relations ensuing between the Cree and the Dene, increased presence of traders in the interior and the adaptation of more Dene to the fur-trade economy, there was a greater Dene presence on the western reaches of the Churchill. After the Cree were decimated by smallpox in the first epidemic of 1781, a group of Dene, called the *kesyehot'ine*, or "Poplar House People," started to summer annually in the Churchill region. The southern regions were much richer in most fur-bearing animals, especially beavers, than the "Land of Little Sticks." These southern Dene made a "round" every summer, travelling from their traplines south of Cree Lake to the Churchill region and back. In the spring they would gather and move south via the Mudjatik (Deer) River, which eventually brought them to the Churchill, 17 km downstream of Patuanak. They proceeded past Patuanak, upstream to Ile-à-la-Crosse for the annual summer rendezvous. At the height of their movement south in the 1790s, some groups carried on as far south as Dore and Smoothstone Lakes via the Beaver River. They returned via the Smoothstone River to the Churchill at Pinehouse Lake. They then ascended the Foster, or sometimes the Belanger or Haultain, back to their wintering grounds south of Cree Lake.

Dene families continued their migratory lifestyle for the next 100 years, but no longer moved so far from Ile-à-la-Crosse. They would gather there four times a year in the late 1800s. The trading houses were made of poplar, thus the name the "Poplar House People." Some families eventually permanently settled along the southern edges of their "round." These were the ancestors of the English River Denesuline First Nation people living along the western Churchill. Patuanak and Elak Dase (Knee Lake, also called Pine River in the past) are the major Dene communities along the Churchill today. There is also a populated reserve at Ile-à-la-Crosse. There were small communities with churches on Dipper and Primeau Lakes, but they are no longer lived in year round. Most families relocated to Patuanak when the school was built there.

For more information on the prehistory of the Churchill River and region consult the following sources: Dale Russell's *Eighteenth Century Western Woods Cree and their Neighbours*, the *Atlas of Saskatchewan*, and *The Handbook of North American Indians: The Subarctic, Volume 6*. I highly recommend you get a copy of Tim Jones's book about the pictographs, *The Aboriginal Rock Paintings of the Churchill River*, before heading out on your trip.

The Churchill River was eventually renamed for John Churchill, first duke of Marlborough, governor of the HBC, after an HBC expedition explored the mouth of the river at Hudson Bay. A number of places on the Churchill have a Dene, Cree, French and English name, while most have at least a Cree, French and English name. Robinson and Marchildon do an excellent job of providing the variety of names for important places along the "voyageur highway."

The Churchill was also called the English River by the French-Canadian fur traders and some Indians because the HBC had its post at its mouth on Hudson Bay, and when Joseph Frobisher crossed Frog Portage to the Churchill, he knew it was the same river. Missinipi, Fidler argues, only refers to the lower Churchill, downstream of the confluence with the Rapid River. Yet, according to some sources, Missinipi only referred to the upper Churchill. The lower Churchill was called *Manitousibi*, or "Danish" or "Strangers' River," by the Cree, in reference to Jens Munk's wintering in 1619–1620. To add to the confusion, the section of the river from the east end of Knee Lake through the Haultain marshes downstream to Dreger Lake was called the Grass or Grassy River during Mackenzie's time.

The Churchill, travelled for thousands of years already, was opened up to the Montreal and European traders by the discovery of a portage over the height of land from the

Saskatchewan to the Churchill drainage system. This Portage du Traite (Trade Portage), or what became known in Cree as *Athiquisipichigan Ouinigam* ("Portage of the Stretched Frog Skin"), links the Churchill to the headwaters of the Sturgeon-weir River, which flows into the Saskatchewan River.

In 1774, Joseph Frobisher, a Montreal trader, arrived at the portage and traded for all the furs he could carry, intercepting Indians who were on their way to trade at the HBC post on the coast. This began the inland trading-post era and changed the scope and nature of the fur trade and the lives of the First Nations people forever.

The portage eventually became known as Frog Portage, for short. Mackenzie recounts in his journal how the Cree name apparently came about. A group of Cree trappers stretched a frog skin, the way one would stretch a beaver skin, and hung it at the portage in order to make fun of the Dene trappers' preparation of beaver furs. When the Dene first entered the fur trade, they had little experience preparing furs the way the European traders wished, especially with beavers, as they were not plentiful in caribou country the way they were in the Churchill region.

Louis Primeau built the first trading post on the Churchill River at Frog in 1774, and also constructed the first trading post on the upper Churchill on Dipper Lake in 1775. At the time, Dipper and Primeau Lake were considered one lake — Primeau. Following in Alexander Henry and Joseph Frobisher's wake, Primeau and Thomas Frobisher opened a post to trade with the Dene, who were travelling south with their furs, at Ile-à-la-Crosse in 1776–1777. Ile-à-la-Crosse eventually became the site of the most important fur-trading post and depot on the Churchill and in the region. Ile-à-la-Crosse was named for the local enthusiasm for playing the game of lacrosse. There were many forts and posts built and rebuilt at the current location of the town of Ile-à-la-Crosse and in the vicinity, including the islands and the mouth of the Beaver River and at Aubichon Arm (Deep River). Fort Black was the NWC post at one time.

Once Peter Pond pushed north from Ile-à-la-Crosse to the headwaters of the Churchill and found the next major portage, the Methy, in 1778, the Athabasca country was the next pie in the sky. Every explorer and fur trader crossed the lakes and portages of the Churchill before you: Turnor and Fidler, Thompson, Fraser and Franklin followed in the wake of the others already mentioned. On a creepy note, the first fatality of Franklin's first ill-fated expedition to the Arctic was at Otter Rapids. The bowman, Louis St. Jean, drowned ascending this large drop on the middle Churchill in June of 1820.

The Churchill eventually became home to missionaries. In 1846–1847, two historic missions were established — one Catholic, St. John the Baptiste at Ile-à-la-Crosse, and the other Anglican, at Stanley Mission. The Holy Trinity Anglican Church at Stanley Mission is the oldest church and the oldest remaining building in Saskatchewan. Small Catholic churches were also constructed at Patuanak, Dipper Lake, Primeau Lake and Elak Dase, but only the ones at Patuanak and Elak Dase are standing today.

More recently, in the 1970s a major hydroelectric project was proposed by SaskPower to dam the Churchill at Wintego Rapids. The public outcry was huge. A board of inquiry was formed to assess the effects of such a project, and though the dam was stopped, there is nothing in place to stop the such a project from happening in the future. In 1993, the Saskatchewan government nominated the Churchill for Canadian Heritage River status, however, unfortunately, the designation has yet to take place. In 1995, the proceedings of a conference held to discuss the issues surrounding the Churchill River's nomination as a Heritage River were published by the Extension Division of the University of Saskatchewan. The document has some interesting information.

Except for National Historic Site markers at Ile-à-la-Crosse and Frog Portage, the provincial plaque at Holy Trinity Church at Stanley Mission, and the pictographs, there is little on the river to guide you in interpreting the prehistory and history of the Churchill River. But you will travel to places where First Nations people gathered in the summer and still continue to live, where explorers searched and voyageurs sweated, and you will paddle past points and coves where famous fur-trade posts were built.

To find out more on the specific historical attractions of the Churchill River downstream to Frog Portage, try *Canoeing the Churchill: A Practical Guide to the Voyageur Highway*, by Sid Robinson and Greg Marchildon. It is an excellent source of river-specific information. For more on the general history of the fur trade and exploration in the Churchill River region consult George Bryce's *The Remarkable History of the Hudson's Bay Company: Including that of the French Traders of North-western Canada and of the North-West, XY, and Astor Fur Companies*. Alexander Mackenzie's journals also make for good reading. Tyrrell's journals and books, including his edited version of the journals of Samuel Hearne and Philip Turnor, are excellent sources of information, and are online at http://digital.library.utoronto.ca/Tyrrell. Another good source of online information is the website of the Canadian Institute for Historical Microreproductions (CHIM) at www.Canadiana.org/. The 1999 *Atlas of Saskatchewan* locates the historic fur-trade posts in Saskatchewan on a map according to who ran them and in what years they operated. I refer to this map regularly in the Trip Notes section.

For more general reading on the river try Sigurd Olson's *The Lonely Land*, about a canoe trip down the Churchill in the 1960s. *Lonely Voyage*, by Kamil Pecher, is about a solo journey on the river. *North to Cree Lake*, by A. L. Karras, is a northern classic and makes many references to the Churchill and its tributaries. S. A. Keighley's *Trader, Tripper, Trapper: The Life of a Hudson Bay Man*, is also about life in the fur trade in the early 20th century in northern Saskatchewan. *The Company of Adventurers* and *Caesars of the Wilderness*, by journalist Peter C. Newman, are entertaining accounts of the fur-trade industry. *Voyages: Canada's Heritage Rivers*, edited by Lynn Noel, has one piece on the Churchill in it. It refers mostly to the Otter Lake area, including the story of how Grandmother's Bay got its name. The book also outlines the purpose and process of nominating a river for inclusion in the Heritage River System, and the stage this system is at in Canada.

Solitude **

On some sections of the river, solitude is more easily found than on others. You will see few canoeists on the upper or western Churchill, but lots of local people in motorboats. Once you reach Trout Lake you will see more fishing and canoeing parties. Then there are two areas that are very busy with traffic, where you will find the least solitude. One is the area below Sluice Falls to Otter Rapids, which is busy with motorboats with people fishing in late May and June and very busy with canoeists on the weekends in July and August. It can be difficult to find free campsites. Then of course there is the extremely irritating commercial jet-boat ride screaming up and down several times a day in the heat of the summer months. If you take the Great Devil–Little Devil Channel down to Devil Lake from Hayman Lake you'll find more solitude, and you won't have the large jet boats in your face.

From Otter Lake to Potter Rapids you will also see a lot of local motorboat traffic, and on long weekends there are hordes of canoeists. One August long weekend I counted 32 canoes from Stanley Rapids to the Rapid River / Nistowiak Falls Channel. After Potter Rapids the scene gets much quieter. The eastern Churchill does not see as many canoeists as the Trout Lake to Stanley Rapids section, and there are no communities past Stanley Mission until you reach Sandy Bay. Local people have traplines and summer camps along the river up to Frog Portage. After that and until Reeds Lake, you will see no one again.

In my opinion, the trip to Sandy Bay is a more exciting and beautiful trip than the western or upper Churchill, from Buffalo Narrows to Pinehouse Lake, though it certainly is a great trip. My favourite section is what I call the middle Churchill, from Black Bear Island to Otter Lake. It has classic big-water rapids and smooth-rock camping areas. Unfortunately some parts of the middle Churchill are seeing too much use and too little care.

Wildlife **

Though the Churchill Uplands has the highest wildlife population and richness of species of the Shield ecoregions, the wildlife resources are under heavy pressure from human activity along the river. Wildlife sightings are therefore rarer on the busy sections of the Churchill than they are on rivers in less rich environments, such as the Athabasca Plain and Selwyn Lake Upland.

Mostly, you will see moose. While woodland caribou are not commonly seen, the river is within their range. This is true of white-tailed deer as well. When I was living in Buffalo Narrows, I used to dread driving from Ile-à-la-Crosse to Beauval at night because of all the deer on the road. The Churchill is also as far north as you will find badgers, coyotes, and fishers.

More common mammals include black bears, timber wolves, red foxes, mink, martens, squirrels, ermine, weasels, wolverines, lynx, skunks, snowshoe hares, beavers, river otters, and muskrats. According to government documents, wild rice was first planted in Saskatchewan in the 1930s as food for muskrats! That's how serious the fur-trade business was in the North.

Between Pinehouse and Otter Lakes is the second-highest concentration of nesting bald eagles in North America, especially along the Black Bear Island Lake to Otter Rapids section. Golden eagles have been sighted on the river, while osprey populations are high. Some years there are lots of pelicans, while other years there aren't. Loons, mergansers, mallards, scaup and Canada geese have a large presence on the Churchill. Ravens, owls, gray jays, spruce, ruffed and sharp-tailed grouse, and hairy and downy woodpeckers are also commonly seen along the river. Breeding sandhill cranes have been located near Ile-à-la-Crosse. Swans and snow geese have been found near Patuanak, and the rare peregrine falcon has been observed on the Churchill. The Caspian tern and great gray owl, considered rare in Canada, also live along the river.

Fishing ***

I have never been skunked for walleye on any trip I have been on, up or down the Churchill. There are some spots where fishing is just plain fun because supper is caught in the first five minutes. The eddies below the large rapids and falls are always home to walleye. Some of the really hot spots have been pinpointed in the Trip Notes section, and include Needle Falls, Rock Trout Rapids, Corner Rapids, Robertson Falls, Twin Falls and Kettle Falls. You can also catch sauger in the fast water. The authors of the *Ecoregions of Saskatchewan*, which I refer to often, say that the occurrence of sauger in the Otter Rapids to Island Falls section of the Churchill River is unusual for the province. In fact, I have caught sauger above Otter Rapids, especially in the eddy in the river-right bend of Corner Rapids and also all the way up to Tuck Falls on the Paull River. They also can be caught in limited numbers on the upper Churchill. According to the book, it is unusual to find sauger anywhere but in the Saskatchewan River and its tributaries. These fish look very much like a walleye, but are smaller, thinner and brown coloured. Maybe you will catch some too — they are just as good to eat!

Lake fishing can be good, though I prefer to fish in current. The huge northerns lurking around in the weedy bays of the lakes on the Churchill are great fun to catch, but should be carefully released. There may be some lake trout left in the large lakes that are very deep — Lac Ile-à-la-Crosse, Shagwenaw, Dipper, Primeau, Knee, Nistowiak and Mountain Lakes — but all are or have been commercially fished, so don't hold your breath; it would be a rare catch indeed. Trout Lake used to have trout, but no longer. Some authors note that lake sturgeon can be found in the Churchill below the Island Falls dam. I can't say that I've had the pleasure, nor have I heard of anyone who has caught one.

Special Equipment

The canoe you choose to take on your Churchill trip must be a proper tripping canoe that can handle big lakes and hold lots of gear. I see no need to go light on extended trips on the Churchill. Portaging is easy most of the time, often over log or roller ramps. For the few long portages where you actually have to carry everything, it's worth the effort to carry the extra luxuries you will want on a long trip like this. A small camp chair is one I would take, as well as a small water-filtration system rather than drops. It's advised that you purify your drinking water on the Churchill, especially downstream of communities.

A spray cover is always fun for advanced paddlers when in big water, and nice on rainy days. A tarp is also important for a Churchill trip, but not just for adverse weather. There is nothing like a good sail across a big lake to make everyone happy. Dave and I sailed from the west end of Trade Lake all the way to Frog Portage in four hours! You will need a compass for the very large lakes, especially Black Bear Island.

Bring books or cards for windbound days. Some campsites lack firewood, so an environmental stove and or gas stove is important. Try to conserve the wood that is available. The bugs are not bad compared to on many other rivers, but you will need repellent.

Trip Notes

MAP NO	GRID REF	FEATURE	DESCRIPTION
73 O/5	173463	Put-in	The Ile-à-la-Crosse public beach, on the north side of the peninsula. You can also put in at the public dock at the Northern store or the dock further east in town.
	2335000	Campsite	On Sandy Point on a sand beach east of the cabins. There are numerous good camping spots on Lac Ile-à-la-Crosse, and the campsites listed below are only suggestions.
	252536	Campsite	On RL or northwest shore there's a sand beach on the south side of the point.
73 O/12	240583	Campsite	On RL in a protected bay is a small beach.
	298756	Campsite	On the west shore of the island just north of Halfway Point, a clearing up on grassy flats.
	288878	Campsite	On RR on Gravel Point. There's a gravel beach for camping.
73 O/13	287877	Campsite	A very good spot on a sandy point on RL.
	284935	Campsite	On RR on a sandy spit. Be warned: there are no good camping spots on Shagwenaw Lake and the next good camping site is on Cross Island above Drum Rapids.
	298007 302006	Shagwenaw Rapids Patuanak Put-in Take-out	**Class 1+** and straightforward. Moderate waves. No portage. At Patuanak there is road access, and supplies are available here. *Patuanak* is Cree for "where the white river flows," or "at the rapid," referring to Shagwenaw Rapids. Pine River was the name of the HBC trading post built here.
74 B/4	331088	Campsite	On the island above Drum Rapids, called Cross Island locally for the metal cross erected in the clearing. Be respectful of this special place.

MAP NO	GRID REF	FEATURE	DESCRIPTION
	345094 351103	Drum Rapids Campsite	**Class 1, 1+, 3 and 2, and 1.** There are five parts to Drum. The first section is fast water. At 350096 there is another section of fastwater with small waves and rocks to avoid. The main part of Drum starts at 351101 where the marked bars are on the map. The **Class 3** rapids start with a large chute, then around the corner are **Class 2** rapids with large compression waves at the narrows and there is a big hole on RL. The **portage (300 m)** for the third and fourth set of rapids is on RR at **352099.** It crosses the point of land. You could camp at the head of the portage in the grassy clearing. The last set of Drum is a **Class 1** chute of fast water (GR 357102).
	363101 370100	Leaf Rapids Campsite	**Class 2** waves with some boulders. A straightforward run of about 700 m. The **portage (775 m)** is on RR about 40 m above the head of the rapids. A large campsite exists at the end of the portage trail.
	381107 385109 388110	Camping	For camping around the confluence of the Mudjatik, an important route to Cree Lake, try one of the points listed; one should suit your group. *Mudjatik* means "bad caribou" in Cree — *atik* is "caribou." It used to be called the Deer River at one time, deer meaning caribou. Tyrrell thought there were too many Deer and Caribou Rivers already, so he changed it. At least Deer Rapids hasn't been negatively affected!
	416123	Deer Rapids Campsite	**Class 2 and 2+.** There are two sets to Deer. The first is short and through the narrows — a chute with standing waves to be avoided, more difficult in higher water. Between the first and second set are some possible rock camping sites on RL at 418125 and 419127. The second set of Deer starts at 421134, and manoeuvring in large waves around rocks is required. The inside of the bend is less pushy. There is an old overgrown **portage** trail on RR around the second set **(175 m).** The fast water continues around the tiny island.
73 O/14	476039 480037	Dipper Rapids Campsite	**Class 3+/4,** large ledgey rapids with violent current and large, irregular waves. There's no clear channel, with a 2.5-m total drop. The **portage (350 m)** is on RL below the preliminary rapids and at the head of the major drop. You can't miss it. There is a fabulous rail setup for rolling your boat and gear to the quiet waters below Dipper. For those who do not feel comfortable coming that close to the head of the rapid, there is a longer alternative that starts at 476040 and within 25 m joins the main portage. There is a nice campsite at the end of the portage on the high, sandy bank. Dipper Lake is where Primeau's House was built, the first trading post on the upper Churchill. Both Dipper and Primeau Lakes were considered Primeau Lake at the time.
	484031	Rapids	**Class 1** fast water.
	548033	Campsite	On a wooded island halfway across Dipper Lake, in a bay on the south side on the western end.
	603985	Campsite	On the RR point on Primeau Lake.
	652954	Riffle	The river narrows, creating fast water.

MAP NO	GRID REF	FEATURE	DESCRIPTION
	663969 674969	**Crooked Rapids Portage Campsite**	There are three sections to the rapids, and the **portage (1,100 m)** bypasses them all. It's on RR below a low, willow-covered island, but before the river narrows again. It cuts off the point of land, and so begins nowhere near the start of the rapids. There is a possible campsite at the end of the portage.
	665977 675968	**Crooked Rapids**	**Class 1, 2+, 2.** There are three obvious sections to the rapids. The first is small waves around a sharp bend to the right and is not indicated on the map. The second set begins at 672978 and is the most difficult — there is a ledge and large stoppers and waves requiring good manoeuvring. The third set is easier, as the waves are more regular. It starts at 675971.
	677943 692936	**Knee Rapids**	**Fast water, Class 2+, and 1+.** There is fast water for 100 m before the Class 2+ rapids marked on the map. The **portage (350 m)** is located at the top of the Class 2+ section at 678944 on RL at the granite ledge. The rapids have a ledge to avoid and a boulder bed to manoeuvre through. There is a fast water section at the small island on RR, that is followed by **Class 1+** rapids at 685938 for almost 400 m — small waves and some rocks.
	712914	**Cabins**	There are seasonal cabins on Knee Lake Indian Reserve. Knee Lake was home to an HBC trading post called Elbow Lake. Knee or elbow, it looks the same on the map!

Note: There are two ways to navigate Knee Lake. One is to paddle southeast to Bentley Bay. The other is to stay to the north and paddle east across Knee Lake, portaging south over the peninsula into Bentley Bay. The wind will determine your best course. If you take the portage (500 m) at 830931, there is a campsite on the way at a small island (731907), and just off the portage trail you can visit the remains of a Beaver that crashed there.

MAP NO	GRID REF	FEATURE	DESCRIPTION
	717895	**Campsite**	On a wooded island, southeast side.
	741871	**Cross**	A large cross sits high on the outcrop.
	743869	**Campsite**	On the south side of the point.
74 O/15	759876	**Campsite**	On a tiny island in Bentley Bay. A nice spot.
	783875 786876	**Campsites**	Two beaches provide nice camping in Bentley Bay.
	792888	**Campsite**	On a tiny, wooded island on the northeast side.
	839900	**Campsite**	On a small island on the east end, facing south.
	884905	**Elak Dase**	A tiny community with an old Catholic church. There is also a bear-hunting lodge. There are no supplies available here and there is no road access.
	880909	**Campsite**	On a large, wooded island across from Elak Dase (residents call their community Knee Lake), facing the community with lovely smooth rocks. Sigurd Olson and the gang camped here. There is very limited camping for the next 38 km. I make some suggestions, but they aren't great. It's swampy — what the voyageurs called the Grass(y) River section!

MAP NO	GRID REF	FEATURE	DESCRIPTION
	893893	Confluence Fishing hole	Paddle up the Haultain a kilometre or so and fish the eddies. There should be walleye to go in late May and the month of June.
	905862	Campsite	On RL where the rock outcrops. Tent sites up top.
	898844	Campsite	On RL at a rock ledge. Tent sites up top.
73 O/10	845775	Potential camping	On the RR just east of the outlet of Gravel Lake. You are in the Haultain marshes. An HBC trading post called Hay River was located somewhere in this area. Maybe the marsh reminded them of hay.
73 O/15	899798	Potential camping	On RR or the northwest shore of Dreger Lake. A good site, but you have to push some bush to get to it.
73 O/10	890747	Rapids	**Class 1**, unmarked, wide, shallow, rocky rapids.
	937767	Campsite	On RR is a lovely beach in the bay.
	000768 010775	Campsites	There are beaches along the southeast shore of Sandy Lake. Pick your spot on this beautiful lake.
	016772 025758	Put-in Hwy 914 Bridge Snake Rapids Campsite	**Class 2, 2/2+ and 1**. From Highway 914 you can put in on the south side of the river and run the first part of Snake Rapids. There are waves and some stoppers. The second part is about 1 km downstream of the bridge, and also Class 2, except in high water where it gets a 2+. It's slightly bigger with a more violent current as the river really starts to pick up steam. There is a **portage (90 m)** on RL over the island, which starts on a sloping rock just above the rapids. There is a fair campsite on this island and you can also scout the lower rapids from here. The third set is an easy Class 1 at 025758, running out into fast water all the way to McDonald Bay. On the east shore of McDonald Bay, a couple of kilometres south of the channel opening to the main part of Pinehouse Lake, there is a pictograph site. The seven paintings start about 1 m up from the jumble of rocks directly below the rock face. The snake figure may have something to do with the fact that the Cree called this lake Snake Lake.
73 O/9	099767	Campsite	On the northeast or RL side of the narrows at a little beach.
	183785	Campsite	On a tiny island off the south side of Cowpack Island.
73 O/16	192801	Campsite	On a north point of Cowpack Island.
	215819	Campsite	On a small island a couple of kilometres downstream of Cowpack, on the south side.
	255827 256828	Campsite Confluence	On a tiny, tiny island just across from the Belanger River mouth. The Belanger River was known as the Souris River during the early fur trade. It was called the Mouse River by the Cree before that. There were a series of important trading posts called Old Souris River here. Old, to distinguish the post from the New Souris or Wakahonansihk Post.
	268817	Campsite	A mid-channel island in the narrows. Try your hand at fishing here.
	268800	Campsite	On a beach on Sandfly just south of where the river comes in.

MAP NO	GRID REF	FEATURE	DESCRIPTION
	280790	Campsite	One beach on the east side of the boot, with a cabin site south of it.
73 O/9	323764	Campsite	On a long, narrow island on Sandfly. Very nice.
	332760	Campsite	On the southwest point of a small, wooded island.
	343746	Campsite	On the south point of small, wooded island.
	355738	Rapids	**Class 3**. At the outlet of Sandfly there are rapids that flow around a small island, steep and fast with large waves. The **portage (40 m)** on RL is over a spit of land to the north of the island at **354740**.
	365741 365740	Needle Rapids	**Class 2+ and Class 3**. These rapids also flow around an island. The north channel is somewhat easier. Both routes have large waves to avoid. The **portage (365 m)** is on RL, the north shore. It begins at about **367744** after running some fast water in the RL or north channel.
73 P/12	372721	Needle Falls Campsite	**Class 5**. A series of wicked ledges that don't line up well at all. The **portage (50 m)** over an old log-roller system is on RR or south shore as marked. There is a nice camping spot in the trees on the rock between the falls and the portage, a good place to stop and fish below the rapids for walleye. You can also check out the eagle's nest at 373708.
	381716	Campsite	On a narrow point on the RL or northwest shore of Kinosaskaw Lake.
	390724	Campsite	On the east point of a large, wooded island.
	400741	Campsite	On a small island off a bigger island off the northwest shore. On the east shore of Kinosaskaw Lake about half the distance of the lake is another pictograph site. The rock paintings can barely be seen from the water. They are 6 m above the water on a 10-m-high rock cliff. There is a jumble of boulders at water level, so go in 6 to 8 m to a broken rock-face. There are four figures at the site.

Note: See the chapter on the Foster River for the significant features, including a pictograph site, to be found at the confluence of the Foster (Fish) and Churchill Rivers.

	456747	Silent Rapids	**Class 1**, mainly boils and whirlpools. At very low water there are some rocks to dodge. Black Bear Island Lake has wonderful camping. Pick your own spot or try one listed below. This lake also is spiritually significant to the Cree people along the middle Churchill. Please leave everything as you find it, whether you are camping or visiting the rock-painting sites. A pictograph site is on the north side of the island, 1 km down a channel from Silent Rapids, about 1 m off the water on a 6-m cliff, with two figures.
	492720	Campsite	On the southwest point of a long, wooded island.
	515705	Campsite	On the shore across from Hadley Island. Another pictograph site is located on the north end of Wamninuta Island, 1.5 m off the water. There are eight figures here.

MAP NO	GRID REF	FEATURE	DESCRIPTION
	535675	Rapids	**Class 1.** I know, how weird! It's a river-lake. At High Rock Narrows there are two pictograph sites. The first one is on a slab of rock 1.5 m above the water. The paintings are quite faint. At the second site there are seven rock faces with figures on them; six of them are 1 m to 1.5 m off the water. The seventh is about 6.5 m up and has the most figures of all. Worth the climb!
	585657	Campsite	A small wooded island on RL. Very nice.
	611656	Campsite	A tiny island.
	682649	Campsite	A tiny island.
73 P/11	699646	Lodge	South side of the island with narrows in the middle. Cabins are right there.
	703633	Campsite	On a point on RR. Smooth-rock camping.
	735634	Campsite	On a pretty, small island between a wooded island on RL and the mainland on RR.
	737626	Campsite	On the west side of Craik Island.
	754603	Birch Falls	**Class 4.** Ledgey rapids with two shelves and nasty holes. The **portage (200 m)** runs over Birch Point on the RR or the south side of this south channel as marked on the map.
	752611	Birch Rapids	**Class 3.** There are ledges, stoppers and large waves to contend with in the northern channel. The standing waves in the final set of rapids are the largest. Scout all three sets before deciding on a plan of action. To portage you must go to the south channel as described above. An HBC trading post was located on Trout Lake somewhere around Birch Rapids.
	758601	Campsite	On a tiny island, the northeast side. Try fishing in this area. A walleye supper should be forthcoming!
	770599	Rapids	**Class 1+,** around an island. The rapids leading into Trout Lake are fast water with some waves and rocks to avoid in the lower water. Either side is navigable. There is a **portage (200 m)** on RR about 40 m above the rapids.
	805634	Campsite	The northwest side of a larger wooded island.
	813643	Campsite	The southwest tip of a long, wooded island.
	820658	Campsite	On the RL shore.
	822661	Campsite	On the point on the RL shore.

churchill river

63

Note: There are two routes to paddle from Trout Lake to Nipew. If you are looking for more solitude, choose the Crew/Torranee option. To continue on in the paddle strokes and footsteps of the voyageurs, take the easier route through Stack and Mountney. Beginners should take this northern route, as there aren't portage trails for some of the rapids on the Crew/Torranee route, so a higher level of skill is involved in navigating the rapids.

Northern Route: Stack and Mountney

MAP NO	GRID REF	FEATURE	DESCRIPTION
	870726	Trout Rapids Campsite	**Class 3+**, steep and rocky with ledges that line up poorly. Swamping is likely with wrapping potential high. The **portage (145 m)** is on RR and starts in a small bay on a grassy, muddy landing above the fast water of the rapids. It is not where it is indicated on the map! The trail is very rocky; be careful of your toes and ankles while carrying heavy loads. Camping is possible at the end of the portage.
	873730	Rapids	**Class 1 and 1+.** Below Trout are small, unmarked rapids at a narrows with a tiny islet in mid-channel. The northern channel is easier. You also have two options for descending the next rapids, which flow around an island into Stack Lake.
	877737	Rapids	**Class 2 and 1.** This northern route has two rapids. The first set is a chute with a big initial drop flowing into a long train of standing waves. In higher water, swamping is probable, in lower water it might be too shallow and rocky. There is no portage around these rapids. **Class 1** rapids follows at 878738. There is a boardwalk portage joining Stack to McIntosh Lake. Boats here are from the outfitter on McIntosh as well.
	880736	Rooster Rapids Campsite	**Class 3.** The southern route is home to a huge chute and very large standing waves that tell the tale of how Rooster Rapids got its name. It flows into Stack Lake. The **portage (90 m)** is on RR. The trail is obvious, and there is a good camping spot halfway through, high and open. The fishing below the portage in the eddies is very good.

Note: Between the outlet of Stack Lake and Rock Trout Rapids there are riffles and a section of fast water through a marvellously scenic channel. Staying to the RR shore will help you navigate. The most difficult riffle is at a bend to the left at 895727.

MAP NO	GRID REF	FEATURE	DESCRIPTION
	901728	Rock Trout Portage Campsites Fishing hole	The **portage (250 m)** is on RR and it starts at a small sand beach 30 m above the flat bedrock ledge that makes the first drop of Rock Trout. It bypasses Class 3 rapids that are potentially very dangerous. There is an undercut in the rock cliff downstream of the first rapids. The strong current can push canoes and people under it and hold them there. There are two great campsites on the portage. My favourite is the first you come upon. The kitchen has a great view of the rapids. There is excellent walleye fishing in the shore eddy on RR of the first drop. It's shallow in places, so you may lose some jigs, but it's always hot if you find the spot.
	902730	Rock Trout Rapids	**Class 3, Hazard.** The undercut is hard to explain because the map does not represent the reality of the rapids. What you will see as you approach the first rapids as marked is a large, shallow chute flowing around the corner to the right. Downstream on RL is a very large recirculating eddy. Downstream on RR is another set of rapids. In between there is the rock face where the undercut is. You will see the main flow pushing up against it. So if you capsize upstream at the first rapids or even trying to make the corner farther down, you will be swept towards the undercut. Most

the trips

			experienced canoeists aware of the danger of the rapids choose to pull over to the log ramp that runs over the flat rocks on RR. Stop on the rocks on RR and carry your gear over and then line your canoe to the ramp to be safe. The landing for the pull over is in the fast water right above the first drop. You will end up on RR below the first chute. Now you can either portage through the campsite if you feel you don't want to run the rest of the rapids or put in and very carefully peel out and run the rest of Rock Trout. Beginners should use the portage and not try to line or run any of this rapid.
	903731	Campsite	On RL, this site is on the other side of the channel of the campsites on the portage. It is rock camping, with tent spots up behind in the trees. It's Brad's favourite. You are still in the fast water below the rapids when you approach the site. You'll have to line up a bit if you come from the portage on RR.
	907728	Rapids	Class 1/1+, around an island. The right channel has the clearest run. There are more sections of fast water as you descend the channel to Mountney Lake.
	910731	Cabin	A trapper's cabin on RL.
	919731 924731	Campsites	On the big island in Mountney. One is on the west side and the other is on the southeast point.
	933701	Rapids	Class 1+/2, with some larger waves in the centre. There are rocks to avoid in low water and waves to avoid in high water. The **portage (200 m)** is on RL and it starts 80 m above the rapids. These are the last major rapids before Nipew Lake. There are small riffles and sections of fast water to pass through before the outlet.

Southern Route: Crew/Torranee

	879694	Rapids	Class 2+. A fast chute with large, standing waves at the bottom and no portage trail.
	884695	Rapids	Class 2+. A series of ledges with several breaks in them. You can line on RL.
	888693	Rapids Campsite	Class 3, with big swamping waves. The **portage (100 m)** is on RL and starts just above the rapids. There is a pretty good campsite on the portage trail.
	894690	Rapids	Class 3+, large ledges and a keeper hole. You can sneak along the shore on RR into a small side channel. There are some small falls, but you can lift over the ledge here into Crew Lake waters.
	915675	Rapids Campsite	Class 2+ and 3. These rapids flow around a good-sized island. The narrow north channel is a Class 2+ chute that is fast. The **portage (150 m)** for this set is on RR of this north channel over the island. At the start there is a good place to camp. The south channel is split by a tiny island. The RL route around the tiny island is Class 3 and tricky, as there are lots of rocks to avoid in the steep drop. The RR route is a fast chute with a long wave train with very large waves. You are pretty much guaranteed to swamp.

Note: The map shows a channel running straight east from these rapids at 931671. This channel is usually dry unless it is a high-water year.

MAP NO	GRID REF	FEATURE	DESCRIPTION
	938681	Rapids	**Class 1 to 1+.** Depending on the water level there is fast water or small waves.
	942685	Campsite	On RR at the outlet of the river channel into Nipew Lake. Fishing can be good here at times. *Nipew* is Cree for "dead." Supposedly, after the smallpox epidemic in 1780–1781, a pile of bones of Cree victims were stacked on the large point, mid-lake and that was how the lake got its present name.
	977698	Campsite	On the north point of a wooded island.
	981699	Campsite	On a tiny island beside the wooded island mentioned above.
73 P/10	009695	Campsite	On the beach on Boyes Island.
	018697	Campsite	Up on the point above the beach on Boyle Island.
	020710	Campsite	For larger groups, on the mainland north of Boyle Island.

Note: There are long stretches of fast water between Nipew and Hayman. The riffle at 058720 is the most significant. Additionally, recognize that you are now approaching a more populated area. Please respect the privacy of the First Nations people who live on Hayman and Otter Lakes. Do not investigate people's camps or cabins, and don't stare.

MAP NO	GRID REF	FEATURE	DESCRIPTION
	113710	Campsite	On Donaldson Island.
	121706	Campsite	On an island above Great Devil Rapids.

Note: There are several route choices at this juncture. The voyageur route through Great Devil and Little Devil Rapids is the fastest. A couple more scenic routes head south into Barker Lake and then on to Devil Lake.

Devil Rapids Route:

MAP NO	GRID REF	FEATURE	DESCRIPTION
	123703 131698	Great Devil Rapids	**Class 2+, 3 and 4.** The **portage (1,100 m)** for the entire rapid is on RL, and starts about 50 m above the fast water. It's wide and well-used, but can be muddy in spots. There are three parts to Great Devil, and some canoeists after scouting will elect to run the top two. The first part is around a bend to the left. A large hole is on RR, and after some rock dodging the real boulder garden begins. Around the corner to the right is a large ledge (among the many boulders) that almost spans the river. For this second part, RL is the only possible run. Be careful though, Wladyka Falls are next and you will want to eddy out on RL in a small cove and pull over the rocks on the RL shore to put back in right below the falls. According to A. L. Karras, an Indian is buried at the bottom of these rapids.
	134698	Campsite	Very nice spot on the island just below the rapids. Good walleye fishing around here.
	139694 144694	Little Devil Rapids	**Class 2**, with three sets of rapids. A **portage (840 m)** can be made around all three sets on RL. The trail starts about 70 m above the first set in a rocky cove at a break in the willows. You can choose to scout the rapids from two portages on RR. The portage for the first set is (90 m). It bypasses a narrow and fast rapid with some waves

MAP NO	GRID REF	FEATURE	DESCRIPTION

at the bottom that are larger on RR. After a brief stretch of fast water, the next set begins, which is a fast chute split by a boulder at the top. The final rapid, the hardest of the three, curves around to the left and then back to the right and is very rocky. The narrowest part at the bottom is the most difficult — there is a large wave to avoid at the bottom. You can portage (120 m) this last set by taking out in the cove on RR after the second drop. The RR channel you see on the map around the island is dry.

Alternate Route: Sluice/Donaldson and Barker Lake

Note: You have two options for navigating the start of the southern route to Devil Lake. One is to portage Sluice Falls and the other is to run Donaldson Channel. Donaldson Channel has no portages and is no place for anybody without advanced whitewater skills. A group with loaded trippers trying to descend this channel is a disaster in the making. I can't count how many canoes have been wrecked in these rapids, and at least one canoeist has lost his life.

MAP NO	GRID REF	FEATURE	DESCRIPTION
	105705 105697	Sluice Falls Campsite	**Class 4/4+.** The falls are in the bottom set and almost span the entire width of the drop, and the hole below is a killer. You could be stuck in there until next Christmas. The rapids above are big water and very difficult, and if you swim above the falls you are looking at a life-threatening situation. The **portage (1,000 m)** is on RR, and starts in a tiny cove just above the fast water of the rapids. Don't pick the blueberries by the trail; local people often harvest them, and it is much more difficult for them to get fruit at a grocery store than it is for you. Small groups can camp at the rock point overlooking the falls.
	113707 110697	Donaldson Channel	**2, 2+/3, 3, and 3+/4.** There are four sets in this channel and they are very technical. The first is not marked and is rock dodging and ledge avoidance. Be careful of the narrow section. The second set at 113705 is a big boulder garden with no clear route — it's a wrap rapid. The third set at 111701 is a rock garden on RR and a huge wave train in RC and on RL. The final set around the corner is the most difficult and dangerous to approach. It begins at 109698 at the top of a boulder garden with tricky ledges. You basically have two choices at this point. You can sneak down the right side to an eddy above the big drop and either pull over the high rock ledge and rocks to the lake below or run the big stuff below if you have the skill. Or, in all but low water, you can paddle to the small overflow channel on RL that starts in a bay above the entire last set of rapids and walk your boats down to the small lake. The maps are very deceiving, because many of the channels they show are dry at most water levels. The RL overflow is the only way to avoid the big rapids at the end of the main channel.
	111694	Portage Rapids Fishing holes	Over the island is the only way to get down dry! The trail is short, only **10 m**, and starts in a cove to the RL of the middle set of rapids. If you want to run, there are three choices: on RL you have **Corner Rapids** at 112694. These are **Class 3** rapids with a large, fast chute and large waves. The rapids head straight into a rock wall and then around the corner. The RR eddy in the inside corner has the best fishing for walleye and sauger around. In RC you have **Ric's Falls** at **110693**. This is **Class 3** as well, but you are much less likely to be upright at the end of it. It has very tricky ledges with holes to

MAP NO	GRID REF	FEATURE	DESCRIPTION
			navigate and is steep. There's good walleye fishing from the island shore. The RR rapids are the **Far Side** at **108692**. This **Class 2+/3** chute is fast with a long, large wave train to follow. There is a violent current, making boils and whirlpools. Again, good walleye fishing from the island.
	112695 113694	Campsites	There are two campsites at Corner Rapids. One is above the rapids at 112695 and the other is below on a rock point at 113694. Be nice to these places. The second site has been overcamped, and people have cut down trees and destroyed much of the moss and lichen covering the rock. Stay on the paths.

Note: There are a number of riffles and small rapids to descend to Barker Lake. The easiest route is to take the north channel all the way via Dieter Rapids or the Shelf. Or, you can go south from Corner Rapids via Carla's Rapids and Surf City. Barker Lake has good northern pike fishing.

MAP NO	GRID REF	FEATURE	DESCRIPTION
	125691	Dieter Rapids	**Class 2**, with boulders to miss at the top followed by a 90-degree turn and a low, broken ledge and waves at the end. There is no portage.
	124689	The Shelf	**Class 2+**. At high water there are several chutes in this broken ledge. The most common run is through the large chute on far RR, but the drop will fill your canoe at most water levels. You can carry your gear over the RR point, and then have a go at it.
	114689	Carla's Rapids	**Class 2**, with a few small ledges and boulders to avoid, and no portage.
	115686	Surf City	**Class 2+**. A large chute split by a boulder in the middle making two Vs and some moderately big waves.
	122685	Campsite	High on a rock outcropping overlooking the south channel.
	124682	Campsite	In the back bay of Barker Island. Walk into the trees for a sheltered spot in bad weather.
	126683	Campsite	An open point on an island with a nice view of Barker Lake.
	135679	Campsite	For more solitude and for a small group, try this camp on the south shore of Barker.

Note: Now you have three choices to reach Devil Lake! A northern, a central and a southern option.

North Route

MAP NO	GRID REF	FEATURE	DESCRIPTION
	136684 150687	Murray Channel	**Class 2, 2+, 3 and 1**. There are four sets of rapids in Murray Channel, and no portage around the first two or the last. The first set is a wide, fast chute with a train of moderate standing waves. The eddy on RR is good for walleye. The there is a section of fast water through a lovely narrow channel. You will soon see a jog to the right the top of Murray Rapids proper. There are some small ledges at the top in low water, so you want to line up carefully. In the guts of the rapids on RL there are several boulders to miss and on RR there is a nasty hole. After descending the second set, make your way to the bay on RL to scout the final big set, which has very large waves and is Class 3. The current is very fast and there are large waves at times between these sets, so head out left early. This last

MAP NO	GRID REF	FEATURE	DESCRIPTION
			big set of Murray is about avoiding the waves in the RC, running as far RL as you can. You can easily portage, however. The trail is on RL at the end of the bay and is only 5 m long. Where the current from Murray Falls joins the current at the bottom of Murray Rapids, dangerous whirlpools can form. Stay RL until you pass Murray Falls, on your right. Class I riffles and fast water bring you to Devil Lake.

Centre Route

MAP NO	GRID REF	FEATURE	DESCRIPTION
	152686	Mosquito Rapids Campsite	**Class 3**. There is a narrow, fast, steep chute at the top on RL of the island, and on RR there is a ledge falls. Near the bottom there are big stoppers and ledge holes. The **portage (200 m)** is on RL in a little rocky cove about 25 m above the fast water. There is a campsite at the end of the portage overlooking the rapids. **Murray Falls** is on your left as you approach Mosquito. This is a steep **Class 4** drop for experts in solo canoes or kayaks only. There is no portage.
	154687	Campsite	On RR on the point.

South Route

MAP NO	GRID REF	FEATURE	DESCRIPTION
	149679	Sister 1	**Class 1**, a minor chute.
	152679	Sister 2	**Class 1**, a slide between two rocks.
	155178	Sister 3	**Class 2**. There is a large rock near the bottom in the main current to avoid. There is no portage.
	157679	Staircase Falls	**Class 4**, with ledges that don't line up well and shallow water. Rocky at the end. The **portage (80 m)** starts about 40 m above the falls on RL and ends at a bank in an eddy. The fast water below the falls takes you to Devil Lake.
	157680	Campsite	In the south channel, high on a rock with a good view.
	159682	Campsite	For a small group, on the point.
	160682	Campsite	For a small group, on the point.
	163680	Campsite	High on a slab of rock on the RR point.
	166692	Campsite	Across the lake.
	171680	Boat Launch Put-in/ Take-out Campground	Road access and a provincial campground on the east shore of Devil Lake.
	166665	Otter Rapids Water survey station Campground Put-in/ Take-out	**Class 2+**. Big, big waves for a long way (650 m). Too much fun! You will probably swamp loaded. Don't worry about hitting rocks. The rapids are very deep. However, avoid the two holes. One is on RR near the top and the other is on RR near the bottom. The **portage (565 m)** is on RL and starts in a rocky cove just above the rapids. It crosses the road where the provincial campground straddles the road. Otter Bridge is a classic landmark. This was always a special place for the Cree in the area, and evidence of hearths has been found here among many other artifacts. Fishing can be good in the eddy below the portage.

MAP NO	GRID REF	FEATURE	DESCRIPTION

Note: There is a phone at Otter Rapids. A short detour can be made to Missinipe to collect supplies or end your trip. Should you want any information on local river conditions, the staff at CRCO will be able to help you. They are located on the northwest side of the peninsula at 145614. There are many fine camping spots on Otter Lake. There are a number of ways to get to Stanley Mission, but this guide describes only the main route. I highly recommend making your own journey here. Practise your canoe-tripping skills. North Falls is beautiful and the French–Ducker route is also great. You can also make a side trip to the pictograph site at the junction of Rattler Creek and the Stewart River at an outcrop about 11 m high. As you pass Grandmother's Bay, I urge you to respect the residents' privacy. Don't stare.

MAP NO GRID REF	FEATURE	DESCRIPTION
175626	Campsite	On a point on RR.
191611 190608	Campsites	Two spots on a wooded island, one on the north side and one on the south.
209595	Campsite	On "T" island, facing south.
234585	Campsite	There are a couple of spots on this island, south and east. MacDonald Channel is well known for its walleye fishing. Find the deep spot by the rock face.
255560 257563 259565	Campsites	There are three spots in this beautiful channel: two on the southeast side of Naheyow Island and one on the mainland.
285565	Portage	You can bypass both Robertson and Twin Falls using this **330-m** trail. As shown on the map, it comes out below Twin, so you can view it, but you'll miss Robertson. You could paddle to Robertson first, then paddle back, carrying only once to see them both!
276564	Robertson Falls Campsites	**Class 4.** This ledgey 3-m drop can be run by experts in solo white-water boats, but everyone else portages. The **portage (75 m)**, called Stony Mountain Portage, is on RL at an obvious break in the trees. There are two campsites off the trail to the right, one up and one down. A toilet was installed in 2001 because this is such popular area with canoeists and fishing parties. Please use it. The walleye fishing below the falls is usually good.
280558 280555	Twin Falls Portage	**Class 6.** This 6-m waterfall can be portaged using **Mountain Portage (300 m)**. The trail is in a small bay of the unnamed lake below Robertson Falls, and is about 75 m to the right of the Beyond La Ronge Lodge, on the point. The landing can be very muddy. There is a log roller ramp for motorboats, which is handy for canoeists with Royalex boats. Carry one load of gear and then push the rest in the canoe York-boat style! Fishing below Twin Falls is usually very good. Most of the small islands on Mountain Lake that are good for camping are used by local people for their summer camps. There is a pictograph site (with graffiti too, unfortunately) on the east side of the northeast tip of Cow Island. The site is facing west 2.5 m or more up the rock face, with two large paintings.
292524	Campsite	A rock point south of Cow Island.
300523	Campsite	A similar camp down the way.
312510	Campsite	The west end of a wooded island, in a bay.

Map No	Grid Ref	Feature	Description
	309516	Campsite	On the north end of a wooded island. A burned area starts on RR at Neufeld Bay.
73 P/7	301501	Campsite	On the southwest tip of a tiny island. On RR or the east side of a long, narrow peninsula there are two pictograph sites 45 m apart. The northern site has two figures about 1.7 m up a 3-m-high rock cliff. The southern site has one about 2.4 m up on the cliff face.
	268442	Campsite	In Chepakan Bay there is a pictograph site. It's on the west shore of a small bay where the Four Portages canoe route from La Ronge comes in. There is a figure on a rock face about 180 cm above the water at a rock slab. There is a good rock camp across the bay.
	283420	Amuchew-aspimewin	The "Shooting Up Place" is at a 60-m-high rock cliff 1 km from Stanley Mission. It is reported to be where, before the Europeans arrived, the migratory Cree would look for an omen as to whether they should move north for hunting that winter or stay near Mountain Lake. A hunter from each family would shoot an arrow up the cliff. If the arrow fell short of the top that meant the hunting would not be good up north and the family should stay.

Note: Stanley Mission has a grocery store for supplies and road access for taking out and putting in. There is an RCMP detachment and various means of communication available. Local guides can be hired for learning about the prehistory and history of this very significant and beautiful area. Ask at the CO-OP who is available. They will take you to the cliff, church and rock painting sites.

Map No	Grid Ref	Feature	Description
	284412	Church	The mission, home of the Holy Trinity Anglican Church, was located on the opposite side of the river from where the current community of Stanley is. Holy Trinity is the oldest church west of the Red River and the oldest building still standing in Saskatchewan. The door is always open. Be respectful of the graveyard. An HBC trading post was built at Stanley Mission in 1853, but the first trading post in the area was built at Rapid River.
	295412 297411	Fast water	Expect fast water around the north channel of Spencer Island. There are three faces of rock paintings 500 m above Little Stanley Rapids, all of which can be viewed by standing on the rocks below the cliffs. The lowest painting is about 1 m off the water.
73 P/8	333427	Little Stanley Rapids Campsites	**Class 2**, with small ledges to negotiate at the top and current pushing up against a large boulder on RL at the end. The **portage (40 m)** is on RR. An amazing new roller ramp for motorboats makes for a good York-boat portage opportunity. There is a tricky landing in the fast water, so stay RR. There is a regular-type trail on RL (100 m) for the cautious. There are many sites for camping on the island between Big Stanley and Little Stanley. If it's crowded go back up to the head of the island; there is a nice high spot there. **Big Stanley** is a **Class 3** rapid with big features. The portage (75 m) is on RL. There is a good campsite at its end.
	332420	Campsites	There are a couple of sites on a small island just off the RR shore of Drope Lake.
	338410	Campsite	On the east side of the island.

MAP NO	GRID REF	FEATURE	DESCRIPTION
	359411	Old Mine	A uranium mine site from the early 1950s, which was abandoned when the grade of uranium proved to be lower than expected. Some remains of the site can still be seen. On the map it shows as two dots in a small bay. Sigurd Olson comments on this mine in his 1961 book on paddling the Churchill, *The Lonely Land*.
	348420	Campsite	On the east side of the L-shaped island.
	361411	Inukshuk	On a tiny rock islet, marking the way to Purmal Bay.
	375415	Fast water Campsite	Camping for two tents is possible on the RR point. There is good fishing in the current and eddies around here, but lots of boat traffic, too.
	377409	Campsite	A very nice island camp on McMorris Bay.
	391406	Campsite	On south side of narrows at rock slope.

Note: Located south of Hall Island is the amazing Nistowiak Falls where the Rapid River (sometimes also referred to as the Montreal River) flows into the Churchill. *Nisto* means "three" in Cree, referring to the three rivers meeting here: the lower Churchill (the Missinipi), the upper Churchill (the English River), and the Rapid River. This was a very important crossroads in prehistory and in the fur trade. From here you can go to all points, east, west, south and eventually north. The cabins here are all that is left of a once-thriving community based around the trading post called Rapid River House. Take a side trip to view the falls. The portage is on the right-hand side (west) as you approach the falls. Jim's Camps is located at the start of the portage, you can't miss it! There is good camping on the islands in north-central Nistowiak Lake, if you are looking for a camp off the beaten path.

MAP NO	GRID REF	FEATURE	DESCRIPTION
	433414	Campsite	On RR in a bay between points.
	455403 456403	Potter Rapids	**Class 3+/4**, with ledges and large wave trains. There is a great ramp-and-roller system **portage (95 m)** on RR. There are also fishing camps on both sides, one of which you portage through. It was closed in August of 2001. The portage ends in Class 1 rapids, which must be navigated through the last narrows and into Drinking Lake. Potter Rapids is also referred to as Drinking Falls. A burn begins here that lasts for many kilometres.
	457404 461400	Riffles	Lots of current, boils and small waves through the narrows below Potter Rapids into Drinking Lake.
	473393	Memorial	A large cross on RR on a high rock outcrop erected in memory of a local man.
	490395	Campsite	On a point on the northeast side of a small island.
	495405	Campsite	A sand beach on the west side of a small island at the mouth of the Drinking River. There are many good campsites in this group of islands below the confluence, just have a look around. It's been an area frequented by the Cree people for a very long time. A mine of some sort (I've heard uranium and copper) was being developed in the 1950s at Hunter Falls, just upstream on the Drinking River, but it didn't meet with success. Some remnants of the operation are still visible.
	514389	Campsite	A small camp is possible on a northwestern point of Reed Island.
	550391	Rapids	**Class 1**. There is fast water to Class 1 around Healy Island.

MAP NO	GRID REF	FEATURE	DESCRIPTION
	568392	Campsite	On the RL point 200 m above Inman Channel.
	570393	Campsite	A nice spot on RL above Keg Lake Rapid. The last good camping for approximately 20 km until the south shore of Trade Lake, if you take the Inman Channel and go north of Grennan Island.
	571396	Rapids	**Class 1.** Shallow rapids where the water runs over slab rock in the first narrows of Inman Channel. On RL 1 km down from the rapids described above there are nine rock paintings on a single rock face, 120–150 cm above the water. You have to walk over rocks to get to them.
	589410	Campsite	A small site, a couple of tent sites at best, located on a rock point on RR.
	591414	Rapids	**Class 2/2+.** A narrow chute with a ledge from RR to RC, steep, with a big waves at the bottom. The **portage (40 m)** for motorboats was blasted through rock on RR. The landing is just above the rapids at the beginning of the fast water. There is a longer portage (90 m) with a path on RL, an easier landing out of current for the cautious.
63 M/5	654396	Old Camp	On a small island at the tip of Grennan Island. Old poles for tents are visible. It's a good place to camp if it's vacant.
	655412	Cabin	A trapper's cabin on a deep bay on RL of Keg Lake.
	676396	Campsite	On an island at the north end of Keg Lake. A clearing in the middle makes an OK campsite.

Note: To portage Keg Falls using the log ramp system, be sure to descend the channel directly south of Greig Island.

MAP NO	GRID REF	FEATURE	DESCRIPTION
	700386 702382	Rapids	Approaching Keg Falls between the islands where the channel south of Grieg Island narrows there are sections of fast water and **Class 1** riffles. Follow the left shore, passing where the north channel joins the south and then keeping to the left into a bay where the Keg Falls Portage is.
	704384	Campsite	A small camp for two tents with a nice view from the high point in the birch trees. But be careful where you put your tent; there are anthills on the sandy areas. Farther back in the blueberries is fine. The best landing is on the north side of the point upstream of the tip, where a path is cut up to the camp.
	702383 702382	Keg Falls	**Class 4,** a ledge falls of 1.5 m. There are some breaks in the ledge, including one on the very far RL. The **portage (85 m)** is a log ramp. It starts on RL at the end of the bay on the left, 50 m before the brink of the falls.
	703378	Rapids	**Class 1+.** About 300 m below the portage at the islands where the two main channels of Keg Falls connect are some Class 1+ waves. The RL route has the most flow and requires the least manoeuvring. The rapids are about 150 m long.
	710355	Camping	On RR, the black spruce and moss bank with a rock shoreline provides camping.

the trips

MAP NO	GRID REF	FEATURE	DESCRIPTION
	720353	Rapids	**Class 2**, a broken ledge that spans the width of the river, with some runnable chutes. We ran the main chute just to RL of the big rock, which is about mid-channel. You can scout and pull over on the rock point on RR.
	728354 734354	Grand Rapids Campsite	**Class 2, 3, 2+, 3+/4.** There are four parts to this long (600 m) ledgey boulder run. The first drop is a series of chutes through boulders. The second section is similar, but you must line up perfectly to catch your next chute. The third section is pivotal: you will have to position yourself in order to stop and scout the large waves, holes and stoppers of the large, nasty ledge that makes up the majority of the final drop. And you must scout the entire rapid before committing yourself to running the first and easier sections of it. If you decide halfway down you can't run the rest, you will have a long, tough, scratchy bushwhack to the portage trail. The **portage (600 m)** is on RL and starts in a small bay 100 m above the rapids. No ramp or rollers here — it's a carry! But better to carry than to end up like the voyageurs who capsized their canoes in these large rapids and drowned. You can camp at the top of the portage.
	738354	Fast water	Between the island and the RL point.
	739354	Campsite	High up on the point on RL there are cranberry flats with birch trees. It's a nice view, but a scramble up, just after the fast water in the channel.
	775351	Campsite	On a rock point on the south or RR shore of Trade Lake.
	788348	Campsite	On a bench on the south or RR shore, to the east of the bay.
	809350	Campsite	On a bench on the south or RR shore on a point in a wide bay.
	870377	Campsite	Rock camping on the north shore of Archibald Island. A well-used spot can also be found on the northeast tip of the island.
	915395	Cabin	A nice cabin on the RR point. There are many summer camps on the small islands here. Peter Ballentyne Cree Nation members come up Frog Portage from Pelican Narrows via the Sturgeon-weir.
	930399	Frog Portage	A must-visit. Portage de Traite, or Frog Portage, was home to the first trading post on the Saskatchewan section of the Churchill River. There is a rail-cart system for portaging heavy loads from Lindstrom, the swampy lake that is the headwaters of the Sturgeon-weir. A historic marker that has seen better days sits high on the height of land. You could camp here, but there is something eerie about the place. It's wide open and too well-travelled for my camping tastes.
	924416	Campsite	A well-used island campsite — you can feel the centuries of use! Lovely smooth rocks to land on, with trees for tarps and level tent sites up in the back. Burn begins again on RR.
63 M/6	984463	Water survey station	On RR in the narrows on a burned point. It is no longer in operation.
	003463	Campsite	An old cabin or camp was here at this cleared land on RL at one time.

Map No	Grid Ref	Feature	Description
	029481 030483	Campsites	There are possible camps on either the southeast or northwest points of this mid-channel island.
	032496	Cabin	A trapper's cabin up on the RL bank. Just south of the cabin on the north shore of Uskik Lake there are two sets of rock paintings 150 m apart on low rock cliffs 5–6 m high. From 1–2 m off the water, on vertical rock slabs facing east-southeast.
63 M/11	045517	Campsite	On the south point of the island, with a nice view back down Uskik Lake. The rock ledges on the east shore of Uskik look good for camping as well.
	079574 081574	Cabins	There are some nice cabins on the north shore. At the mouth of the Conjuring River there are rock paintings on a low cliff of gneiss rock about 1 m off the water on a vertical face facing west-southwest.

Note: Approach Kettle Falls on RL. The current is very strong above the falls and the channel is wide. You don't want to be trying to make it over to the portage at the last moment here. There is some current to negotiate along the RL shore above the portage landing, but nothing to be overly concerned about. *Uskik* means "pail for boiling water" or "tea boiling pail" in Cree, and as you near the falls, you'll see why these falls are called Uskik or Kettle Falls. This is one of my favourite places in northern Saskatchewan.

Map No	Grid Ref	Feature	Description
	109571 110571	Kettle Falls Fishing hole Campsite	**Class 5.** The **portage (100 m)** is on RL, 20 m north or right of the falls. You will see the log ramp as you approach. Fishing in the eddy right beside the bottom of the falls is fabulous, even in the dog days of August. There is also a five-star campsite below the falls on RR — it's the best around. Ferry across the current below the portage and above the downstream island into the bay behind the flat rock point at 113571. There is good parking on the smooth rocks in the bay. Pitch your tent anywhere facing northeast and enjoy the amazing view of the falls.
	114574 115575	Little Kettle Falls	**3, 3+, 4, and 2+.** There are four drops in this island string. The far RL drop is where the main flow is and the **portage (25m)** over a log roller ramp goes around it on RL. This drop is a big chute with a large wave train; a loaded canoe will swamp at most water levels. The RL of centre channel has a 3+ ledgey drop. The RR of centre channel has a steep, Class 4 boulder jumble. The far RR channel is a tricky Class 2+ rock dodge. All the drops can be scouted by landing on the islands.
	144587	Campsite	On the north point of Nairn Island.
	149595	Confluence Campsite	Where the Reindeer joins the Churchill River. The Cree called it Atik or Caribou or Deer River. The HBC trading post Fairford House was built just up the Reindeer from the confluence in 1795, and a NWC Fraser House was located in the same area. A hunting camp on the west side of the island makes a good spot for camping. There are few sites suitable for camping on Iskwatam Lake, and a burn begins on RR at Wapumon Lake. The next recommended campsite is below Wapumon Gorge.
	160596 163594	Fast water	There is fast water in the narrows leading to Iskwatam Lake, which means Doorway Lake in Cree. It was the entrance to the Churchill from the north via the Reindeer River.

Note: There are a number of routes to choose from to navigate Iskwatam Lake. The most northerly is the most scenic, but it is also the most difficult in terms of rapids. But you may want to make a detour to visit the culture camp on the southeast point of Romuld Island. You can arrange to stay at the camp before your arrival and study any number of things about traditional Cree life.

North Route

MAP NO	FEATURE	DESCRIPTION
208594	Culture camp	The kitchen and cabins are clustered on the point. The main lodge is in the back bay.
226606	Portage	There is a **portage (60 m)** that bypasses both the sets of rapids at 223604 and 224604. It is on RL across the narrow neck of the peninsula. The trail was being widened and refurbished in August 2001. Perhaps there will be a log ramp for you soon!
223604	Rapids	**Class 4, 2+/3, or 2.** Big water — waves, current and boils start to become the issue in most of the rapids from here on in, as the water flow almost doubles with the inflow of the Reindeer River. Here there are three rapids flowing around two islands. The RL channel is a steep, narrow, rocky drop and probably unnavigable at most water levels. The RC rapid is a steep drop with rocks and large waves to avoid. The RR channel has the main flow and is the easiest of the three: but the large standing waves need to be navigated. You can scout from the islands.
224604	Rapids	**Class 2+.** Immediately after the preceding rapids is a drop in the narrows; it is a large wave train and swamping is a possibility. Fast water continues around the island in mid-channel. To avoid these rapids, you can portage as described above at 226606.
241600 245599	Rapids	**Class 2 and 2+.** There are two sets to this rapid. The first is a chute with a wave train, and so is the second, but it has larger standing waves and more violent current. These drops are characteristic of what is to come. There are no portages, but lining is possible from the rocks on RR shore.
249602 252603	Rapids	**Class 2+ and 3.** There are two sets here. Both are chutes dropping over ledges, creating stoppers and wave trains. The second is by far the most difficult of the last five rapids. Be sure to scout both these sets on the rock points on RR. You can also pull over on each of the RR points to bypass each of the rapids completely. At high water levels these rapids have violent currents, and small whirlpools are created in the eddies; big-water paddling skills are required to avoid swamping and capsizing. Exposed camping is possible on the bare rock point on RR.

South Route

There are no portages around the rapids in the south channel, but two of the rapids may be bypassed easily by pulling over bare rock points.

MAP NO	FEATURE	DESCRIPTION
203574 207576	Fast water	There is only fast water where the two sets of dashes indicate rapids.
239576	Rapids	**Class 2 and 2.** The rapids flow around an island, and both channels are the same difficulty — they are ledge chutes with wave trains. But you can pull over on RL, so this is the best place to scout and

MAP NO	GRID REF	FEATURE	DESCRIPTION
			the RL channel rapid is the most likely run. Exposed camping is possible on the bare rock point.
	246581	Rapids	**Class 2**, more of the same here — a ledge chute and wave train.
	246584	Rapids	**Class 4, Class 2+/3 and Class 1**. The Class 4 ledge can be by-passed by carrying 50 m over the rocks on RL. The second part of the rapid splits around a small island, and the RL channel is the most easily lined or run. Scouting is mandatory and possible from the RL shore. The third and final part of the rapid is split by a large island and starts immediately after the second part. The easiest route to run is the RR channel, which is a shallow riffle.
63 M/10	271578	Fast water	Marked as rapids on the map by bars, but in reality there is only a section of fast water.
	282588	Rapids	**Class 2, 2 or 3**, with an island string here. The RL channel has a fast chute around a bend to the right, with a few rocks to avoid below. The RC channel has a straightforward chute with a wave train at the bottom. The RR channel has a steeper ledge drop. There is no portage here, but scouting and lining are possible using the islands.

Note: You again have a route choice. You can portage once into Wapumon Lake or twice. If you take the 1,100-m portage to the north you will miss viewing the Wapumon Gorge unless you paddle back upstream from the lake. To reach this portage you must run or line the RL rapid, and partway down the rapids eddy out into a cove on RL (283589) just below the tiny island shown on the map. The trail ends at a grassy bay on Wapumon Lake at 290594.

MAP NO	GRID REF	FEATURE	DESCRIPTION
	284584 286583	Rapids	**Class 3**. Wide rapids with a clear route, but potentially very dangerous, as the Gorge is just downstream. You do not want to swim here. Scouting is possible from the RL shore, where you can climb up a high rock outcrop. The **portage (110 m)** is back in the bay on RL at 285585. The trail starts in the willows about 400 m in from the beginning of the fast water, and ends in the big bay between this drop and the Gorge. This is where you want to be next so you can carry around Wapumon.
	289584 292583	Wapumon Gorge Campsite Fishing hole	**Class 4+**. There is one nasty ledge on RR, but really these rapids are one gigantic set of compression waves. The entire flow of the Churchill and all her tributaries thus far squeezes between narrow rock walls — probably over 700 cu m/sec flow through on an average late July day. You do not want to mess around above these rapids! The **portage (300 m)** is on RL in the big, weedy bay. You will probably have to wade and drag to get to the trailhead, which is on the east side of the bay approximately 300 m to the left of the head of the gorge. You can camp on the rock ledges that line the shore at the end of the portage. There is violent current in the eddies below the rapids, and cautious canoeists may wish to continue down the rock ledges until they pass the rock point on RL and reach the slow water behind it. Of course, the walleye fishing here is very good!
	296584	Fast water	The dashes across the width of the river represent fast water in the narrows.

churchill river

77

Note: You can choose to run the eastern channel or the western channel if the water is high. In low water the rapids are too shallow in the western channel and there is no portage. The rapids are at 300586 and are Class 2 with a narrow chute, which turns sharply to the right, making a miniature headwall rapid. It is followed by 150 m or so of rock dodging.

MAP NO	GRID REF	FEATURE	DESCRIPTION
	305587	Rapids	**Class 2 followed by Class 1+.** In the eastern channel is a small, broken ledge followed by shallow, rocky rapids.
	300593	Rapids	**Class 1+/2.** This 250 m rapid is very wide and very shallow and rocky. There are a number of small ledges with chutes.
	311599	Campsite	On a point on RL — a rock point with a grassy clearing.
	363609	Campsite	On the west side of the island above Wintego Rapids. High, flat rocks make for exposed camping, but what a view, and it's difficult to find camping out of the burn for the next 12 km. On the east side of the island, 500 m above Wintego Rapids, there is the last pictograph site on this trip, on a rock facing east, very faint, 2 m up from the water.
	364603	Fishing camp	On a sand beach on the east shore of Wintego Lake.
	369607	Wintego Rapids	**Class 3**, with big water waves following a large chute. The **portage (65 m)** is on RR in a bay above the rapids at 368607.
	381616	Rapids	**Class 2+**, the first of three large rapids in quick succession. This first drop flows around a small island at the top, making two chutes and irregular standing waves. You can scout and or pull over on the rock point on RR.
	383616	Rapids	**Class 2+**, and also divided by an island. There are two main chutes with standing waves. You can scout and or portage on the RR point. In high water it is key to end up on RR in order to eddy out before the last and most difficult rapids in this set.
	385617	Rapids	**Class 3+.** This rapid consists of one large chute falling over a ledge with a big stopper at the bottom. There's really swirly, violent current here. Scouting and a pull over is possible on RR.
	385615	Fast water	There are fast water sections through the islands.
	398616	Rapids	**Class 2, 2+ and 2+.** The river splits around an island and a rocky islet, creating three channels with rapids. The RL channel is narrow and rocky, but the easiest to run and line. The RC and RR channel rapids are steeper.

Note: There are northern and southern routes around Duncan Island on Pita Lake, neither more scenic or difficult than the other. Most of Pita Lake's shoreline is burned.

North Route

MAP NO	GRID REF	FEATURE	DESCRIPTION
	412631	Rapids	**Class 2 or 3+**, these unmarked rapids flow around an island at the north end of Pita Lake. The RL or north channel is a Class 2 chute around a corner with some rocks below to avoid. The RR channel is steep and rocky.

South Route

MAP NO	GRID REF	FEATURE	DESCRIPTION
	398592	Rapids	**Class 2**, a chute with a few rocks to avoid. Lining is possible on RL.

MAP NO	GRID REF	FEATURE	DESCRIPTION
	414583	Rapids	**Class 1** and straightforward.
	445616	Campsite	On a rock on RL in an unburned area.
	440594	Cabin	A small cabin high in a cleared area. In a pinch, northern hospitality will allow you to pitch your tent in the vicinity, as camping is so limited on Pita.
	444585	Marker	Your first barrel marker — you will see many from here on in. They are to help the tourist fishing parties find their way back to camp.

Note: You can go west or east around the large unnamed island into Pikoo Lake. To the west is a beautiful channel I really recommend. It gets the least boat traffic and is a joyride.

Western Route

	455596	Rapids	**Class 1**. A big fast water chute for 150 m or more.

Eastern Route

MAP NO	GRID REF	FEATURE	DESCRIPTION
	458592	Cameron Falls	**Class 2**, just a standing wave run. No falls!
	509631	Cabins	These are local fishing guides' cabins.
	515617	Campsite	On the flat rocks on the north side of Johnson Peninsula.
	519642	Fishing camp	A large lodge on Reeds Lake.
	525618	Cabins	More seasonal cabins.
	525608	Campsite	In a sheltered bay on RL there is a beautiful sand beach with tent sites in the trees. Lots of traffic around, though.
	532560	Campsite	On RR at a high rock outcrop. Up on top of the outcrop are a couple of tent spots and down below in the trees are a few more. There is a small, flat rock landing.
63 M/7	555527	Campsite	On the north end of the island.
63 M/8	586482	Campsite	On the east side of the island on a point.
	614488	Campsite	On RL high up on a rock, with a nice view.
	645521	Cabin	On a tiny island.
	651530	Campsite	A small site on the southeast point of the island.
63 M/9	668566	Island Falls Dam	The **portage (325 m)** is at the far northeast end of Sokatisewin Lake on RL. Keep paddling north past the powerhouse (the large prison-like pinky-grey building). To the left of the spillway is a large rock outcrop. The portage is to the left of the hump in a bay full of logs and old metal. Land at the grassy clearing. The trail is in fair condition but is growing over in places. It ends on a large, smooth whaleback rock outcrop.
	676573	Rapids	**Class 2**. One more large chute with a wave train so you can say good-bye to the Churchill in style. Lots of swirly, sucky water on the eddylines of the wave train. You can pull over on the bare rock on RL.
	692563	Sandy Bay Take-out	There are two docks across from the island: one is for the float-plane base and the other is public.

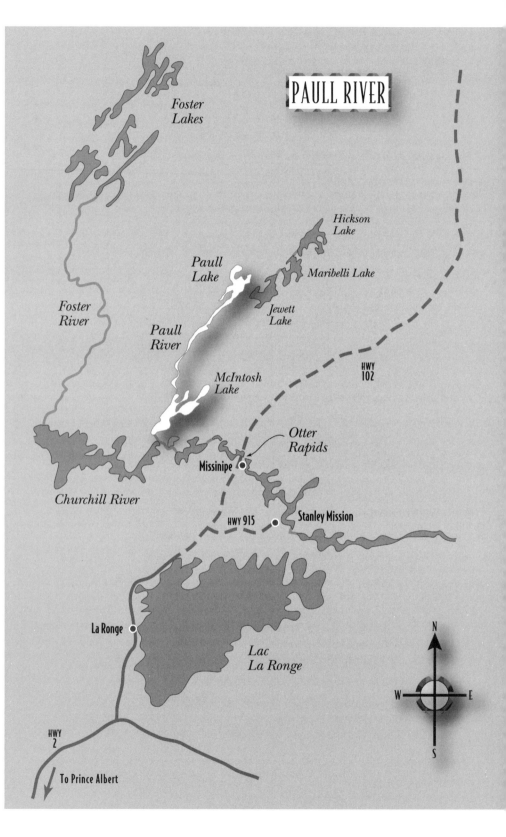

PAULL RIVER

This was my first fly-in trip, and the second river Brad and I paddled together. It's still one of my favourite shorter trips, and I've paddled it five times since 1988. The beauty of the Paull, a tributary of the Churchill River, is in its Precambrian Shield drop-pool nature. But it's not a large-volume river. There are scenic, narrow sections along the river, and the Paull's granite outcrops and flat, smooth-rock shores make for good camping along the route. There are a variety of rapids on this river, some shallow and rocky and some drops with ledges and bigger waves.

On the lakes, you will find great sand beaches for relaxing and swimming and lovely, high, rock and moss banks to admire as you glide by. And, as a bonus, most of the lakes on the route have islands to nip around should the wind come up. Tuck Falls (also known as Whitefish Falls) is a draw for photographers and for the adventurous. Brad's claim to fame here in 1988 was the first solo descent of the falls, while together he and I have the honour of the first tandem descent (it was all in the Royalex!). The falls are great for exploring, fishing and swimming. You can cross them almost to the other side of the river if the water level is right. Sliding down them on your behind into the large pool below has even been accomplished (though perhaps not enjoyed) by my mother-in-law!

The Paull is also known for its walleye and northern pike fishing. On this route there are three major fishing holes that rank with the best I have ever found. Brad and I have flown to Tuck many times just to fish for the day. And to top it all off, the Paull flows into the best part of the Churchill for rapids and fishing!

Length

The trip described here is approximately 105 km long. It is a fly-in trip that starts at a beach about midway down Paull Lake and ends at Missinipe, a community on Otter Lake on the Churchill River. The Paull section of the trip is 65 km long, while for the remaining 40 km of the trip you navigate the Churchill.

It is possible to shorten the trip by landing farther down the river or on any of the lakes along the route. To extend the trip, canoeists can land farther upriver on Taylor Bay, or take the opportunity to see the rock paintings between Hickson and Maribelli Lakes by flying in to Hickson Lake. Canoeists can then paddle through Smith Narrows to Maribelli and then up a creek to Johnston Lake and through a series of small lakes with portages in between to Paull Lake. That was the trip we did in 1988, and the rock paintings and trout fishing were worth the strenuous portaging!

The shortest time you should consider for the route described in the Trip Notes, from Paull Lake to Missinipe, is five whole paddling days. You will need to scout a good portion of the rapids, which takes time. Be sure to check the water levels: some of the rapids on the Paull can become too shallow to navigate, and that could add an extra day to your trip. Plus, the wind can get up on McIntosh and Nipew Lakes.

Paull Lake to Missinipe*	105 km
Taylor Bay to Missinipe	122 km
Hickson Lake to Missinipe	155 km

* This is the trip down the Paull described in detail the Trip Notes section of this chapter; the Churchill section is described in the Churchill Trip Notes.

Topographic Maps

I would recommend 1:50,000 — 74A/2, 74A/3, 73P/14, 73P/11 and 73P/10. If you are thinking of going in at Taylor Bay, you have all the maps you need above, but for the Hickson Lake route you will need 74 A/8 and 74A/1 as well. In order to make the best use of the information provided in this chapter, canoeists should purchase the required maps in advance and use the grid reference coordinates in the Trip Notes section to mark in the rapids missing on the maps. Classification of the rapids and other features of interest from the Trip Notes section can be marked on your maps as well, including the portages, fishing holes and nice campsites.

There is a SERM canoe trip booklet available for the trip described in this chapter. It is number 36 and is available via the Canoe Saskatchewan website or by calling SERM for a copy.

Getting There and Away

You must fly into the Paull, but you can drive out from Missinipe, making for an easy shuttle if you fly from Missinipe or La Ronge. The easiest and cheapest option is to leave your car at Churchill River Canoe Outfitters or at Osprey Wings, the aviation charter company in Missinipe, and simply paddle back to your vehicle(s) via Otter Rapids and Otter Lake. The contact information is in the Directory of Services.

When to Go

The beginning of June to early August is best. The ice is usually off the big lakes along the Churchill by the third week of May, but go too late in the season and low water levels may make some of the rapids unnavigable. There is no water-gauging station on the Paull River, but if the water is low on the Churchill you should be concerned. You can check the flow of the Churchill at Otter Rapids on the SaskWater website. In order to put the cu m/sec reading you get in context, that is, to see if the water is high or low, check the Canoe Saskatchewan website chart on the Churchill's average monthly flow at Otter Rapids.

Additionally, you can try calling Churchill River Canoe Outfitters for Paull River water-level information. Someone there generally knows what the water levels are like on any given river in northern Saskatchewan. Many canoeists stop there and share their recent trip information, and CRCO runs guided trips down the Paull. See the Directory of Services for contact information.

Difficulty of the River **$^{1}/_{2}$

The Paull gets a two-and-one-half-star difficulty rating because of the numerous rapids, its isolation and the big lake crossing of McIntosh. The rapids average a solid Class 2. At low water levels, some rapids will have to be portaged or waded, even by skilled paddlers. At high water levels the large number of rocks combined with relatively steep gradients result in more demanding rapids. However, scouting is not difficult, as the rapids are not continuous, and the portage trails are in good condition; less-skilled whitewater paddlers are encouraged to use them. I've personally seen three Royalex canoe wrap in the rocky rapids of the Paull. The river is suitable for guided beginners paddling with intermediates, and the rapids will challenge intermediate paddlers.

The gradient of the river from Paull Lake to McIntosh Lake is 0.78 m/km (4.1 ft/mi), a fairly moderate gradient for northern Saskatchewan. The difficulty rating of the Churchill section you must travel to reach road access is also two stars. However, the volume of water is much higher when you reach the Churchill. Almost all of the rapids can be portaged on very good trails, but some of the portages are quite long. Nipew Lake is relatively exposed open-water paddling.

Character of the River and Region

The moderate volume of the Paull doesn't change much as you descend, but the Churchill is a large-volume experience. Both riverbeds are Precambrian rock for the most part. Boulder rapids prevail, with beaver-sized rocks to bear-sized boulders. There are also ledge formations where the river flows over exposed shelves of Precambrian rock.

The Paull lies completely within the Churchill River Uplands ecoregion. The landscape appears rugged, though local relief rarely exceeds 25 m. Wetlands are numerous, and varied outcroppings of Precambrian rock, especially a pink-coloured granite, are predominant. There are some glacial deposits, and most of the soils are sandy, supporting low stands of black spruce and jack pine. The understory of the forest is usually a mix of feather mosses and lichen, blueberries, pin cherries and small shrubs and herbs.

Local History **

The Paull River was an alternate route between Reindeer Lake and the Churchill, but its importance was minimal in early exploration and the fur trade. However, it was an area much used by the ancestors of the Woods Cree. One of the largest single pictograph sites in Canada is the narrows between Hickson and Maribelli Lakes, northeast and over a height of land from Paull Lake. The Cree travelled this lake route from the Churchill via the Paull River to reach the lower section of the Wathaman River, which flows into Reindeer Lake.

The Dene that wintered south of Cree Lake and travelled to the Churchill to trade at Ile-à-la-Crosse and summer in the south used the Foster River, which is just west of the Paull, to return to their wintering grounds. This annual "round" started later in the 1700s and continued throughout the 1800s, but I have not been able to discover any evidence of them using the Paull River. This area southeast of the Foster appears to have been primarily used by the Cree. The prevalence of the rock paintings seems to support this, as it is generally accepted that the Cree made the pictographs found in northern Saskatchewan. McIntosh Lake, the last lake on the Paull River route, is called *Numekos Sakuhikun* by the Cree, or "Trout Lake," for the trout that can still be caught there.

In 1790, Alexander Fraser built a trading post called Fraser House on the southeast shore of McIntosh Lake, somewhere by the portage into Stack Lake. Those were the early days of the inland posts, and they were built quickly and abandoned even more quickly if they failed to show promise.

Level of Solitude ***

The Paull River is a good trip for wilderness solitude, though it has become much more popular with canoeists since I first paddled in the area. The section of the Churchill you will travel sees a lot of traffic these days, thus the two-star ratings for solitude on that stretch (see the section on the Churchill River). There are no communities along the Paull, and there is only one fishing lodge. On McIntosh Lake there is a large fishing lodge and some cabins. On the Churchill you will find local trapper cabins and two fishing-camp outposts. In peak season you will likely see other canoeists, or local people and fisherpersons, but not many until you near the area upstream of Devil Lake.

Wildlife ***

The Churchill Uplands is a rich ecoregion for all the common fauna of the Boreal Shield. Wildlife sightings of moose, bears, timber wolves, beavers and otters on the Paull are quite possible. On the sand beaches you will often see bear, moose and wolf tracks, and there are lots of game trails around the marked campsites. Keep your tent away from these paths to avoid any unwanted disturbances in the middle of the night!

The first time I was on the Paull River was also the first time I had ever heard nighthawks diving after insects in the dusk. The zipping, buzzing noise was a complete mystery to me. I had to ask Brad what it was, and when he told me birds were making the sounds, I thought he was pulling my leg!

Eagles are especially numerous on the Paull. As you approach the Churchill, the hunting activity becomes more intense, and the chances of seeing wildlife later in the trip are lessened. But the eagles are always there.

Fishing ****

The fishing on the Paull gets four stars, as the walleye and northern pike fishing is normally excellent. There are deep pools below the rapids in which the fish can feed. There is also fine lake fishing, including trout fishing at McIntosh. An interesting note on the types of fish you may catch; sauger, which looks like a small, thin, brown-coloured walleye, is unusual to find on any river but the Saskatchewan River and its tributaries. However, I've caught many sauger below Tuck Falls, and in the eddy on river right at Corner Rapids on the Churchill.

There are three walleye fishing holes of particular note on the Paull: two are in bends of the river below or between rapids, and the third is Tuck Falls. Coordinates for these spots are in the Trip Notes. Huge northern pike can be caught below the falls, and in the weedy bays of the river, Nipew Lake, and farther on down the Churchill. But the sheer number of walleye that can be caught in the pools below the rapids is really amazing. One year Brad and I took a group down the river, and by jigging Brad and I caught thirteen walleye in a row — each! We threw them back as we caught them, as it was all just for fun. But it was astonishing to our guests.

The fishing on the Churchill is almost as good as that on the Paull. See the chapter on the Churchill for more details.

Special Equipment

The best choice for a canoe is a Royalex-hull tripping canoe with Kevlar skid plates to protect it from the inevitable hard knocks. A Royalex canoe is ideal for this kind of shallow back-country river — it is a slippery toboggan when you run out of water, and if you do happen to wrap it around one of the big rocks, it will quite often regain its shape again, if you can get off the rock to carry on down the river. The worst choice of material for a canoe for this river is aluminum; it will stick to every rock you touch, and it is impossible to slide over rocks and ledges in the shallows. Plus, if it wraps, it's almost impossible to get off the rock. And aluminum tears. You could also paddle a Kevlar or fibreglass canoe. Either will skid over rocks, but both are vulnerable to crushing if pinned hard on a boulder. Like I said, I've seen three wraps on the Paull and some on the rapids of the middle Churchill too.

Bring insect repellent. The Paull is pretty good in July for blackflies and mosquitoes, but they will be there. June is the worst for blackflies. In July, the mosquito population begins to go down as the dragonflies come out. Of course, then the horse flies and deer flies come out.... The bugs are at their lowest levels in August, but the water might be too!

Trip Notes

MAP NO	GRID REF	FEATURE	DESCRIPTION
74/A/2	149236	Fly-in, put-in point	This beach, at the northeast end of the lower half of Paull Lake, is the common put-in if you fly with Osprey Wings. But they will drop you anywhere they can.
	090179	Campsite	On a rock point on RL.
	070173	Fast water	Approaching the river at the southwest end of Paull Lake there is a narrows and the current increases.

MAP NO	GRID REF	FEATURE	DESCRIPTION
	048145 049144	Stewart Rapids	**Class 2/2+** narrow, shallow rapids with boulders to avoid. The **portage (120 m)** is on RL, and starts 40 m east of the beginning of the rapids.
74 A/3	986092	Campsite	On RR in a bay as the river widens again.
73 P/14	971045 971044	Rapids Fishing hole	**Class 2+**, a shallow, L-shaped rapid that splits around a small island at the 90-degree bend in the channel. This bend halfway down the rapid is home to 6-lb walleye! The first section is fast and steep, with the waves larger in the RL channel, as it has the greatest flow. There is a big eddy in the fishing-hole bend. The second part of the rapid is a bit hairy. You have to work to get RL to avoid the rocks in the main current on RR. The **portage (150 m)** is on RL on the east side of a flat rock immediately above the first drop of the rapid. There is a trail back to the great fishing eddy in the bend.
	966027	Rapids	**Class 1**. A riffle.
	960008 958007	Rapids	**Class 2**. A shallow, wide, and rocky set of rapids approximately 200 m above a larger rapid described below. The **portage (200 m)** is on RL starting just southeast of a flat rock landing above the rapids. The trail runs along a rock ridge.
	957006 955004	Rapids	**Class 3-/2**. This second set starts off narrow, the rapids are steep and fast and there are a few big boulders at the top to navigate. After the boulders the rapids become Class 2. The **portage (325 m)** starts on a flat rock on RR about 40 m above the start of the rapids.
	955004	Campsite	On RR at the bottom of the portage is a poor campsite (for the Paull), but you can play in the rapids, fish or watch the eagles.
	952001	Rapids	These rapids, 200 m below the end of the portage, are shallow **Class 1/1+**. At low water they may become unnavigable, and wading may be required.
	935963 936962	Falls Campsite Fishing hole	**Tuck Falls** is a river-wide, beautiful granite ledge (5 m) with numerous cascades along its width. The **portage (40 m)** starts on the rocks on RL at the top of the falls. This is where the good campsite is. There is no trail for the portage, it is over bare rock with a steep descent to the bottom of the falls. Below the falls there is great walleye and northern pike fishing. You could catch sauger too.
	946943 947942	Rapids	**Class 3**. Narrow, fast and steep with numerous boulders. The rapid starts out easy, then drops over a 30-cm ledge and then without warning drop over another larger ledge (1 m or 3 ft). It's more difficult at higher water levels. The **portage (310 m)** is on RR just past a big boulder 75 m above the start of the rapids.
	924904 924902	Rapids "The Gorge" Potential camping	**Class 4**. A winding gorge with a steep rock wall on RL. The **portage (300 m) starts at 925907** in a grassy cove on RR, not at the top of the rapid. The path you will find there is a fishing trail that runs along the gorge's RR bank. It is possible to camp along this trail on the banks of the river, but it's squishy. Depending on the water level, there may be intermittent areas of fast water and some

MAP NO	GRID REF	FEATURE	DESCRIPTION
			riffles in between the next three sets of rapids that make up Campbell Rapids. This is another stretch where wrapping your canoe in low water is a concern.
	931898	Campbell Rapids 1	**Class 2**. Rock dodging is required. These are fast and shallow and may require wading in very low water.
	936883	Campbell Rapids 2	**Class 2/2+**, shallow and rocky, and may be unnavigable at very low water. The **portage (250 m)** is on RL about 20 m above the start of the rapid after a section of minor rapids at **937884**. The second part of the rapid is more rocky and difficult.
	934876	Campbell Rapids 3	**Class 1+**. It's shallow and rocky, and may have to be waded at low water. The rapids are the outlet of the Paull River, and flow into a small lake above McIntosh Lake. The **portage (25 m)** starts on RR at a break in the willow-lined shore.
	924854 924852	Rapids Campsite	**Class 3**. This rapid connects the small lake to McIntosh Lake and is a drop over a large, broken ledge. Sheila smacked her hip against the rear thwart but good running this in 1988, so it has been dubbed "Broken Hip Rapid." The **portage (95 m)** is on RL beginning at a flat rock and is across open rock. The open rock is a nice campsite at lower water levels. There are some cabins around the corner on the north end of McIntosh, and the area is frequented by fishing parties, so bears may be around.
	916832 912825 911830	Campsites	There are three good island campsites out on McIntosh Lake for those who prefer camping on islands.
73 P/11	875732	Portage	From a small beach on the southeast shore of McIntosh to Stack Lake, it's **260 m** long. There is a boardwalk for your portaging ease!

* Follow the Churchill Trip Notes from here on in starting with the fishing holes below the rapids dropping into Stack Lake. Below are notes on the alternate route to Stack.

MAP NO	GRID REF	FEATURE	DESCRIPTION
73 P/11	864725	Rapids	**Class 2**, shallow, rocky, winding rapids that connect McIntosh Lake with the Churchill River just before Trout Rapids (Chipewa Falls). I prefer this route over portaging straight into Stack Lake because there is a great spot to fish as you leave McIntosh and enter the channel. Try above the rapids and below for great walleye fishing. You can often see fish in the water below you as you enter the channel. The **portage (175 m)** starts on RL down the channel, just before the rapids begin. It is in fair condition, ending in the fast water on a rocky shore.

* Follow Churchill Trip Notes from here, beginning with Trout Rapids and Trout Portage.

FOSTER RIVER

The Foster River is a tributary of the Churchill and shares its Precambrian Shield character-istics. Like the western Churchill especially, it can be rugged and swampy. The Foster has a Jekyll-and-Hyde nature. In a matter of an hour you can go from beautiful granite cliffs to twisty low-relief monotony. A new burn on the lower part of the river in 1998 really emphasizes the contrasting landscapes of this river. The camping potential follows from the landscape; there is great camping on rock ledges and jack pine benches, then nothing for campsites but marshy shores or burn. The rapids also exhibit extreme characteristics. They are either easy and fun, or really difficult and intimidating. Since the burn, the portages have two definite natures as well. There are excellent portages and then there are some burned-out messes. Finally, as with the Churchill, the water can be really high or really low in any given year. All in all, it's a river with great variety and some marvellous scenery. The north shore of the unnamed lake above Eulas Lake is stunning with its rock ledges. Spiral and Diagonal Waterfalls are exquisite. There are no overly large lake crossings to worry about, there is good current in many stretches, and there are rock paintings to ponder.

There is true wilderness and solitude to be found here. The Foster is not a river particularly in vogue with canoeists at this time. Lots of eagles and osprey live along the river, and the marshy areas of the Foster, along with the burn, make for good moose habitat. Finally, flying into the Foster gets you to the best part of the Churchill, the final reason for doing this trip. Black Bear Island Lake is magical beyond belief.

Length

The trip described in detail in the Trip Notes section of this chapter is 260 km long, of which 153 km are on the Foster, starting at Lower Foster Lake, and 107 km are on the Churchill River from Black Bear Island down to the community of Missinipe on Otter Lake. You could shorten the trip and fly out of Eulas Lake or the Churchill once you reach it, or you could lengthen the trip by starting on Middle or Upper Foster Lake.

Lower Foster Lake to Eulas Lake*	125 km
Lower Foster Lake to the Churchill River confluence*	153 km
Lower Foster Lake to Missinipe on the Churchill River**	260 km
Middle Foster Lake at Grand Rapids to Missinipe	280 km

  * These trips down the Foster are described in detail in the Trip Notes section.
 ** The Churchill part of the trip is described in the chapter on the Churchill.

Topographic Maps

I recommend 1:50,000. From Welsh Rapids on Lower Foster Lake to Otter Lake on the Churchill River, the entire trip described in this chapter, you will need 74 A/3, 74 A/4, 74 A/5, 73 P/11, 73 P/12, 73 P/13, 73 P/10. If you go up to Middle Foster Lake to start at Grand Rapids you will also need 74 A/11. To find out what maps you need for a shorter trip, look in the Trip Notes.

In order to make the best use of the information provided in this chapter, canoeists should purchase the required maps in advance and use the grid reference coordinates in the Trip Notes section to mark in the rapids and falls missing on the maps. Classifications of the rapids and other notes can be added as well. It is important to note the camping opportunities, as there are stretches on the Foster where finding good campsites is difficult.

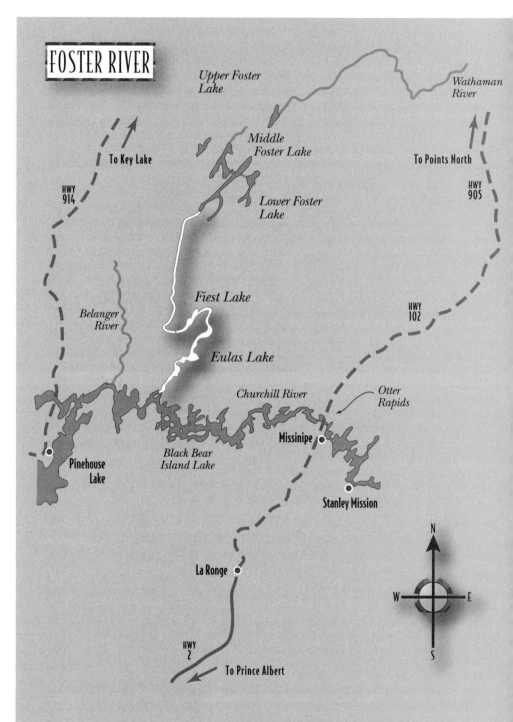

There is a SERM canoe-trip booklet for the Foster, number 57. But it has not been updated since the Robin Fire in 1998, so some of the information is outdated. It is available by calling SERM or by printing it off the Canoe Saskatchewan website.

Getting There and Away

The trip described here is a fly-in only, but getting a floatplane charter out of La Ronge or Missinipe is easy. Safe parking is available at both places. If you decide to fly with Transwest in La Ronge, you may be able to catch a backhaul from Foster Lake Lodge, which is on Lower Foster Lake, just down from Grand Rapids (grid reference 735649 on 1:50,000 74 A/11). A shuttle back to La Ronge with your canoes and equipment can be arranged by contacting Churchill River Canoe Outfitters. If you are taking out at Eulas Lake, you may be able to get a backhaul to La Ronge via Transwest as well, through an arrangement with the people who own Foster River Camps, the fishing camp on Eulas.

Finally, you can paddle right back to your vehicle in Missinipe if you fly with Osprey Wings. Thompson's Camps has an outpost camp farther north on the Foster Lakes, and you could try to arrange for a backhaul with Osprey Wings to there. Contact information for all the companies mentioned in this section is provided in the Directory of Services in the back of this guidebook.

When to Go

Late May to the end of July in a normal-water year; in a high-water year the beginning of August is a possibility. The Fraser, Lewis and Jones Rapids in the upper reaches and many of the rapids from Fiest Lake down are the problem in low water. They are very shallow and rocky in places, and you may have to wade and drag for quite a stretch. The river peaks in May, as does its sister river, the Haultain, but unlike the Haultain it drops significantly in August and September. I paddled it in late May and early June 2001 at a fairly normal water level, judging from high-water marks on the rocks and the very full creeks running in. The rapids weren't pushy, and no wading was required. Lower water makes many of the rapids easier — you have less chance of swamping, as a number of the drops involve steep chutes with standing waves. However, the steeper, rockier rapids become more difficult to navigate in low water.

There is no longer an operating water-survey station on the Foster. You can check the current water level on the Churchill, however, and if the Churchill is low in July and August, you can bet its feeders are too. Call SaskWater at 306-694-3966 or fax them at 306-694-3944 for the current water levels on the Churchill at Otter Rapids, and then compare the cu m/sec rate you get from SaskWater to the monthly average mean chart of the Churchill at the Canoe Saskatchewan website at www.lights.com/waterways/local/church.htm.

Another way of checking the current water levels on the Foster is by contacting Churchill River Canoe Outfitters. Someone there generally knows the state of the water levels in the Churchill region, as they have lots of canoeists coming through their office sharing their recent trip experiences. Maybe you'll get lucky and a group will have been through and passed on the scoop on the water levels. You could also try calling some of the fishing-camp operators and the SERM office in La Ronge.

Difficulty of the River ✱✱✱

The Foster gets three stars for difficulty. It is a remote wilderness river with many rapids, and is not a good choice for inexperienced canoe trippers. It has been said that the Foster is the most difficult to travel of all the major tributaries of the western Churchill. It's a toss-up between the Foster and the Haultain, and I'd say the Haultain wins by a hair. The Haultain has some difficult rapids and portages like the Foster, but not as many runnable rapids. Although now that the Foster is burned, it's more like the Haultain in that some of the portages are just a bushwhack in places.

In the first section, Fraser, Lewis and Jones Rapids, there are no portages and the canoeist is required to read and run Class 1+ rapids in order to make any timely progress. The larger rapids can be portaged, and most of the portages are in good to fair condition. As such, the Foster is like the Paull, averaging a class 2/2+, but there are many more rapids on the Foster, and more and longer portages to be made around the significant number of falls and larger, difficult rapids that only very advanced and expert paddlers are going to be able to run successfully. The Foster is a strenuous trip, and it is one of the longer trips in terms of distance. I have noted the changes in the trip since the Robin Fire that burned part of the river in 1998. Be warned — while some of the portages that were burned out have been recut and were in fairly good condition when I was there, some were still very difficult to find, much less traverse. Furthermore, trees will continue to fall across the trails. This makes the Foster even more of a strenuous trip than it was before. I encourage you to do your part and help maintain the portages that are there compliments of a trapper's hard work.

The gradient of the Foster to its confluence with the Churchill is 0.83 m/km (4.4 ft/mi), making it one of the steeper rivers. But it has larger falls and drops that make up some of the total drop. Once the Foster gets rolling it is a drop-pool river, and is a good choice for canoeists with intermediate whitewater skills looking to run a river with a variety of kinds of rapids, but who are prepared to portage the more difficult rapids. Advanced and exceptional paddlers can enjoy the serious challenge of the big rapids on the Foster.

Character of the River and Region

The Foster gradually increases from a small-volume river, reminiscent of the Montreal, to a more moderate volume like that of the Sturgeon-weir above Amisk Lake. There is a lot of variety in the nature of the riverbed. It's shallow with small rocks at the beginning, then it's full of moose food, then the rocks get bigger, then there is moose food again, then big boulders. Throw in some smooth granite ledges.... You see what I mean.

This changing riverbed accounts for the variety of kinds of rapids the canoeist will encounter on the Foster. There are the shallow, small, rock rapids of Fraser and Lewis, and slightly bigger rocky rapids later on. There are chutes with large standing waves, ledges and steep boulder aprons, and finally, some smooth-rock ledges and falls. Quite a mix. See the Churchill chapter for the nature of the river and rapids of the middle Churchill to complete an overview of the kinds of rapids to expect on the next section of the trip.

Like the Mudjatik and the Haultain, the Foster was a former glacial meltwater channel. It carried meltwater from the ice during the formation of the Cree Lake moraine. You actually feel as if you are in a river valley in some places along the Foster; this is unusual for northern Saskatchewan rivers.

The river is completely within the Churchill River Upland ecoregion, and it has a dose of the wetland in one long stretch. However, it has a smaller dose than its two previously mentioned sisters! It is very rugged in a number of places, with high granite cliffs and lots of reddish and dark gray outcroppings of gneiss — this is quite characteristic of the Churchill Uplands. There are rocky shorelines and sand plains. I've mentioned the Dr. Jekyll and Mr. Hyde nature of the Foster, haven't I? The lakes follow the northeast-southwest pattern of the Shield, and black spruce dominates in the swamp and out. I was surprised by the number of birch and aspen trees that are also a significant part of the landscape in places. Jack pine is common where there is sand and outcropping. The understory of the forest is feather mosses, Labrador tea, bog cranberry and various shrubs and herbs. Lichens and alder occur where there is more sunlight.

On the Foster, campsites are either open jack pine bench areas or rock ledges. And be warned, they are plentiful in a few areas, but then are non-existent for many kilometres. I highly recommend your group take as few tents as possible and plan where you will stay each night according to the notes provided. Camping is not at all easy to find in many places on the Foster, especially now, because of the Robin Fire in 1998.

Local History ✱✱✱

The Foster is interesting in that historically both the Dene and Cree of northern Saskatchewan have used it. There is some question as to how early the Cree people arrived in northern Saskatchewan, but some put it as early as AD 1000. Regardless, it is now generally thought that the area south of Lake Athabasca and southwest of Wollaston Lake down to the Churchill was actually Cree territory before the Europeans came and for the first 100 years of the fur trade. The three pictograph sites on the Foster are evidence of the importance of the route for travellers moving north and south before the European influx. It is generally thought that the Cree were the authors of the rock paintings, making it seem even more likely that the river was in Cree territory when the fur traders arrived. There are pictographs below a double set of rapids (before Scott Rapids) on a high rock cliff on river right. The second set is on Eulas Lake, on the west shore at the outflow of the lake before the river begins to narrow. The third site is at the mouth of the Foster where it joins the Churchill.

However, during the 1800s and into the early 1900s the *kesyehot'ine* Dene, or "Poplar House People," ascended the Foster on their return trips to caribou country from the Churchill River and points south. Families from this group of Dene wintered up at Cree Lake, and their annual "round" took them south in the spring, descending the Mudjatik to Ile-à-la-Crosse. There they gathered to socialize and trade. Some carried on south to Dore and Smoothstone Lakes. This group would then return north via the Smoothstone River to the Churchill. From the Churchill they would ascend either the Belanger River or the Foster to get back to their wintering grounds by freeze-up. See the chapter on the Churchill for more about these ancestors of the Dene, who live on the upper Churchill today.

The Foster is also the first leg of some other very old canoe routes. From the Foster Lakes you can eventually access the Geikie, Wheeler and Waterfound Rivers and Highrock, Big Sandy, Russell, Cree and Wollaston Lakes. You can also travel to the Wathaman River via the Foster Lakes and another chain of small lakes.

Joseph Burr Tyrrell, a surveyor for the Geological Survey of Canada, was probably the first person to write about the river, and it was he who changed its name; it was once called Whitefish or Fish River. Tyrrell, claiming there were already too many Whitefish Rivers, renamed the river after George Eulas Foster, the finance minister of Canada in the early 1890s and MP from New Brunswick. One would think this is how Eulas Lake got its name as well. But Eulas Lake had a much more interesting name previous to Tyrrell — Jumping-into-the-Water Lake! Perhaps from the high cliffs that one could jump from? Obviously, the Little Whitefish River that joins the Foster midway through the trip was at one point aptly named. Do I hear Little Foster?

There were, at times, trading outposts on the Foster Lakes, and there was one at the confluence of the Foster and the Churchill, called Fish River. It was home to a small community of the same name. It was a village with cabins and a graveyard, and this is where many Native people would wait for friends and relatives to come in from their winter trapping grounds. Today, members of the Ratt family are still taking advantage of the resources of the Foster River, and have been for at least 100 years. The camp south of the pictographs at the end of the peninsula is theirs.

Though the river has always been used as a canoe route, that doesn't make it easy to travel. Ed Theriau, a white trapper in the Russell Lake area in the 1930s, wrote in his journal about ascending the Foster to his trapline. He wrote, "It is the worst river on which I have ever travelled, full of rapids and with several waterfalls. In one place you have to pack everything almost straight up over a rocky hill." The other interesting thing I discovered was that one man portaging his canoe around one of the rapids on the Foster stepped in a hole on the rough trail. One of the paddles he was using for a yoke broke on his shoulder, and the canoe fell sideways, breaking his neck. Apparently he is buried on that portage. Watch out, all canoeheads!

Doug Chisholm, a La Ronge resident, told me that in the early 1970s a group of hippies homesteaded on the island on Eulas Lake where Foster River Camps is now located. There is still rhubarb growing back behind the outhouse!

You might want to read Tyrrell's account of his 1892 journey up the Geikie from Wollaston Lake down the Foster to the Churchill. See the References pages for bibliographical details of his report. There is also an online version available, and the website is listed as well. *Face the North Wind* and *Lost Land of the Caribou* are interesting accounts of two trappers who used the Foster to access their traplines in the area north of Foster Lakes.

Level of Solitude ✳✳✳

You may meet another party of canoeists on the Foster, but don't expect to. The Foster is not what I call a "sexy" river to paddle right now. It used to be more popular, but lots of canoeists have been focussing on the Far North for their longer expeditions in recent years — the William and the Waterfound / Fond du Lac, for instance.

There is a fly-in fishing camp on Eulas Lake, so you will probably encounter people in motorboats. The trappers along the river are not trapping during the summer months, and there are no communities on the Foster, so the river is not going to be crowded by any means. All in all, the solitude rating is pretty high on the Foster. Once you reach the Churchill the traffic really picks up, especially after you reach the east end of Trout Lake. You will usually encounter local motorboat traffic and fishing and canoeing parties as you descend, especially just upstream of Devil Lake.

Wildlife ✳✳✳

The Churchill Upland ecoregion has large populations of common northern wildlife. There is a good chance you will see a moose or a bear on the Foster, as it's not travelled extensively. You will certainly see lots of eagles and even an osprey or two. Timber wolves are common, but usually keep out of sight. Beavers and even otters are also a good bet. Once you reach the more heavily trafficked areas of the Churchill, your chances of seeing large animals are at least halved, as the populations in these areas are under much more pressure from human activity.

Fishing ✳✳

Like the Haultain, and unlike the Paull, fishing for walleye is basically a fruitless enterprise on the Foster until you get to Eulas Lake. From then on the walleye fishing is pretty good, becoming excellent in places along the Churchill. On the Foster, however, northern pike are readily available for supper or a shore lunch. Trappers net a lot of whitefish on this river, as they do on the Haultain.

Special Equipment

My bias is towards a Royalex boat with Kevlar skid plates, especially when I'm tripping for a longer period of time on a remote river with shallow and rocky rapids. It slides over shallow rocks and ledges, and regains its shape if it gets wrapped around a rock. Very unlike aluminum canoes, which are not recommended.

There is lots of portaging to be done, so a Kevlar boat becomes more attractive, but only if you stay away from the more difficult rapids, and make sure you don't go in low water conditions. Your gel coat will pay, and there is always the chance of hitting that one rock, and "goodbye." Lots of canoes have been beaten up in the Foster.

You will be portaging lots no matter how good you are, so be sure to pack for it. A spray skirt in high water would be lots of fun for exceptional and advanced whitewater canoeists. I had a lot of fun in a whitewater solo boat in 2001, except on the lakes!

The bugs can be bad on the Foster, both blackflies and mosquitoes. I recommend a bug jacket with a head net, especially in June and early July.

Trip Notes

MAP NO	GRID REF	FEATURE	DESCRIPTION
74 A/5	639546	Put-in point	A little beach in a protected bay next to Welsh Rapids. There is a trapper's cabin here.
	607523	Put-in point	Another little beach in a protected bay. This is where I flew in on my solo trip because of the wind. There was evidence of spring birchbark collecting back of the beach.
	597527	Campsite	A small site on a rock point. Tent sites are up top.
	587507	Campsite	For those who prefer island sites, I call this one Ant Island. This small, sandy island has some large ant hills, but lots of flat and open space for tents away from them. A scramble up the sand bank on the southeast side brings you to this nice high camp spot.
	582494 583493	Rapids	**Class 3+**, starting out with a ledge on top, then dropping over a steep boulder apron at the end. The **portage (90 m)** has two landing areas, one for high water and one for normal and low levels, and they are approximately 50 m apart. The first landing (for high water) is before the fast water at the beginning of the bay on RR. The trail starts in a jumble of rocks in front of an opening in the trees. Stay to the left on the path. The trail is wet and rocky in places. The shorter alternative portage starts at the far end of the bay in a shore eddy (thus the problem landing when this is flushed out in high water) on RR, and you must descend the fast water above the main rapid to catch it. The start is again a jumble of rocks in front of an opening in the trees.
	583492 560430	Fraser Rapids	Fast water and riffles make up these long, very shallow rapids. The biggest problem is finding the deep water in order to navigate them without grounding out, especially in a low-water year. The bars marking the rapids appear rather arbitrary, as there are many similar sections of fast water and riffles that are not marked, especially after the bar mark at 565440. The hardest section to navigate in general is around bar mark 572462. There is a very shallow rock apron that may require wading at lower water levels, or it can be portaged on RR. Below are a couple of campsites located in the Fraser Rapids stretch.
	580483	Campsite	On RL by a beaver lodge. A nice jack pine bench.
	573464	Campsite	On RR on a rock outcrop.
	560433	Lewis Rapids	More of the same water (or lack of it!) as in Fraser Rapids. Slightly more water, but no rapids more difficult than Class 1+, and that would be at higher water levels and therefore pushier. Below are some campsites located in the Lewis Rapids stretch.
	550382	Campsite	On RL after an easy S-turn rapid. A high bench with a view of the lakelet.
	542371	Campsite	On RR at flat rocks in a pointy bay just after a section of fast water at 543372 in the narrows.

MAP NO	GRID REF	FEATURE	DESCRIPTION
	539364 539346	**Jones Rapids**	More substantial whitewater in these rapids. Some Class 1+/2 in higher, pushier water, with continuous rapids in places. You know you've reached the end when you drop into a lakelet after a long, continuous stretch of narrow, fast water to Class 1+/2 rapids at 533346. The river calms down for about 5 km until it picks up again into fast water and Class 1 rapids at the top of Mackenzie Rapids.
74 A/4	544305 540302	**Rapids**	The marked bar is the beginning of a long **Class 1**, S-turn rapid that ends at a small bay just above Mackenzie Rapids.
	540301 539299	**Mackenzie Rapids Campsite**	These **Class 2+/3** are made up of some waves and rocks, pillows and stoppers with a rock garden at the end. The **portage (300 m)** is on RL and the trail begins at a grassy opening just before the fast water in the wide entrance to the rapids. The portage is in good shape and ends in a campsite on the jack pine bench. There isn't any good camping for almost 7 km from here.
	536287	**Rapid**	This unmarked rapid is a good example of how a river can change. Where there once was only fast water there is now a **Class 2** beaver dam to negotiate. I ran it on far, far RR after being quite surprised by it as I came around the corner to the left. The dam rapid is followed by a riffle that is easily navigated.
	533278 531274	**Rapid**	An unmarked **Class 1/1+** rapid starts shortly after the river narrows again.
	533273	**Rapids**	The two marked bars actually represent continuous, 450-m long **Class 1+** rapids that start with a **Class 2** drop around a big rock in the middle of the channel, located about 100 m before first marked bar.
	532262 532260	**Rapids**	**Class 1+**, an S-turn rapid at the marked bars.
	527242	**Campsite**	Bench camping on RR. It is 11 km before any more good camping opportunities.
	525225 525223	**Rapids**	**Class 3+**. Rocks and pillows with a ledge at the bottom. The **portage (235 m)** is on RR and begins at an opening in the long grass and reeds above the fast water.
	531222	**Rapids**	A short **Class 2+** drop with large pillows. Scout from the RL shore for an entry line. The **portage (40 m)** starts right before the rapids on the RL riverbank.
	525192	**Rapids**	**Class 3+/4**, depending on the water level. It's fast, with many boulders and pillows to avoid in canyon-like narrows. The **portage (300 m)** is on RL and starts at a break in the trees just above the rapid. The trail follows the river, getting steep at the end, and ends in a jumble of rocks in the fast water.
	534153 534151	**Diagonal Falls**	**Class 5**, amazing 3.5-m diagonal ledge waterfall. The **portage (220 m)** is on RR and starts on a rock shelf right above the start of the fast water at the beginning of the rapid. The trail ends in the rapids below the falls, and they are fast water or Class 1 depending on flow and easily negotiated. Three rock camping sites are in the Diagonal Falls area, see the notes below.

the trips

MAP NO	GRID REF	FEATURE	DESCRIPTION
		Campsite	On the portage trail and overlooking the falls at a clearing on the rocks two-thirds of the way down the trail. There are only a few, flat tent spots, but it's a nice spot from which to view the falls.
		Campsite	On the west side of the first island, immediately below the falls. You can see it from the end of the portage trail.
		Campsite	On the RL shore, behind the first island if you're looking from the portage trail.
	537132 536131	Rapids Campsite	**Class 3+/4**, many boulders, pillows and waves, with no clear route. The **portage (225 m)** is on RL, and begins at a clearing on the river bank approximately 75 m above the start of the rapids. It ends in a grassy landing where fair camping can be had. This is the last site for more than one or two tents for approximately 14 km.
	534130	Rapids	**Class 2.** A straightforward run. The **portage (185 m)** starts in the willows on RL, just above the start of the rapids.
	527110	Campsite	A small camp on a jack pine bench on the RL shore. Several kilometres downstream you are in the 1998 burn.
	496076	Falls	**Class 5**, a waterfall. **Portage (150 m)** on RL. Luckily this portage was not burned, and it is in good condition. The trail begins just above the rapids.
	494075 488071	Portage	This **portage (700 m)** on RL bypasses a long set of **Class 3/3+** rapids, which are rated with a higher level of difficulty because you must catch an eddy on RL just above a dangerous set of **falls** at **488076. CAUTION:** The eddy is only there in lower water, and gets flushed out in higher water. Additionally, if you choose not to portage, you must pull over the first falls on RL and then paddle down and bushwhack portage on RR the second set of **falls** that the portage bypasses at **487073**. Then there are **Class 2+ rapids** (**488072**) with a small ledge at the bottom at the end, just before the portage reaches the river. The end of the portage was slightly singed by the fire, but it is has been refurbished and is in good condition. The 700-m portage trail around all the falls and rapids starts on RL at a blazed jack pine about 75 m above the Class 3/3+ rapids.
	487072	Campsite	On the RR shore below the Class 2+ rapids described above and across from the end of the 700-m portage trail. The area is partially burned, but open and flat.
	482063	Cabin	A log trapper cabin still standing on RR at the confluence of Little Whitefish River in the midst of the burn. The sandy area around it provides potential camping.
73 P/13	485060 488060	Spiral Falls Campsite	**Class 5.** Wonderful S-turn waterfall with smooth, swirly rock. It drops some 16 m. The area was partially burned in 1998, but the RL side is still untouched by the fire and lovely to spend time at. The **portage (490 m)** was burned out, but has been fairly well maintained (to June 2001). It is in good condition and not difficult to follow, except at the end, where deadfall is thick and one must find a way through to the river off trail. The trail starts on RR at a

| --- | --- | --- | --- |
			flat rock about 25 m above the falls. The landing is in current in higher water. A lovely campsite still exists on RL at the bottom of the falls.
	500050 503049	Rapids	**Class 2+**. A tricky 200-m-long S-turn with numerous rocks and stoppers to avoid. The **portage (250 m)** is on RR starting at **499050** on the rocky shore. It was burned in 1998, and the trail is only distinguishable by the opening in the standing burned trees. It was re-cut at some point and was in good condition in June 2001, with little deadfall to contend with.
	524047	Cabin	An old trapper cabin on RR.
74 A/4	591065	Eagle Nest	The nest is on a point on RR in a burn on the extreme south end of Fiest Lake. The northwest end of Fiest Lake is not burned and still very attractive. In fact, you come out of the burn altogether for about 20 km after Fiest.
	596092	Campsite	Island camping on high rock. Approach the southeast side of the island.
	607090	Campsite	On a rock point on RL at the outlet of Fiest Lake into the Foster.
	612099	Campsite	A rock shelf on RL shore of a gorgeous channel.
	614104	Campsite	A very nice spot on RL, in a bay on a rock shelf.
	615105	Campsite	On RL on a point in the same channel.
	633129 635129	Portage	This **portage (375 m)** is on the RL shore of the north channel of the river, a secondary channel that under normal and low water conditions does not have much flow, or none at all. Look for the trail 30 m to the left or north of this channel; it begins to the left of a rock outcrop at a break in the willows and trees. This portage bypasses two sets of rapids, a **Class 3/3+** and a **Class 2+**, depending on water levels, as the first rapids are easier at lower levels and the second rapids are more difficult at higher levels. **CAUTION:** You will have difficulty portaging the second set of rapids if you do not use this portage for both rapids, unless the water is very low and you are able to line on RL. It is highly recommended that you scout the second set of rapids using the portage trail described above. Head south a third or so of the way down the trail to get to a high rock-face overlooking the beginning of the second set.
	633128	Rapids	**Class 3/3+**, depending on the water level. First, there is some Class 1 fast water, with an eddy on RL before the big drop. The main rapid is a steep drop over a 1-m, slanting rock shelf with some chutes in it. There is an easy pullover spot on RL.
	634128	Rapids	**Class 2+**. Big waves and stoppers for about 75 m. If the water is high and you decide not to run this rapid, you are looking at a tough portage on RL on a huge rock slab and a bushwhack after that, or an awful clamber over boulders on RR. So make sure you evaluate carefully your ability to run the second set and your other

MAP NO	GRID REF	FEATURE	DESCRIPTION
			options by scouting as described above, before pulling over the first set. There is a pictograph site on the rock cliff on the RR below this rapid.
	638129 640126	Scott Rapids	**Class 4**, 800 m of very challenging rapids. They begin with a three-part series of 2+ drops, then get more difficult after a big chute on RL, where continuous rapids with large, irregular waves, big holes and boulders go around corners, and so on. A real boat-wrecker set. The **portage (450 m)** is on RR and starts at a break in the shoreline reeds about 50 m above the start of the rapids. The trail can be very boggy and wet in spots.
	655133	Rapids	Just below the Sandy Creek confluence. The two marked bars indicate **Class 2** rapids that can be pushy at higher water, so scout the rocks to avoid from RR. A portage can be made on the RR shore as well.
	659130	Rapids	**Class 2/2+**. A marked bar indicates a ledge that can be scouted on RR, where a portage can be made as well. I ran the RR break. Watch for swirly, sucky water at high water levels.
	664129 665131	Rapids Campsite	**Class 1+/2 followed by Class 2+**. The first of the two sets of rapids is just a big rock dodge, which is harder at lower water levels. The second set is narrow and fast and requires some manoeuvring. It's more difficult at lower water as well. A **portage (75 m)** exists on RR, and starts in the fast water above the first rapids at an obvious opening in the trees. At the end of the trail is a campsite.
	673134	Rapids	**Class 1/1+**, easy, unmarked rapids in the narrows at the sharp bend to the right.
74 A/3	695130	Rapids Campsite	**Class 4/4+**. Big drops and big waves. The rapids split around an island and are very difficult. The **portage (350 m)** is on RR and starts at a grassy opening below a jack pine bench. A jack pine bench overlooks the rapids and makes a great campsite. The portage trail ends in the rapids below the big drops, but there are shallow, rocky rapids to be negotiated still. There is a narrow channel to the right of the main flow that can be lined or run depending on water levels.
	695125	Rapids	This unmarked **Class 1+** chute comes about 75 m after you descend the rocky rapids below the previously discussed portage.
74 A/4	687115	Rapids	**Class 3+/4**. Rocks, holes, stoppers and waves, and a difficult, steep, boulder apron at the bottom requiring precise manoeuvring. The **portage (130 m)** on RL was not burned out and is good condition. The trail starts at a clearing on the riverbank just above the rapids.
73 P/13	680043	Campsite	Beautiful rock ledges, the best of camping in the Precambrian Shield, on RL or the south shore of an unnamed lake before Eulas Lake. The south shore was not burned in 1998.
	670042	Campsite	More great rock-ledge camping to be had on RL or the south shore of an unnamed lake.

MAP NO	GRID REF	FEATURE	DESCRIPTION
	649036	Rapids	**Class 2/2+.** A marked bar with an R beside it on the map indicates a tricky, narrow chute with a few big waves and pillows. There are more obstructions in lower water. I ran it RR making a hard right at the bottom. It can be scouted from the rocks on RR. The old portage (SERM Booklet number 57, Portage 18) on RL is burned out. A new **portage (275 m)** was cut on RR in 1999, but it was barely distinguishable or useable in June 2001. The supposed trail is steep at both ends and rough in spots, plus there is lots of deadfall. It starts at the right bank to the right of the rocks at the head of the rapids.
	644038	Rapids	**Class 2**, at the second marked bar with an R beside it on the map indicates a wide turn with some waves and pillows to avoid. The **portage (135 m)** on RL is burned, but still useable. There was little deadfall in June 2001. The trail starts about 30 m above the start of the rapids at a break in the burned trees still standing.
	637029 633023	Rapids	**Class 2+/3.** A long and windy rock garden in a gorge-like area, approximately 1 km in length. There are two basic parts to the rapid. The first part is a Class 2 rock dodge, with the flow getting faster and rocks bigger until the boulder drop (Class 2+, maybe more in higher water) just before the sharp bend to the right. The second part begins after the corner to the right where there is slow water. This set is a Class 2 rock dodge. Then there are shallow rapids at the end around the islands at the bottom of the gorge where the river begins to widen and eventually becomes Eulas Lake. The portage (640 m) (SERM Booklet number 57, Portage 20) was on RR until it was completely burned out in 1998. When I checked the trail in June 2001, the portage was in terrible condition. It was impossible to follow the trail in many places, as there was so much deadfall. There was some flagging tape along the way, but all in all, the trail was a serious mess. Let's hope it will be re-cut and maintained again. You can scout from the burn on RR, and there is flagging tape to indicate where the portage used to start, just above the rapids.
	612983	Fishing camp	Foster River Camps is located on a small island with a sandy beach. Eulas Lake is known for its walleye fishing. On a large rounded outcrop on the west shore of Eulas Lake, there is a pictograph site with two sets of figures. They are on a light-coloured vertical face about 2 m up as you leave Eulas, before the river narrows.
	610980	Campsite	In a pinch, a small camp is possible on the long southwest point of the small island with Foster River Camp on it. Campsites are limited on Eulas and the section of the river before the Churchill due to the 1998 forest fire. Ask for permission to camp on the island from the people at the camp.
	581945	Campsite	On a point in the burn on RR. It's level and open and has good access to the water.
	540925	Campsite	In the burn on RL, but flat and open with good access to the water.

MAP NO	GRID REF	FEATURE	DESCRIPTION
	534914 535909	Rapids	Following a brief riffle are **Class 3+/4** rapids. They are difficult, winding, and steep with big rocks and waves and a rock apron at the bottom. The **portage (275 m)** (SERM Booklet number 57, Portage 21) on RL was burned in 1998, but has been re-cut and is now in fairly good condition. Some deadfall is to be expected. The trail starts on the rocks, where trappers have cleared a small channel for boats. The portage is steep at the far end.
	542885	Rapids	**Class 2.** A fast, steep chute where the river narrows again.
	526864	Rapids Water survey station	**Class 4.** Heavy water with large drops, boulders and waves. The second set is more like a Class 3, narrow and fast. The old **portage** was burned out (SERM Booklet number 57, Portage 22) and a new one is cut on RR **(220 m)**. It bypasses both sets of rapids, and was in good condition in June 2001. The trail starts well above the rapids at a clearing in the burn that has been flagged. The trail is steep at the far end, and one must depart in the fast water below the second set of rapids. The water survey station (no longer operating) is above the first set of rapids.
	512850	Rapid	**Class 2.** A marked bar indicates a short and straightforward rapid, the last rapid of any note on the Foster.
	499839 497837 495833	Riffles	For the last 1-km stretch before the confluence with the Churchill there are several narrows with fast water and riffles. Their size depends on water levels, but none are of concern to the alert canoeist with moving water experience.

* See the Churchill River Trip Notes if you are continuing on through Black Bear Island Lake and to Otter Lake. There is another pictograph site below the confluence of the Foster and the Churchill and before the cabin at Fish River. It's on RR on a rounded outcrop, 8 m high, and the paintings are on a vertical rock-face formed by a slab of rock falling off the outcrop.

foster river

99

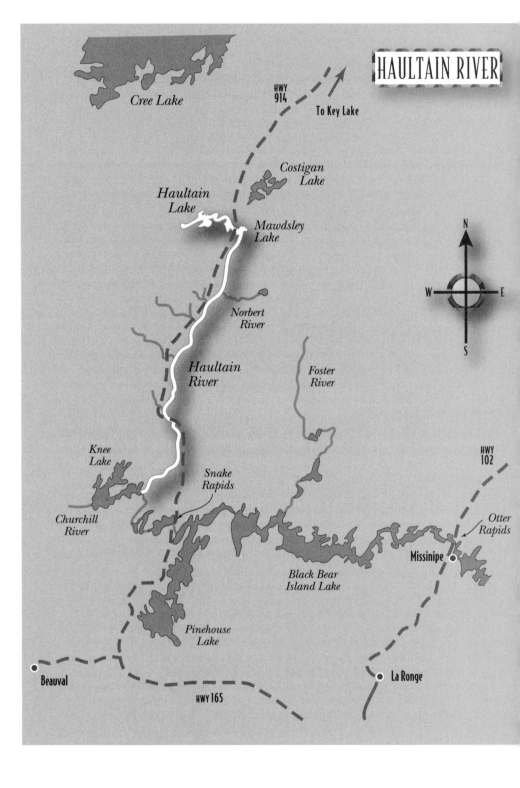

HAULTAIN RIVER

Cree Lake

HWY 914

To Key Lake

Costigan Lake

Haultain Lake

Mawdsley Lake

N
W E
S

Norbert River

Haultain River

Foster River

Knee Lake

HWY 102

Snake Rapids

Otter Rapids

Churchill River

Missinipe

Black Bear Island Lake

Pinehouse Lake

Beauval

La Ronge

HWY 165

HAULTAIN RIVER

The Haultain River is a major tributary of the Churchill. It sits between the Mudjatik and the Foster and has the most extreme landscape characteristics of both. Like the Foster, the upper Haultain flows south through rugged Precambrian Shield country, and the river is dotted with many large rapids and falls, including a large granite gorge. The southern portion of the river has the lowlands and oxbows of the Mudjatik. The draw of the Haultain is in its waterfalls and wilderness.

The amazing moose population matches the amazing rock formations. I encountered more moose on an eight-day trip down the Haultain to Knee Lake than I usually see in a season! The number of osprey I saw was also staggering — one nest was sitting high above Lewis Falls. Having lunch atop a cascade of orange-coloured water rushing over red granite slopes while watching osprey fish is about as much as you can ask for on most days.

Finally, you get a chance to taste the canoe country to the northwest of the Churchill without having to fly in. Moreover, even though a road runs along much of the Haultain's length, you can expect to see virtually no one until to you approach the Churchill. It is not an easy trip, though; portages are the rule rather than the exception, and much of the forest along the river has been burned at different times over the past 30 years. But you feel as if you are on a journey back in time, when there was uncharted wilderness and you could expect anything around the next corner.

Length

The trip described in the Trip Notes section is approximately 150 km. It starts at a bridge on Highway 914, the gravel road to the Key Lake Mine, and ends with access to 914 via a short path up from the river. The trip can be done in eight days. The Haultain has good current, and there are no lakes to cross after Mawdsley, but the portages are in poor to fair condition and there are lots of them. Portaging takes time.

It is easy to shorten your trip, as the river runs close to the road in a number of places. Potential put-in and take-out spots are indicated in the notes. To extend the trip, you can paddle to the Churchill River, and once you reach it, many destinations are possible. You can paddle upstream to Patuanak, where there is road access, or you can paddle downstream to the bridge at Sandy Lake where Highway 914 crosses Snake Rapids. If your trip includes a section of the Churchill, you will need to plan for the possibility of being windbound on its big lakes.

Mawdsley Lake to the Highway 914 bridge above oxbow section*	130 km
Mawdsley Lake to the last Highway 914 take-out before the Churchill*	150 km
Mawdsley Lake to the Highway 914 bridge over Snake Rapids**	239 km

* These trips are described in detail in the Trip Notes section.
** The Churchill section of the extended trip option is described in detail in the Churchill Trip Notes.

Topographic Maps

You require 1:50,000 scale maps, in my opinion. They provide the level of detail necessary to locate yourself in terms of all the rapids and falls. This is especially true for this trip, as there are many incorrectly marked features, and the portages are not really trails in most places. For the trip described in detail you will need 74 B/16, 74 B/9, 74 B/8, 74 B/7, 74 B/2 and 73 O/15. For the shortest trip option you will only need the first four maps. If you plan on paddling to Snake Rapids on the Churchill you will need 73 O/10 as well.

In order to make the best use of the information provided in this chapter, I suggest you purchase the required maps in advance and, using the grid reference coordinates in the Trip Notes section, mark in the rapids and falls that are either missing or mislabelled on the maps. There are a number or significant errors, not the least of which is the misrepresentation of the location of three sets of falls. And, in one case, no indication of one large drop at all! You can also note in the locations of the portages (or what constitutes a portage), classifications of the rapids and other features of interest, so that while you are paddling the river the information is in front of you. Campsites can be hard to find on certain sections of the Haultain because of the old burns and the swampy nature of the oxbow lowlands, so be sure to plan your stops ahead of time where possible.

Getting There and Away

To drive to the put-ins and take-outs on gravel Highway 914, you must first access gravel Highway 165, either from Beauval or Highway 2 to La Ronge. Then you take the turnoff north to Pinehouse, Highway 914 — or what is known locally as the Key Lake Road. The road is pretty bad, especially once you pass Pinehouse. You should take jerry cans, two spare tires, and be sure you have a tire iron that fits your tire nuts (and your trailer tire nuts if you take one). When you drive on gravel in the North you must be prepared. You can get gas at Beauval at the gas station on 165 by the Hall Lake turnoff, and at Pinehouse. But be warned, none of them will be open late.

The farthest north put-in at Mawdsley Lake is 160 km north of Pinehouse, and the take-out for the trip (described in detail in the Trip Notes) is 60 km north of Pinehouse, making for a shuttle 100 km one-way from Pinehouse. I don't advise leaving your vehicles in the bush, even up there. Call in your favours with your friends or be prepared to pay for shuttles. You can usually hire long-distance taxis to take you back to the put-in after dropping off your gear and to pick you up at your take-out of choice. You should be able to arrange for safe parking and a taxi from Pinehouse, but call ahead to book. Remember, sometimes organizing for services in remote areas like this can be different from what you may be used to. Have some realistic expectations.

If you have more money than time to spare, you can always fly to Mawdsley Lake, where there is a fishing lodge, from Ile-à-la-Crosse or Otter Lake and paddle out to a road. Or, go for the easiest and most expensive option and get picked up by floatplane from Elak Dase (Knee Lake) or virtually anywhere on the Churchill.

When to Go

From mid-May to mid-September. In a normal year, the small-to-moderate-volume Haultain can be paddled throughout the canoeing season. However, if it is a low-water year and you are going later in the season, you should put in below Thomas Falls somewhere. If you take out before the Churchill, there are no lakes to wait for the ice to come off in the spring, so it can be an early season trip. The river is at its highest at spring runoff — late April and early May. Be cautious of flooding conditions if you go early in the season, as the portage landings become more difficult in high water. It would be a very pretty trip in the fall, as it has a significant deciduous element to its forests, especially in its lower reaches.

There is a "real time" operating station on the Haultain, meaning you can call SaskWater at 306-694-3966 or fax them at 306-694-3944 and get an up-to-date reading on the current flow of the river. You can also check the last month's flow on the website by clicking on hydrology and then Churchill River Basin. To put the cu m/sec reading in context, I paddled the Haultain in the third week of May 2001, and the flow varied from 15.5 to 14 cu m/sec. The water was low, but below Thomas Falls there were no sections that required wading. The river would normally flow at around 30 cu m/sec on average in May. In June and July a normal flow is around 25 cu m/sec, and in September the water level drops to 19 cu m/sec on average.

Difficulty of the River ✳✳✳

The difficulty of the Haultain is in the mandatory portages around waterfalls. There are 20 to 23 of them, depending on which route you take at the two large islands and the Gorge. On top of that there are some rapids too difficult for most canoeists to run, unless they are exceptional paddlers. Plus, most of the portages are in poor condition, some are burnt out, and all of them seeing little use. On the other hand, there aren't any large lakes to cross on the Haultain, and there is potential for road access at many points along the river. This river trip gets a three-star rating, mostly because the portages are not in good shape, and canoeists must use them extensively. One hazard of note is that a very high water level will make landing at the portages above the falls more difficult. Extreme caution and solid paddling skills will be required to approach them safely.

To compare it to the other three-star rivers, it is like the Foster, because you must portage a number of times a day. It is not like Clearwater, in that most canoeists will not be able run the majority of the rapids. The whitewater and landscape of the Haultain have the same Jekyll-and-Hyde character as the Foster's. The average rapids rate Class 2 on the Jekyll hand and Class 4/5 on the Hyde. There's not much for Jekyll on the Haultain, making it a poor choice for canoeists wanting a whitewater bonanza but without the skill to paddle Class 4.

What this all means for the canoeist looking to choose a trip from the smorgasbord is this: you don't need extreme whitewater skills to paddle the Haultain, you just have to be prepared to portage. Extremely! It is a good choice for experienced canoe trippers who want a rugged wilderness experience, but who don't necessarily want to run lots of rapids. Several seasons of tripping experience are required to do the trip safely, but the whitewater skill level required is only intermediate. Guided beginners with basic skills will find this river very challenging.

The gradient of the river is only slightly less than that of the Foster, at 0.80 m/km (4.24 ft/mi). Of course, the last part of the Haultain, the second oxbow section, is without rapids, making the upper Haultain, in reality, a steeper river than the Foster. There are more falls making up the drop in elevation than rapids.

Character of the River and Region

The Haultain begins as a very small-volume river, with only one line representing it on the map. But by the time it joins with the Norbert River, where the water survey station is, it is almost a moderate-volume river, with an average flow similar to the Foster just before it joins the Churchill. The Haultain is always picking up steam, as many creeks flow into it all along its path. It isn't deep, but has good flow between narrow banks.

The riverbed is generally sandy or mucky, with lots of moose food. The rapids are steep and full of rocks — from breadbox to VW Beetle size. Ledges of exposed Precambrian rock nearly spanning the width of the river are fairly common. Some of the easier rapids are wide and quite shallow rock gardens at low water.

Like the Foster, the Haultain is a former glacial meltwater channel that carried meltwater from the ice during the formation of the Cree Lake moraine. It is completely within the Churchill Uplands ecoregion, and has three characters to it, clues of which are evident just from looking at the map. The top section of the river down to the Highway 914 bridge is all rugged granite and spruce or jack pine and sand, except in the burned areas, where thick, immature jack pine forest dominates. The next section is a maze of oxbows, willows and swamp, and wet alluvial terrain with black spruce and birch trees, until the river straightens again and the road splits away to the east. The last section before the Churchill is less swampy, with more sand and evidence of glaciation providing for a mixed forest of jack pine, white and black spruce, poplar, aspen and birch. This last section is home to a billion beavers, I'm sure.

What I will always remember about the Haultain is the red-orange colour of the water. I have yet to find the likes of it on any other river trip in northern Saskatchewan, though the Mudjatik comes close with its tea-coloured waters.

Local History **

It seems probable that the Haultain was used to access the Churchill from the Cree Lake region, as there was a Dene name for the river before it was called Pine River during the fur-trade days. The Mudjatik (Deer), Belanger (Mouse/Souris) and Foster (Fish/Whitefish) Rivers were used to travel north and south by the Dene trappers, so it seems logical that they used the Haultain as well. Tyrrell notes in his report on his travels in 1892 that while on the Churchill he met a group of Dene on their way from Ile-à-la-Crosse to their hunting grounds north of the Haultain and Foster Rivers. Ed Theriau, in his book *Lost Land of the Caribou*, also says Cree Lake Dene trappers used the Haultain as an alternative travel route to the Foster, and that at one time there was a white trapper trapping on it. Artifacts of the Dene ancestors' tool traditions have been found along the Haultain.

Elak Dase is a small Dene community on the Churchill at the extreme east end of Knee Lake and just west of the Haultain. It's called Elak Dase on the map, but the people of that community refer to it as Knee Lake. The Reserve is part of the English River First Nation, a Dene-speaking people who are descendants of the "Poplar House People." This Dene group was one of the bands that began to travel south in their annual round and eventually settled on the Churchill (see the Churchill for more information on the movements of the Dene during the fur trade).

The fur traders didn't use the river, but the Haultain was definitely a travel route and important source of furs for local trappers. A small HBC winter outpost was located at the mouth of the river at one time, and the fur trade was economically important to the people at Knee Lake.

According to Louis George, an elder from Knee Lake whom I met when I was paddling on the Haultain, Patuanak eventually became home to the families from Knee Lake. That is where Pine River House, the main HBC trading post in the region, was located, as well as a school. When the Knee Lake people's children were required to go to school, families moved there.

Louis also told me the Haultain was a travel route and an important hunting and trapping area for the people of Knee Lake in the recent past. There was a series of big fires starting about 20 years ago that burned out the portages along the river and disrupted the wildlife populations. He said the portages were like highways before the fires. Hard to imagine today!

After trapping alone could no longer could sustain local families, commercial fishing grew in importance. Whitefish from the Haultain were shipped over to Buffalo Narrows, according to Etienne George, Louis's nephew. He still fishes commercially on the Haultain in the winter.

The river got its present name courtesy of Joseph Burr Tyrrell, as did a number of others in this book. He thought there were already too many Pine Rivers in the North, and renamed the river in honour an old college mate — Sir Fredrick W. Haultain. This would seem strange had his friend Fred no other claim to fame. But in 1897 Haultain became the first premier of the Northwest Territories, and was key in getting provincial status for Alberta and Saskatchewan, though he advocated that one province be formed, called Buffalo. He eventually became the chief justice of the Province of Saskatchewan.

Level of Solitude ***

Considering that this is a drive-in and drive-out trip with a road always close by, it's a remarkably "out there" trip. I felt as if I were the only person who had run this river for years, and saw no one until the last section of the river, where I met Louis and Etienne and Louis's two granddaughters.

While paddling, I heard a truck or two on the way up to the mine, but it did not take away from the wilderness experience I had on the river. The only traffic you may encounter will be motorboats below the last falls. The residents of Knee Lake net fish below the smaller rapids on the lower section of the Haultain. They also use the river to drop off or pick up people at the road access I suggest as a final take-out before the Churchill. It is one of the places that people from Knee Lake use to access Highway 914 when the wind is too bad to cross Sandy Lake to reach the Snake Rapids Bridge.

Wildlife ✳✳✳✳

This is another area in which the Haultain really shines. It is a great river for moose watching, especially as you descend the lower parts of the river. It rates up there with the Cree and the Wathaman, which are rated best for seeing moose in this book. The grassy, willowy reaches of the Haultain, bordered by burn, make great havens for moose populations, and there is lots of food in the river and along the shores. I encountered nine adult moose in six days, and all but one had a calf with her — that's seventeen!

Always keep your distance from a cow and calf, especially in May when the babies are very young. I came as close as I have ever been to being attacked by a wild animal one day on the Haultain (except for a polar bear on Hudson Bay, but that's a whole other story). I rounded a corner while looking at the map and surprised a mother and baby moose lying on the grassy shore. The cow jumped up and grunted at me with all her might, the hair stood up on her shoulders, and I thought she was coming into the shallow water after me. Luckily, I was drifting away from her while she decided what to do, and I was able to make a non-threatening exit out of her sight, behind an island. It took me about ten minutes to get my shoulders back down from around my ears and for my hands and knees to stop shaking! I was about 15 feet from her front hooves!

There is an amazing osprey nest at the "real" Lewis Falls, and osprey and eagles abound on this river. There are so many beavers on the lower reaches that I can hardly believe it. I assume there is a good bear population as well, though I did not encounter any. These are the animals most commonly seen on the Pinehouse Plain, through which the Haultain flows.

Fishing ✳✳

The fishing on the Haultain isn't what you would expect, much like the Foster. There is no resident walleye population in the river; walleye fishing is only good once you are 4 or 5 km upstream from the confluence with the Churchill. Fish the eddies on the corners of the oxbows.

There are northern pike in the eddies and weeds, but not as many as you would expect and not very big ones either. The Haultain is commercially fished for whitefish, and that seems to be its most plentiful species. I've been told that in the very upper stretches of the Haultain you can catch grayling, but since I didn't, I can't say for sure. It's certainly worth a try.

Special Equipment

For those who are expecting to portage and line most of the rapids, I recommend taking a lightweight tripping canoe, preferably Kevlar, with a strong and comfortable yoke. Pack carefully for portaging. Royalex is the only way to go if you have the skill to run the rapids that are runnable.

Bring lots of insect repellent if you are going in June. And a bug jacket with a hood or a bug hat will be put to good use, so don't go without them.

Trip Notes

MAP NO	GRID REF	FEATURE	DESCRIPTION
74 B/16	300945	Put-in	Approximately 159 km north of Pinehouse Lake on Highway 914. Put in at the small bay just south of the bridge and paddle east through Mawdsley Lake, or you can put in right at the bridge. There is good camping on sandy eskers on the way to the outlet of the Haultain.

the trips

MAP NO	GRID REF	FEATURE	DESCRIPTION
	322930	Campsite	On RL, a nice sandy esker camp across from the outlet. Catch your supper just across the way!
	321929	Rapids	**Class 4 to 2**, narrow, steep and rocky at the top, getting easier at the bottom. You can **portage (70 to 200 m)** on RR. Line the bottom if you don't feel confident running the last section of the rapids. There is a **trail** on RL **(500 m)** that bypasses the entire rapid. Start fishing for grayling!
	308905	Campsite	On RL at the esker. The next 12 km has many good campsites. Take your pick.
74 B/9	300892 299889	Rapids	**Class 1+**. Straightforward rock dodging. Shallow. **Portage (240 m)** on RR.
	300887	Rapids	**Class 1**, fast water in the shallows.
	265808	Rapids	**Class 1+**. Long, shallow and rocky. A **portage (400m)** is on RR. Make your way to RL after this rapid. The portage for the falls is on RL, 50 m downstream.
	266807	Portage/Falls Campsite	The **portage (50 m)** for the falls that are improperly marked as a rapid, with one bar, is on RL before the sharp bend to the right. There is a good camping spot on the portage up the hill.
	255782	Rapids	**Class 2+**. Rocky, with a tricky corner to negotiate. The **portage (325 m)** is a bushwhack on RR. After the rapids, move RL to catch the portage for the upcoming falls.
	254780	Portage/Falls	The **portage (175 m)** is on RL over rock, starting before a sharp turn to the left.
	253774	Rapids	**Class 2**, rock dodging for 350 m. You can **portage (450 m)** over a sand ridge on RR. The portage starts before a creek coming in on the left. There will be fast water and riffles for the next kilometre until the river widens into a lakelet.
	227696	Possible put-in Campsite	A small sandy beach on the south end of an unnamed lake. You could fly in here. Camping is possible, too, though it is in the burn of 1981.
	216685 214684	Thomas Falls 1	There is a riffle right above the portage landing for the first of the three sets of Thomas Falls. The riffle is around the unmarked island above the falls. Stay to the far RR and catch the eddy at the **portage**, landing on RR. The trail **(75 m)** starts in the burn at an opening on the river bank directly across from the unmarked island. Cautious canoeists may want to land farther upstream and not pull out in the fast water. The trail is indistinct, over bare rock and around deadfall. It ends in the fast water below the falls.
	212682 211680	Thomas Falls 2	Rapids above the second set of falls make the take-out for the portage approximately 200 m above where the falls are shown on the map. The **portage (275 m)**, as such, is on RR and begins where the river turns to the left before going back right where the falls are marked. The trail has been burned out, and the landing is simply a break in the vegetation on the bank. Bushwhack your way to the other side of the point and put in again downstream of the rapids following the falls.

MAP NO	GRID REF	FEATURE	DESCRIPTION
	208676 205675	Thomas Falls 3 Campsite	After a 90-degree turn to the right is the third set of falls. The **portage (365 m)** on RL begins in the fast water just above where the preliminary rapids leading to the big drop are marked on the map start. The landing is in a small break in the shoreline vegetation. The beginning of the portage is up a steep outcropping through the burn. The trail is burned out, but it is not difficult to portage through the jack pine and over the bare rock following the steep beginning. You can put back in at the weedy bay following the rapids, below the falls. Just before the weedy bay, by the rapids, is a flat area of bare rock that makes a decent campsite.
	184673 182663	Rapids Campsite	**Class 4.** These 700-m-long rapids begin with a large chute below the creek coming in on RR, and go on to drop over large boulders. There are large holes and irregular waves. The **portage (650 m)** is on RL and starts before the creek coming in on RR, about 75 m before the beginning of the rapids. The first part of the portage is up the ridge through standing, burned trees, but it is open and easily negotiated. Once you achieve the ridge, the new growth of jack pine begins to close in. But it is not difficult to descend to the river bank above the unmarked island, where you can put in below the major rapids. The rapids around the island are shallow Class 1. Camping is possible overlooking the rapids just below the large chute. The trees are burned, but it is level and sandy.
	179659	Riffle	A riffle goes around both sides of an unmarked island.
	178659	Potential put-in	The river meets the road at a mossy bank on RR just below the unmarked island with a riffle around it. Approximately 131 km north of Pinehouse.
	174647 173645	Rapids	**Class 1+/2.** Waves and boulders for 300 m.
	168634	Potential put-in	River meets road with an open area to put in. Approximately 128 km north of Pinehouse.
	167624	Rapids	**Class 1+.** Strong current. There is a point on RR where the river takes a sharp turn to the left, creating a small whirlpool at some water levels.
74 B/8	167619	Falls Campsite	Improperly marked as rapids, these are falls (considered any drop of 1 m or 3 ft). A steep **(50 m) portage** is possible on RL. Camping is possible just down off the portage, overlooking the falls, or on RR below the falls.
	168617	Riffle	
	170615	Riffle	
	145579	Potential camping	There's open bench camping on RR just before a high hill at the bend to the right.
	143574	Potential camping	Open bench camping on RR. A scramble up the bank, but not in the burn.
	136563	Potential put-in	From the bridge this fast-running creek can be used to reach the Haultain. It is approximately 120 km north of Pinehouse.

MAP NO	GRID REF	FEATURE	DESCRIPTION
	137556	David Rapids	**Class 2 and /2+.** After a blind entrance there are three chutes around two rock islets. The RC chute is a Class 2, while the RL has the most water and is Class 2+. The RR chute is Class 2, has the least water, and is probably dry in low water. Eddy out RL before or after the rock point at the turn to the left to scout from the RL shore. A **portage (25 m)** is possible on RR, but difficult, as there is an old burn and lots of blowdown.
	135554 126552	Potential camping	Large, open jack-pine-bench camping area.
	104529	Campsite	A flat level site up on a sand bank.
	099524 097523	McKenzie Falls	**Class 3+.** Two drops with boulders to avoid. It looks as if it would be easier in higher water. The **portage (165 m)** is on RL, and is in poor condition. It starts right above the rapids in an opening in the shoreline vegetation and ends in the fast water below the second drop.
	096522	Campsite	On a sand bank on the east side of the island 150 m after McKenzie Falls.
	103520	Rapids	**Class 1+.** These rapids are represented by a bar, and go around an unmarked island. **CAUTION:** You are approaching three waterfalls in a gorge. You have two options for portaging. One involves two portages and paddling a section of Class 3 in between the first two falls. The other option is to do one long portage around all three falls and associated rapids.

Note: There are two options for navigating up to Evans Rapids.

Option 1: Two Portages

This option entails two portages, 265 m and 575 m, and paddling a Class 3 rapid that comes at the end of the first falls. You then portage the second and third falls in one fell swoop. You can either run Evans Rapids, the Class 2+ rapids at the end of the gorge just down from the third falls, or portage them along the trail that follows the riverbank.

MAP NO	GRID REF	FEATURE	DESCRIPTION
	105521 108523	Portage	After the **Class 1+** rapids around the island at 103520, keep to the RL shore for the next 125 m. Land on the bank at the sloping rock before fast water at the beginning of the falls. **Portage (265 m)** down the shore on an indistinct trail to the bay on RL where you can put in to run the Class 3 rapid at the bottom of the falls. This rapid is represented by the third bar in the series of three that are marked on the map before the dogleg to the right. The first two improperly marked bars are the falls.
	108523	Rapid	**Class 3.** Full of rocks and stoppers. Climb up the ridge on RL to scout the bottom drop. There are several large boulders to be avoided. I ferried out to RR and ran the RR side, moving father RR for the final section. The second portage landing is on RR before the dogleg to the right.
	109523 111519	Portage	The second **portage (575 m)** begins at a sand beach on RR about 100 m above the second set of falls, which flows around an island. These falls are also improperly marked as rapids. The bar following the island falls is actually a rapid. This Class 3 rapid should not be

| | | | run, except by exceptional paddlers, as the third and most deadly of the falls are at the end of it. If you don't catch the eddy on RR before the turn, you will go over a Class 6 falls, with little chance of surviving it. This Class 6 vertical drop is also improperly marked as a rapid. The portage around the two falls is basically a bushwhack up a ridge and along it until the ridge ends, and then you descend to the river below the ledge falls. |

Option 2: One Long Portage

This kilometre-long portage bypasses the three falls and all associated rapids, except the last rapids in the gorge, Evans Rapids. The portage cuts off the looping corner the falls go around. It ascends the shoulder of the high ridge and then descends back down to the river. You will eventually end up at the rapids between the second and third falls, and can continue down the side of the river to the put-in below the ledge falls described above, or below Evans Rapids.

MAP NO	GRID REF	FEATURE	DESCRIPTION
	105520 111519	Portage Campsite	A **portage (1,000 m)** around the entire gorge, except the final rapids. The trail starts on the RR shore after the Class 1+ rapids around the unmarked island. Stay to RR and look for the trailhead, which starts long before the fast water of the falls. It is a break in the vegetation with an obvious clearing. After ascending the ridge, the trail falters and an old streambed and a short bushwhack take you down to the rapids above the last set of falls, the deadly ledge falls. Follow the river, carrying on over the next small ridge to the fast water below the falls. The trail along the river below the falls allows you to scout or portage Evans Rapids. There is a nice place to camp below the ledge falls.
	111522	Evans Rapids	**Class 2+.** A drop at the end of the gorge represented by the last bar before the small island mid-channel. There are several chutes to choose from around large boulders. These rapids can be scouted from RR. I ran far RR over a rocky ledge. RL has more water and more of a drop. These rapids can be portaged on RR using the trail from the ledge falls and carrying on past it to the bottom of the gorge. There isn't a good put-in below Evans at higher water, as the willows have grown back thickly.
	113516 113511	Camping	Open bench camping all along the shore on RR for 500 m. Pick your spot to recover from the gorge!
	109499 107497	Rapids	**Class 2+.** Represented by three bars and 275 m long, this is a boulder garden, becoming more difficult at the end. I ran it far RR after scouting from the ridge on RR. It is possible to portage on RR, but it would be a bushwhack, as the portage is burned out and jack pine are coming back in thickly. There is a good landing spot at the big rock right above the rapids.
	106483	Rapids	**Class 1+/2.** Waves with a few big rocks. I ran RC at the top, moving to far RR for the final section. No portage was found, but the rapids can be scouted from RR.
	079470	Campsite	A nice, long, open jack pine bench with hiking potential.
74 B/7	071463	Rapids	**Class 4 and 5 drops: falls** around both small and large islands. The easiest **portage (50 m)** is on RL of the farthest left channel. It starts on a point above the channel and across from the beginning of the small island.

haultain river

109

MAP NO	GRID REF	FEATURE	DESCRIPTION

Note: You must choose from two routes around the large island. The western or RR channel has two rapids (Class 1+ and 2+), and a campsite, and one falls. The eastern route or RL channel has one rapid (Class 2), two falls and a campsite. The western channel has more runnable rapids and is easier to navigate.

Western Route

	068463	Rapids	**Class 1+**, shallow rapids around an unmarked rocky islet occur in the narrows at the beginning of the western channel. They are marked by one bar, and can be run on RR.
	067463	Rapids	**Class 2+**. About 100 m down from first rapid is another set of unmarked rapids. It is made up of three chutes where the river goes around a corner and flows around another islet. The RL has the easiest run; on RR there is a ledge. Far RR is an overflow channel that in high water is runnable. Scouting is possible on RL or RR. No portage was found, but lining the overflow channel is possible at certain water levels.
	066463	Campsite	Nice camping on a point on RL right below the rapids and before the island marked on the map. There is fast water around the island.
	065464 063465	Falls	An improperly marked **Class 6** falls is represented by the two final bars. The falls begin approximately 100 m downstream of the island. The **portage (250 m)** is barely discernable and starts on RR just above the falls. It goes through an old burn, running along the bank for the most part, to a bay just below the end of the fast water. This is the last drop in the western channel.

Eastern Route

	065458	Rapids	**Class 2**. There is a 2-m-wide chute in the RR channel on the west side of the small island. Be sure to scout, as very dangerous falls are just downstream. There is a good **portage (150 m)** on RL around the drop in the RL channel.
	064457	Falls	The highest falls so far. **Portage (50 m)** on RR through the 1980 burn. This was a very thorough burn compared the 1981 burn found upstream.
	063454	Falls	The **portage (50 m)** in on RR over bare rock.
	056449	Campsite	On RR at the bottom of the large island. The two large island channels join here.
	047434	Rapids	**Class 1+**, with small waves and some rocks to avoid for 150 m. They start earlier than indicated on the map.
	045421	Observation Rapids	**Class 4 and Class 6**. There are two obvious parts to these rapids. The first is a ledge with a large hole in the middle, and the second is a set of falls. There are Class 1+ rapids in between, which can be lined or waded by the cautious canoeist. The first **portage (a few metres)** is a pullover on bare rock on RR, and the second **portage (50 m)** is also on RR, but slightly longer, with a tricky put-in down a rock ledge.
	045419	Campsite	On the largest island below Observation Rapids there is an open clearing on the west side that provides good island camping.

MAP NO	GRID REF	FEATURE	DESCRIPTION
	042407	Riffle Campsite	The bar on the map is only a riffle. On RR is an open jack pine bench for camping.
	025385	Campsite	For those who like beach camping there is a nice sandy point on RL, although it's exposed.
74 B/2	031343	Water survey station Potential campsite	A tin shed on RL. Possible camp on the sandy knoll by the survey station.
	032342	Rapids	**Class 1+**, a 200-m straightforward stretch with some waves and rocks, starting just below the survey station.

Note: Only the western channel, with Lewis Falls on it, is described in detail. Neither channel is easy to descend, so you might was well enjoy the marvellous scenery at the "real" Lewis Falls! See below for more serious mapping errors.

	035313 037313	Rapids Campsite	**Class 2 and Class 4.** There are two sets of rapids in this stretch, **not a falls and a rapid as is marked on the map. Lewis Falls is downstream from here.** The first rapid is a small Class 2 ledge that can be run or lined on far RL or far RR. Downstream 100 m is the larger rapid, consisting of a couple of ledges and holes. There is a **portage (40 m)** on RL that starts about 40 m above the rapids. There is a small campsite at the portage on the point.
	036305 037305	Rapids Lewis Falls	**Class 1 and then 5.** The first marked rapid is at the hairpin bend in the river at the bottom of the western channel. **CAUTION:** This small rapid is at a blind corner to the left, with the first drop of Lewis Falls starting about 100 m downstream of it. The falls are improperly marked by the second bar where the river widens. Run the small rapid on RL to get into the eddy on RL. Then stick to RL in order to reach the portage landing for the falls on RL. The **portage (250 m)** starts at the granite outcrop at the top of the falls and runs through the jack pine over sections of bare rock down to the pool below the falls. Follow the bare rock along the shore to below the large eddy, which will take you back up to the falls if you put in too early! Check out the osprey nest across from you. What a colourful, amazing falls. What a great lunch spot!
	038305	Falls Fishing hole	The second and last set of Lewis Falls, unmarked on the map, is at the narrows of the pool below the first set. It is a steep drop, and is only apparent from the horizon line dropping. The **portage (30 m)** is basically a pullover on RL. Land on the rock point and look for the break in the jack pine — there is even a proper trail cut in the trees. There are some northerns lurking in the eddies here.
	038296	MacDonald Falls Campsite	These lovely falls have an easy **portage (60 m)** on RL. Land at the overflow channel and carry over the smooth rocks to the incredible sand beach that comes as a big surprise. A perfect place to camp, take photographs, swim and fish. I call it Otter Beach for all the evidence of otters I saw. It's my favourite place on the Haultain, only slightly ahead of the granite falls (Lewis Falls) and Osprey Bay area you just came from.

haultain river

111

MAP NO	GRID REF	FEATURE	DESCRIPTION
	035284	Ford Falls	The **portage (175 m)** is on RR, and there is an obvious landing on the flat rocks above the falls. Look downriver and you can see the beginning of the next falls. They are improperly marked as a rapid, of course.
	032278	Falls	These unnamed falls are the last drop before the bridge on Highway 914. The **portage (100 m)** is on RL, and there is a perfect landing rock at the top of the falls and a genuine portage trail to follow to the end.
	032276	Campsite	On the farthest south of the three islands. The campsite is on the north side.
	026266	Riffle	
	998235	Bridge Potential take-out	There is a sandy landing area and path up to the road on RL, immediately downstream of the bridge over Highway 914. The next section is snyes and oxbows for 40 km. Campsites are limited, to say the least. Welcome to moose land, though!
	995194	Riffle	
	995195	Campsite	Just after the riffle. An open bench on RL.
	045109	Campsite	Open bench camping on RR.
73 O/15	045058	Falls	Another improperly marked, unnamed falls! You can portage this falls and the next in one carry on RR if you wish. The landing for the **two-in-one portage (550 m)** is at a flat rock about 60 m above where the first falls start. The trail is quite steep at the start. You could put back in after 150 m of portaging and paddle the short distance to the top of the next falls but be very careful. You will be paddling in current above another set of falls. Keep to the RR shore to get to the next portage.
	045055	Falls Campsite	The last falls on the Haultain. If you didn't do the two-in-one portage described above, you can land on the flat rocks right above the falls (perhaps not in very high water, so check this out by scouting from the long portage) on RR and carry (75 m) over bare rock. Good rock camping here.
	040034	Potential take-out	A trail **(350 m)** leads up to Highway 914. This is a wide, well-worn path, and is used by Knee Lake residents to access the road when the wind is up on Sandy Lake.

Note: If you are carrying on down to the Churchill, you will encounter three small sets of rapids, which can be easily navigated, Class 1+ being the most difficult. Camping is limited, but there are some sand escarpments and open jack pine benches. There are two large loops that can be cut off to the right. The short cuts were bulldozed out in the spring of 2000, according to Etienne. One has a sign, Cut Off 2000. This will save you a couple of kilometres, so keep your eyes peeled. As you approach within a few kilometres of the Churchill, try fishing the eddies for walleye. There is nice smooth-rock camping just upstream of the confluence of the Haultain and the Churchill. See the Churchill Trip Notes for details on the Churchill River stretch from Elak Dase to Snake Rapids.

CLEARWATER RIVER

This river simply has it all — great beauty, big whitewater and a long history. Everybody loves the Clearwater for its variety of landscapes and amazing geology, so evident as you travel the river. There are countless photographic opportunities.

When someone says Clearwater River, I picture a bird's-eye view of Smoothrock Falls, with its boiling cauldrons and golden sinkholes. Or I see Skull Canyon with its towering black and orange lichen-painted cliffs, the flowerpot island standing tall between twin ribbons of green entwined with white. Birch trees rooted in cranberries sigh in the breeze from the falls, and the eagles wheel above the yellow speck of my tent perched on the edge of the shining gorge.

The river changes as you descend into a genuine river valley, unusual for northern Saskatchewan. The landforms you pass are records of Saskatchewan's geological and glacial history. The Earth's natural forces have produced a wide variety of rapids: there are bouncy boulder runs, tricky granite ledges, fast, shallow rock gardens, and steep chutes with standing waves.

On the upper river, pictographs decorate vertical cliffs. Deep in the lower valley lies the northern terminus of the Methy Portage, the long-ago overland highway of the original inhabitants of the Northwest. In 1778, by this trail, Peter Pond became the first white man to cross over from the Churchill into the Peace River and Mackenzie Basins. Suddenly, the fur trade became a whole new venture.

If you had to pick just one river to paddle in Saskatchewan, this might well be it. The river is the basis of the Clearwater River Provincial Wilderness Park and is a Canadian Heritage River. It is well travelled, but it captures all that is wonderful about wilderness canoeing on northern Saskatchewan rivers.

Length

The trip described in detail is 240 km. It starts in Gibson Bay of Lloyd Lake and ends below Cascade Rapids. Technically, you end in Alberta. I don't recommend doing this trip in less than two weeks. You want to plan for 20 km a day, but don't forget to stop early at least one day and camp at either Smoothrock Falls or Skull Canyon; they are not to be missed. Also note that many canoeists will have long portages around the difficult rapids. Less-skilled whitewater paddlers may want to add one or more days to their trip.

There are a number of good options for shortening or lengthening the trip. To shorten the trip, you can fly into a deep bay at the confluence of the Virgin River and the Clearwater. You can also put in or take out at the Highway 955 bridge over Warner Rapids. Flying out below Contact Rapids or at the Methy Portage are two other possibilities, and below Whitemud Falls is another. A couple of popular options for extending the trip are putting in farther north and west on Lloyd Lake, perhaps at the outfitter on Ferrie Peninsula, or paddling all the way to Fort McMurray.

Virgin River to Warner Rapids*	55 km
Virgin River to Contact Rapids*	105 km
Warner Rapids to Cascade Rapids*	120 km
Virgin River to Cascade Rapids*	175 km
Gibson Bay to Whitemud Falls*	222 km
Gibson Bay to Cascade Rapids*	239 km
Lloyd Lake Lodge to Cascade Rapids	251 km
Lloyd Lake (from road) to Cascade Rapids	263 km
Gibson Bay to Fort McMurray	333 km

* These routes are described in detail in the Trip Notes section.

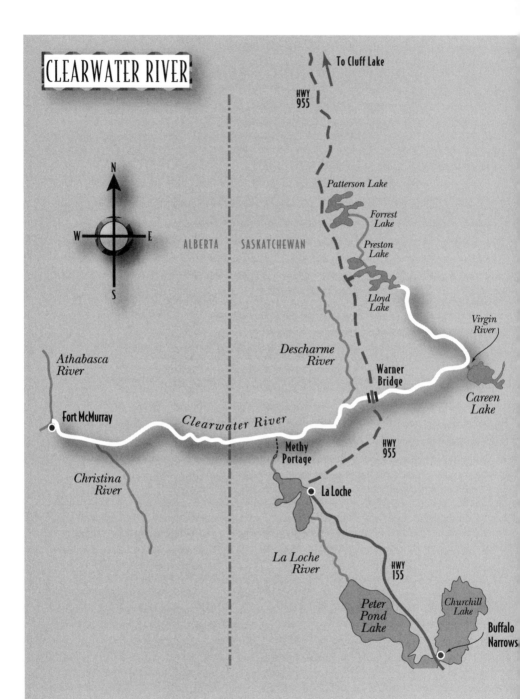

Topographic Maps

I recommend 1:50,000 maps for this trip because of the level of detail they provide. You can actually use the maps to assist in navigation. For the trip I highlight you will need 74 F/7, 74F/2, 74 F/1, 74 C/16, 74 C/15, 74 C/14, 74 C/11, 74 C/12 and 74 D/9. If you start from the lodge or the road at Lloyd Lake you will need 74 F/6. If you go on to Fort McMurray you will also need 74 D/10, 74 D/15 and 74 D/11. You may want to buy the 1:250,000 scale 74 D instead, as there are no rapids to speak of from Cascade down. If you start at the Virgin River you won't need 74 F/7, 74 F/2 or 74F/1. Warner Rapids are on 74 C/15 and Contact Rapids on 74 C/11 and 74 C/12. You can figure out the rest of the trip options from that information, as the maps are in the order you need them on the river, and the put-in and take-out points are in the Trip Notes.

I suggest you purchase your maps in advance and, using the Trip Notes, mark in all the rapids that are missing from the originals. Also, some of the falls are improperly marked as rapids. Plan your days so you can camp at either Smoothrock or Skull. There are more potential campsites than are listed in the Trip Notes, but you may want to mark in a couple of possible camps for every night. There are some areas along the river that have burned in the past twenty years that aren't great for camping. In general, camping on the Clearwater can be good, but most of the spots aren't the five-star-hotel kind you find on the Fond du Lac.

SERM canoe trip booklets are available for the Clearwater. Number 58 covers Lloyd Lake to Warner Rapids, and number 40 covers Warner Rapids to Fort McMurray. You can print them from the Canoe Saskatchewan website or phone SERM for them.

Getting There and Away

The trip as highlighted here is a fly-in and fly-out trip, but you have other options. The most convenient plan for the highlighted trip is to drive to Fort McMurray, Buffalo Narrows or La Loche and charter a floatplane to Gibson Bay on Lloyd Lake. You can leave your vehicles in the air service compound and charter your return flight back. The trick is to get back to your vehicle if you don't start and end at Fort McMurray.

There are options. If you drive to La Loche, you can charter a flight in and out with Air Mikisew. They have two nesting Royalex canoes for rent, as well. They will also help you arrange for a shuttle up the road if you want to drive to put in at Lloyd Lake and fly out with them. They also have floatplanes at their waterbase in McMurray, making it cheaper to fly from there back to La Loche.

Voyage Air has a waterbase about 110 km south of La Loche at Buffalo Narrows. Starting at Buffalo Narrows may save you some time and money. If you have six in your party, check the price difference between flying in and out with Air Mikisew's Beaver and Voyage Air's Otter. Voyage Air has a waterbase at the Snye in McMurray that you can paddle right to. I recommend you check around to figure out your best option for the size of your group.

If you are thinking of driving in and out from your Clearwater trip, you can do it, but it requires shuttling vehicle(s) long distances. There is road access to Lloyd Lake, but the last 3 km or so are very sandy, and you will need four-wheel drive. To get to the access road, drive 120 km north of La Loche on gravel Highway 955 (the Semchuk Trail or Cluff Lake Mine Road). Start looking for a tiny, unmarked dirt road on the right or east side of 955. Turn right and drive east on this sandy trail for 3 km down a hill to the west end of Lloyd Lake. There are private cabins at the end of the road. If the road looks bad down the hill, portage your boats and gear instead of driving down to the lake. I tried it in 1989 and got good and stuck on the way back up. Using some boards I luckily had in the back of the truck, Craig and I managed to get my truck back up the sand hill.

It's not a good idea to leave vehicles unattended anywhere in the North. You will probably want to organize a shuttle to get your vehicle to either La Loche or Buffalo Narrows or McMurray, depending on how and where you end up taking out. If you are paddling to

Fort McMurray, you have access to a new scheduled flight service to Buffalo Narrows via Voyage Air. Or you could charter a floatplane to fly back to La Loche or Buffalo from one of the earlier take-out points and have your vehicle shuttled to the air services in those towns. Or long-distance taxis can be chartered pretty near anywhere in the North, and you could have one take you back to Lloyd Lake after you drop off your vehicle.

You can also drive to Warner Rapids (approximately 65 km north of La Loche) to put in or take out, but you will have the same shuttle problem. You just can't leave a vehicle by the bridge. The key to shuttling on the Clearwater is call in all your favours and get one or two friends to shuttle your vehicles around. Or, you can pay to have a taxi service take you back to your put-in after leaving your vehicles at the take-out. Of course, the question becomes how much cheaper is it to drive in and out?

Backhaul possibilities with Lloyd Lake Lodge and the outfitter at Careen Lake may be worth investigating. As always, the best option for putting in and taking out on a trip is the one that suits your group's size and priorities.

When to Go

Late May to mid-July. This is not a river you want to paddle if the water is too low. Wading and dragging is likely in most of the lower rapids if the water is too low, and you will not be able to fly out because the floatplane landing spots will be too shallow for the plane to land.

The lowest I've paddled the river was in mid-June 1993, when Sheila, Craig and Brad and I took our solo boats. The river was running around 70 to 75 cu m/sec at the water-gauging station above the confluence of the Christina River and the Clearwater, which is on the Alberta section of the river. That is the only survey station currently in operation. The monthly mean for that June was 67 cu m/sec. It was definitely a low-water year, but all the rapids were runnable and the plane picked us up at Contact Rapids. Compare that to the whopping 133 cu m/sec flow of June 1991, when I paddled solo in an Old Town Tripper! The average mean for June for the past 30 years is 99.4 cu m/sec, the maximum flow 153 and the minimum 65.8.

If you are planning on going before mid-July you should be okay in a moderate- or higher-water year. You can call Environment Alberta for current flows at 780-427-2046, or better yet, check their website at www3.gov.ab.ca/env/water/overview.html. Double click on Hydrometerological Data and scroll down to the Clearwater at Christina River heading and double click.

It's probable that you will not be able to fly out of the river if the water level is below 60 cu m/sec. Call the air service you are planning to charter with to see if they are willing or able to pick you up. If you are driving, just remember, it's too good a trip to have to be a drag! Don't go too late in the season unless it's a high-water year.

Difficulty of the River ✳✳✳

The Clearwater probably has more canoe wrecks along its shores and in its depths than any other river in Saskatchewan. The river gets a lot of press, and maybe what happens is people think, "Well, if it's so popular or well-known then it can't be that difficult." Well, that's not at all true. This river deserves your ultimate respect. I've seen a really nasty swim and had my own Zen-Karma-Buddha moment.

The rapids are quite long in places, and they usually are at least Class 2. Often, they are more difficult than that. There are some continuous sections, also Class 2 or more. On average, the difficulty rating of the runnable whitewater is Class 2+ and approaching Class 3; there are some really dangerous ledges with killer holes. Swamping large waves are also a potential hazard. Numerous rapids in the highlighted trip have no portages at all.

There are five mandatory portages around falls, unless the cheat creeks are running high and you have the skill to navigate them. Then you will have two fewer portages. But intermediate canoeists without more advanced paddling partners will portage maybe seven to nine more times than that, and some of them are quite long. The real problem for the less-skilled canoeists comes in the middle section of the river, where there are no portages around many tricky rapids. The long portages are in fair to good condition.

The trip is remote and rather long. There are few sources of emergency help, and there is only one point where a road crosses the river. Depending on where you start you will not have to worry about large lakes being a hazard; Lloyd Lake is the only large lake on the river. However, when the wind starts to howl down the valley, you can lose ground — it can be a strenuous paddle in the wide sections of the Clearwater.

This river will challenge intermediate paddlers with solid whitewater skills, and you are recommended to have a more advanced leader or a guide in the party. This is not a river for a group of beginners. The river will challenge beginners paddling with advanced and exceptional paddlers in the same canoe. Advanced and exceptional paddlers really find this river very stimulating to run; it keeps them coming back. Sheila, my sister, has paddled this river at least five times!

The gradient of the Clearwater section highlighted in this book is 0.87 m/km (4.58 ft/mi). This compares to the Foster, and there are similarities between the rapids. There are tough ones and a few large falls, but many of the river's rapids are runnable by experienced paddlers.

Character of the River and Region

The Clearwater really gains volume as it runs first southeast and then southwest towards the Athabasca River. It starts at Lloyd Lake, with an average flow of 33 cu m/sec in June. Just upstream of the Christina River confluence in Alberta, the Clearwater is flowing at an average of 99.4 cu m/sec in the same month. The Clearwater is a drop-pool river with large rapids followed by pools of slow water. Ledges and boulders dominate the rapids. Frequently, the river is split by islands, and rapids swing around both sides, resulting in blind corners. Gorges are also more common than on most rivers in northern Saskatchewan, except perhaps the Wathaman.

The Clearwater's character comes from a combination of ice and water erosion. In some places the powerful meltwaters cut much deeper into the sediments than in others, exposing the rock of the Precambrian Shield. At the beginning the riverbed is rocky, and in quintessential Canadian Shield style the river rushes over granite ledges and through a gorge. It flows over bedrock with scattered rocks and boulders from the deposits of the glacier-scoured plain. Then the riverbed becomes sandy and mucky for a 35-km stretch, with low banks and few rapids. The river is slow moving and winds around low islands.

As the river changes course below the Virgin River confluence, the riverbed becomes a mass of medium-sized rocks and boulders, passing through more moraine areas before cutting deep into the bedrock again. There are large cataracts in these canyons. The drops in elevation are followed by flatwater. Rock and boulder gardens, big ledges and ledge falls characterize the middle section. But you won't see basement rock again after Contact Rapids, where the river leaves the Shield for good. After the sculptured sandstone cliffs of Pine Portage and the sandstone ledges of Cascade Rapids, the river slows its pace and flows over small rocks and sand. It eventually meanders through alluvium cutbanks to its confluence with the Athabasca.

The Clearwater's variety of landscapes comes from the fact that it runs through two ecozones and two ecoregions. It also shows evidence of four major time periods in the Earth's history: Precambrian, Mesozoic, Devonian and Pleistocene. The river begins at Broach Lake in the Boreal Shield, and runs through the Churchill Uplands. It crosses two different plains before dropping into the Boreal Plain ecozone. Lloyd Lake sits in the sandy Black Birch Plain, where a thin veneer of sandy glacial till covers the Precambrian bedrock, though outcropping is very common. Jack pine mixed with black spruce make up the forest in most areas. Open jack pine is found on the outcropping and in the sandy, dry areas. The understory is generally lichen and blueberry. Black spruce predominates in the boggy lowlands, along with tamarack in fens. The transition area between bog and upland has a forest of black spruce and white birch with an understory of Labrador tea, bunchberry, twinflower and feather mosses.

The Clearwater drops into the Frobisher Plain after making the turn at the Virgin River confluence to head southwest. This section begins in low hills that are the result of the glacier waters. You are no longer following the path of the ice, but the meltwaters of the last glaciers. Here the river drops through major gorges and canyons — a giant spillway carved through the soft sediments left by the glacier and cut deep into the bedrock. From Warner Rapids to the confluence of the Descharme River, the valley takes shape. Skull Canyon is actually a valley within a valley. Glaciers cut U-shaped valleys as they move slowly along the land surface, while rivers cut V-shaped valleys with the force of the continuous rushing water. The Clearwater exhibits this phenomenon at Skull.

This amazing geological area is characterized by extensive jack pine forest on sand plains and glacial till ridges that are shallow and in some places showing bedrock. Black spruce forests become predominant where the glacial till deposits are thicker. Stands of white spruce, birch and poplar are also found in areas where there is good soil and drainage.

Following Contact Rapids, the Boreal Shield gives way to the Boreal Plain, and the river flows through the southern Firebag Hills. The Clearwater's deeply incised river valley, which in places is up to 250 m deep, is characterized by diverse vegetation, with trembling aspen often mixed with jack pine and white birch. The lower areas are full of sedges, grasses, willows and stands of tamarack and black spruce. The underlying bedrock is sandstone. The soils are sandy and organic, alluvium deposits of the glacial spillway the Clearwater once was. The grassy slopes of the valley on the Alberta section below Cascade are survivors of the great grasslands of the Pleistocene.

"River Relicts," by R. Johnson and L. Noel, is an interesting piece on the geology of the Clearwater, and can be found in *Voyages: Canada's Heritage Rivers*. The other good source on the forces creating the present geological formations in Saskatchewan is the *Geological History of Saskatchewan*.

Local History ✳✳✳✳

It is now generally thought that the Clearwater River area was first inhabited around 5,000 years ago by the Athapaskan-speaking Beaver people. Following them, the Cree people lived here. The Dene are now the First Nations people most associated with the area. The Clearwater River Dene Nation has its central administration and principal reserve in La Loche, a community on Lac La Loche. *La loche* means "loach," or "slug," in French, and loach is the English name for burbot (*Lota lota*), also known as maria or freshwater cod. If you've ever seen one of these fish, you'll know where the slang usage of slug comes from! *Mithiy* is the Woods Cree word for fish, thus the name for the Methy or La Loche Portage.

There are four pictograph sites on the upper Clearwater between Lloyd Lake and the Virgin River confluence. They were the most northwesterly of the known rock-painting sites until another site was found on the MacFarlane River in the Far North in the early '90s. What is unique about one of the sites on the Clearwater is that it is reported to be of Dene authorship, whereas the Cree, it is generally agreed, created all the others in northern Saskatchewan.

The story of the Dene rock painting on the Clearwater, as told to Tim Jones by a Dene man from La Loche, is that "a young Chipewyan [Dene] boy being pursued on water by some Crees came to a place on the river where there was flat rock face that went straight into the water. He painted some figures on the rock and continued on. When the Crees came to the place the figures on the rock came to life, frightening them, and they fled back from where they came."

In 1778, Peter Pond, following in the Frobishers' footsteps, made his way up to the headwaters of the Churchill, where his guides told him about the Methy Portage. He crossed the height of land and became the first of many European fur traders to go north to Lake Athabasca. He travelled via the lower Clearwater to Fort McMurray, where it flows into the Athabasca River. Up the Athabasca Pond founded the first Fort Chipewyan, predecessor of the great "Emporium of the North." From there, Alexander Mackenzie would go farther north, eventually exploring the river named after him and reaching the Arctic Ocean. On his map, Pond labels the Clearwater the Pelican River, though it was always known as *Washacummow*, meaning "clear water" in Cree. Mackenzie also said that the river was known as the Swan, Pelican or Clearwater. Tyrrell notes that Turnor, who followed Mackenzie up the Clearwater to the Athabasca, also called the Clearwater the Pillicon River, "From a Mr. Dalrymples chart." But according to Tyrrell, the river has always been known as the Clearwater. The Dene call the Clearwater "The Great River."

Philip Turnor and Peter Fidler surveyed the area for the HBC, and John Franklin travelled the river on his ill-fated expedition to find the Northwest Passage. David Thompson also travelled the Clearwater, calling it the Methy Portage River. George Simpson, the bigwig of the newly merged HBC, visited Fort Chipewyan via the Methy Portage and Clearwater River.

The Methy Portage and the Clearwater River were very important links between Hudson Bay and the Athabasca District. The only link for 40 years, they were still in use until the late 1800s. A National Historic Site plaque commemorates the Methy's significance in the history of Canada. This 20-km portage provided an overland link between the Churchill and Athabasca Rivers that allowed the traders to avoid the Clearwater's difficult Precambrian upper section. And an HBC post was situated on the portage. At Rendezvous Lake, the Mackenzie brigade would exchange their heavy packs of fur for heavy packs of trade goods brought there by the southern brigade.

From the river, the lake is about 6.5 km up the portage, which is more like a road. This is not surprising, given that packhorses and ox carts were used in the mid-1800s. After the wet part you ascend a steeper section, but then the path gradually slopes upwards until you come upon a view of the lake. It's well worth the time to hike that far. It's really just a pleasant walk on a wide path through spruce and jack pine. Now, if you were carrying two 90-lb packs, it would be a completely different sort of beast! There are more voyageur portages on the river downstream from Methy that you can still trek as well.

In the late 1700s and into the 1900s the Clearwater became the basis of the travel route of a group of Dene who wintered west and southwest of Cree Lake, trapping and hunting. This was the southernmost stop on their nomadic "round." They summered in the north, near the edge of the barrens land, instead of going south, as did the "Poplar House People," whose descendants are now part of the English River Dene Nation (see the Churchill chapter). After spring breakup, they would assemble at the headwaters of the Clearwater and descend the river to its confluence with the Athabasca to Fort McMurray and then up the Athabasca to trade at Fort Chipewyan. These Dene were the ancestors of the people of the Clearwater Dene Nation. By the late 1800s, the Dene were wintering in the south as well. With the change in their lifestyle, no longer moving so far with the seasons, their permanent settlements ended up being in the southernmost area of their round, Lac La Loche.

In 1986, the Clearwater was designated a Canadian Heritage River. In the same year, the Province of Saskatchewan established the Clearwater River Wilderness Park. It is 200,000 hectares and is designed to protect the natural and historic resources and recreational opportunities that are to be found on this great river. Canoeists should be aware of the guidelines pertaining to the park, including the following: all garbage should be packed out; the digging of garbage pits is prohibited; no cutting of live trees for tent poles is permitted; mandatory use of portable stoves may be instituted at any time by park managers. You are also expected to avoid interfering with traditional resource-use activities of the First Nations residents. For more information contact Parks at 306-235-1740 or SERM as listed in the Directory of Services. The CHRS has a website, www.chrs.ca, where you can read about the CHRS and the Clearwater and other rivers in the system.

The best practical guide to visiting the historic fur-trading sites on Saskatchewan's voyageur routes, including the Methy Portage, is the book by Robinson and Marchildon, *Canoeing the Churchill: A Practical Guide to the Historic Voyageur Highway*. A more general description of the Clearwater's significance in the history of the fur trade is Eric Morse's *Fur Trade Routes Then and Now*. There are also a number of books on general fur-trading history listed in the References. Other interesting reading on the river includes *Clearwater Winter* by E. Engstrom, "A Valley View in Verdant Prose: The Clearwater Valley From Portage La Loche" by W. D. Kupsch, and the article in the Heritage River book called "River Relics."

Solitude **¹/₂

There are lovely wilderness stretches on the Clearwater, but the river sees a significant amount of use on its lower reaches, since it was a First Nations and fur-trade highway. Lloyd Lake has a fishing lodge and private cabins, and the Virgin River area is a grayling fishing spot for fishing parties from Careen Lake. The Warner Rapids bridge and provincial park campground also see a lot of use. A rafting company runs trips on the river, and the Whitemud Falls area has a semi-developed campground maintained by the Alberta government. It is from here, downstream to Fort McMurray, that you are most likely meet up with other people. Jet boats come up from McMurray, and there are a number of campgrounds and cabins along the stretch after Cascade Rapids. It's not as probable that you will bump into anyone if you paddle the upper Clearwater and move quickly through Warner Rapids, and then take out at Contact Rapids.

Wildlife **

As there is a significant human presence on the river, the wildlife is pretty wary of the open. Black bears and beavers are very common. Be cautious about camping at the semi-developed campsites frequented by fishing and jet-boating parties — they attract bears because of garbage.

You might see a moose or a wolf in the upper reaches, most likely above the confluence of the Virgin River. Woodland caribou, elk, white-tailed and mule deer could be sighted in the lower river valley. Bald eagles, osprey and white pelicans can be observed at close quarters along the river.

Wolverines have been seen in the area, so you may see them, but sightings are rare. I once saw a pair on the side of the road while travelling the gravel highway between Beauval and the Key Lake turnoff.

Fishing ***

The variety in the landscape is matched by the variety one can find angling on the river. Walleye hang out below most of the major rapids. Pike, well, they live just about anywhere. Grayling can be caught in Virgin River, and Brad and I have often flown there just to fish for grayling. The best place to fish for really big northerns and walleye is below Skull Falls, in the big, round lake of small rapids. In the slow water and eddies of the very southern reaches are huge pike. On our 1993 trip, they pulled Brad around in his solo boat all day! Sheila tried to help him land them, and I caught 5-pound walleye, one after another, while sitting in a mid-river eddy watching the show. It was hilarious!

Special Equipment

If you had seen the number of wrecked aluminum and fibreglass canoes on the Clearwater that I have, you would not go on a trip on this river without a Royalex-hull canoe and good whitewater skills. There is just no question in my mind — you should take advantage of the plastic technology on whitewater rivers like this.

A spray cover is a handy item on this river if your whitewater skills are sufficiently advanced to run some of the big rapids. Advanced and exceptional paddlers will also enjoy the solo boating opportunities there are on the Clearwater. The blackflies and mosquitoes can be horrendous some seasons, so bring a bug jacket and or hat. You will need protection.

A number of people I know have contracted giardia or "beaver fever" from drinking untreated water on the Clearwater. It is best to take precautions against this. Bring a filter system or some drops to purify your drinking water.

Trip Notes

MAP NO	GRID REF	FEATURE	DESCRIPTION
74 F/7	254590	Campsite	On a point on RR or the south shore of Lloyd Lake, with a sandy jack pine bench. The Lloyd Lake Lodge is over on the southwest side of Ferrie Peninsula (198566 on 74 F/6).
	274584	Campsite	On a long, pointy spit on RR, with a nice view and a bench.
	313566	Campsite	On a tiny point on RL at the head of the Clearwater River proper.
	343565 348564	Lloyd Rapids Water survey station/cable	**Class 2, 2+ and 3**, a series of drops around curves in the river that increase in frequency and difficulty, becoming steeper towards the end. A low-hanging cable crosses the river at the tin water-survey station on RR between the first two chutes. The entire rapid is shallow, with numerous holes and large, closely spaced waves created by boulders. The last drop is very narrow, fast and steep. The **portage (535 m)** is on RL, and starts in a bay above the first drop (344566). If you are interested in the pictographs keep your eyes on RL after navigating Lloyd Rapids. One site is directly after the rapids, and another site is at the narrows just downstream of the small lakelet. The third site is also on RL about 6 km downstream, just before a good-sized creek comes in. The final site is on RL after a small rapid upstream of the Virgin River confluence.
	354556	Campsite	At the narrows on RR. Try your luck fishing here.
	360545	Rapids	**Class 2+.** A big, irregular chute, with large waves. It's very steep at the start. A poor **portage trail (70 m)** is on RR, starting at a break in the willows just up from the beginning of the rapid.
	358543	Rapids	**Class 1+.** A fast channel, but mainly clear.
	353524 354524	Rapids Campsite	**Class 2+/3.** This marked rapid starts as a big chute in the narrows followed by large waves piling onto big rocks, with a boulder garden at the end. A **portage (600 m)** is on RL, and starts 75 m above the rapid. A sandy, level area with mature jack pine provides good camping at the end of the trail.
74 F/2	365448	Campsite	On RR on a jack pine bench just before the island. Good camping and moose country, but poor whitewater prospects for the next 30 km!
	319413	Campsite	On RL on a sandy bench.
	469375	Campsite	At a bend to the right, on RL.
74 F/1	574354	Campsite	On RR in the RR channel on a jack pine bench.

clearwater river

121

MAP NO	GRID REF	FEATURE	DESCRIPTION
	572351	Rapids	**Class 2**, with a slight curve to the right. A fairly clear channel.
	598337	Rapids	**Class 2**, with some large rocks and waves. After the rapids make your way to RR for scouting/portaging First Gorge.
	599336 613327	First Gorge	**Class 4, 2/2+, 3+, 3, 3+ and Class 2+**. A long series of drops through the first gorge of the river. Scouting the big drops in the "canyon" is difficult, as the portage trail cuts off the point of land and there is an old burn. This gorge is the site of many accidents and canoe wrecks. Canoeists are strongly urged to portage the Class 3+, 3, and 3+ rapids in the canyon unless they are advanced or exceptional whitewater paddlers. The **portage** around the entire rapid is **1,375 m** long and starts in the narrow bay on RR on the right bank. The left bank trail goes to a lookout. If you are going to run part or all of the gorge, you can be creative about pulling over the first drop. Then you can paddle the 500 m 2/2+ section and take out or scout at the easy landing spot on RR before the river narrows in the canyon.

You can see First Gorge in six sections:
- **Class 4.** Steep falls (1.25 m or more) with a keeper hole at bottom.
- **Class 2/2+.** 500 m of boulders and waves through a wide area with an easy landing area to get back to the portage on RR.
- **Class 3+.** The river narrows to drop over 1.25 m of broken ledge on a curve with steep sides. It's a difficult drop to stop above or scout.
- **Class 3.** Big waves and many large holes.
- **Class 3/3+.** The river turns right sharply. A large, steep chute is at the end of the canyon with large waves at the bottom.
- **Class 2/2+.** A wide, steep, and very shallow boulder fan, which may have sweepers and snags from the old burn.

	GRID REF	FEATURE	DESCRIPTION
	604323	Rapids	**Class 1+.** Fast water and small waves.
	624304	Campsite	On RR.
	628300	Rapids	**Class 1.** Fast water.
	648236	Campsite	On RL in a very old burn with new jack pine. On a sandy flat above the river. It has a small sand beach landing.
	651215	Confluence Campsite Fishing hole	On the left side, looking upstream at the Virgin River Falls is a small campsite in the trees — a great place to stop and fish. Head up the Virgin on foot for grayling. Stay down below for walleye and pike. The Virgin River is also a fun solo boat run. Sheila, Craig, Brad and I had a blast running it from the bottom of the first nasty section right below Careen Lake to just above the bottom falls.
	643237	Rapids	**Class 2+.** A broken ledge with large waves. The **portage (75 m)** is on RL, and starts about 10 m above the rapid's head.
	618222	Rapids	**Class 1+/2.** Fast water with large waves.
	607218 606217	Beauty Rapids Campsite	**Class 4, 3, 2+, and 2**. A long series of drops beginning with falls between the islands. The **portage** for the Class 4 falls **(115 m)** is on the RR shore of the RR channel, starting in a small bay just above the falls. There is a campsite on the portage.

You can see Beauty Rapids in four parts:
- **Class 4**. Big ledges between islands with boulders, keepers and large waves meeting in a turbulent area below.
- **Class 3**. Big irregular waves, rocks and boils where the channels rejoin and head off to the right-hand curve.
- **Class 2+**. Steep, fast waves and holes on a corner.
- **Class 2**. Slows and widens through a boulder garden to the end of the portage.

MAP NO	GRID REF	FEATURE	DESCRIPTION
	604215 602215	Rapid	**Class 3**, deep and fast. The obvious V leads into large, irregular standing waves and some large stoppers. Watch for the large rock in the main current outflow to the right of RC. There may be a sweeper on it. The **portage (135 m)** is on RR, and starts in small bay immediately above the start of the rapid.
	554203 552202	Granite Gorge Campsite	**Class 2+, 2+, 3 and 3**. A series of drops through a constricted elbow-shaped gorge. Marked R on the map.

You can see Granite Gorge in four parts:
- **Class 2+**. Fast chutes around small rock islets.
- **Class 2+**. Big holes and a fast current; you need to set up for the next corner.
- **Class 3**. Narrow, violent currents, with a big stopper in the centre of the main flow.
- **Class 3**. Another stopper at the head of a chain of large, standing waves that mark the end of the rapid.

MAP NO	GRID REF	FEATURE	DESCRIPTION
			The **portage (300 m)** is on RR, and starts about 15 m before the gorge. The gorge starts about 50 m before the rapids. Do not pass the head of the gorge if you are looking for the portage! There is a campsite just off the portage trail, set on a high sand bank overlooking the back bay.
74 C/16	527197	Rapids	**Class 2+**. Marked with an R and a bar, the rapid starts with an irregular chute. The main flow has large waves at high water. The RL side of the main flow has an obvious V. The **portage (95 m)** is on RL, and starts just above the rapid.
74 C/15	517187	Campsite	On RR on a jack pine bench just before the bend to the left.
	478134 475135	Bielby Rapids	**Class 2**, rather small and very shallow, marked with dashes on the map. You may have to wade in low water.
	465137 463138	Anniversary Rapid Campsite	**Class 2 or 2+**. Here the map shows two islands that in reality are more like one. They divide this rapid into two parallel channels. The RR channel is Class 2; it starts shallow, gets faster, and becomes rocky, with waves at the end of the second island. Often it is too shallow to navigate. The RL channel curves away to the right to begin with, and the current piles up towards the RL bank. Then it gets rocky, increasingly so towards where the end of the first island is marked on the map. There is a campsite in the burn at the bay on RL. Land below the RL point at the end of the rapid to get to it. Camping is possible on the downstream end of the "two in one" island as well, as it is not burned.
	450140	Rapids	**Class 2**. Marked with dashes on the map. It's a long boulder run. Easy manoeuvring but shallow near the end.

clearwater river

MAP NO	GRID REF	FEATURE	DESCRIPTION
	429126 426125	Rapids	**Class 2**, and unmarked rapid around the island. The main current runs RL, but this channel is more difficult because of the curve and the number of boulders to negotiate at a higher speed. The RR channel is very shallow, but slower.
	402113 372103	Olson Rapids	**Class 2.** This section is approximately 3 km long. It is winding and boulder strewn, with lots of room to move around in moderate current. A good place to practise those midstream-boulder eddy turns!
	378105	Campsite	In Olson Rapids on RL at a small point with a bay behind it.
	351094 350094	Rapids	**Class 2**, with a few boulders to dodge in moderate current.
	345096	Rapids	**Class 2+**, around an island. Both channels have Class 2+ rapids. The RL channel has little flow. The RR channel is a tight drop with fast current requiring good manoeuvres. There's a strong current pushing you to the outside.
	335102	Rapids	**Class 2.** A very low, broken ledge with several chutes. The largest and deepest chute is on far RR.
	313105 304104	Upper Mackie Rapids	**Class 2 to 2+.** There are many boulders, the river winds a bit, and there is moderate current.
	298102 296102	Lower Mackie Rapids	Made up of two channels, as the rapids flow around a large island. The main flow goes to the left. Both routes are blind corners. **RL channel: Class 3, 3, and 2+.** The rapids begin with a steep ledge with a narrow chute right of RC. A larger main-flow chute is on RL (the outside of the curve). There is a high, broken shelf halfway down on RL, and boulders on the inside where the flow is slower. The rapids end as a Class 2+ boulder garden with major waves and holes in fast current. **RR channel: Class 3.** Possible only at medium-high to high water levels, as this is a minor-flow channel with a fast drop in elevation and many boulders. Very technically challenging, as it is so tight and fast.
		Portage Campsite	The **portage (450 m)** is on RR and starts at a campsite that is visible from the water, about 20 m from where the channel splits. Watch for a double blaze on a birch tree 200 m down the trail. You want to follow the right fork. The left fork follows the shore and ends in a swamp!
	278095	Campsite	On RR. It will do in a pinch, especially if you have to dry out after Mackie!
	269074 241076	Rapids	**Class 2 to 2+.** About 3 km of winding boulder gardens becoming faster with more obstacles towards the end. Good manoeuvring is required.

MAP NO	GRID REF	FEATURE	DESCRIPTION
	231077	**Bridge Warner Rapids Campground**	Gravel Highway 955. You can take out before or after Warner Rapids on RR. This is where the **portage (100 m)** is located. The rapids under the bridge are **Class 2/2+**, a mainly unobstructed deep-water channel creates moderate to large standing waves, which can be avoided. There is a provincial park campground on RR 500 m upstream of the bridge.
74 C/14	215075	**Rapids**	**Class 1** where marked with dashes, about 200 m. Straightforward.
	209070	**Rapids**	**Class 1.** Riffles.
	206068	**Rapids**	**Class 1.** Riffles.
	168060 167060	**Tricky Ledges Rapids**	**Class 2+ or 3**. An island splits the rapid. The RL channel is your best bet in low or moderate water. Once you enter the channel, the current speeds up and the river swings around a big curve to the right. Several broken ledges and strings of boulders cut across the channel throughout the curve. No direct line exists. Back paddling and back ferrying are required. The RR channel is Class 3 and a high-water run — very steep with lots of rocks. The **portage (125 m)** is on the RR shore of the RR channel, starting 25 m above the head of the rapid.
	128035 117027	**Rapids**	**Class 1+**. These rapids flow around a large island. Taking the more scenic route, the RL channel at 129036, you will encounter riffles to Class 1+ rapids along its length. The RR channel is similar in nature.
	099026	**Rapids**	**Class 1/1+**, marked by a bar. This is a 50-m-long rapid. A wide and shallow boulder garden with more rocks on RL.
	095034	**Campsite**	On RR on a jack pine bench below with the main flow in the a sharp bend to the left or southwest. The camp is above the confluence of the Descharme River, and easy to miss. Look for the pink, sloping rock.
	082024	**Riffle**	800 m down from the Descharme confluence.
	077015	**Rapids Campsite**	**Class 2+**. This is a 75-m boulder garden with waves in the middle. You can **portage (100 m)** on RR. A campsite is right below the rapid on RR on an open, sandy jack pine bench. It's on the point before the cove where the portage ends. There is a small riffle 250 m down from the camp.
	074981	**Cabin**	On RL a trapper cabin on a sandy open flats.
	066955 066944	**Gould Rapids Campsite**	**Class 2, 2+/3, 3/3+ and 2**. A series of drops in a "canyon." Very difficult to scout properly from land. To **portage** all but the first Class 2 rapid is **1,275 m**. This trail begins on RR at 066953, across from a tiny islet. It is in the fast water above Gould Rapids and canoeists should be very cautious on their approach. There is a campsite at a clearing about 300 m upstream of the portage. It's a short walk into the trees. The cautious canoeist could start their portage from here as well.

You can see Gould Rapids in four parts:

♦ **Class 2**. These are the rapids in the RR channel around the island before the canyon. Deepest water is right of RC, with some boulders. Stay right to catch the portage.

♦ **Class 2+ to 3**. A series of drops from the start of the portage to the point of no return below a small island where there is a last chance to scout or portage (GR 068946) in a small bay on RL. You will have to choose between working the left shore to the bay or making your way left after the small island. We usually run the small island on the right and work left after it. Eddy in to the shore eddy just before the really hairy section begins after the right turn. Where the channel walls rise so does the difficulty of the rapids. Scramble up the steep back and take a good look, and or portage (150 m) through the open jack pine to below the last major chute of Gould Rapids.

♦ **Class 3 to 3+**. Large waves with many rocks and stoppers to avoid. Fast current increasing in intensity. Choose a good line, as the current is fast for a long way.

♦ **Class 2**. Fast water and waves with some obstacles.

Note: The current is fast for 1.6 km before reaching the portage for Smoothrock Falls. Stay near the right shore as you approach the portage trail on RR, which starts between a very old beaver lodge on the right (upstream of the trail) and a rock outcrop on the left, downstream of the trail — do not pass! **Be very careful. Smoothrock starts with innocent-looking rapids, and the sound of the almost 20-m drop beyond may not be audible because of the wind direction.**

MAP NO	GRID REF	FEATURE	DESCRIPTION
	057930 047932	Smoothrock Falls Campsite	**Class 6, 5, 4, 5, 2+ to 3, 2+, 3 and 2**. The falls consists of three drops, the third being the Class 6 plunge into the "boiling cauldron of death," according to Sheila! The **portage (1,300 m)**, as mentioned above, is on RR and starts just past the old beaver lodge, about 125 m above the falls in a small cove. There are two sites to camp — one high at the top overlooking the falls (150 m up the portage trail and to the left) and a bigger, more luxurious one near the bottom of the portage. The falls are followed by Class 5 rapids pounding over huge boulders to a curving fan running off to the left and continuing on through an increasingly narrow boulder run. Advanced and exceptional paddlers with solo boats or tandem boats with spray skirts may elect to carry their gear and then run parts of the lower rapids. There is a rough trail down to the river where the Class 4 rapids start, where canoes can be put in for this extremely difficult and dangerous run (GR 055933).

You can see the rapids right below Smoothrock in six parts:

♦ **Class 4**. Fast, steep, many obstacles, requiring precise manoeuvres.

♦ **Class 5**. A big ledge creates falls, with most of the water going over the main drop on the RR. A very violent chute with boulders hidden in the backwash and a nasty swim below. There are small falls on the RL, a tight job with lots of twists and turns.

♦ **Class 2+ to 3**. Numerous obstacles and waves, gradually smoothing out to the next corner.

♦ **Class 2+**. The river turns right and heads north after this set. We caught some nice walleye off the point.

♦ **Class 3**. The final set has large rocks and stoppers in the main flow.

♦ **Class 2**. Easier rock-dodging signals the end. The bottom of the portage is on RR. A grassy opening with a rocky shore.

MAP NO	GRID REF	FEATURE	DESCRIPTION
	010932	Riffle	Short.
	994937	Rapids	**Class 2/2+**, around a large island. Take the RR channel, where there is a low ledge with a break on RL that can be run. Caution is required, as you are approaching dangerous falls. Line or carry over the rocks if you feel unsure.
	986931 982932	Skull Canyon Campsite Fishing hole	A series of rapids leading into a huge gorge, with twin falls dropping around a huge, tower-like island. The Dene call these rapids Bald Eagle Rapids. The **portage (350 m)** on RR starts about 125 m above the small rapids leading to the falls. The trailhead is in thick bush and hard to see — watch carefully and stay right. A small campsite at Skull overlooks the falls. To get to it you turn left about 50 m from the bottom of the portage trail and go up the steep hill. There is a larger camping spot in the bay just before the next rapids, about 250 m down the portage trail. The best fishing is in the eddies and pools of the lake area below Skull.

Option: Crazy Man's Creek, Class 3, rated for conditions as much as technical difficulty, this route is only possible at moderate to high water and only suitable for advanced paddlers and inter- mediates willing to wade. This cheat creek starts above the Class 2 rapids, beginning at GR 993935. The creek steadily increases in speed, slipping over and around rocks so that you become so busy rock dodging through the zigzagging channel that you might not see the 1-m ledge until you are almost over it (GR 989931). There is a pool of quiet water below to bail. The cautious will stop to drag over the ledge. The creek gets slower and shallower from then on. Expect to scrape bottom at times. You end up in the lakelet below the twin falls. Getting back up to the portage to camp can be difficult because the current is very fast and right below the falls. You may have to walk your boat.

	980933	Campsite	On RR at the northwest end of the lakelet below Skull. There is a tiny, sandy beach landing and the site is up on the steep bank on an open jack pine bench. This is a five-star spot!
	979932	Rapids	**Class 2**, marked with a bar around a large island. As you leave the lake area below Skull Canyon using the RR channel around the island, there is a rapid with a low ledge, broken along its length, but especially at extreme RL. It's more difficult to run at low water. The RL channel around the island is also Class 2 and runnable after scouting.
	964933	Riffles	Fast water and riffles around a bend to the left.
	939919 929893	Simonson Rapids	**Class 2 to 3, Class 2 and Class 3 to 4.** A series of rapids stretching over 5 km.

There are three basic sections to Simonson:
◆ **Class 2+/3, Class 2+, and Class 2**. Heading south there is a three-way split around islands. The main flow is in the centre channel. There is a ledge in the main flow and large waves and stoppers. The rocky side channel on RR is the easiest route. There is a **portage (80 m)** around this top drop on RR about 50 m above the rapids at a grassy spot with a break in the willows. About 200 m downstream is another drop past an enormous boulder in the main current. The rest of this section to 942914 is Class 2 boulder dodging.

- **Class 2.** Heading northwest, about 1 km of boulder dodging, with some ledge-like formations at 941906 to 933913.
- **Class 3 to 4.** Depending on the route chosen at 933914. The rapids are created by a high, steep and sloping granite shelf that spans the river, and there are five channels cutting through it. The extreme RR channel is Class 3, taking a left-hand curve around a blind corner. There are lots of rocks, and good manoeuvring is required. There is a ledge three quarters of the way down, too. We run the extreme RR channel inside to outside of the curve to set up for the ledge drop. You can portage the granite shelf drop by portaging (50 m) the northeast tip of the small, farthest RR island or by pulling out at the lip of the ledge on the left side of the island and carrying on down the indistinct portage trail to the downstream end of the island. The remainder of Simonson from 924907 to the confluence of the McLean River (GR 925893) is Class 2 and 1.

MAP NO	GRID REF	FEATURE	DESCRIPTION
74 C/11	922893 910888	Contact Rapids Campsite	**Class 2 to 5**, a series of five drops. You can't scout from the **portage (1,250 m)** on RR. The trail starts at the obvious cut in a high, sandy bank, across from the mouth of the MacLean River. This portage bypasses all five rapids. Portaging your gear is advised, even if you decide to run parts of Contact. The trail is flat and sandy, and makes the mandatory carry at the falls much easier. There are two sites at which you can camp — top or bottom of the trail.

Those wishing to take the more scenic route through Contact Rapids should head south. There are five parts to Contact:

- **Class 2.** With fast water and small waves around the first island to the second island.
- **Class 2+.** At the second island, the far RL channel is the easiest and safest option. Go with the main flow around the tight bend to the right. Vision downstream is restricted, so watch for sweepers and rocks on the outside of the turn.
- **Class 4+ and 5 falls.** Around another island. Both drops are dangerous. Portage over the island at 922887.
- **Class 2.** A boulder garden.
- **Class 4 and 3+.** To navigate the last island string you have two options. There are Class 4 rapids in the RR channel. It is a steep boulder spillway, only runnable at high water. The RL channel is home to the Class 3+ "Around-the-Corner-Down-the-Drain-to-Hell" rapid, a personal favourite of mine, since I spent a long time in 1991 in the triangular ledge hole on RR! All joking aside, approach these rapids with extreme caution. The majority of the rapids are hidden by a very tight right-hand corner. The current is so fast that the water banks up on RL like a bobsled run. Landing on RL to scout is not advised; scouting is best done from the island. Follow the shore of the island until you can see the corner in the distance, and then stop. Don't pass the island thinking you can scout from the boat, or you may end up in the hole on RR before the turn, like I did. It's not a good place to be. The rapids consist of a huge chute that forms a huge pyramid wave followed by many large standing waves. On either side of the chute are holes. Downstream the rapids are rocky and long, so prepare for rescues before attempting this rapid. You can carry over the island instead of running this drop. Say goodbye to the Shield bedrock. It ends here.

MAP NO	GRID REF	FEATURE	DESCRIPTION
	857884	Campsite	On RR up a sand bank. Grassy flats up top. More like this up ahead to just before trapper's cabin at 706867.
74 C/12	706867	Cabin	A trapper's cabin on RL.
	696865	Methy Portage Take-out	The famous portage starts on a grassy bank on RL. You can follow it with your finger on the map to Wallis Bay or stretch your legs and at least check out the view above Rendezvous Lake — about 6 km of good trail. In fact, it's like a road once you pass the wet

MAP NO	GRID REF	FEATURE	DESCRIPTION
			spots at the beginning, and there's only one steep section. No camping is allowed here, by park regulations. Floatplanes will land downstream of the Methy Portage if there is enough water. Arrange for a spot with your charter pilot.
74 D/9	609846	Border	Voila Alberta! Now you are on the track to the Mackenzie Basin. Check out the historic voyageur upstream portages to come.
	574834	Whitemud Falls Campground Take-out	**Be cautious approaching falls.** The **portage (450 m)** is on RR and starts at a creek opening. The current is strong above the falls, and cautious canoeists can land on the RR shore before the creek and begin their portage 300 m early. This trail starts right beside the flowerpot island. There is a semi-developed campground on the trail about halfway, overlooking the falls. Bears are a problem because of the garbage left here. Be alert for jet boats downstream of the falls. Floatplanes will land in the deep channel below the falls if there is enough water. Have your gear at the end of the portage. This was the first upstream portage for the voyageurs.

Option: Bradley Creek, Class 2+. Paddling this creek allows you to avoid the portage around Whitemud Falls. Navigable at medium to high water levels, it starts at 575835 and ends at 559833, and it's a scenic trip past high cliff walls. The rapids are not as challenging as Crazy Man's, but be prepared for tight corners. This creek should be named after me, not Brad. I was the one who fell in and lost my fishing rod!

	543850	Upper Pine Rapids	Class 1. You may want to check out this upstream portage. The **portage** is on RL **(125 m)**. The names of the portages are from the days when the northern or Mackenzie brigade paddled up the Clearwater to rendezvous on the Methy. This would have been Pas Rapids and Pas Portage in the voyageur days. Pas comes from *Pasquia*, which is Cree for "where the river narrows." That's what it is — a narrows with fast water.
	537852 525855	Pine Rapids Portage de Pins	Class 2+/3, with ledges and waves. The rapids can't be scouted from the the **portage (1,000 m)** on RL at 537851. But, if you decide to run, there are places to scout along the way. The current is moderate, so descending through the low shelves using a back ferry works well. There are nifty sandstone formations in the area — hoodoos, overhangs and cliffs. This is another historic upstream portage, and it is the Portage of the Pines in English.
	487859	Gros Roche Rapids	Class 2. Wide, with few obstacles and moderate waves. Big Rock or Big Stone Rapid, to those whose French is weak. The **portage** is on RL **(425 m)**.
	477853	Un Coup Rapids	Class 1, with fast water. The **portage (180 m)** trail is on RR. Another historic upstream portage, and I assume the name relates to a blaze or lobstick that was present to mark the portage. Coup means "cut" in French, but it can also mean "cup." I've read it was called "The Nurse" portage, so maybe it's where they had a good stiff drink before the next upstream adventure?
	474848	Le Bon	Class 2+. A very long stretch, 3 km, of shallow ledges. Bottom is

MAP NO	GRID REF	FEATURE	DESCRIPTION
	474848 456844	Le Bon Rapids Campsite	**Class 2+.** A very long stretch, 3 km, of shallow ledges. Bottom is visible most of the time. Good read-as-you-run practice, as scouting is difficult because of the width of the channel. The **portage (2,000 m)** is on RR, starting 150 m above the rapids. Camping is possible on the sandy, open jack pine bench at a clearing near the end of the trail. It was called Long Rapids by English paddlers, but was the Good Rapids in voyageur times, because you can wade your canoe up the rapids instead of portaging, and that's good for any voyageur, then or now!
	446843 435844	Cascade Rapids Campground	**Class 2+ to 3.** A simple run, except for the Class 3 ledge about one third of the way down. It's an easy scout from RR using the trail branching off to the shore from the portage. The **portage (1,250 m)** is on RR and starts above the sharp bend to the right. The provincial park semi-developed campground is at the end of the portage. This was the last of the voyageurs' upstream portages, the Cascades.
		Take-out	Floatplanes will land on the stretch of river approximately 2 km down from Cascade, if there is enough water. There is a section where there are no midstream islands. Ask your pilot exactly where you should be for pick up.

Note: It's 90 km or so to Fort McMurray. You will soon come to the end of the wilderness section of the Clearwater. Beware of jet boats and don't drink the water without purifying it first. There are only short, easy rapids ahead of you. Three semi-developed Alberta provincial campgrounds are along the way. The Voyage Air waterbase is in the Snye, a dead-end side channel at McMurray on RL after the big island and before the golf course. In case you are wondering, a snye is an oxbow that has been cut off from the main flow so that it becomes a little, separate lake.

the trips

WATHAMAN RIVER

The serious challenge, the incredible geological features, the wildlife and the wildness of the Wathaman are the reasons to go on this trip. This narrow river zigzags northeast, crossing the grain of the Precambrian Shield in many places and dropping into gorges with steep, vertical walls over blocks of rock hardly worn by the river's low-volume flow. In places the river is barely 3 m across, with granite cliffs five times as high. The rapids are extremely technical — mostly long and continuous boulder gardens. It's like mountain creek boating. In northern Saskatchewan? Who knew!

Much of the forest is new-growth jack pine due to forest fires over the past 20 to 30 years, making portaging very tough. But the vibrant green of the new trees that mottles the orange-red Wathaman Batholith outcropping contrasts beautifully. In the golden evening light, the cliffs and lakes can send a photographer into an ecstatic frenzy. The water is so warm in July that Sheila and I called it the Wathaman Bathtub.

Finally, it's only you and the moose out there. It takes strenuous effort to get down the Walk-a-man — our other pet name for the river. But it could be the most intensely satisfying wilderness trip of your life.

Length

The trip described in the Trip Notes section is approximately 162 km long. It starts at an unnamed lake (marked 505 m above sea level) just north of the Wathaman River and north-east of Burbidge Lake. It ends at the Highway 905 bridge at Wathaman Lake. You should not attempt the route in less than ten whole paddling days. At the beginning of the trip, making 15 km a day is too much to ask — there are too many tricky rapids and bushwhack portages. If you try to rush this trip, you'll just end up exhausted and frustrated.

The trip could be shortened and made somewhat easier by flying in farther downstream at a long, narrow lake, in the sandy section of the river marked 438 m above sea level. The trip can be extended on both ends. You could start at Burbidge Lake if you had good water levels and were prepared for some added strenuous wading, lining and portaging. Better yet, you could start at Upper Foster Lake, then portage into Rupert Lake and skip from lake to lake down into the Wathaman via the 438-m unnamed lake. Or you could cut across Wathaman Lake and paddle into Davin Lake to the road access at the campsite there. To really add some distance, you could carry on past the Highway 905 bridge on Wathaman Lake and paddle all the way to Southend, on Reindeer Lake.

Unnamed lake (438 m) east of Pendleton Lake to Wathaman Lake*	126 km
Unnamed lake (505 m) northeast of Burbidge Lake to Wathaman Lake*	162 km
Burbidge Lake (oufitter's camp) to Wathaman Lake	180 km
Unnamed lake (505 m) to Davin Lake Campsite	184 km
Upper Foster Lake (Miller Island) to Wathaman Lake	195 km

* These trips are described in detail in the Trip Notes section of this chapter.

Topographic Maps

For this trip, 1:50,000 maps are essential. This scale is the only one that can provide you with enough detail to locate yourself in terms of all the rapids and falls on the river, many of which are not marked on the map. You will need 74A/15, 74A/16, 74H/1, 64D/13 and 64E/4. If you start at the outfitter's camp at Burbidge or Upper Foster Lake you will also need 74 A/14. If you go the Davin Lake route, you don't need 64E/4.

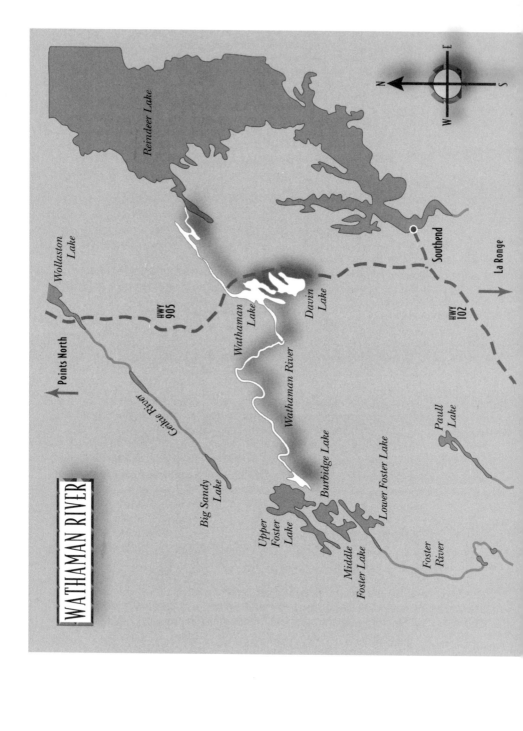

In order to make the best use of the information provided in this chapter, I suggest you purchase the required maps in advance and use the grid reference coordinates in the Trip Notes section to mark in the huge number of rapids and falls that are either missing or mislabelled on the maps. There are a number of significant errors, not in the least the misrepresentation of numerous sets of falls as rapids. There seems to be no rhyme or reason for the way rapids are marked, or not marked! You can make note of the classifications of the rapids and other features of interest, so that while you are paddling the river the information is in front of you. Campsites can be especially hard to find on the upper Wathaman because of the old burns, and are often small and rustic. You will be going slowly in the first couple of days, and will be tired at the end of the day. Be sure to plan your stops ahead of time where possible.

Getting There and Away

This is a fly-in only trip, but you can choose to drive out via the Highway 905 bridge at Wathaman Lake or the Davin Lake Provincial Campsite just off 905. Logistically, there are two good options for shuttles. The first option is to drive to Missinipe, leave your vehicle(s) there and fly out. Then have a vehicle shuttled up to you by Churchill River Canoe Outfitters on an arranged date. The drive to Wathaman Lake is 220 km from Missinipe one way. The Davin campsite take-out is approximately 190 km one way.

The second option is to fly from Southend. You can arrange a floatplane charter with Lawrence Bay Oufitters and Air Services at Reindeer Lake. You would drive to Southend to meet the plane (the SERM fire cache may be a good place to leave your vehicle — you will have to arrange for safe parking at Southend), and then fly to the river. Then fly or paddle back from Wathaman Lake or arrange for a ride from the Davin Lake Lodge to Southend to pick up your vehicle. These options should be cheaper than flying from Missinipe. However, it may be possible to catch a backhaul flight with the outfitters on either Burbidge or Upper Foster Lake. See the Directory of Services for contact information.

When to Go

Late May to late August. You want to go when the water is not too low or too high. The reason Sheila and I called it the Walk-a-man is because some rapids are unnavigable even at normal water levels, and you must line and wade them. But you don't want to have to wade or line half the river, which may happen if you go in a low-water year. I wouldn't want to paddle the Wathaman in flood either, however; the river is too narrow and full of boulder rapids and falls to be safe in pushy water, whether you are paddling, wading or lining. In flood, the river would be dangerous and shouldn't be attempted.

The water survey station on the Wathaman is still in operation, and you can call SaskWater for a "real time" water-level reading. Sheila and I paddled the Wathaman in mid-July in 2001 in a fairly low-water year. The flow was 60 cu m/sec just downstream of Wathaman Lake, where the survey station is. This was a decent level to paddle the entire river, but slightly higher flows would have been better. We left some Royalex behind and had to wade some bits. The July ten-year average flow runs around 75 cu m/sec.

That being said, high water in June would be very pushy. The ten-year average flow for June is 100 cu m/sec, and that is when the river peaks. I wouldn't want to paddle the Wathaman that high. The average August flow is 65 cu m/sec, making it a good month to paddle the river in a normal year. The water will be like a hot tub by then, and the bugs will have settled down too!

Difficulty of the River ✱✱✱✱

No doubt the Wathaman gets the four-star difficulty rating. You do not want to go down this river if you are not ready for the challenge. I think the Wathaman is the toughest trip in this book. Unlike some of the other more difficult trips, it requires a very advanced skill level in all areas of canoe tripping. Not only do you need a high level of physical fitness and bushcraft, but also a very advanced level of whitewater skill to descend it in a safe and timely manner. On top of that, it is a very remote river, where the only way out of most stretches is by helicopter.

The portages are non-existent in the upper reaches, and this is where there are some serious gorge-type falls and rapids, so the trip is physically demanding. You will be bushwhacking through burn, big time. My line was, "Every moment without a bushwhack portage is a good moment." Sheila would laugh. It's not that bad, but be prepared to work extremely hard for the first three days or so. About 60 km downriver, the portage conditions improve. By improve, I mean that there is a trail in most places. You will also work hard wading and lining unnavigable rapids. The river starts off like a creek, with too many big rocks.

The whitewater is tough, the average rapids reaching Class 3. The rapids are long, rocky and shallow to start with. Some have more rocks than water. Once I cracked Sheila up completely when I turned back to look at the rapids we had just run and said, "If that had more water, I'd give it a four." The rapids remind me of the William in that way.

As you descend, the flow increases and ledges come into play. So do bigger waves. Scouting from shore is difficult to impossible on most stretches. The most challenging rapids come at the end: Bell, Stuart, Cowan and McKenzie Rapids.

Your map-reading skills will also be challenged. The constant rapid running tends to make it difficult to pinpoint where you are. But keeping tabs on your location is very important because the river is so twisty. There are lots of blind corners, and falls can appear out of nowhere. One hazard to note is due to the narrow and steep nature of the river: you must be extra vigilant about sweepers and strainers. Some rapids go around tiny islands, and with the burn there can be dead trees in and across the channels. The only lake crossing to worry about is Wathaman Lake; it is long and exposed in places. Sheila and I were windbound on our last day and had to paddle until dark to reach the take-out.

This is a trip only for advanced and exceptional paddlers. You do not want to run the Wathaman tandem without another advanced boater. You must be able to read and run long and continuous Class 2+ and 3 rapids. The rapids are extremely technical, and there is no time to be indecisive or ineffective with your strokes. This is not a river where you plunge through the standing waves and make it or not. If you wipe out in this river, your boat will be pinned, wrapped and trashed, unless you are very lucky.

The gradient of the Wathaman from Burbidge Lake to its outlet at Wathaman Lake is around 1.05 m/km (5.5 ft/mi). This is a very steep gradient for a river in northern Saskatchewan. On the highlighted trip there are eight falls, all mandatory portages, a few of which are large drops. But the change in elevation is mostly made of long, rocky rapids — lots of them.

Character of the River and Region

The small volume of the Wathaman is a result of its location. It is a trickle of water filling the fractures in the Precambrian bedrock. Each time the river crosses a fault in the bedrock structure, there is a steep drop. The volume of the river increases significantly as it flows northeast, fed only by the inflow of creeks and streams, but there are lots of them. By the time you reach Wathaman Lake, the Wathaman can be considered a moderate-volume river for northern Saskatchewan. The average flow below the lake in June, when the water levels peak, is around 100 cu m/sec.

The riverbed is generally made up of small rocks and sand. In the swampy areas the bottom is mucky with lots of moose food. I noticed many more sedges, snails and fresh-water clams than in any other river in northern Saskatchewan; the warmer water seems to agree with these lifeforms. It's hard to believe the Wathaman drains into Reindeer Lake, which is such a large, cold body of water.

The unique aspects of the Wathaman are directly related to its geology. For one, the rocks are more square than round. Huge car-sized chunks of rock have dropped out of the canyon walls, and sit where they landed. Slightly smaller rocks crowd the riverbed, left over from the movement and melting of the glaciers. Normally, rocks in a meltwater channel would be more eroded, but not on the Wathaman. The rock was too hard and the water flow was too limited in this crack-trickle type of river system. This makes for lots of tight chutes, S-turns galore, and crowded boulder gardens. We ran lots of rapids on the outside of the bend because that was the only place where deep-water Vs could be found.

The river runs through the Churchill Uplands and shares its diverse characteristics. There are ledges of exposed Precambrian bedrock at the falls and some minor rapids more towards the middle and end of the river. The last unnamed lake before Wathaman Lake and Wathaman Lake itself have lovely smooth rock and ledge camping.

There are also intermittent areas of glacial deposits, moraine and eskers. The sandy areas have some good campsites. There are a number of small, marshy lakes and peat and wetlands, but you don't paddle through them for extended stretches like you do on the other rivers in the Foster Uplands — the Haultain or the Foster, for example. The river will wind through some swampy areas, but will then drop almost immediately into another canyon between two points of high relief.

The most amazing feature of the Wathaman, though, is the Wathaman Batholith. It is a formation of mainly granitic rock that was formed in the first mountain-building stage and the island arc collision preceding the continental collision. This red-orange rock was formed below the Earth's surface 1,860 to 1,850 million years ago, and you are surrounded by it. Huge outcroppings, cliffs and escarpments tower over you. The area around the river is high relief, and it is the most rugged Shield country south of the Taiga Shield. In this book, only the Porcupine River compares in terms of high relief.

The old-growth forest you encounter farther down the river is mostly black spruce with some jack pine. All in all, however, the sandy areas, the exposed bedrock, and the 1982 burn make jack pine the predominant forest along the river. There are a number of birch trees as a result of the fire as well. The understory of the black spruce old-growth forest is feather mosses, Labrador tea, bog cranberry, various herbs, lichens and alders. In the jack pine you will find lichen, mosses, low shrubs such as blueberry and bearberry, and herbs.

Some good sources on the geology and ecology of the Wathaman include the *Geological History of Saskatchewan*, the *Atlas of Saskatchewan*, and *The Ecoregions of Saskatchewan*. Full bibliographical details are in the References list at the end of the book.

Local History **

The Wathaman is in what is generally considered Cree territory. The upper Wathaman is too rugged and too remote from the major waterways to have been a major travel route in prehistory or in the fur trade. But the lakes of the lower river are good hunting and fishing areas, and they can be accessed via the river or through chains of lakes and creeks in the summer and by trails in the winter. This is where you see signs of human habitation, cabins and blazes, and in some spots, thank you, portages!

In fact, the lower Wathaman was part of an alternate route from the Churchill to Reindeer Lake. Instead of travelling the Reindeer River, the Cree went up the Paull River to Paull Lake, through a chain of lakes to Maribelli and Hickson and then another chain of lakes to the lower reaches of the Wathaman. The Wathaman took them to Reindeer Lake via Wathaman Lake. This route must have had some importance to the Cree — the narrows between Hickson and Maribelli Lakes (northeast of Paull Lake and the Paull River) is home to one of Canada's largest single pictograph sites. Reindeer Lake is home to the Cree community of Southend.

In 1790, in the early days of the inland trading posts, there was a North West Company trading post by the mouth of the Wathaman on Reindeer Lake called Paint River House.

David Thompson refers to it in his journals. When surveying for the Canadian Geological Survey in 1892, Tyrell thought he had reached the "Vermilion River," as he calls the Paint or Wathaman River, when he had actually reached the Foster (White Fish / Fish River). He eventually figured out that he wasn't heading east to Reindeer Lake. But he was right in that the headwaters of the Wathaman are just east of the Foster Lakes.

It makes perfect sense that the river was called the Vermilion or Paint River, vermilion being the colour of the Wathaman Batholith. It gets better, though. According to Tim Jones's research on the rock paintings of northern Saskatchewan, *Wathaman* is the Woods Cree word ("th" dialect) signifying ochre, the iron oxide thought to make the paint, usually red, for the creation of the pictographs. Indeed, there is a Paint Lake on the Grass River in Manitoba that is mentioned frequently in the HBC explorer journals, which the Cree called Withaman.

Once you have seen the red cliffs of the Wathaman Batholith, it's hard to imagine any other name that could suit this river better. Though I heard something that sounded almost as good on my drive back to La Ronge after two months of canoeing in the Far North. I was stopped by construction on the road, and got to chatting with Rob Clarke, a young man from Southend working as a flag man for the construction crew. I asked him about the river and the origin of the word *wathaman*. He said his father was born in a cabin on Wathaman Lake, but he wasn't familiar with the meaning of the word. Then he told me that *athiman* meant "difficult" in Cree. I couldn't help but laugh out loud! Yes, the Wathaman is *athiman*, and it is also totally amazing.

Later in the summer of 2001, I found a deposit of *wathaman* on the eastern Churchill — an unforgettable moment. This hole in a rock was filled with a rust-coloured material. I reached down and rubbed some of it between my thumb and two first fingers, and it was thick and red, just like paint. Magic.

Solitude ★★★★

Not many people canoe trip down this river — maybe one group every couple of years, if that. It's just too rough. There are no fishing lodges on the river, and only one or two traplines. You can count on not seeing anybody until Wathaman Lake. Dave Bober, an enthusiastic wilderness canoeist from central Saskatchewan, bumped into a group from Wisconsin in 1996. As of 2001, those are the only two groups I know that have made the trip at all. What are the chances they would be on the river at the same time? What are the chances that the Wisconsin group would be going upstream? They were headed to the Foster Lakes. I shudder to think of it. It's a very difficult river to descend — why would anyone want to ascend it? I don't think they had any idea what they were in for.

Wildlife ★★★★

You will encounter more wildlife on the Wathaman than on any other river in this book. One area we called Mooseville, because Sheila and I saw eleven moose in three and a half hours. It makes sense. The burns are rejuvenating the landscape, there is intermittent swamp, lots of moose food in the river, and there are no people around.

The day after seeing the eleven moose, we saw five more moose, once thinking a cow's head was a rock to be avoided. Then, being on moose alert that afternoon, we thought we saw a small blonde moose. But it was actually a wolf in the willows. It loped up the nearby outcrop and stopped to watch our passage. We floated by, admiring it all the way.

I'm sure there are also lots of bears around, as we saw signs. We did see two mink. They are always fun to meet, as they are so curious and such good rapid swimmers. One swam up to the boat from an eddy to check us out as we ran the top of a Class 3 rapid. There were some big beaver lodges, and some tail-slapping at night indicated that other fur-bearing creatures are doing well on the Wathaman.

We saw a large, gray owl in one of the early gorges. It was surprising that there weren't more fishing birds on the river, since it is in the Churchill Uplands, which has a high population of bald eagles and osprey. But, as the fishing wasn't much to write home about, I can see why there weren't as many as expected. The numbers did pick up as we reached more of the small lakes downriver.

Fishing **

As with the Foster and the Haultain, there is no resident walleye population on the Wathaman; the rapids and falls are too much of a barrier. As you reach Wathaman Lake, however, you come into good walleye fishing, especially below McKenzie Rapids.

The weedy bays of the shallow lakes on the Wathaman are home to large northern pike. You won't be disappointed or go hungry.

Special Equipment

You simply must have a Royalex-hull canoe for this river. I'll leave it at that. Solo whitewater boats would be an absolute hoot. Those awful bushwhack portages are the only thing that makes me think twice about running this river in a playboat. I would definitely bring a beefed-up repair kit, including epoxy, extra string and rope, and a good axe and saw. You may need to repair or replace parts of your canoe. The axe and saw can also help make some better portages and get you through the worst of the deadfall. And, should you need to get out, you can use them to clear a helicopter pad.

The bugs weren't too thick in mid-July when we ran the river, but my bug jacket was appreciated on those bushwhack portages, believe me. Bring some insect repellent and good hiking shoes for those babies, and pack carefully.

Trip Notes

MAP	GRID	FEATURE	DESCRIPTION
74 A/15	023033	Put-in Campsite	A point on the east shore of a long, narrow unnamed lake north-east of Burbidge Lake, marked 505 m above sea level. There is an old exploration drill camp on this point with an old dock, and there are numerous level places to set up tents among the stuff left from the camp.
	027021	Campsite	A jack pine bench on RR.
	035034	Rapids	**Class 1**, an unmarked chute at the narrows.
	037037	Power line	Watch for this line to cross again. It's a good reference for a steep drop to come.
	038038	Rapids	**Class 1+**, a narrow, shallow channel with rock dodging required.
	041040 042038	Rapids	**Class 1+ to Class 2**. Narrow chutes with rocks. Where the river narrows is a Class 1+ rapid ending as a Class 2 rock-dodging exercise.
	046038	Rapids	**Class 2**, a rock garden. After a tiny lakelet the river narrows and doglegs to the left.
	048039	Campsite	On RR, rock with jack pine bench in the back.
	053041	Rapids	**Class 2**, a short, unmarked rock garden.

MAP NO	GRID REF	FEATURE	DESCRIPTION
	054040 054029	Rapids	**Class 2+**. In the beginning of the gorge there are unmarked, continuous rapids for 1,100 m. Some sections are unnavigable and require wading to descend. The last kilometre of the high-relief section is fast water. The rapids begin again where the river narrows and becomes a single line on the map again.
	055019 056014	Rapids	**Class 2+**, with 650 m of really narrow "creeking" rapids. Some sections must be waded.
	055013	Powerline	A landmark for the upcoming section with a potentially dangerous ledge drop.
	055011 057003	Rapids	**Class 2+**, marked with three bars, this is a creeking exercise that ends just before a Class 3+/4 ledge rapid at the extremely narrow point in the river indicated by the one bar (after the creek coming in on RR).
	057007 059001	Rapids	**CAUTION: Class 3+/4 ledge drop**. An extremely narrow chute through a gorge. It can be lifted over on RR. Followed by 700 m of **Class 2+** rapids ending with an amazing channel with towering vertical walls leading into a tiny lake.
	061997 062998	Rapids	**Class 2** unmarked rapids sweep to the left and then an island rapid starts. Watch for sweepers in the island channels. We waded the RL channel to avoid sweepers. **CAUTION:** The next 600 m contain a Class 3 rapid, two small falls, a Class 2+ rapid, and one more small falls, all before the river widens again!
	065999	Rapids	**Class 3**. An unmarked rapid. A short rock dodge after the blind corner to the left.
	066999	Falls Campsite	The marked bar on the map on the bend to the right indicates small falls. You must bushwhack portage on RR through an old burn about 75 m. Though it is not very pretty, it is possible to camp here.
	067000	Powerline Falls	Once you see the powerline you are almost on top of the next falls. This 2-m falls must be bushwhack portaged (100 m) on RR through the old burn.
	067001	Rapids	**Class 2+**. Short.
	068002	Falls	We lined and pulled over this falls on RL with great difficulty. This tough section ends in a beautiful fast-water gorge with high rock walls.
	072001	Campsite	A rock outcropping on RR at the far end of the tiny lake is the site of an old drill camp. There is room for a couple of tents in the back and a kitchen on the nice slab of rock overlooking the river. Don't let the small jack pines covering the front of the rock outcrop fool you into thinking you can't camp here.
	073000	Fast water	In the narrows at the outlet of the tiny lake. It goes around a corner to the right.
	073999 074998	Rapids	**Class 1**. Wide rapids around islands. Watch for sweepers.

MAP NO	GRID REF	FEATURE	DESCRIPTION
	079002	Rapids	**Class 1**, at the bend to the right.
	082002 083003	Rapids	**Class 2**. A rock garden splitting around low islets. We waded the RL channel for most of this section because of sweepers.
	084004	Rapids	**Class 3**. A boulder dodge.
	085006	Falls	The bar marked on the map indicates a 2-m falls that must be bushwhack-portaged on RR (175 m).
	088007 088010	Rapids	**Class 2+**, a 225-m rock dodge that we eventually had to line on RL, as the channel became too choked with rocks to navigate.
	085013	Campsite	On RL in the back of a bay where an esker ends there is a small bench.
	097015	Campsite	On RL on a flat rock. A small camp, with room for two tents only.
	099014	Falls	A very big drop represented by the six bars crossing the single line. This is one very long bushwhack portage (600–650 m). We snuck up RL through the preliminary rapids on top of the first big drop to a large, high outcrop. From there we crashed up to the top of the rock ridge and on over the bare rock through the small jack pine. Heading a bit left, we descended into a sphagnum bog with standing deadwood, moved over left again to higher ground on the side of a ridge until almost reaching the small lake. Then we ascended a rock ridge with lots of deadfall. Then it was a short descent to the river just below the falls in a little cove. RR looked better on hindsight (600 m), and to tell you the truth, it couldn't be worse than RL — that was the worst portage I've ever had to make! Dave Bober's group bushwhacked the RR side, we found out after the fact. It's definitely worth a try.
	105010	Rapids	**Class 3**. A 150-m rock dodge.
	110010	Falls	The bar marked on the map is a small falls that we lined on RR.
	155065	Campsite	On RL, the jack pine bench in the small bay looks good for camping. There is old-growth forest for the next 6 km, providing more spots to camp. At least one should suit the size of your group.
	161067	Campsite	On RR. A rock landing with a bench for tents in the back.
	172076	Campsite	On RL just after the islands is a bench for camping.
	178077	Campsite	On RL on a jack pine bench just before the river winds to the right.
	203073 205076	Rapids	**Class 1+/2**. Just when you expect another horrible bushwhack, the spot where the river becomes one line is an easy creeking exercise, about 350 m long. Excellent!
	214095	Campsite	A lovely, open jack pine bench on RL, but it's messy getting through reeds and swampy shoreline. Maybe not worth the effort if you can make another few kilometres today.
	229111 229113	Fast water	At the S-bends there are sections of fast water.

MAP NO	GRID REF	FEATURE	DESCRIPTION
	238122 240122	Campsites	On RR there is a high, open, jack pine bench with good access to level tent sites.
	241124 246127	Campsite Potential Put-in	For those who prefer rock, check out the point on RL. In order to miss the really tough portaging conditions of the upper Wathaman, or if you don't have time for the whole river, you could fly in to this nice lake. There is a sandy beach landing for the plane. Across this narrow lake is a trapper's cabin.
	242130	Cabin	In a bay on RL.
	300150	Rapids	**Class 1+**. Short.
74 A/16	307147	Rapids	**Class 2 becoming Class 3**. A marked bar represents a rock garden followed by a tricky boulder drop. The entire rapid is 150 m long.
	309145	Rapids	**Class 1**, a straightforward chute.
	307140	Rapids	**Class 2+**. A rock dodge that precedes 250 m of difficult whitewater. Caution is advised.
	307142 306139	Rapids	**Class 3+ followed by Class 4**. The marked bar represents a Class 3+ rapid with large rocks in a very twisty section. Right after this drop is another even more difficult one. Lining or wading this section is strongly recommended.
	305136 305133	Campsites	On RL an open jack pine bench provides a number of possible sites. The only drawback is the bank of willow that you must navigate to get to the bench. But on the Wathaman, one can't be too picky!
	313122	Campsite	A small site for two tents on RL. A flat rock kitchen with one tent spot behind and one to the side.
	312119	Rapids	**Class 1**, an easy rapid just before a sharp bend to the left.
	314120	Campsite	High on RL is an outcrop that is flat on top for tents.
	316117	Rapids	**Class 1+**. Two chutes.
	316114 316112	Rapids	**Class 2+/3**. Rock dodging and waves for 200 m. The rapids go around a blind corner to the right and then back to the left.
	317111	Falls	The falls are represented by one bar mark on the map. Now, believe it or not, there is a trail of sorts on RR. Dare I say, **portage**? The falls actually start 100 m above where the mark is on the map, and the portage starts about 20 m above there. The cut trail begins on a mossy bank opening and ends **200 m** later in minor rapids below the falls. These minor rapids can be lined or run.
	321110 321103	Rapids	**Class 3+ on average**. This last section of narrow, twisty river before the junction with a long lake is about 900 m of steep creeking. Wading and lining is required to negotiate some sections, even by exceptional canoeists. Boulders and blind drops abound. Go slowly and carefully.
	325105	Campsite	A bench with good water access provides camping on RL.
	329104	Campsite	A smaller site on open old-growth forest bench on RR.

MAP NO	GRID REF	FEATURE	DESCRIPTION
	363128	Campsite	An open area on an esker on RL.
	377152	Campsite	A nice bench on RR with old-growth spruce and jack pine mix.
	380167	Campsite	A nice spot on an esker in old-growth jack pine on RR.
74 H/1	377190 373194	Rapids	**Class 1.** Three class 1 chutes in the narrows, about 150 m apart.
	375204	Campsite	On a point on RR on an old-growth jack pine bench.
	379210	Campsite	More bench around the corner in a protected bay on RR.
	403222	Rapids	**Class 2,** a rock garden.
	405225 407225	Rapids	**Class 2+,** 175 m of rock dodging in the narrows.
	418229	Rapids	**Class 2 followed by Class 2+.** The bend to the right of the S-turn is Class 2. The marked bar is a Class 2+ rock dodge on the turn to the left.
	423232	Campsite	A nice old-growth jack pine bench on RR. In the next 15 km, Sheila and I saw eleven moose!
	431225	Campsites	A long stretch of open old-growth jack pine bench on RL. There's good camping along here.
	428205	Rapids	**Class 1+/2.** Short.
	455197	Rapids	**Class 2.** Short.

Note: According to my reading, there's a map error. The two bars marking rapids at 457194 and 460193 are in the wrong place. The rapids are actually as indicated below:

	461188 462187	Rapids	**Class 2+.** At a bend to the right is a ledge that can easily be scouted on RR. It can be run far RR or far RL. A Class 2 rapid follows the ledge, becoming a Class 2+ as it ends above the islands indicated on the map.
	463186	Campsite	On RR at a rock outcrop.
	464184	Riffle	A shallow riffle downstream of the first island.
74 A/16	479141	Campsite	A great camp on an esker on RR in the far north end of a bay, with a great view down the lake.
	481135	Campsite	A campsite on a high rock outcrop on RR. There is a tiny beach for those who prefer the sand or who want a dip in the bathtub. There's a nice view of cliffs and moose.
	491137	Rapids	**Class 2+ becoming Class 3.** The five marked bars after the lake, a set of three and then two, represent in reality an almost continuous 600-m stretch of Class 2+ becoming Class 3 rapids where the last two bars are. There are two good places to scout on RR using eddies and outcrops. One spot is at the top of the first rapid and the other is before the final drop. In higher water, the waves may make this a more difficult rapid.
	497133	Rapids	**Class 1+.** Short.

the trips

MAP NO	GRID REF	FEATURE	DESCRIPTION
	503133	Rapids	**Class 1+**, an easy chute.
	504134	Campsite	On RL there is an old-growth jack pine bench for camping.
	512136	Campsite	In a bay on RR facing east is the shoulder of a long jack pine bench that makes for good camping.
	514124	Campsite	On RL at a corner by a rock outcrop is a jack pine bench for camping.
	520104	Falls	This is the first of two falls in the section we dubbed Double Falls. This pretty, improperly marked waterfall goes around both sides of the island shown on the map and continues to just past the marked bar. The falls can be portaged on RR, but it is a tough bushwhack of about 350 m through old burn. It starts above the fast water of the falls and ends below the falls in a bit of a cove. Not very pleasant, to say the least. But the falls run over lovely smooth rock. Take a break on the island below the falls and enjoy the place.
	522102 523101	Rapids Falls	Around the next island, the second of three islands in this stretch, there is a **Class 2** rapid. It must be navigated to reach the third and last island where the portage is for the second falls that flow around the island. You can stop to scout this preliminary rapid on a large rock point on RR. You want to take the RR channel around the island to reach the **portage (523100)**, which is over the smooth, bare rock on the island's right side and around to the back of it to below the main channel of the falls **(75 m)**. We camped on the right side of the island on the rocks. There's not room for more than one or two tents, but it's a great spot to stop for a while.
	531097	Rapids	**Class 2+**. This 800-m-long rock garden starts 100 m above the four marked bars and ends where the river widens after the solitary bar mark. There is a break of slow water at the hairpin turn, and there are lots of eddies to scout from. You can **portage** the majority of the rapid on a trail (!) cut on RR. It is about **450 m**.
	534092	Campsite	In a bay on RL there is a rock outcrop with tent sites up top and behind where it is flat; three tents maximum.
	545070	Campsite	A nice, high, old-growth jack pine bench on RL at a bend to the right.
	538044	Campsite	This lovely lake is so Shield. The first of two camp spots is a rock outcrop on RR with old-growth jack pine in behind.
	540041	Campsite	On RL on a cozy little point with rock and old growth.
	548025	Campsite	On RL up in birch trees there is a grassy opening.
	547020	Cabin	An old trapper's cabin sits on a point on RR at a narrow outlet of the channel from Evelyn Lake.
	554024	Campsite	On RR on a rock shelf. Small, with only room for a couple of tents.
	555028	Eagle Nest	On RL, on the point by the rock outcrop. A swampy area begins shortly and lasts for approximately 7 km, and there is no camping again for almost 10 km.

MAP NO	GRID REF	FEATURE	DESCRIPTION
64 D/13	620060 622055	Bell Rapids	Class 2/2+. An 1,100-m rapid with three parts to it. The first part flows east and is a difficult Class 2 rock dodge — more like Class 2+ in high water. The second part is Class 2, and it comes after the flatwater at the bend to the south or right. There is a chute at the top and there are some shallow rocks at the end. This section can be scouted easily from RR. The final part is Class 2 and begins after a stretch of fast water. There is a small ledge with a rock apron following it at the end. There is a good **portage** trail (**500 m**) on RR (compliments of the trappers) that goes over the saddle and cuts off the piece of land that Bell Rapids wrap around. The landing is on RR in the bay before the rapids start (**620058**).
	624047	Campsite	On RR at flat rocks facing upstream. Tent sites are in behind on moss.
	635055	Fast water	
	639053 654056	Stuart Rapids	This is longest, and I consider the most difficult rapid of the four named rapids that make up the last of the whitewater. Exceptional paddling skills are required to navigate Stuart Rapids. There is a **2,000-m portage** on RL that starts just above the rapids at a cut opening in the jack pine.

There are five parts to 1,600-m-long Stuart Rapids.

- **Class 2.** The first section begins 150 m before the bars marked on the map. This rock dodge goes around the first bend to the left.
- **Class 3.** Where the river turns to the right is a Class 3 rock dodge with big waves (at the "S" in Stuart).
- **Class 3+/4.** This third section is almost continuous with the second section, but it comes where the river is narrowest (at the "A" in Stuart), and there is a Class 4 drop. It is a boulder ledge right at the narrows with big waves. It is possible to eddy out just before the drop on RR and scout, and the RR chute is possible at certain water levels. This is a very difficult place to line, and I don't recommend running this rapid to anyone who is not willing to take on the potential danger of this section of gorge.
- **Class 2+/3.** The fourth part of the rapid begins at the bend to the left after the extreme narrows (between the "R" and "A" in Rapids) and works up to a Class 3 boulder dodge.
- **Class 2.** The final section is where the river widens out and there are some rocks to avoid (at the "S" in Rapids).

	666057 673060	Cowan Rapids	Class 2+/3. This set is 900 m of continuous rapids. It has some big waves like Stuart, but the rapids are mostly technical rock dodging. There is a steep boulder apron at the end. There is a **portage (1,000 m)** on RR that goes through the muskeg. It starts in a little bay to the right of the beginning of the rapids.
	678062	Camping	It is possible, in a pinch, to make a camp high up on a rock outcrop on RR where it is flat.
	687077 689082	McKenzie Rapids	**Class 3 and Class 4 followed by Class 2+.** This last of the named rapids has two sections. The first begins in the channels around the mid-river island. The right or southeast channel has a Class 3 rapid, with a boulder ledge in the middle, which can be scouted on rocks on RL (the right shore of the island). The left or northwest channel begins with a Class 1+ chute, but has a Class 4 ledge rapid

MAP NO	GRID REF	FEATURE	DESCRIPTION
			at the bottom of it. This first section of the McKenzie can be portaged on RR **(250 m)**. After the island is the second section of the rapids, and there are two bars that represent a Class 2+ rapid that actually begins 100 m before the first bar. This section can be portaged on RR **(175 m)** by the cautious canoeist using the trail cut by the trappers. It starts at the head of the rapids.
	689086	Riffle	There are small, easy rapids in the final narrows before reaching Wilson Peninsula on Wathaman Lake.
	690088	Campsite	On RL at the widening of the river is a rock outcropping with some flat tent sites in behind. There's good fishing for walleye and pike in the eddies here.
	710113	Camping	A rock point on RL.
	716125	Cabins	Two cabins belonging to Robert McLeod, the trapper in the area.
	737133	Cabin	An old trapper cabin, well hidden in the bush in a small bay.
	738137	Campsite	A sandy beach on RL in a bay.
	748125	Camping	This group of broken islands is absolutely stunning. Check out the smooth-rock camping available; exposed, but exquisite.

Note: The length of Wathaman Lake has great rock and beach camping opportunities and very little burn. A nice lake with good fishing. Enjoy!

MAP NO	GRID REF	FEATURE	DESCRIPTION
64 E/4	757208	Possible fly-out point Campsite	Sand beach, and great camping too.
	764267	Bridge Take-out	On RR is good access to Highway 905. Camping on RR is possible if you have to wait for your ride.

Left: Author admiring the bounty of the boreal forest on a Paull River trip.

Below: Mirror image: Photograph of a pictograph of a canoe taken from a canoe at Smith Narrows en route to the Paull.

Above: Flowing over smooth rocks, chocolate-coloured rocks, and through red granite gorges, the Haultain River is home to many spectacular falls.

Left: A fair-weather camp on Wintego Lake on the eastern Churchill. Nothing makes for a sounder sleep than billion-year-old Precambrian bedrock.

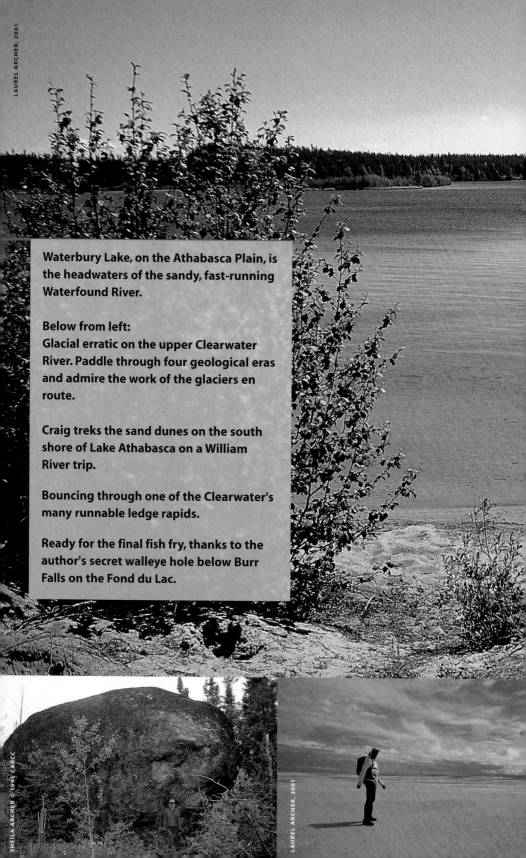

Waterbury Lake, on the Athabasca Plain, is the headwaters of the sandy, fast-running Waterfound River.

Below from left:
Glacial erratic on the upper Clearwater River. Paddle through four geological eras and admire the work of the glaciers en route.

Craig treks the sand dunes on the south shore of Lake Athabasca on a William River trip.

Bouncing through one of the Clearwater's many runnable ledge rapids.

Ready for the final fish fry, thanks to the author's secret walleye hole below Burr Falls on the Fond du Lac.

LAUREL ARCHER, 2001

Into the blue: Flying across magical Wollaston Lake to run the Fond du Lac.

LAUREL ARCHER, 2001

Above: What's a few hay-stacks between friends? Running the big water of Otter Rapids on the Churchill River.

Right: The impossibly green waves of the Churchill will steal your heart and expand your soul.

SHEILA ARCHER © 1991 CAR

GEIKIE RIVER

The Geikie River is an excellent, short, wilderness canoe trip for those looking for a bit of a whitewater rush. Besides having lots of rapids, it has a variety of scenery, good fishing and high potential for wildlife viewing. The Geikie flows northeast into Wollaston Lake, a wonderful gateway to the Far North.

The river is of medium volume for northern Saskatchewan, and the rapids are technical. It's a river for canoeists who thrive on back ferries and boulder gardens. The landscape of the Geikie has a nature all its own, as it sits between the Athabasca Plain and the Churchill Uplands. There is much evidence of the glaciers, with long eskers snaking along the river. Frequent Precambrian rock outcroppings, mottled with orange and black lichen, dot the landscape. Unfortunately, the Geikie has been burned quite often over the past twenty years, and again in 2001. This makes for fewer nice campsites in places. Moreover, many of the rapids no longer have portages, making the trip more difficult for less experienced whitewater paddlers.

In 1992, Brad and I had a big black bear chase us out of our campsite below the Wheeler River's last set of rapids, lost the lid to one of our barrels while photographing a moose on Middleton Lake, and caught a big trout on a small lake off the confluence of the Wheeler and the Geikie — thanks to a lure given to us by some fishermen we bumped into. We had forgotten all the fishing tackle at our last campsite! My second trip in 2001 was less entertaining, but I did paddle past a forest fire. And I saw another bear. It was on the side of the river above the second set of falls, which has a tricky blind-corner portage landing at the best of times!

Length

The trip described here is approximately 85 km. It starts on Big Sandy Lake at an island at the northeast end of the lake and ends at Highway 105 just before the river reaches Wollaston Lake. It is possible to do this Geikie trip in five or six days, if the water level and your whitewater skill level allow you to run most of the shallow, rocky rapids. Wading and lining takes much more time. Portages on the Geikie are not easy, and some are no longer in existence. Bushwhacking is very time-consuming!

An option for extending the trip is to fly into Highrock Lake and paddle via the fast and rocky Highrock River to Big Sandy Lake. That will add approximately 35 km to the trip outlined in the river notes and a couple of long days. You could also choose to paddle more of Big Sandy Lake, or you could take out at a fishing camp with road access or a provincial campsite on Wollaston Lake. To make a really long expedition that was drive-in and drive-out you could start at Otter Rapids and ascend the Churchill and Foster Rivers to Foster Lakes and portage over into the headwaters of the Geikie and paddle its entire length to Wollaston Lake. That would be an adventure!

Big Sandy Lake to Highway 105*	85 km
Wilson Bay via Highrock River to Highway 105	120 km

* This is the trip described in detail in the Trip Notes section.

Topographic Maps

I recommend the 1:50,000 scale, maps 74H/2, 74H/7, 74H/8, 74H/9 and 64E/12. I suggest you purchase these maps in advance and use the map coordinates in the Trip Notes section to mark in the rapids missing from the originals. There are a number of them. An error of note

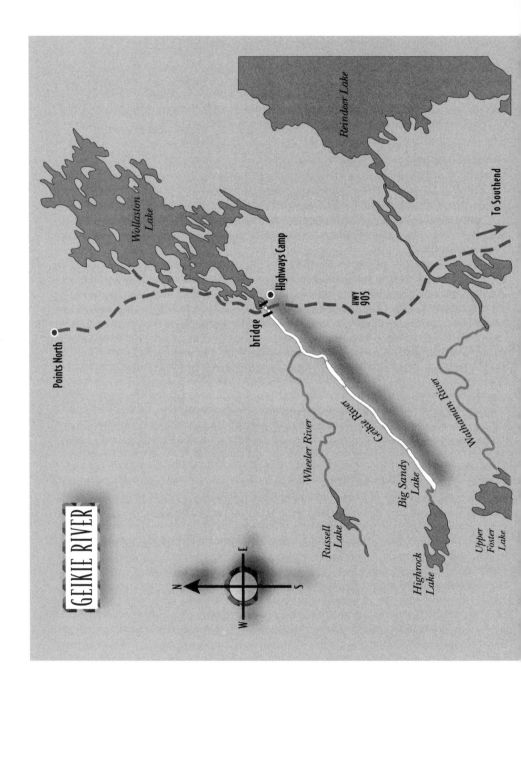

GEIKIE RIVER

Points North

Wollaston Lake

Reindeer Lake

Highways Camp

bridge

HWY 905

To Southend

Wheeler River

Geikie River

Russell Lake

Big Sandy Lake

Wathaman River

Highrock Lake

Upper Foster Lake

N
E
S
W

is that the first falls is mislabelled as a rapid. As well, campsites are sparse in places, so marking in the campsites from the notes is a good idea. Plan your stops ahead of time where possible. You will need 74H/3 if you plan to paddle from Highrock Lake, and beware, the rapids are not all marked on that map either! There is a SERM canoe-trip booklet for the Geikie trip described here, number 38, however it has not been updated since the last burn on the lower Geikie. You can print it from the Canoe Saskatchewan website or order it by calling SERM.

Getting There and Away

Most people fly in to the Geikie. The most convenient way to do a fly-in and drive-out trip is to arrange to fly out from the Saskatchewan Highways camp on the right or east side of Highway 105 just before the bridge. A couple of the larger fishing lodges on Wollaston Lake have their own floatplanes, and Points North has an Otter and a Beaver for charter. You can drive to the Highways camp, leave your vehicle there, and fly out to Big Sandy. Then you paddle back to the camp, pick up your vehicle, and away you go.

The other fly-in, drive-out option is booking a floatplane with Osprey Wings, which is based in Missinipe. You can leave your vehicle there or at Churchill River Canoe Outfitters. You paddle to the bridge and either hitch a ride back down to Missinipe to get your vehicle or arrange for a shuttle. Churchill River Canoe Outfitters offers a shuttle service. They will pick you up with your vehicle or theirs for a fee. You may be able to get a backhaul with the outfitter on Highrock Lake, making for a cheaper flight from Missinipe. See the Directory of Services for contact information.

When to Go

End of May to July. If you go too early in May, the ice may still be on Big Sandy Lake. If you go too late in the season, this lower-volume river running through fast-draining, sandy country will be very difficult to navigate. I've paddled the Geikie twice, once at higher water in June 1992 (57 cu m/sec) and once at low water in July 2001 (42 cu m/sec). Other paddlers familiar with the Geikie agree that normal to slightly higher water is better for running the river than lower levels.

There is a "real time" water-level gauging station in operation just after the confluence of the Wheeler and the Geikie, so you can call SaskWater at 306-694-3966, or fax them at 306-694-3944 for current water levels. You can get last month's flows off their website by clicking on hydrology and then Reindeer River Basin. To put that reading into context, see the monthly and yearly mean discharge charts that include the Geikie River on the Canoe Saskatchewan website, at www.lights.com/waterways/local/various.htm.

If the river is running at less than 35 cu m/sec, I would choose another river. The lower water will increase your chances of a canoe wrap remarkably, and it will be a lot more work getting down the river wading and lining.

You could also call Churchill River Canoe Outfitters about the water level on the Geikie. Someone there generally knows what the water levels are like on any given river in northern Saskatchewan, as many canoeists share their recent trip information with the staff. You could also try the SERM field office in Wollaston.

Difficulty of the River ***

The Geikie gets three stars because of its isolation and the long, winding, shallow rapids where even the best read-as-you-run paddlers will be challenged. The rapids average is Class 2/2+, but they are on the longer side — 500 m on average. They usually open out into wide boulder fans at the end, where the water is shallow, and navigation becomes a real challenge. At low water levels many rapids will have to be waded, even by highly skilled paddlers. At high water levels the large number of rocks, combined with little opportunity to get out and scout or line easily from shore, result in demanding rapids, which canoeists must carefully pick their way down either by paddling or wading and lining. There are also a number of tricky ledges to negotiate.

There are few portages on the Geikie anymore. The ones that are there, except for the two around the falls, are in generally poor condition, having been burned or not used frequently. The two mandatory portages of the falls are in relatively good condition, but the portage on river left of Big Baby Rapids, the almost 2-km set in the last section of the river, was burned in 2001. It will be very difficult to traverse for the next few years, even if it is recut.

There are no large lake crossings to make. Of course, you can expect wind on Middleton Lake, but it is narrow, and a storm coming up fast is not a hazard.

Do not make the Geikie your first major wilderness river trip; it is too difficult for inexperienced whitewater paddlers by themselves. It is a good choice for intermediate paddlers wanting to challenge themselves. Cautious and less-skilled paddlers will have to choose between the challenges of trying to wade or line and bushwhacking. Recognize that you will be wading in moving water on a rocky river bed, and the potential for ankle and knee injury or entrapment is high.

The Geikie drops 95 m from Big Sandy Lake to Wollaston Lake. The gradient for the river section of the trip is 1.12 m/km (5.89 ft/mi), which is a steep gradient for a northern Saskatchewan river, especially considering that only two falls occur along its length. The steep, rocky rapids make up the majority of the drop.

Character of the River and Region

The Geikie starts off fairly narrow, and most of the rapids are narrow in the upper reaches of the river until the moderate volume of the river increases slightly after the Wheeler River junction. Though the river becomes wider, it is shallow from start to finish. The riverbed is a mixture of sand and erosion-rounded rocks, ranging from small, egg-shaped rocks to large, Volkswagen-sized boulders. There are also ledge formations where the river flows over exposed shelves of Precambrian rock. The boulder and rock gardens of the Geikie are tight, and some require instantaneous decisions and precise manoeuvring to run. The majority of the rapids end in a big fan, making the bottom sections of most of them harder to navigate than the top. I think the Geikie is a great solo boat run for canoeists making the step up; there are few lakes and good current.

The Geikie lies completely in the Boreal Shield ecozone. However, it is in a transitional area between the Churchill Uplands ecoregion to the south and east and the Athabasca Plain ecoregion to the north and northwest. This makes for a varied environment. Compared to southern rivers in the Churchill Uplands, there is more sand and glacial till, with fewer wetlands and smaller trees. The landscape is less rugged, and there are fewer lakes.

Sediments originating from the Athabasca sandstone to the west and north largely cover the area, but the underlay is Precambrian Shield rock. The relief is made up of hummocky moraine with some drumlins and prominent eskers, some of which are as long as 50 km. The glacial deposits mark the northeast-southwest direction of the ice movement. Soils along the Geikie are more sandy, making jack pine the dominant forest. As fires are very common on the Highrock and Wollaston Lake Plains, the jack pine forests are at different stages of regeneration all along the river.

There are rock cliffs of red granite and foliated dark gray gneiss, mottled with orange and black lichens. Sometimes the riverbank hosts black spruce in beds of feather mosses. Old man's beard or witch's hair hangs on them, as is common in the wetter areas of the Churchill Uplands. There are also a few weedy, marshy shores interspersed along the banks of the Geikie.

Ironically, though there are many fine campsites on the river, when you really want a campsite, it is sometimes hard to find one. This is because of the transitional nature of the environment of the river, and the fact that the Geikie has borne the brunt of many forest fires over the past twenty years, taking another hit in the summer of 2001. The area around the Wheeler confluence burned, as did the lower Geikie around Big Baby Rapids. All in all, though there are still some pretty sections, the Geikie isn't in the top ten for amazing camping or scenery, but it is an interesting river in terms of natural history. Plus the rapids are lots of fun!

Local History ✱✱✱

The Geikie River lies in an area that might have once been a buffer zone between traditional Cree and Dene territory before the arrival of the fur traders from Europe. At this time, Dene territory is thought to have extended from north of the Clearwater River to south of Cree Lake to northern Reindeer Lake. It is of note that Wollaston Lake was called Manito Lake in David Thompson's day, as *Manitou* is Cree for "creator or spirit." The lake was an object of awe, as two rivers flowed out of it yet the lake was never drained. Manito Lake was renamed Wollaston by Sir John Franklin. He travelled overland from Cumberland House to Fort Chipewyan in the first winter of his ill-fated first expedition to the Arctic. Franklin named the lake, which is the largest lake totally within the boundaries of Saskatchewan, for William Hyde Wollaston (1766–1828), an English chemist and physicist.

The Dene people traditionally moved with the seasons and the caribou in the transitional forest and barrenlands. However, sometime around the mid-1700s some Dene bands began to winter south of Cree Lake and summer in the upper Churchill region. This move south was more evident after the smallpox epidemic of 1781 decimated the Cree. In the late 1700s, this group of Dene are thought to have summered as far south as Dore and Smoothstone Lakes. They would descend the Mudjatik River to the Churchill, and then take the Beaver River south. To return to their wintering grounds south of Cree Lake, they would return via the Smoothstone River to the Churchill. They would then ascend the Foster River or one of its sisters to their hunting and trapping areas.

Evidence suggests the Dene from the Wollaston Lake and Reindeer Lake regions used the Geikie and the Foster to reach the Churchill to get to Ile-à-la-Crosse. The Geikie might also have been an alternate route for the Fond du Lac Dene communities in the Lake Athabasca region. Instead of travelling the MacFarlane or the Cree to Cree Lake and on down the Mudjatik to the Churchill, they could take the Fond du Lac/Geikie/Foster route. There was also a canoe route from Cree Lake to Wollaston Lake via the Wheeler (Poorfish) River and the Geikie. Once at Wollaston Lake, travellers could reach the eastern Churchill via Swan River / Reindeer Lake / Reindeer River and all points west, south and east from there. The Geikie was a river of some importance for the people of the Far North — a gateway to all points south. For more information on the research into the prehistory and history of the region around the Geikie, consult Dale Russell's *Eighteenth Century Western Cree and their Neighbours*, the *Atlas of Saskatchewan*, and the Canoe Saskatchewan website.

In 1892, Tyrrell and Dowling reported finding old portage trails on the Geikie, evidence of First Nations' use of the river. They were searching for a southward-running river to access the Churchill while collecting information for the Geological Survey of Canada. Tyrrell decided to name this river after another man of the hour, this time a geology professor of his, a Professor James Geikie of Edinburgh, whom Tyrrell noted had "done so much to foster the study of glacial geology," and who eventually became "the eminent director of the Geological Survey of Great Britain." From Tyrrell's notebooks and an earlier map he had of the river, it appears the Geikie was once known as the Drifting River. I can't help wondering about his renaming so many amazing places in northern Saskatchewan, as most were already aptly named. Regardless of my views on Tyrrell's choice of names for geographical features in northern Saskatchewan, his *Report on the Country Between Athabasca Lake and Churchill River* is a gold mine for canoeists interested in the rivers of northern Saskatchewan. You can read about Tyrrell's survey of the Geikie in the report, or check it out online. See the References pages for the website.

Trappers Ed Theriau (for which Unknown Lake was renamed) and Fred Derbyshire trapped in the Russell (Poorfish) Lake area to the northwest of the Geikie. The books *Face the North Wind*, by A. L. Karras, and *Lost Land of the Caribou*, by Patricia Armstrong and Ed Theriau, make for interesting reading about the Geikie River region. They can be found online at deep-river.jkcc.com/face.html and deep-river.jkcc.com/lost.html respectively.

Level of Solitude ✱✱✱

The Geikie is a very good short trip for wilderness solitude. There are no communities along the river, and signs of modern human activity are in evidence only as you paddle the last flatwater section to Wollaston Lake. A few cabins along the way and a campground just before the bridge aren't much to quibble about. Chances are, if you have company at all, it will be a bear or a fishing party. The Geikie and the Wheeler confluence is an Arctic grayling hotspot. Walleye fishing is big on the Geikie in June. You may see a fishing party if you visit the final rapids on the Wheeler, and you will probably meet a party at the bottom of the Big Baby Rapids or at the last rapids before you reach the bridge. In June or July, the peak season for paddling, you may see another party of canoeists, but I doubt it.

Wildlife ✱✱✱

Since travel is difficult in this remote country and the river runs through the rich Churchill Uplands, wildlife is plentiful. Moose, black bears and timber wolves are your best bet for wildlife sightings. Beware of campsites near good fishing spots (such as below the Wheeler's last rapids). This is where a big, and I mean big, black bear chased Brad and me out of our camp. It was early in the morning, and when he looked in our tent he woke me up. Needless to say, I was surprised to awake face-to-face with a large bear with a fish carcass in his mouth. I quickly roused Brad, and we tried everything to get him to go away, but to no avail. He licked our environmental stove grate for a while as we took the tent down, and then as we packed the rest of the gear up he lay around, napping. We chucked our poorly packed bags and barrels into the canoe and skeedaddled!

There are woodland caribou in the area, but it would be very rare to see them. There are lots of eagles on the river.

Fishing ✱✱✱

The fishing on the Geikie can be very good. In the shallow, rocky, fast water, you can catch Arctic grayling. Or try fishing below the creeks running into the river with small spinner spoons, unless you have a fly rod and flies. Fly-fishing is best for grayling. Walleye and northern pike can be found in the usual locations, but the walleye are not in the upper reaches. Don't bother looking for them until you have portaged the second falls. Hereafter they can be found in the eddies below rapids. Fish the eddy line. The northern pike are everywhere, but especially along weedy shores by rapids.

Special Equipment

The best choice for a canoe is a Royalex-hull tripping canoe with Kevlar skid plates to protect it from the inevitable hard knocks. A Royalex canoe is ideal for this kind of shallow, back-country river — it is a slippery toboggan when you run out of water, and if you do happen to wrap it around one of the countless big rocks, it will quite often regain its shape again if you can get of off the rock and carry on down the river. The worst choice of material for a canoe for this river is aluminum. It will stick to every rock you touch and is impossible to slide over rocks and ledges in the shallows. You could also paddle a Kevlar or fibreglass canoe; either will skid over rocks, but both are vulnerable to crushing if pinned hard on a boulder. The canoe-wrapping rapids found on the Geikie are the reason why they make Royalex canoes, so use the proper tool for the job.

Bring insect repellent. The Geikie is normally run early in the season and that means the blackflies will be bad. Bring a bug hat or jacket. A good axe and saw to help with the portage clean-up after the burn is recommended.

Trip Notes

MAP NO	GRID REF	FEATURE	DESCRIPTION
74H/2	032355	Put-in point	On the northeast side of the island at the northeast end of Big Sandy Lake, approximately 2 km from the narrows where the Geikie flows out.
	044358	Campsite	A high campsite on a rock outcropping on RR just before the narrows.
	053365	Rapids	**Class 1**, an unmarked riffle.
	063372	Rapids	**Class 1+**, where the river narrows. Rocky.
	066374	Rapids	**Class 2**. This unmarked, easy Class 2 rapid occurs where the river narrows and begins to curve to the north or your left, **but caution is advised. You are approaching a Class 5 falls.** Immediately after the Class 2 rapid you must catch the eddy on RL in order to portage the Class 3 rapid at the top of the Class 5 falls (improperly marked as rapids) that begins as the river bends to the right.
	067375 068379	Falls Campsite	The **portage (525 m)** is found in a small bay on RL and is indicated by an opening in the willows. The path is steep at both ends and is only in fair condition. There is a campsite halfway through the portage.
	119429 124432	Rapids	**Class 2**, where the river narrows again. The rapids are 500 m long and rocky.
74H/7	143452 153456	Rapids	**Class 2**, 900 m of winding rapids that become more shallow and more difficult as you descend. The first half is easy boulder dodging, but the second half becomes more and more of a boulder fan, making for a more difficult run.
	170475 174477	Rapids	**Class 2+/3**. The rapids start with a narrow, fast channel that turns sharply left. Just after the tight bend there are ledges, creating holes in higher water. One ledge extends from the RR shore to RC. The rapids end in a Class 2 boulder fan. The original portage was lost in a forest fire, so it's a bushwhack, and the bush is thick and difficult to walk through.
	178481 178485	Rapids	**Class 2**. A 400-m rock garden with small ledges to avoid.
	185485	Campsite	On RR an esker provides good camping.
	186495 190495	Rapids	**Class 2+**. Very rocky rapid above an island. RL has the channel with the most water for navigation; the RR channel is shallow, and better for lining and wading. There's no portage.

Map No	Grid Ref	Feature	Description
	207502 210503	Falls	The **portage (225 m)** starts on RL after some Class 1 fast water. There is a blind corner before the small eddy that you must catch on RL to land at the portage. In high water conditions and if you are concerned about locating and catching the eddy, you should land before the sharp corner to scout the location of the eddy and the portage. Then carefully descend the fast water above the falls. Watch for wildlife! I call it Surprise Bear Falls.
	219512 220513	Rapids	**Class 1+**, very rocky and shallow; wading may be necessary. These rapids may be unnavigable at low water.
	220513	Campsite	On an esker on RL following the rapids above. Burn for the next 2 to 3 km makes for poor camping.
	238540	Rapids	**Class 1, 2, 3+.** The rapids begin with a section of easy, fast water. The second section is Class 2, and begins after approximately 175 m of quieter water. The third section is Class 3 because of ledges, which can be difficult to navigate depending on the water level. There is a particularly nasty one to run or bypass on RR at the sharp turn to the left. The high rock banks and speed of the river make it almost impossible to line or wade this ledge in high water. You can **portage** using the old riverbed that begins on RL approximately 30 m above the sharp turn to the left. The dry riverbed brings you out to the top of the small island in the middle of the last section of the rapids. The left channel can be run or waded depending on the flow, but the right channel is shallow and unnavigable at most flows.
	248550 252552	Rapids	**Class 2+.** There are 250 m of straightforward rapids with some small holes and rocks to be avoided.
	256557 252552	Rapids	**Class 2+.** These rapids are similar to the previous ones, but the last half of the set is more difficult than the top, as a number of small ledges create holes near the bottom.
	265568	Campsite	On the northwest side of a small island on RL, approximately 1.25 km downstream from the last rapid. Middleton Lake is next.
74H/8	389709	Campsite	In a small bay on RL at the north end of the lake.
	417718	Rapids	**Class 2**, a short rock garden.
	421715 423714	Rapids	**Class 2+**, with ledges to avoid. You may have to line or pull over in higher water. Rock gardens follow for 125 m.
	424714	Campsite	On RL below the rapids is a good campsite.
	432721	Rapids	**Class 1**, a riffle
74H/9	441736 442740	Rapids	**Class 3, 2.** A big S-turn rapid. The main channel has two Class 3 ledges just below a side creek on RR. In higher water, you can sneak down the side creek, or in lower water line it. The bottom of the set is Class 2. A rock garden.
	451797	Campsite	On an esker point on RL. The 2001 burn starts.

MAP NO	GRID REF	FEATURE	DESCRIPTION
	459811	Confluence Fishing hole	The Wheeler River enters the Geikie here, and if you like fishing there are a couple of places to try. For grayling, proceed approximately 1.5 km up to the Wheeler's last rapid. Camping at the jack pine bench there, which is now partially burned as of June 2001, is not a great idea, as the bears may come to visit to see what the fishermen left them to eat. On your return to the Geikie, try the unnamed long lake running parallel to the Geikie for lake trout. Its entrance starts at 471818.
	489825	Water survey station Rapids	**Class 2.** A straightforward run just after the water survey station on RL. Rocky in lower water levels.
	493829 508838	Big Baby Rapids	**Class 2+/3, 2.** This is an almost continuous stretch of whitewater for nearly 2 km. RR is the most obvious run. About 800 m down there is a difficult spot where the river curves to the left. The rapid then gets easier (Class 2) and ends in a boulder fan. There was a portage of sorts on RL, however the 2001 burn is going to do that in. In the future you are looking at an 1,800-m bushwhack through burn, unless someone recuts it. Additionally, lining or wading this rapid is going to become more and more difficult as the burned trees fall along the shore. Be sure to allow for extra time to descend this section. Fishing is good in the fast water.
	527866	Rapids	**Class 2 and 3.** The last rapids before the bridge are divided by an island. The right channel is Class 2, while the left side is Class 3 with ledges.
	525868	Campsite	A nice site on RL in the old burn.
64E/12		Take-out	15 km of flatwater paddling and you are at the bridge where Highway 105 crosses the Geikie. There are three cabins along this stretch. The provincial campground is on RL before the bridge, and the Saskatchewan Highways buildings are on RR after the bridge.

geikie river

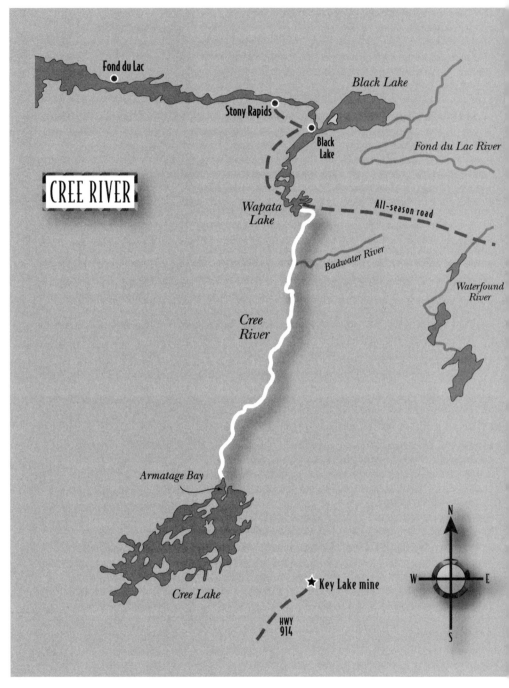

CREE RIVER

You don't so much paddle the Cree River as cruise it. The current is fast, and it can be a quick trip if you don't have to face a strong north wind. Solo tripping, I easily did 40 km a day. But you don't want to rush this gem of a true wilderness trip. There is great esker hiking and fabulous fishing on the Cree. You get to run lots of small rapids, and there are no mandatory portages!

Flowing north in a fairly straight line until Wapata Lake, this river eventually feeds into Black Lake. The Cree passes through the epitome of the Athabasca Plain landscape. There are black spruce lowlands along the river, but it flows mostly through moraine. Drumlins and eskers are the main features of this level landscape. There is often little underbrush in the mainly coniferous forests, making short hikes an option in many places. Marvelous jack pine bench campsites are all over in the high sandy areas. Sometimes it's difficult to choose between them!

Because there is no access to the Cree Lake area other than by floatplane, and there are no communities anywhere between there and Black Lake, the wildlife and fish populations are high. The river is very shallow in places, and I saw thirteen moose standing in the water eating. I spent as much time moose watching as I did enjoying the excellent grayling and northern pike fishing.

The whitewater isn't a stretch — running out of water is your main concern. Beyond a few ledges, the rapids never exceed Class 2. It's just plain fun to run the Cree.

Length

The trip described here is approximately 200 km long. It starts in Armatage Bay at the far northwest end of Cree Lake and ends at a small beach on the east end of Wapata Lake. The trip can be done in five days — Tyrrell did it in less than four in a birchbark canoe! But it is such a great trip and you are out there already, why not make a holiday of it? Take a week.

You can't really shorten this trip, and nor would you want to. There are few places, if any, where you would want to land a floatplane; it's too shallow. It's easy to extend the trip. You can keep paddling through Wapata Lake to Giles Lake and finally on to Black Lake, adding another 54 km to the trip.

Cree Lake to Wapata Lake*	200 km
Cree Lake to the community of Black Lake	254 km

* This is the trip described in detail in the Trip Notes section.

Topographic Maps

You should have 1:50,000 maps 74G/9, 74G/16, 74J/1, 74I/4, 74I/5, 74I/12 and 74I/13. If you are carrying on to Black Lake you will also need 74P/4. I suggest you purchase these maps in advance and, using the Trip Notes, mark in all the unmarked rapids missing from the originals. Almost every rapid, even the smallest, is marked for the first little while, and then nothing is. Go figure. There are also a few low or burned sections along the Cree that don't have good camping, so you will want to mark in some potential campsites as well. And don't forget to note the fishing holes!

Getting There and Away

This is a fly-in and fly-out trip, as there is no road access to Cree Lake, and shuttling your vehicle to take out at Stony Rapids via the all-weather road would be a nightmare drive of about 25 hours roundtrip (see the Fond du Lac, MacFarlane and Porcupine trips for more about shuttles using the new road to Stony Rapids). I don't think it would be worth the drive there and back. You would spend a pretty penny on gas and then on the floatplane charter to put in at Cree Lake — back down south!

You have a couple of good options for flying in and out to look at, though. The simplest option is to drive to either Buffalo Narrows, La Loche or Points North and charter a floatplane from there. Park your vehicle in the air service's compound, fly to Cree Lake, and then have a floatplane pick you up from either Wapata or Black Lake. Presto, you get in your vehicle and drive back home. You can also fly to and from Points North on a scheduled flight from any southern city or La Ronge and rent canoes from CRCO right at Points North. A convenient and timely option, but not cheap.

The other possibility is to try to arrange with one of the outfitters on either end, Cree Lake Lodge on Cree Lake or Cree River Lodge on Wapata Lake, for a backhaul with their airplanes, or the companies they charter with. This possibility may include a drive to Key Lake Mine at the end of Highway 914 (gravel). It is a short flight to Cree Lake from there. For contact information see the Directory of Services.

When to Go

The beginning of June to August. Go earlier, rather than later in the season. The problem with the Cree, as with many other rivers in northern Saskatchewan's Athabasca Basin, is that runoff water drains quickly from the sandy soil. In a dry year the river just keeps going down — quickly. I was on the Cree in the third week of June in 2001, a low-water year in the Far North. The river was shallow, but navigable in all places. However, I don't think it would have been fun to take a loaded Tripper downriver by August — major wading would have been required.

In high water, many of the rapids would wash out. Then standing waves would become an issue in some rapids. The ledges would become more difficult to avoid and things are going to happen much faster in pushy floodwaters. If you have limited whitewater experience, think twice about running the Cree for the first time in flood.

Normally the Cree peaks in May, with flows averaging 176 cu m/sec. Much as on the Waterfound in a normal year, the water levels don't drop as much as you'd expect over the summer months. June's average flow is 152 cu m/sec, July's 144 cu m/sec, August's 135 cu m/sec and September's 129 cu m/sec. I was surprised there was this much flow in the river normally. It really seems like a smaller-volume river when you paddle it.

The water-gauging station on the Cree is no longer in operation, unfortunately. However, you can check the water levels in that general area of the Athabasca Basin by calling SaskWater and getting a current water-level reading for the Fond du Lac, and then compare it to the average yearly flows by month on the Canoe Saskatchewan website. If the Fond du Lac is running less than 300 cu m/sec at the outlet of Black Lake, I would choose a different river that you know has a good water level. It's best to ask a local source about water levels before making a final decision. Call the SERM office in Stony Rapids, the aviation services, or the outfitters on Cree and Wapata Lakes.

Difficulty of the River **

The Cree gets two stars because it is so remote and difficult to access if an accident happens. The rapids are often long and continuous, but they are not difficult. There are lots of rapids, but the average class is Class 1+. They are usually shallow, often fanning out around rocky islets and willow-covered islands. Hawk Rapids and two other rapids with ledges are the only places where you will find water more difficult than an easy Class 2. The tricky parts can be lined after scouting which side of the river or channel is easiest at what water level.

There are no falls on the river, and thus no mandatory portages. There are no big water crossings in the trip described in detail in the Trip Notes section either. You start at the end of a big lake and end at the start of one, with the option to paddle them if you like. Perfect.

This is a good river for wilderness canoe trippers without extensive whitewater experience, but who are comfortable in fast-moving water and shallow Class 2 rapids. In this guidebook, the Cree is the best trip for canoeists without a lot of whitewater experience wanting to challenge themselves by paddling a river in the Far North. You may want to take a guide or paddle with other intermediate canoeists comfortable in whitewater to be sure you have a good experience. The difficulty level is similar to that of the Montreal River and lower Sturgeon-weir, with the added bonus of the wonderful parkland country of the Athabasca Plain.

The gradient of the Cree reflects its fast current and many small rapids. In the length of the route described in the book, it falls at a rate of 1.08 m/km (5.64 ft/mi). That's one of the steeper gradients in this book, but because there are so many small rapids, the drop in elevation is not a difficult one to descend. The Cree runs at an average of 10 km/hr (6 mi/hr), according to Tyrrell. He estimated that the speed of the current gets up to 16 to 20 km/hr (10 to 12 mi/hr) in the swiftest rapids!

Character of the River and Region

The character of the Cree River reminds me of the Waterfound, except it has a much greater flow. The water is usually very clear, running through wide banks. The riverbed is usually small rocks or sand, and the shallow rapids often fan out into wide channels around islands. The current is fast, with flat sandstone ledges here and there to keep you awake. No falls, with lots of fast water. In the slower sections and where the river widens around grassy islands the bottom has lots of vegetation. Moose food galore.

The Cree runs north through the heart of the Athabasca Plain. Welcome to the land of the caribou! The land can be low with black spruce bog, or high with a parkland of open jack pine forest. The forest is carpeted with lichen (also called reindeer or caribou moss) underfoot. Blueberry, bearberry and sand heather are also common understory. On some larger islands and along some of the river's channel you can find white birch or poplar, the light green catching your eye.

The open woodland makes for great short hikes along eskers and on open sand plains. You can see why the Dene in this region, depending on their destination, quite often walked rather than paddled. The camping can be spectacular — huge sites with great height. Both black spruce and jack pine can be found on the north-facing slopes of drumlins and eskers. There are a few large burned areas typical of the Athabasca Plain, especially the Cree Lake Upland, in the first few days and then again as you approach Wapata Lake.

The geology of the Cree is very interesting. Cliffs, cutbanks, eskers and knife-edged drumlins along the riverbank reach 3 to 9 m high at times, making for a scenic trip. Sandstone cliffs, white and salmon and red coloured, dot the river too. The horizontally bedded sandstone is especially prevalent at Hawk (Epèrvier) Rapids. In the middle of the rapids there is an island called Hawk Island, which Tyrrell eloquently described as follows: "While in the middle a little island of similar sandstone presents its vertical sides to the rapid raging around it." At one point on the river there is a shattered, red rock cliff at a corner to the left. There's a ledge to run there too, and you can scout it atop this ledge. You won't miss it!

The predominance of sandy glacial deposits contributes to the strongly rolling nature of the terrain. You can see all these hills as you fly into Cree Lake. There are mounds of moraine and large ridges with boulders all over. The hills are also evident from the river, especially as you approach Wapata. Some of these are what Tyrrell deemed *ispatinow*, the Cree word for a "conspicuous hill." He described an ispatinow as a steep, narrow ridge of glacial drift, parallel to the direction of glaciation, with the sides joining in a crest that may be less than a metre in width. They are like drumlins and kames, but not really. The fact that he had never seen such a feature before prompted him to bestow the name. I like it! The largest ones are between Cree and Black Lakes. You'll also see them on the Fond du Lac and Waterfound.

For more information on the Athabasca Plain ecoregion consult *The Ecoregions of Saskatchewan*, by Acton et al. It describes in almost layman's terms why you see what you do in the landscape. For a play-by-play account of the river, print and bring along a copy of Tyrrell's notebooks from his Cree River descent in 1892. It's very good on-the-river reading and can be obtained online at http://digital.library.utoronto.ca/Tyrrell. If you are especially interested in the ispatinow, do a search of the site, as he refers to them in a number of documents.

Local History **

It is difficult to say why Cree Lake, the Cree River and the Little Cree River are so named. I've come across three references to Cree Lake being named for the Cree. The first is from Erik Munsterhjelm's account of trapping in the Far North in the '40s, *The Wind and the Caribou*. He says Cree Lake was so named because it was so important to Cree in prehistory. A second reference is found in Bill Barry's book about Saskatchewan place names. He states, "It is interesting that this far northern lake was once so associated with the Cree that it bears their name, yet the reserve there is held by a Dene Nation." The third account of the name is more detailed. Ed Theriau, once a trapper from northeast of Cree Lake, says there is a Dene legend about Cree Lake.

> The Crees would push northward and have to be driven back again below the Churchill. From the beginning of time these wars apparently went on, and the memory of ancient wrongs and triumphs was kept green as the old stories were handed down. According to these tales, the land around Cree Lake was always Chipewyan (Dene) hunting territory. They claim that the lake got its name through the great battles that drove the invading Crees back southward and restored the land to its owners.

The original territorial boundaries before the Europeans arrived are still not clear, as the first peoples' oral histories are lost in many cases, and there was very little written about it during the fur trade. However, it is generally accepted that the area north of Cree Lake has been predominantly Dene territory only since the late 1700s. The tiny community at Cree Lake is mostly populated by members of the English River First Nation. They were part of a larger group of Dene that wintered south of Cree Lake from the mid-to-late 1700s until permanently settling along the upper Churchill in the late 1800s. See the chapter on the Churchill for more information on the history of this First Nation.

Tyrrell indicated that the Dene rarely ascended the Cree River to go south to Cree Lake. They went up the Trout and Pipestone Rivers and then portaged into Cree Lake instead. Tyrrell descended the river to Black Lake on his travels for the Canadian Geological Survey in 1892. He thought it a sandy, stony and sterile environment. The river he called a "wild and impetuous stream," elaborating that "the many dangerous rapids are caused by the presence of these broken angular masses of sandstone as well as by sudden contractions and expansions of the channel." His notebooks number two and three from 1892, and his final report on his travels that year makes for good reading on the Cree River and the region it flows through. They are listed in the References section. Both can be read online as well.

Tyrrell was right in that the country is not bountiful like the Churchill region. Its wildlife populations would not have compared to the riches of moose and waterfowl to be found there. The dry Cree Lake Upland is not good beaver country, either, but other fur-bearing animals such as the otter do well. The Cree Lake region had a couple of trading posts in 1803: an independent house, Mowatt's House, and one belonging to the NWC. The HBC reopened the Cree Lake Post in 1925, and then again in the '30s and '40s for a number of years. One independent post was also in operation in the late '30 to early '50s, called Weitzel's Post. It was located on the Cree River several kilometres up from the lake on the west shore. There appears to be a camp at that spot still. In 2001, it looked well-used, and there were some fairly new cabins.

There was also a tiny Dene settlement on the mainland northwest of Armatage Bay, a couple of kilometres west of the outlet of the river. The settlement was occupied from 1937 until 1946, when it was destroyed by a forest fire.

You can read more about trapping and the last days of the fur trade in the Cree Lake area in three books, *North to Cree Lake* and *Face the North Wind* and *The Lost Land of the Caribou*. All three are available online. See References.

Level of Solitude ✳✳✳

You will see very few signs of human activity on the river. The Cree River Lodge on Wapata occasionally sends guided fishing parties up the river a ways, but not when the water is low. You probably won't see anybody else paddling the river; the only signs of people are one or two hunting camps, or maybe an old campfire ring. However, the Cree is becoming a more popular route with canoeists now. Let's hope everyone practises no-trace camping, so that the wilderness of the Cree remains pristine. Once you reach Wapata you will encounter signs of the outside world. The new road to Stony Rapids crosses the narrows of the lake.

Wildlife ✳✳✳✳

This river is great for seeing big mammals because it is so difficult to travel in the region other than by canoe. I saw thirteen moose, with seven in one short stretch. There have been woodland caribou sightings as well. Barren ground caribou will sometimes winter in this region. Black bears and timber wolves are common, and you may see otters and porcupines. I'm still waiting to see a porcupine anywhere in the North! Tyrrell saw lots on the Cree in 1892, when he noted: "Porcupines were about the only living things to be seen on these sandy plains, and where these animals are plentiful you may be sure that human beings rarely come, for they are easily killed, and the Indians are very fond of a nice roasted porcupine."

Seeing a lynx or a wolverine is a remote possibility. Bird diversity is low because of the dry pine uplands, but you will see hawks, eagles and osprey. There are fewer waterfowl than in other regions as well. Ed Theriau writes that there was at least one documented sighting of a grizzly bear in the Cree Lake region and that they are "almost unknown there." In *Face the North Wind* he says they were confirmed to have lived in the high hills north of Cree Lake. Hmm.

Fishing ✳✳✳

There is some great fishing on the Cree. It's not the greatest river for walleye, though there is one hot spot. But the grayling and northern pike potential make up for it. Plus, you can catch trout to your heart's content at the outflow of the river into Wapata Lake.

The key to finding the grayling is fishing the eddies in the rocky rapids and using fly-fishing tackle or tiny, tiny spinners with little lead weights. The northerns are really big. You must debarb your hooks so you can let the far-too-big-for-dinner ones go. Jigs are good for pike, and you might get lucky with the walleye. Look for the pike in deep, weedy places and at the confluences of the tributaries of the Cree.

Special Equipment

I'm normally partial to plastic on remote rivers, but the Cree at higher water is an exception — Kevlar is fine if you have solid whitewater skills. The rapids are very runnable and are not generally the wrap-o-matic kind. But if you are more of a beginner or the water is low, definitely take a Royalex boat. The river has lots of shallow areas, and you must read the deep-water channels expertly not to run aground at times. Besides, there are no mandatory portages, so weight doesn't matter. Finally, don't take an aluminum canoe if the water is low!

The bugs can be bad on the Cree. The blackflies and mosquitoes were both in fine form by the time I came along in the third week of June. Take a head net, and or bug jacket, and lots of repellent.

Trip Notes

MAP NO	GRID REF	FEATURE	DESCRIPTION
74 G/9	Armatage Bay	Put-in	It's impossible for a floatplane to get to shore near the mouth of the Cree River. But you can load your boats from the plane and carry on down the river, or go to shore and camp at any of the nice beaches on the northwest end of the bay.
	225885	Put-in	Cree Lake Lodge has a dock. Maybe call them ahead of time about landing here.
	233983	Cabins	On RL is a hunting or fishing camp. Well-maintained log cabins, but an old dock in disrepair in 2001.
	224015	Camp	On RR is a hunting camp. Structures for shelter, hanging and drying can be seen just before the turn to the left.
74 G/16	224017 227023	Fast water/ Riffle	800 m of shallow, fast water with a Class 1 rock apron at the end. Grayling fishing commences!
	234032	Campsite	Open bench camping on RR.
	235035	Rapids	**Class 1**, and straightforward.
	242045	Riffle	At the end of the channel around the island.
	242046	Campsite	On RL, open bench camping.
	245058	Rapids	**Class 1**, and straightforward.
	243061 238069	Rapids	**Class 2**. A ledge on RR signifies the beginning of a stretch of rapids that lead into Hawk Rapids. The ledge can be run on RL. Class 1 rapids follow until another Class 2 ledge occurs on RR. It can also be run on RL. The rapids that follow are Class 2 becoming shallow Class 1 as the river narrows before Hawk.
	239069 226095	Hawk Rapids	**Class 2.** Hawk Rapids are continuous for almost 4 km, but are never more difficult than Class 2. See the following highlights:
	239078	Ledge	About 1 km into Hawk the river takes a turn to the left or west, and there is a **Class 2** ledge running from RC to RR. It is marked by the bars at the "P" in RAPIDS on the map. Stay to the inside of the corner or RL to run the ledge.
	229085	Island Rapids	At the "HA" in HAWK are two bars. These signify **Class 2** rapids preceding and around a mid-channel island made up of shelves of sandstone (Hawk Island). The rapids are wide, and most of the water runs to the outside of the channels, both on RR and RL. There are small ledges to navigate and very shallow places to avoid as well. Take your time and scout if you feel the need. Definitely fish for grayling in the fast water. Hawk ends with shallow Class 1 rapids and the river widening into a bay with a wonderful esker deep in on RL.
	223096	Camping	The esker on RL in the sheltered bay provides many campsites. You can stretch your legs.
	225098	Campsite	For those who prefer island camping, there is an excellent, established campsite on the small island mid-channel after Hawk. The north side of island has the best path up to the site.

MAP NO	GRID REF	FEATURE	DESCRIPTION
	224104	Fast water	Where the river narrows again.
	224106	Fast water	At the narrows.
	220108	Riffle	A rock shoal on RL where the dashes are on the map.
	218113 228119	Camping	A low esker provides camping for almost a kilometre down RL.
	235124	Campsite	Open bench camping on RR.
	239130	Rapids	**Class 1 with a Class 2 ledge**. These continuous rapids begin at the bar marked on the map at the narrows and culminate in a tricky Class 2 ledge 400 m downstream. The ledge is RC and runs almost the width of the river. It occurs at a sharp bend to the left, making it hard to see until you are on top of it. It can be run far RL or far RR.
	238136 260144	Riffles	Approximately 400 m after the ledge you will encounter a long stretch (almost 3 km) that has numerous fast water sections and riffles. Where there are deep, weedy bays the northern pike fishing is good.
	269153 272155	Riffles	Where the river narrows for approximately 350 m.
	274165 279177	Riffles	As the river narrows again for approximately 1,300 m.
	279178	Campsite	Open bench camping on RL in a bay.
	281180 291183	Fast water	The three marked bars are fast water for 1 km. Where the river narrows there is a shallow riffle.
	293193	Fast water	The marked bar is only fast water.
	294202	Riffle	The marked bar is just a riffle.
	292199 288199	Camping	Nice bench camping along the south shore of the bay. Pick your spot.
	287200	Riffle	The marked bar beside the BM 437.7 arrow is only a riffle where the river narrows again.
	286202	Rapids	**Class 2**, with ledges on RL. Run RR to avoid them.
	285205 284214	Rapids	**Class 1**. Very shallow rapids around willow – covered islands for 1,200 m.

Note: These rapids are very characteristic of the rest of the Cree River. In low water, what look like open flatwater sections on the map are actually shallow rapids flowing around willow-covered islands. These rapids are usually continuous and long — the trick is to find the water. Take the channel running to the outside of a turn if possible. It usually has the most water.

| | 283214 | Campsite | Open jack pine bench camping on RL in a narrow section of river. |
| | 278225 | Campsite | Very nice bench camping in a partially burned area. On RL in a bay, with room for lots of tents. |

MAP NO	GRID REF	FEATURE	DESCRIPTION
	279233	Campsite	A third option for the night is an open bench on RL in a bay just before the island. The next 15 km of the river are burned, with few nice campsites.
	300267 316284	Rapids	**Class 1 and fast water** for approximately 3 km. There are numerous shallow rapids, riffles and sections of fast water. Low water may make some sections unnavigable.
74 J/1	328292	Fast water	Where the river narrows.
	339300	Riffles	For a short stretch.
	342308	Fast water	Where the river narrows again.
	348313	Riffles	Riffles and fast water for 700 m.
	364317	Campsite	Very nice, open jack pine bench camping on RL (BM 407.5 arrow). A very large site, where you can stretch your legs and watch moose. One walked right through my camp at 3:30 A.M. to have a snack out in the shallows!
	374324 376324	Rapids	**Class 1**, and straightforward for 250 m.
	387326 389325	Rapids	**Class 1**, and straightforward for 225 m.
	390326	Campsite	Open jack pine bench on RL in a nice bay.
	392323	Rapids	**Class 1**, 550 m of continuous rapids, beginning with a Class 1 chute. Then there is only fast water, ending with a shallow Class 1 rock dodge as the river widens again.
	399324	Campsite	Open bench camping in a bay on RL.
	404322	Riffle	Where the river narrows.
	408323	Fast water	Around the island.
74I/4	410324 430351	Rapids	**Class 1+**. Almost 4 km of fairly continuous rapids that begin with a shallow riffle as the river narrows, becoming Class 1/1+. The last third or so of the rapids are through and around low islands. The shallow rapids require you to choose the channel with the most flow. I ran the main RL channel in the first section of islands and then far RR in the last island section.
	437383 445395	Rapids	**Class 1 and 1+**. A section of Class 1 waves followed by continuous, very shallow and rocky Class 1+ rapids, where rock dodging is key. Don't be fooled by the map, in lower water the islands in the lakelet are surrounded by rapids until almost the end of the open section.
	448404 449406	Rapids	**Fast water and Class 1**. After some fast water sections is a narrows where there are 250 m of Class 1 rapids, with rock dodging.
	449408	Campsite	Open bench camping on RL.

MAP NO	GRID REF	FEATURE	DESCRIPTION
	452411 453412	Rapids	**Class 1 and Class 2.** The first marked bar is a Class 1 chute, and the second bar is a Class 2 ledge on RL that can be run on RR.
	453416 454421	Rapids	**Class 2.** About 500 m downstream of the preceding ledges are more ledgey rapids, represented by three marked bars. There is a series of three ledges across RC and RR. They can all be run on RL. But after the ledges you must find the main, deep water channel, as the rapids become shallow and rocky Class 1+, Class 1 and then end as riffles. These rapids are marked by double bars and are continuous with the ledge rapids.
	455423 462445	Rapids	**Class 1+.** Just downstream of the above rapids in another long rapid around willowy islands. It's about 2.5 km long. There are many more islands than are shown on the map, but you will locate yourself again easily where the river widens. The rapids are never more difficult than Class 1+.
	463453 470460	Rapids	**Class 1.** A 1-km-long S-turn rapid that becomes shallower at the very end where the river widens. There are waves where the river narrows and turns.
	471465 468465	Rapids	Class 1, beginning at the left-hand bend following the long island and ending 200 m later.
	465468	Riffle	Where the river narrows and bends to the left.
	462480	Campsite	On RR on the west end of a long island is a lovely, high esker camp. A scramble up, but camping along this section is limited. You will notice that the map shows many islands, but there are none in reality!
	460484	Campsite	On the RL is another chance to camp. Open bench. The next good camping is approximately 8 km downstream.
	460486 461487	Rapids	**Class 1.** Two sets of Class 1 waves in succession.
	462488	Riffle	After the left bend as you go back right.
	461490	Rapids	**Class 1,** shallow and rocky.
	463513 465517	Rapids	**Class 1.** Waves to fast water to riffles, ending in Class 1 waves again where the river widens to a tiny lake with numerous islands. Good northern pike fishing in the deeper, weedy bays.
	463535	Campsite	On RR the end of an esker provides camping opportunities. It's definitely a scramble up, but a dream of an esker hike once you get there.
	467546	Riffle	Around a tiny island in mid-channel.
	475557 484564	Rapids	**Class 1.** Waves at the top around mid-channel island. Followed by riffles and then a shallow and rocky Class 1 rapid, just before the river widens into a tiny lake.
74I/5	503593	Riffle	After a bend to the left.

cree river

163

MAP NO	GRID REF	FEATURE	DESCRIPTION
	505599	Riffle	Where the river narrows in between two sections of bays.
	528635	Campsite	The best open jack pine bench camping for a long while, right across from the island on RR, where the river bends to the left sharply before reaching the Rapid River junction. A big fishing eddy is right out front!
	530636	Fishing hole	Where the Rapid River joins the Cree. There is grayling fishing up the Rapid River, walleye fishing below it on the Cree, and in the deeps the northerns lurk.
	535639	Campsite	Open bench camping on RR.
	542644	Campsite	Open bench camping on RR.
	553688	Rapids	**Class 1** waves around the bend to the left and then some rocks.
	553692	Fast water	For 100 m.
	552698	Rapids	**Class 1**, very shallow and rocky, and may require wading at low water.

Note: In the next 10 km, I saw seven moose. One young bull decided to check me out and ran along beside me in the shallow water on the other side of an island as I paddled away! Be cautious around these magnificent, large animals, especially if they are cows with a calf.

	558720 558723	Rapids	**Class 1.** Fast water followed by Class 1 rapids.
	558732	Riffle	
	558743 561746	Rapids	**Class 1/1+.** A wide, shallow rapid with a few boulders to dodge.
	559750 560751	Fast water	For 100 m.
	557754	Campsite	On RL is a bench camping spot that will do in a pinch.
	558755 559759	Rapids	**Class 1** waves for approximately 450 m.
	563765	Rapids	**Class 1**, wide and shallow for 325 m.
	565774	Riffle	
	563783	Campsite	Open bench camping on RL in a wide section of river.
	568788	Fast water	In the narrows.
	570796	Campsite	Esker camping on RR. Bushy to get to, but nice, open camping on the top.
	567803 566804	Riffles	
	561816 562817	Riffles	
	560820 561822	Rapids	**Class 1+** waves with big rocks on RR.

MAP NO	GRID REF	FEATURE	DESCRIPTION
	563824 560830	Riffles	All around the big bend to the left.
	561829	Rapids	**Class 1**, shallow and rocky, at the end of a big bend.
	560830 539830	Riffles	Through a gorge-like straightaway for 2 km.
	539830	Rapids	**Class 1+**. Waves are all there is to worry about.
	534834	Campsite	An esker on RR. There are three main spots to choose from. There are some bushy willows to get through, but nice airy views of the big bay on RL. The first spot is in the first bay and the last spot in on the third point down. You'll notice some birch trees for a change.
74I/12	553865	Campsite	On RR there's a bench that will do in a pinch. You'll have some bush to push to get to it.
	547875	Campsite	On RL, with a bit of bush to push again, but it is good and open on the north end of the bench for camping.
	553878 554880	Campsite	On RR. For a change, how about black spruce with bearberry and lichen flats for camping? No heights to climb here, and lots of room.
	557888	Riffle	Shallow, before a big bend to the left.
	559890	Campsite	Good jack pine and sand bank camping on RR.
	555890	Riffle	In the narrows.
	548892 547893	Rapids	**Class 1**. A shallow rapid around a rock islet. The RR channel has the most flow.
	556894 556895	Fast water	On the bend to the right following the islet rapid.
	549900	Campsite	On RL, an easily accessible open bench on a small point.
	551902	Riffle	
	553905	Riffle	
	555908 555916	Rapids	**Class 1**. 1 km long, continuous, and very shallow around and between islands. Some parts would require wading at lower water.
	560920 567928	Riffles	Continuous and shallow for 1,100 m.
	568934	Riffle	Where the river narrows significantly. Be sure to try fishing at the confluence of the Badwater River and the Cree!
	568940	Riffle	Just after the junction of the Badwater and Cree.
	570946 570954	Fast water	The narrow S-turn is fast water.
	572957	Riffles	Around a small mid-channel island.
	574960	Fast water	As the river narrows.

Cree river

165

Map No	Grid Ref	Feature	Description
	570975	Rapids	**Class 1**, around islands, there are 500 m of rocky rapids, becoming more difficult to navigate at the bottom.
	570980	Campsite	On the south end of an esker island. Nice and airy with a bit of a scramble up. A primo view.
	570987	Campsite	On RL in a bay, an esker provides open, flat camping with a view.
	576996 575997	Rapids	**Class 1+** waves ending in a riffle around the bend to the left.
	573045	Campsite	On the shoulder of a high sandy point on RR. There's a bit of willow to push, but there are great breezes and a view.
	595073	Riffles	Very shallow riffles around the island.
	601089	Campsite	At the south end of the island, with a sand beach to land on. Birch trees and a view, with only a bit of a scramble up.
74I/13	615137	Campsite	Open bench camping on RL, with easy access.
	664160	Campsite	An esker campsite at a bend on RR. You have to scramble up, but it's very nice.
	678170	Campsite	Pick your spot along this esker on RR.
	603185	Take-out Campsite	Just south of the where the Cree River flows into Wapata Lake. There is a sand beach with an old, dilapidated log cabin. Minus the junk, it would be a really nice campsite.
	544238	Cree River Lodge	There's an optional take-out at Wapata Lake at the lodge. Call ahead for a meal and bed!

WATERFOUND RIVER

The Waterfound is a quick little river with lots of small rapids, fantastic fishing, excellent esker camping, and good wildlife viewing potential. It's one of those trips that makes you love the Far North. It's all about sand, parkland and grayling. Fast, shallow rapids and sandstone ledges make the Waterfound a great river to work on your whitewater skills. You may never want to portage on this sweetie, but you easily can. It's easy going through the rolling, open jack pine and spruce forests. The one big rapid, "Ledge-o-matic," will make your blood run cold. It adds the necessary thrill or sweat factor, depending if you run it or walk it, to make the Waterfound a true northern river adventure. The added bonus is that grayling live in all those long, continuous rapids. Plus, the rapids downriver of Durrant Lake eventually house walleye!

The beach-and-bench combo campsite — a sandy landing with level tent sites up in the open forest behind, is the classic Waterfound Special. The eskers are great too, providing high views and photo and hiking opportunities. Track your favourite northern mammal on the sand ridges as you stretch your legs after dinner.

This short trip is very accessible, and should you have the skill and time you can carry on down the Fond du Lac. You will then get the chance to enjoy more amazing camping. Yes, it gets even better.

Length

The trip described in the Trip Notes section is approximately 105 km long. It starts at the northwest end of Waterbury Lake and finishes on the northeast end of Waterfound Bay at the confluence of the Waterfound and Fond du Lac. If you really had to shorten this already short trip, you could fly out of Durrant Lake at the Hatchet Lake Lodge fishing outpost camp. Some parties will want to extend their trip to carry on down the Fond du Lac from Waterfound Bay, given that they have the skill or a competent guide. This adds around 155 km to the trip. The Fond du Lac trip is described in detail in the next chapter.

The Waterfound is fast-flowing in most places, and the majority of canoeists will easily paddle 25 km a day. It can be a four-day trip, depending on the winds when you cross Theriau (Unknown Lake) and Durrant Lakes. But take your time. Enjoy the fishing and camping now that you have come all this way!

Northwest end of Waterbury Lake to Durrant Lake camp*	85 km
Northwest end of Waterbury Lake to Waterfound Bay*	105 km
Waterbury Lake to Black Lake via the Fond du Lac River**	260 km

* These trips are described in detail in the Trip Notes section of this chapter.
** The Fond du Lac River to Black Lake route is detailed in the Fond du Lac Trip Notes.

Topographic Maps

In order to get the level of detail required to find your location in the many rapids that are not marked on the maps, 1:50,000 scale maps are recommended. You will need 74 I/8, 74 I/1, 74 I/2, 74 I/7, 74 I/10, 74 I/9 and 74 I/16. The reason there are so many maps for this short trip is that the river twists off the main maps for a few kilometres in three places. If you are a really good navigator and experienced in paddling on northern Saskatchewan rivers, you may want to run off the map and not buy 74I/2 and 74 I/10, but I don't recommend it. You will need 64 L/13, 74 P/1, 74 P/2 and 74 P/3 for the Fond du Lac River extension.

I suggest you purchase these maps in advance so, using the Trip Notes, you can mark in the rapids that are missing on the maps. Only one rapid is marked on the original maps — you guessed it, Ledge-o-matic! You may want to indicate on your maps where the rapids end

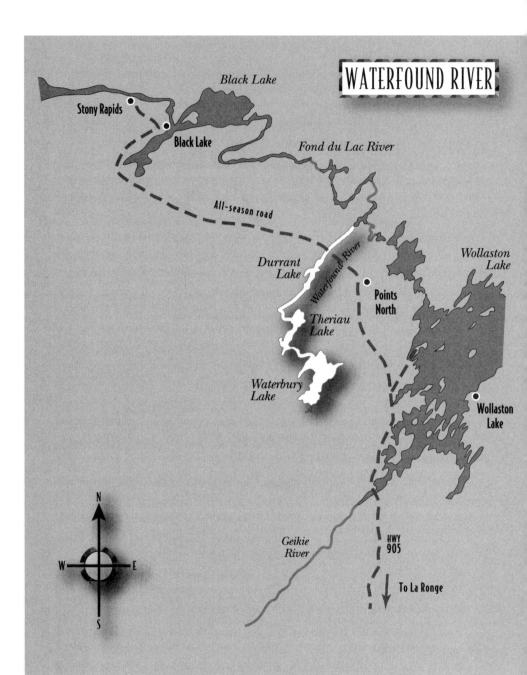

and begin, as some are long and continuous. Classifications of rapids and the one portage location can be noted as well. There are some burns on the Waterfound, so you may want to mark in the good campsites too. Don't forget the fishing holes!

Getting There and Away

Getting to and from the Waterfound is cheaper than most other Far North trips, and you have a number of options. The easiest option, not overly expensive, is to drive to Points North, which is located just off gravel Highway 905 before it becomes the all-season road to Stony Rapids. Then fly via a floatplane charter from Points North to the put-in at the outlet of the river on Waterbury Lake. Then fly out from Waterfound Bay back to Points North. No shuttle required and good parking — very convenient.

You can also fly to Points North via scheduled flights from Regina, Saskatoon, Prince Albert and La Ronge with Transwest. And you can rent canoes from Churchill River Canoe Outfitters right at Points North, so no shipping of canoes is required. Expensive, but easy.

Another option, but one very hard on your vehicle, is to arrange for a shuttle from Points North to Waterbury Lake via an old winter road. I haven't gone this route, but Andy Eikel from Points North Air says it's a very rough road. He has taken people in this way before, and if you fly with Points North on your return trip they will help you get your vehicle back to their compound. There is a controlled road to Cigar Lake, where there is a uranium mine being developed that passes by Waterbury Lake, but at this time Cameco is not giving the public permission to use it. It may be an option in the future, however. Getting back from Waterfound Bay is a fly-out only proposition. It's a short floatplane flight to Points North from Waterfound Bay.

When to Go

June to August. This river's water level doesn't fluctuate much over the summer, though you would think it would, being a shallow, small-volume river. But it is fed by a large lake and aquifer, so its season is long compared to a number of the other rivers in the book. Don't go too early, however. You can't get into Waterbury until enough ice is off the lake above the river outlet to land a plane. Theriau and Durrant Lakes must be ice-free as well, and this is often not until early June. If you go too late in the season or in a low-water year you may have to wade some of the long, continuous and shallow rapids.

The water-gauging station on the Waterfound is still in operation. In mid-June, 2001, a low-water year in the area, I ran the river at a flow of 18 cu m/sec. That is fairly low for June, but I had no difficulty running all the rapids at that level. To get a current water-level reading call SaskWater, check the Canoe Saskatchewan website for average yearly and monthly flows on the Waterfound from 1974 to 1993. They will help you determine whether the current water level is high, low or average. You could end up wading some of the river if the water was too low, making the trip longer and less fun. You can also call the SERM office at Wollaston or Andy at Points North to double-check the water levels in the region.

Difficulty of the River**

The Waterfound is not a difficult trip. Its rating of two stars warns less-experienced white-water paddlers to be cautious. The whitewater reminds me of the Cree, with the usually shallow and fast rapids averaging Class 1+. There are numerous rapids, and they can be long and continuous in places. It's a good river to work on your burgeoning whitewater skills, as the rapids are not too steep, violent or overly demanding. The Montreal River at an average water level is good practice for this Athabasca Basin trip. Most canoeists will elect to portage the tricky upper section of Ledge-o-matic, but there are no mandatory portages.

The river is fairly remote. If an accident happens, help is far away. If you go in at the northwest end of Waterbury you avoid the one exposed open lake crossing, but there are two lake stretches yet that are somewhat exposed. However, on both lakes you can pull off to the shore in a short time if the wind comes up quickly.

This river is appropriate for all canoeists with experience in moving water, but it is recommended that less-skilled paddlers have intermediate-level whitewater canoeists in their group, or a competent guide. The Waterfound is a very good introduction to the type of river you can expect on the Athabasca Plain. The Cree, the Fond du Lac, the MacFarlane and the upper William, among other far northern rivers, share many of the Waterfound's characteristics.

The gradient of the Waterfound is 0.83 m/km (4.59 ft/mi). That's a good gradient for northern Saskatchewan; it reflects the clip of the current. There are only two moderately long lakes and no falls, so the numerous rapids make for a fairly consistent and very paddleable drop in elevation.

Character of the River and Region

The Waterfound is a tributary of the Fond du Lac, the mother river of the Far North. It runs northwest from Waterbury to Theriau (Unknown) Lake, then basically north, then northwest again for a bit until it turns and runs straight northeast, flowing into Durrant Lake and then the Fond du Lac. This small-volume river starts skinny and rock-choked out of Waterbury Lake. Downstream, shallow, rocky fans become the most common feature of the rapids. Like the Cree, there are also rapids that braid around low islands. And there are some wicked-shaped sandstone ledges here and there. Ledge-o-matic has three big ones! But for the most part, the river is fast and shallow, running over sand or small rocks with a few bigger rock gardens.

The Waterfound flows through the Athabasca Plain of the Boreal Shield and this ecoregion is characterized by drumlin and moraine. There are many prominent eskers in the area, some up to 80 km long. The soil is sandy, and the dryness of the area makes for extensive forest fires. Thus, jack pine is the dominant forest along the river. This open parkland commonly has an understory of lichen, blueberry, bearberry and sand heather. Some black spruce occur on north-facing slopes of drumlins and eskers, while bogs are full of stunted black spruce with some tamarack.

The beginning of the river is in lowlands with black spruce, but the banks quickly become higher and sandier. There are some interesting small cliffs; the layered sandstone you see more of on the Cree. Much of Theriau Lake is burned, and the moraine hummocks are very evident. The last half of the river is dominated by eskers and open jack pine forest. Durrant Lake has some lovely sand beaches, as does Waterfound Bay.

Local History **

Not much has been recorded or written about the Waterfound River's use in prehistory. It was certainly a good landmark when travelling overland between Black Lake and Wollaston Lake, as the Dene did. It must have been of some importance, as it was one of the few landmarks that appeared on early maps of the area. That was before the aerial photographs were taken in the late '30s and used to create scaled maps like those we use now.

J. B. Tyrrell, in one of his 1892 notebooks, writes that an Indian guide told him of a canoe route to the Churchill from the headwaters of the Waterfound. The route went over the height of land to the headwaters of the Haultain (Pine) River, and then down that river to the Churchill. It was a route that brought the Dene to the trading post at Ile-à-la-Crosse. By the late 1700s, two groups of Dene began to winter in the area south of Cree Lake. This route probably was used as an alternate to the Mudjatik/Churchill route used by the Dene who moved south for the summer, as far south as Dore and Smoothstone Lakes at one time. They often returned to their Cree Lake wintering grounds via the Foster. See the chapter on the Churchill for more about the change in the Dene's lifestyle and territory as they entered the fur-trade economy.

I spoke to an old trapper, George Sanderson, in Robertson's Trading Post in La Ronge about his trapping days in the Waterbury Lake region. He told me it took him 75 portages and one month to get there from La Ronge via the Geikie River. The trapping in the area must have been good, as other trappers also spent a lot of time just south of there. Ole Jacobsen, Ed Theriau (Unknown Lake was renamed for him) and Fred Derbyshire all trapped around the Waterbury, Russell and Close Lakes area. Three books dealing with trappers' experiences in the region make for good river reading: *North of Cree Lake*, *Face the North Wind*, and *Lost Land of the Caribou*. See the References section for full bibliographic details. If you are carrying on to the Fond du Lac, there are more books and articles to consult on its history.

Solitude **

The Waterfound has evidence of modern human activity along its length, but there are not a lot of people around. There are at least three fishing camps or lodges on Theriau Lake and one on Durrant Lake. The all-season road to Stony Rapids crosses the river later on, and just after there the skies are full of planes heading to and from Stony Rapids and points north. It's still wilderness, but you can expect to bump into fishing parties and maybe another group of canoeists.

Wildlife ***

Moose, bears and otters are frequently sighted on the Waterfound, and I think everyone I've spoken to has seen a moose. I've seen otter families too. They like to play in the current. If you huff at them sometimes they will come up to the canoe and pose for a close-up! Try a half snort and huff at the same time — it usually works. There are many eagles and osprey on the river, because the fishing is so good!

Fishing ****

There are lake trout in Waterbury Lake and some big northern pike. And every time I have fished on the Waterfound, the grayling have been biting. You can't go on the river and not catch one, unless you don't have the right tackle. Take a fly rod and reel or your favourite rod and some tiny spinners. I also often use a clear bobber half full of water with a wet fly on the end of four feet of line with my regular rod. Cast upstream and let the bobber float your fly in front of all those beady little eyes. The walleye after Durrant Lake are marvellous, and jigs and twisters always work in the eddies. The pike like them too, and anything shiny, of course. The Waterfound is simply a fishing bonanza.

Special Equipment

I would highly recommend a Royalex boat, especially if the water is low. An aluminum boat and low skill levels will guarantee a much longer trip! The blackflies can be merciless in June and July; take a bug hat and or a bug jacket with full head gear.

Trip Notes

MAP	GRID	FEATURE	DESCRIPTION
74 I/8	333565	Put-in	A small, sandy beach in front of a couple of trapper cabins at the northwest end of Waterbury Lake.
74 I/1	324563	Rapids	**Class 1**. A shallow chute at the first narrows. Start grayling fishing now!
	319564	Rapids	**Class 1**, shallow and rocky. This set follows the previous rapid after a section of fast water and is indicated by an Inukshuk on the rocks in a little bay on RL.

MAP NO	GRID REF	FEATURE	DESCRIPTION
74 I/8	317565 316567	Rapids	**Class 1+.** A fast chute with waves at the corner, followed by shallow, rocky rapids to where the river widens into a tiny lake. Good grayling fishing at these rapids.
	311569	Rapids	**Class 1.** A fast chute around a tiny, rocky island. The rapids sweep to the left and become shallower at the end. Run RR in lower water. There is no navigable channel to the left of the island in moderate to low water levels. Good grayling fishing at these rapids.
	309568	Rapids	**Class 1.** An S-turn, and a combination of fast, narrow chutes with shallow rock aprons at the end.
	296568	Cut line	An exploration gridline cuts through the trees on either side of the river. There are posts, blazes and flagging tape. You are in the heart of uranium country, don't forget.
74 I/7	291563	Fast water	On RR you will see an Inukshuk just before a small island. Take the RR channel, as there is more water. Just after the island is a fast water chute.
	287563 286563	Rapids	**Class 1** and straightforward. About 175 m long.
	286564	Campsite	On RL in a bay just after the rapids is an open bench with good access to the river. Stop here and fish for supper.
	281578 280583	Rapids	**Class 2**, about 450 m long. The rapids start shallow and rocky around a rock islet. The RR channel has the most water. The rapids get more difficult to navigate as they become a rocky fan where the river widens.
	277584 273582	Rapids Campsite Fishing hole	**Class 1+.** 500 m of continuous, rocky rapids where the river narrows considerably. You can find camping on RR on a level grassy bank or rock shelf along this stretch. Fish the whole rapid from the shore!
	272582 262595	Rapids Campsite	**Class 1.** Just down from the above rapids, where the river widens, is an almost 4-km-long, continuous section of shallow rapids, broken up by sections of fast water. The rapids end where the river makes a sharp turn to the left before it widens and drops around an island. There is a campsite on RR. Look for the outcropping at GR 263580.
	261597	Rapids	**Class 2**, and very shallow. The RL channel around the island has the clearest route, and I ran it far RL. Only fast water and riffles from here until the river's outflow from Theriau Lake.
	237598	Campsite	On RR, a sandy esker spot.
	218601	Fishing camp	Points Unknown Camps is on a point in Mitchell Bay on Theriau (Unknown) Lake.
	220617 224619 223620	Camping	Within half a kilometre there are three potential camping sites, one of which should suit your group. It may be desirable to choose from these or three others farther north if you are planning on stopping on Theriau Lake for the night. The north end of the lake is badly burned, and there is little for nice camping. The first is a

MAP NO	GRID REF	FEATURE	DESCRIPTION
			sand beach, the second is an esker island site with a steep bank up to it, and the third is also an esker island site.
	242664	Campsite	A small site with room for only two tents, on a small point on the southeast side of a forested island in the middle of the channel at the north end of the lake. Fairly exposed.
	239670	Campsite	Rock camping on the eastern mainland across from the forested island.
	250676	Campsite	On the eastern shore in open jack pine forest on a point.
	248685	Marker	A red pylon hangs on a burned tree so that fishing parties can find their way back to the lodge! It indicates to canoeists that they are on their way to the northwest end of Theriau Lake and the outflow of the Waterfound.
	244719	Hunting camp	At a beach at the west end of the lake. A potential place to camp, but there may be unwanted visitors looking for scraps.
	242721	Fishing camp	An outpost camp of the Cree River Lodge sits on a point of the island.
	230713	Riffle	A fishing spot!
	231718	Rapids Water survey station	**Class 1+.** A set of waves at the narrows. A cable runs across the river here. On RL the water-survey station tin hut can be seen. There is a cut line and a cleared area that make for potential camping. A portage of the rapids is possible down the cut line. There are more fishing spots at these rapids.
	220717	Rapids	**Class 1.** The rapids are shallow and go around a rocky islet. Run the RL channel for the most water flow. There's more good grayling fishing here.
	206717	Rapids	**Class 1.** A chute with small waves occurs at the outflow of Theriau Lake proper.
	199729 199747	Rapids Portage	**Class 1+/2 to Class 3+ to Class 2. CAUTION:** Ledge-o-matic Rapids coming up! There is a preliminary Class 1+/2 chute around the sharp corner to the left, and the Class 3+ ledge section follows almost immediately. After the ledges the rapids get easier. But the entire rapid is over 2 km long and very rocky. You do not want to swim here. You and your canoe are going to take a beating. You have three options for navigating the first two sections of Ledge-o-matic Rapids. One is that you run the Class 1+/2 chute and eddy out RL above the ledges, then scout from the RL shore. Note that this is an advanced move that should only be attempted by advanced paddlers who can back ferry in Class 2 rapids. You can portage through the jack pine near the shore or walk in to the regular portage trail if you decide not to run the ledges. Put back in anywhere where you feel confident about running the rest of the rapids. The second option is to stop at the overflow channel on RL above the chute and walk over the point and down the shore to scout. If you decide to carry, follow the shore or walk in to the portage. Put in again where you feel comfortable. The third option is to just head straight to the **portage** trail, which is on RL 60 m or

MAP NO	GRID REF	FEATURE	DESCRIPTION
			so above the point. The path is obvious in the open jack pine. It will peter out, as people have put back in after the ledges where they felt comfortable. The pike fishing in the lakelet below these rapids is good. You can also walk up the river to fish for grayling.
	201750 203748	Camping	Excellent jack pine bench camping along the north shore of the lakelet. Pick your spot. Fish for supper. Does it get any better than this?
	194747 182748	Rapids	**Class 1 to Class 2.** There are 1,400 m of continuous rapids following the lakelet. The rapids are shallow in spots and through the islands. You will always be looking for the channel with the most water flow.
	184749	Campsite	On RR just after the end of the long island-choked rapid. A long, open jack pine bench. Not the nicest camp on the river, but it will do.
	233799 237799	Rapids Camping Fishing hole	**Class 2**, shallow and rocky continuous rapids for about 600 m that end in a bay with camping on either side. The power line and fire-singed areas are the only blots on this great section of the river.
	240798	Fast water	At the outflow from the bay.
	242803	Campsite	On RL is open bench camping in the bay.
	255822	Campsite	Esker camping on RL.
74 I/10	283845	Road	On RL you will see the white backs of traffic signs! The all-season road to Stony Rapids is up ahead. It's a sand pit here, as it is built on a beautiful esker, which is still worth a hike for the views of the river. There is a small beach to park your canoe on, and the top of the esker is still a nice place to camp. But there are many esker camping spots to come that don't have roads beside them.
	291845	Bridge	The only bridge I know of that joins two eskers. A road built on the top of eskers? Sacrilege.
74 I/9	305865	Campsite	Esker camping on RL on the northeast side of the point. There are better spots a couple of kilometres down on Durrant Lake.
	308865	Campsite	Esker camping on RR. Nice, but better just ahead.
	315883 315888	Camping	Esker camping galore in the bays on RR. A beauty spot. Gets four stars.
	318891 322892	Camping	Esker camping on RR in a bay. Nice spots.
	325915	Campsite	Beach camping on an island — just for a change!
	369976	Campsite	This is the five-star baby of them all! Beach-and-bench, the Waterfound Special. On a point on RR across from the island. Beauty, just beauty.
	372991	Fishing camp	Hatchet Lake Lodge outpost camp on the beach on the west side of the peninsula.

MAP NO	GRID REF	FEATURE	DESCRIPTION
	390014	**Fast water** **Fishing hole**	This is the walleye hole you have been hoping for, and Brad's favourite spot. You can see the walleye in the narrows where the esker almost crosses the river. Fish the eddy lines with jigs and twisters. Try the bay following for big northerns.
	387017 390019 392018	**Camping**	All three sites listed are on an open jack pine bench on RL.
	402027	**Fast water**	Fishing potential.
	405031	**Fast water**	Fishing potential.
	409037 420043	**Rapids**	**Class 1+** rock dodging for 1,100 m. It gets shallow and more difficult as you approach the end, where there is a bay on RL.
	418044	**Campsite**	Four-star site on RL in a beautiful bay with nice esker camping and walking, and great views of the rapids.
	421045	**Riffle**	
	427048	**Campsite**	Excellent open jack pine bench camping in the tiny bay on RL.
	428049	**Rapids** **Fishing hole**	**Class 1** and straightforward. Stop and fish now; there are all kinds of fish here.
	428053	**Riffle**	
	435058	**Fast water**	There's a sharper corner here than appears on the map.
	448068	**Riffle**	
	449069	**Campsite**	On RL just before the turn and the start of the rapids. You can fish from this camp.
	449069 450070	**Rapids**	**Class 1/1+**, shallow, rocky and 250 m long around the bend to the left. There's a rock apron at the end.
	449071	**Campsite**	On RL in a nice bay after the rapids.
	470089	**Campsite**	On RR in a tiny bay after the island. Fine open bench camping.
	471090	**Fast water**	Where the river narrows again.
	472090 480098	**Rapids**	**Class 1**, shallow and rocky for 1 km. There's a rock apron at the end.
	493114	**Campsite**	On RL is a very nice spot on the shoulder of the esker. Hiking is good along the esker. An added bonus.
	505119	**Eagle Nest**	On a point on RL where the river narrows. The other riverbank is burned.
74 I/16	514132	**Campsite**	Esker camping in a sheltered bay on RR.
	562188	**Campsite** **Take-out**	This is Cat's Meow campsite and pick-up spot! Five stars for this beach-and-bench special. On RL at the end of Waterfound Bay. To your right is the Fond du Lac.

waterfound river

175

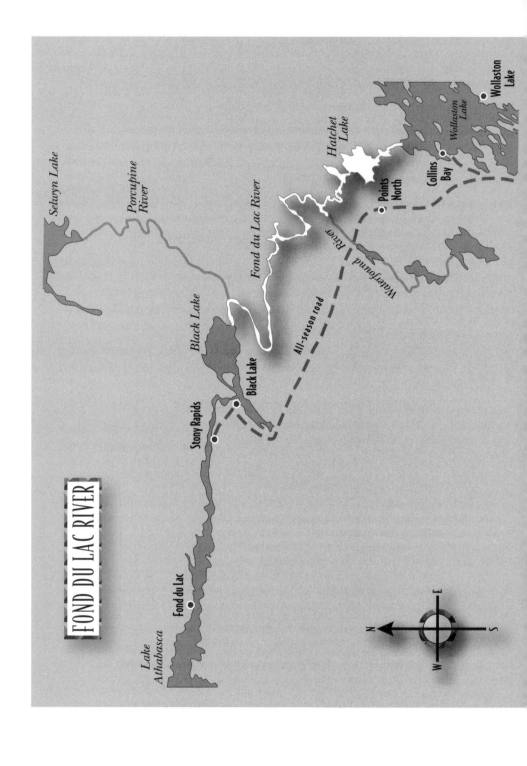

FOND DU LAC RIVER

The Fond du Lac is the mother river of the Far North. This magnificent silver ribbon ties together vast, clear lakes — Wollaston, Hatchet, Black and Lake Athabasca. It is a premier wilderness canoeing experience.

The sandy Athabasca Plain is home to most of the river's length, but it also runs through the Shield in places, making for contrasting scenery and a variety of types of rapids. The south shores of both Black Lake and Lake Athabasca are gentle and sandy, while their north shores are extremely rugged, with gneiss boulders and soaring granite cliffs. A number of famous cataracts grace the Fond du Lac's flow, including Manitou, Burr and Elizabeth Falls. Most of the river's rapids are quite runnable, however. Rock gardens, boulder aprons, and smooth sandstone ledges make the Fond du Lac a fun and challenging river to paddle.

You can angle for Arctic grayling, walleye, northern pike and lake trout on this trip, plus enjoy the best camping there is. I don't think you can find better camping than on the Fond du Lac; it's even better than on the Churchill, much as I love it. Moose and bears are known to amble by in broad daylight for your viewing pleasure.

But for me, it's the landscape that draws me to this river. Once you have drifted by the yellow cliffs of layered sandstone rising high into the blue, northern sky and climbed to view the vista of Black Lake beyond the gorges of Burr Falls, you are hooked. The Fond du Lac is one of the most beautiful rivers I've ever paddled, and there have been a few.

Length

The trip described in detail is approximately 222 km. It starts at a small island in Cunning Bay on Wollaston Lake and finishes on the south shore of Black Lake. You can easily shorten this trip if you don't have twelve days to paddle the majority of the river. I strongly recommend that you do not plan to do more than 20 to 25 km a day. Being a wide, slow-moving river, it can be a tough slog in many places if the wind is against you.

You can fly into Crooked Lake, Waterfound Bay or Kosdaw Lake to shorten your trip. To avoid the kilometre-long portage of Burr Falls and to shorten the trip even more, you can fly out at the confluence of the Fond du Lac and Porcupine Rivers. This takes off 12 km, but really saves you almost a day. I recommend the whole trip, though!

To extend the trip, you can start on the Waterfound River. This option adds around 30 km, though you miss the beginning of the Fond du Lac. The Waterfound is prettier, in my opinion, and is often a better option in a moderately low-water year because the first couple of rapids out of Wollaston Lake are very shallow. However, when it's a really low-water year you may want to go with the top of the Fond du Lac. At least you can portage the dry rapids, whereas you would have to drag and bushwhack on the Waterfound. There is only one portage on the Waterfound and many, many kilometres of shallow rapids.

To add more length and to travel only on the Fond du Lac, you can paddle the northwestern shore of Wollaston Lake from Collins Bay. This option adds 20 km of open lake paddling. Then you can also paddle across Black Lake to the community there, making for an additional 35 km of very exposed lake paddling. Or you can paddle and portage (oh, yes — big time!) another 32 km to Stony Rapids, where the road and airstrip are. Finally, you can do the whole Fond du Lac River, right to the community of Fond du Lac on the east end of Lake Athabasca; this trip is approximately 395 km. Keep in mind that if you paddle the large lakes you may be windbound for one or more days, and open-water crossings such as these are potentially dangerous.

Kosdaw Lake to the south shore of Black Lake*	132 km
Crooked Lake to the confluence of Porcupine and Fond du Lac*	155 km
Waterfound Bay to the south shore of Black Lake*	155 km
Crooked Lake to the south shore of Black Lake*	167 km
Cunning Bay to the south shore of Black Lake*	222 km
Cunning Bay to the community of Black Lake	257 km
Collins Bay to the community of Black Lake	287 km
Collins Bay to Stony Rapids	313 km
Collins Bay to the community of Fond du Lac	395 km

* These routes are described in detail in the Trip Notes section.

Topographic Maps

For routes ending at the south shore of Black Lake, 1:50,000 scale maps are recommended. After that the 1:250,000 are sufficient. For all the routes putting in at Wollaston and taking out at the Porcupine or the south shore of Black Lake you will need 64 L/5, 64 L/12, 64 L/13, 64 I/16, 74 P/2 and 74 P/3. If you start at Crooked Lake, you don't need 64 L/5. If you start at Kosdaw or Waterfound Bay, you won't need 64 L/5 or 64 L/12. For the trips to the community of Black Lake or to Stony Rapids, you will need the 1:250,000 scale map 74P. To carry on to the community of Fond du Lac add 74O.

I suggest you purchase these maps in advance and, using the Trip Notes, mark in all the rapids that are missing on the maps. And put Manitou Falls in the right place – it's disturbing that it is marked one rapid too far upstream. I guess it could be worse. It might have been marked too far downstream!

There have been extensive forest fires along the Fond du Lac, but most of the burn comes at the beginning and the end, with the exception of the burns just before the Pilot's Lodge and around the Perch River confluence. I'd think about marking in the good camping in these areas. Plus, you just don't want to miss some of those five-star hotels I've listed!

Getting There and Away

The trip I have highlighted starts and ends with a floatplane charter from Points North. It's not a cheap option, but it is extremely convenient. All you have to do is drive the gravel highway to Points North (about six hours from La Ronge, depending on road conditions). Park your vehicle in their safe compound, and charter a floatplane to your put-in from there. Then charter your return trip, flying back to your vehicle from your take-out of choice. It's as easy as it gets.

You do have other options. You can put in at the Collins Bay or anywhere along the southwest shore of Wollaston Lake where a road leads to the water — the bridge at the Geikie or Hidden Bay Provincial Campground, for example. Arranging for parking with a fishing lodge that has road access is a good possibility. Check out your options by calling around.

If you paddle all the way to the community of Black Lake or to Stony Rapids, there are a number of return trip options. The difficulty lies in getting your canoes back to Points North. This information applies to all the Far Northern rivers in this guidebook — the Cree, the Fond du Lac, the William, the MacFarlane, and the Porcupine. Shuttling vehicles to Stony is a nightmare drive of twelve to thirteen hours one way from La Ronge, but it is possible. You must have a four-by-four, heavy-duty vehicle in top running condition and jerry cans of gas. You can't buy gas past Points North, and you still have six hours of driving from there. Then you would fly out of Stony to the Wollaston Lake put-in and paddle to the community of Black Lake. From there you could carry on to Stony Rapids via the river or a half-ton "taxi" from Black Lake to get back to your vehicles. Ask around for a "taxi," and someone will take you and your gear in their truck to Stony at a reasonable cost. Gas is not cheap, nor is maintaining a vehicle in such a remote location.

Another option is to drop your canoes and gear off at Points North, drive the vehicle up to Stony so you can take all the canoes back, and then have the driver fly back to Points North on a scheduled flight and charter a floatplane to your put-in. It's an option, but in the end it might not be all that much cheaper than just chartering a floatplane in and out.

If you want to fly on a scheduled flight out of Stony, whether you paddle there or take a "taxi" from the community of Black Lake, you will have to arrange to ship your canoes from there, and they may take a while to catch up to you. Renting canoes from Churchill River Canoe Outfitters at Points North will save you this hassle. Scheduled flights for passengers are available to and from Regina, Saskatoon, Prince Albert, La Ronge, Points North and Stony Rapids via Transwest. Call Points North about freighting canoes.

Basically, when it comes to doing Far North trips, you should know it's going to require time and money. Which of these you have to spare and the number of people in your party determine your best option.

When to Go

June to September. The Fond du Lac reaches its peak water level in June (415 cu m/sec on average) and doesn't lose that much volume over the summer months (July, 400; August, 360). Since it is a large-volume river for northern Saskatchewan, you can also paddle it in September. But I don't recommend it in a really low-water year. In early July of 2001, when I tagged along on a Churchill River Canoe Outfitters trip, the water was low. The flow dropped from 351 to 333 cu m/sec in the nine days, and the first rapids out of Wollaston Lake were basically dry a couple of weeks later.

There is a water-gauging station at the Fond du Lac's outflow into Black Lake. To check the current water levels on the river call SaskWater. Then compare the cu m/sec reading you get to the charts displaying the average monthly and annual flows from 1973 to 1993 on the Canoe Saskatchewan web site. This will tell you if the water is low, and whether an alternative plan is required. Also call a local source to double-check. The pilots at Points North and the resource officers in the SERM office in Wollaston or Stony Rapids should know the general water level of the river.

Difficulty of the River ✳✳✳

The Fond du Lac is a long and remote river, and sources of emergency help are few and far between. It's a large-volume river and very wide in spots. The river is actually like a lake in many places, so there is little current. You also change direction several times. Your chances of getting headwinds are pretty high, and all these factors can make for a strenuous paddle. Depending on the route you choose, there are also a number of open-water crossings.

The rapids of the Fond du Lac are usually followed by flatwater. However, there are some long and continuous sections of rapids. The average rapids are Class 2, and there are several common types. The trickiest are the ledges that nearly span the width of the river or come in multiples. The other interesting ones are the steep, wrap-o-matic boulder aprons at the end of chutes and rock gardens. The tops of the rapids are quite often deeper than the bottoms. And though the river is shallow, it has significant volume, making for large standing waves and stoppers in some places. When the Fond du Lac is in flood, it roars.

The portaging isn't all that strenuous. In the route described in detail there are only two mandatory portages — Manitou and Burr Falls. However, the trail around Burr Falls is about a kilometre long, and most canoeists will portage at least three or four times, including the two falls and the large ledge just before Manitou. Some will choose to run some rapids empty, or what the voyageurs called demi-chargé; Thompson Rapids is one I would recommend you don't run loaded. The mandatory portages are in good shape, but some of the ones on the upper Fond du Lac are burned out, and for some rapids there just isn't a trail. In low water you can usually line, but in high water you may have a tough portage if you decide not to run the rapids.

The Fond du Lac trip as highlighted in the Trip Notes is a good choice for intermediate paddlers wanting to make a step up. The river will challenge guided beginners. This is not the Far North river you want to be learning to paddle whitewater on. If your whitewater and bushcraft skills are limited you should have a guide or more experienced paddlers in your party. Be cautious, especially at high water. The gradient of the river is a mere 0.54 m/km (2.83 ft/mi), but that is not at all indicative of the challenging whitewater that can be found along its length. There are a number of lakes, large and small, that skew the figure.

Characteristics of the River and Region

The Fond du Lac twists and turns on its course northwest from Wollaston Lake to Lake Athabasca. It drops into large lakes on its way, and only the Reindeer and the lower section of the Churchill have more water flow. The riverbed is predominantly either sandy — a jumble of rocks or boulders — or smooth sandstone slabs with scattered rocks. Thus, the rapids are usually not large abrupt drops, but are often long and shallow with ledges.

For the most part, the Fond du Lac flows through the Athabasca Plain, except for a short distance from its headwaters and near its end, where the familiar outcrops of Precambrian bedrock and black spruce of the Taiga Shield appear. This makes for the variety in scenery and river characteristics. The first section of the Fond du Lac borders the Selwyn Lake Upland of the Taiga Shield, which lies to the east until just after Hatchet Lake. The river bumps up against the Shield again above Burr Falls, but in a much more dramatic fashion. Where the river intersects the harder rock of the Tazin Lake Upland there are large rapids or falls, as the rock is not easily eroded.

Though bordered on the north and east by Shield, the river is best characterized by its glacial-till features, including Tyrrell's *ispatinows* (meaning "conspicuous hills" in Cree), drumlins, and hummocks of moraine. As well, there are many prominent eskers in the area, some up to 80 km long. The soil is sandy, and the dryness of the area makes for extensive forest fires. Thus jack pine is the dominant forest along the river. This open parkland commonly has an understory of lichen, blueberry, bearberry and sand heather, among other small shrubs and herbs. Some black spruce occur on north-facing slopes of drumlin and eskers, while bogs are full of stunted black spruce with some tamarack.

At its headwaters, the river is wide with low banks of willow and black spruce, boulders of gray granite and gneiss. Much of the area is burned. After Hatchet Lake's beaches and sand come the lovely eskers and drumlins of the Waterfound Bay area. Then the yellow-and-red sandstone banks that are so characteristic of the Fond du Lac begin to show sporadically. The volume also increases greatly. The river runs through scrub banks again through Kosdaw, but the sand and sandstone return again at Red Bank Falls. The middle section of the river is the most scenic, where the layered sandstone cliffs and overhangs really come into their own. Nests perch upon tiny ledges high above the river, and caverns and crannies draw the eye. The erosion of the soft sandstone is art, as far as I'm concerned.

Manitou Falls is a photographic highlight, with its whirling green waters and spectacular sandstone formations. Then the river winds again through some low areas until sandy Otter Lake and the eskers above the Perch confluence. There is another large burn here. After you pass through the low, sandy area at the Porcupine confluence, the Shield outcropping begins and the granite cliffs rise, announcing Burr Falls. After the gorges and cataracts of Burr, the south shore of Black Lake is gentle and sandy. You can see the black rocks start again across the lake from your five-star hotel balcony of jack pine bench overlooking the beach.

Local History ✳✳✳

Wollaston Lake was called Manitou Lake in Thompson's day. It was named thus by the Cree, as it had two rivers, both flowing out of it in two different directions, yet it never ran dry. It is interesting that Thompson refers to its Cree name, as the Wollaston Lake area has generally been regarded as Dene territory, and he was travelling with Dene guides. He notes that, "while the Nahathaways [the Cree] possessed the country, they made offerings to it [Manitou Falls], and thought it the resident of a Manito; they have retired to milder climates; and the Chipewyans [the Dene] have taken their place who make no offerings to anything."

Today, there are three Dene communities along the Fond du Lac. The Hatchet Lake Denesuline Nation is based at Wollaston Lake, across the narrow bay from Wollaston Post. The Black Lake Denesuline Nation is centred on the northwest shore of Black Lake. The Fond du Lac Denesuline Nation is on the north shore of Lake Athabasca, at the community of Fond du Lac. Certainly the northern areas of the river have always been used by the Dene, though they did not use canoes to travel to Hudson Bay or Ile-à-la-Crosse to trade in the days of the early fur trade. They went overland on foot. Later, however, the Fond du Lac was part of the canoe route for Dene hunters summering in the south to head north to their wintering grounds to hunt caribou. Tyrrell met a group in the fall of 1892 enroute from Reindeer Lake to Black Lake.

According to Tyrell, Black Lake was called *Dess-da-tara-tua* by the Dene, meaning "the Mouths of Three Rivers Lake." The Cree, Chipman and Fond du Lac Rivers flow into the lake. Black Lake and its rivers were and still are the basis of important travel routes; hunters from Black Lake and the surrounding area still use the Fond du Lac today. Along the lower reaches of the river, I've often been asked if I saw any moose upriver! There are traplines along the river as well. For more information on the prehistory of the Black Lake area, consult Sheila Minni's published thesis, listed in the References.

According to Tyrrell, David Thompson renamed Black Lake for the "dark hills of norite," which overlook its northwest shore. However, another source indicates that the lake was actually renamed for Samuel Black (1780–1841), who was an HBC fur trader.

In written history, the Fond du Lac itself has had a number of names. Fidler, Turnor, Thompson and Tyrrell all refer to it as either the Black or Stone River. Tyrrell, in one of his reports published in 1895, also calls it the Hatchet River. But by 1896 he is consistently calling it the Stone River. How it eventually was named the Fond du Lac, I don't know. I've read that the French phrase means "neck of the lake," "end of the lake," or "the end of a waterway." Sigurd Olson states that it is "a voyageur's term for a place where a river flows in or out of a lake." If you look at the map, they are all good interpretations. Fond du Lac was originally the name of the HBC trading post at the far eastern end of Lake Athabasca during their years of competition with the NWC.

The most well-known exploration of the Fond du Lac was Thompson's ill-fated 1796 trip from Wollaston Lake to Lake Athabasca and back. He was trying to find a shortcut to the Mackenzie Basin from Hudson Bay. The accident happened on the return trip from Lake Athabasca. Thompson's two Dene guides, Paddy and Kosdaw, were lining the canoe up what is now called Thompson Rapids, when they lost control of it. Thompson was in the canoe steering it at the time. He was swept downstream, the canoe overturned, and he had a nasty swim through the rapids. They lost everything but the canoe, Thompson's papers and sextant, an axe, tent, rifle and knife. Worse yet, Thompson and Paddy ate immature eagles and became violently ill. Had the three men not come upon a Dene family camped upriver, they likely would not have survived.

Fidler explored the river in 1807 and wrote about it in his journals. Then Tyrrell and Dowling surveyed the river for the Geological Survey of Canada in 1892, the same expedition during which Tyrrell travelled the Geikie and the Foster. He had a hand in changing the names of the some of the Fond du Lac's landmarks as well. He renamed Kosdaw Lake (Black

Lake according to Thompson) for one of Thompson's guides. He named Elizabeth Falls after his sister, whose birthday it was while he was there. And there must be some reason the name Burr Falls came about, considering that his full name was Joseph Burr Tyrrell? He certainly admired the falls, writing, "Seen on a clear bright day towards the end of summer, the falls were perhaps the most beautiful that I ever beheld."

There is a quite a bit of reading material on the Fond du Lac. Thompson's diaries, edited by Tyrrell, provide the reader with the details of his nearly disastrous expedition in Thompson's own words. There was an article in *National Geographic* in August 1994 about a Fond du Lac canoe trip organized to celebrate the 200-year anniversary of Thompson's explorations. Sigurd Olson's account of his experience running the river is in *Runes of the North*. Joanie and Gary McGuffin's book, *Where Rivers Run: A 6,000 Mile Exploration of Canada by Canoe* also has some interesting anecdotes about their journey through northern Saskatchewan and paddling the Fond du Lac.

Tyrrell's report on the Athabasca region is the best book for those interested in the geology of the area. *The Wind and the Caribou*, by Erik Munsterhjelm, a trapper in the region in the '30s, also refers to interesting aspects of the Black Lake and Lake Athabasca region. *The Prospector: North of Sixty* is Ted Nagle's story of his experiences in the North and the mining industry. In a time when canoes were still used in prospecting, he took a trip down the Fond du Lac. For another perspective on uranium mining in the Wollaston Lake region read *Wollaston: People Resisting Genocide*, by Miles Goldstick.

Solitude ✳✳

The trip described in detail is a good one for solitude, considering how long it is. There are five communities along its length: Wollaston Post and the Lac La Hache Reserve on Wollaston Lake, Black Lake, Stony Rapids and Fond du Lac. It supports activity from numerous fishing and hunting camps and local trappers. You may see a fishing party on and around Hatchet Lake. And as you approach the confluence of the Perch River you may see some Camp Grayling boats. The Pilot's Lodge is a hunting camp on the river before Brink Rapids. Once you reach the Burr Falls vicinity, you may meet Dene hunters from Black Lake, some of whom have boats above the falls. The Fond du Lac is also a popular route with canoeists, so you may see another group of paddlers.

Wildlife ✳✳✳

I'm sure everyone who paddles the Fond du Lac sees a moose, and I'll bet you see more than one. Black bears are also very common. Your next likely bet is a family of river otters. In 2001, the group I was with was lucky enough to see a lynx on shore. That was only the second time I've seen one in the North in seventeen years of canoe tripping. And although it's unlikely, you may see woodland caribou.

We saw two trumpeter swans on Otter Lake, which is rare. There are large numbers of osprey and eagles, and you will observe raven and eagle nests on the sandstone cliffs.

Fishing ✳✳✳

I have fished on the Fond du Lac a number of times and always had good luck with most species, if not all of them. The spectacular and unusual thing about this river is that you can catch all the typical northern fish on one trip: walleye, grayling, northern pike and trout! There are a couple of really good walleye holes, one right below Red Bank Falls on river right, and another below Burr Falls. Manitou Falls can also be a hot spot. Grayling fishing is best in the shallow rapids, and there is good trout fishing at the outlet of the river at Wollaston and again at Hatchet. Black Lake is famous for its lake trout, as is Lake Athabasca, which you should check out if you go that far.

Special Equipment

A Royalex-hull tripping canoe is the best boat for the Fond du Lac. It's a long trip with some tricky boulder gardens and aprons with high wrap potential. You'll want a boat that will regain its shape so you can carry on down the river. Plus, most of the rapids are shallow, and you'll want to slide over those rocks and hidden sandstone ledges, not stick and flip! Kevlar would be my second choice.

Bring a bug jacket and or head net — the blackflies can be voracious. Maybe also bring a couple of sheets of paper or a little notebook and a pencil to keep the guest book supplied.

Trip Notes

MAP NO	GRID REF	FEATURE	DESCRIPTION
64 L/5		Camping	There are nice beach campsites along the western shore of Wollaston Lake from Collins Bay to the river outlet in Cunning Bay, such as 827690 to 837720 and 837725.
	834762	Put-in	Cunning Bay floatplane put-in. On a sand beach in a small bay on the east side of a small forested island.
64 L/12	824860	Red Willow Rapids	**Class 1**, rocky and shallow. If the water is low you will be dragging and wading. This is the shallowest rapid on the river. Do not despair!
	791883 790882	Rapids	**Class 1+, Class 1+ and Class 2**. The first two parts of the rapid are straightforward shallow chutes. Find the deep-water V. The last section is Class 2 with boulders in the middle and on RL. It may need to be lined or waded in low water.
	779897	Rapids	**Class 2**, unmarked, shallow, and rocky. There's a boulder ledge on RR in low water.
	779915	Cabins	On RR as you enter Hatchet Lake via Tromburg Bay.
	762914	Campsite	On an island in Tromburg Bay. On rock flats in the most northerly bay on the east side of the island.
	759918 759919	Campsite	On RL. Take your pick of the beach-and-bench specials in the double bays. This is your introduction to Fond du Lac's famous camping.
	760969	Campsite	Another Hilton on the beach. This time you have a whole island to call home.
	825005	Fishing lodge	The famous Hatchet Lake Lodge. Five-star accommodations with 87 buildings! It runs on Manitoba time.
	736015	Campsite	A protected spot on the northwest tip of a small island at the northwest end of Hatchet Lake.
	710049	Rapids	**Class 2 and 2+**. There are two channels to choose from in the first of two parts of the Hatchet Lake outlet rapid. An island splits the river, and the two rapids going around it are about the same level of difficulty. The RL or west channel has a **portage (610 m)**, which is in poor condition and begins at a dilapidated dock and ends below both sections of the rapids (709055). If you portage here you bypass both parts of the rapids. The rapids in the RL channel

MAP NO	GRID REF	FEATURE	DESCRIPTION
			are 300 m long and start with a Class 2 chute. The rapids end in a Class 2+ boulder garden. The rapids in the RR or eastern channel are 450 m long and Class 2. They start with a chute and some rock dodging follows. The second part of the outlet rapid starts at 711053 and comes almost immediately after the two channels join. There is a chute with boulders near the bottom and big waves. Class 2+ in lower water and 200 m long.
	687053	Campsite	In a deep bay on RL. Grab a spot out of the burn. This beach is the last unburned camping area for the next 8 or 9 km.
	664059	Rapids	**Class 3+ and Class 2.** This two-part rapid flows out of Corson Lake. The first section has a Class 3+ ledge that can be lined down on RL. In high water you can pull over the rocks on RL. The second part of the rapid is a Class 2 boulder-dodging exercise. You could portage through the burn on RL if the water level leaves you no other option. There is no trail to speak of.
	658068 655076	Rapids	**Class 1 and fast water** for about 900 m. There are several sections of shallow rapids.
	655077 653079	Rapids	**Class 2+, Class 2 and Class 2+/3 or Class 3+/4.** This large, unmarked rapid begins about 100 m after the above riffles. There are three parts to it. The first part is before the bend to the left and is a **Class 2+** drop. The second part that goes around the bend is a shallow and rocky Class 2. The last set flows around an unmarked island. The **Class 2+** RL channel is smaller volume and has a boulder ledge that can be run if there is enough water. In low water it is unnavigable except by lining and wading. The RR channel has a large ledge, Class 3+/4, and is difficult to line or wade. There is a **portage (375 m)** on RL that was burned out, and the trail is hard to find. It starts in a weedy bay just above the first set and ends below the boulder ledge in the RL channel.
	631091 636100 610108	Campsites	On the RR shore of Crooked Lake there are numerous beaches at which to camp. These are the best spots for camping in the next 10 km or so until you reach Waterfound Bay, as the area downstream is burned.
64 L/13	598138	Rapids	**Class 1 and Class 1+/2.** Class 1 and fast water for approximately 300 m before the six bars marked on the map. The bars represent easy Class 1+/2 rapids, which get very shallow at the end. No portage was found. Enjoy the marvellous sandstone formations so characteristic of the Fond du Lac.
	587148	Rapids Fishing hole	**Class 2+.** This next marked rapid (one bar) is a short Class 2+ boulder run, with a boulder apron at the bottom that can be tricky in low water. There's good walleye fishing in the eddies below. Hatchet Lake Lodge boats gather here, and the guides say it's always good!
74 I/16	562180	Campsite	Just around the corner is Waterfound Bay. This beach-and-bench camp is on the southernmost island, and is a great spot to camp, as is most everywhere around here!

the trips

184

MAP NO	GRID REF	FEATURE	DESCRIPTION
	561189	Campsite	On RL is the supreme beach-and-bench camping spot, high over Waterfound Bay. Hilton says it all!
74 L/13	579199	Put-in Campsite	On RL is another beauty. It's also an optional put-in spot, and is where people fly out from the Waterfound River trip.
	604220	Campsite	Yet another beach-and-bench combo on RL. It's too good, and faces northeast this time. The last nice camp for 12 km.
	607247 605252	Rapids	**Class 2+\3**. Marked by five bars, these rapids can be scouted from RL, where a **portage** of sorts (**375 m** and in poor condition) begins about 50 m above the rapids. There are tricky ledges at the bottom and big waves to be negotiated.
	614287 605295	Fast water	The fast water flows around large, wooded islands. The left channel around the first island has the most water, while the right channel around the second island is best in lower water.
	607300 608311	Rapids	**Class 1**. There are several sections of small rapids where the river narrows after the islands.
	599319	Riffle	After a narrows with riffles there is a nice bench to camp on.
	599320 595324	Camping	A long bench provides lots of sites on RR. Try fishing the fast water.
	591324 587325	Flett Rapids	**Class 1+**, a 400-m boulder run.
	587331	Fishing camp	In a bay on RR. Though a nice spot to stop, don't camp here — there have been bear problems.
	585333	Fast water	As the river narrows before entering Kosdaw Lake.
74 I/16	572364	Riffles	Wide and shallow outlet rapids from Kosdaw Lake.
	573366	Rapids	**Class 1**. A chute at the bend to the left.
64 L/13	573372 576378	Red Bank Falls	**Class 2**. This is not a falls, but there is a ledge at the top of this 850-m-long rapid. The rapid begins with fast water as you approach the turn to the right. The ledge follows and extends across RL and RC. It can be run on RR. Waves and a boulder garden follow. The boulder garden gets more difficult towards the end, where there is a shallow apron to be negotiated.
	577376	Campsite Fishing hole	On RR, at the peak of the bend to the left in Red Bank, about 500 m down the rapid, is a beautiful birch tree and red sandstone campsite. Eddy out on RR. You can fish for walleye, pike and grayling from this camp too! Fish the eddy at the bottom of the rapid on RR for walleye, fish the weeds in the deep part of the bay for pike and the shallow rapids for grayling.
74 I/16	543363	Rapids	**Class 1+**. This marked rapid in the narrows has shallow ledges on RR and RL in lower water. We ran left of RC.
	530360	Raven Rock Channel	The river divides here, and the northern channel is the most beautiful by far, and not to be missed unless there is no water in it! The channel starts out as a narrow creeking exercise with numerous **Class 1 and Class 2** rapids. You'll want plastic here! Then the

fond du lac river

185

MAP NO	GRID REF	FEATURE	DESCRIPTION
			characteristic Fond du Lac yellow sandstone beauties begin at 523364. The name of the channel comes from these amazing sandstone cliffs, which overhang the river, and the raven's nest that is perched on a tiny ledge high on RL (522364).
	518364	Campsite	Just after the sandstone is an esker on RR. Camping here may make for good wildlife viewing. Lynx, moose, bears, eagles and osprey have been sighted in this area, and there's good fishing.
	517363	Eagle nests	There are two nests on RR just down from the esker camp. As I said, a good fishing opportunity.
	516363	Riffle	Between the two islands after the point with the nests.
	510359	Rapids	**Class 1+**. At the end of the north channel and 250 m long. The rapids become an S-turn as the south channel joins.
	508358 500355	Fast water	Around the island after the junction rapid. It continues until you see sandstone cliffs again.
	498355	Rapids	**Class 1+**, with shallow areas to be avoided.
	495357	Riffles	After the sandstone cliffs there is a 750-m section of riffles and fast water.
	485356	Campsite	On RL where rock is showing.
	484357	Campsite	On RL. On the point is open bench camping.
	480361 478363	Riffles	Where sandstone cliffs begin again on RL. The river splits around islands, and there are many small rapids that are easily negotiated.
	477363	Campsite	On RL is a large site above a rock outcrop.
	475371	Rapids	**Class 1**, rocky and shallow where the river enters Otter Lake. This lake can be very shallow in spots.
	427378 425377	Rapids	**Class 1+**. An S-turn chute joining the east and west parts of Otter Lake.
	420387	Campsite	On the RL shore on the west end of Otter Lake is a four-star campsite. Beach-and-bench combo. If you don't like the southeast exposure, keep going around the point.
	422391	Campsite	On RR is rock ledge camping at its finest.
	419388	Inukshuk	On the RL point is a large and elaborate Inukshuk on the rock overhang. Right beside it is a great rock campsite.
	418386	Campsite	On RL in a tiny cove just after an Inukshuk. Very nice rock shelf camping.
	414383	Campsite	The five-star baby. On RL is a very large beach-and-bench site. Stretch your legs.
	409384	Campsite	The same as above, also on RL, but with a penthouse suite on top of the high bench.

MAP NO	GRID REF	FEATURE	DESCRIPTION
	400384	Rapids	**Class 1+.** The marked rapid on the map where the river narrows again after Otter Lake is a straightforward run.
	398383	Riffle	At low water there is a small rapid at the second narrows. You can see the sandstone cliffs marking the beginning of Thompson Rapids from here. Stay RR to get to the portage and scouting spots.
	395382	Thompson Rapids	**Class 2+/3, Class 2, and Class 1+.** Thompson Rapids can be described in three sections. The first part is a series of tricky ledges. The second part starts after the large eddy on RR. It consists of shallow rapids with a ledge on RL and a chute on RR, with boulders to avoid at the corner. The last part after the sharp turn to the right is a shallow rock-dodging exercise. These rapids eventually become riffles until the river widens into the bay at 386377. The **portage (550 m)** on RR bypasses most of the rapids, except the Class 1+ and the riffles at the end. The trail begins in a tiny cove right before the sandstone point where the fast water picks up above the rapids. You have to carry up a sand bank, but the trail is excellent. It ends on the rocky shore below the point of the sharp turn to the right at 390379.
	361376	Riffle	At a turn to the right where the river narrows.
	362377 361378	Rapids	**Class 1** for 200 m after a bend to the left.
	359379 355379	Rapids	**Class 1 with a Class 2 ledge.** Class 1 rapids start just before the marked bar on the map, which indicates the Class 2 ledge in the north channel around the mid-river island. Several riffles follow as the river begins to narrow again before the rapid indicated by six bars, which is mistakenly labelled Manitou Falls.
	355380	Rapids	**Class 2.** A small ledge must be navigated just before the widening of the river to the right and before the six bars. It must be navigated on far RL in order to catch the portage for the incorrectly named rapid indicated by the six bars.
	355381	Rapids Campsite	**Class 4 and Class 1+.** The six bars represent a 1-m-high ledge falls followed by long, shallow rapids. The **portage (400 m)** starts on RL in a small, sandy cove. The trail is a steep sand bank at the beginning, which you can spot from just after the small ledge described above. The rest of the trail is in good condition, going through an old burn. Stay to your left down to a rocky cove. You could put in earlier if you wanted to use ropes to lower your boats and gear down from a rock cliff before the cove. The rapids below the rocky cove are not difficult, but be on the lookout for a hidden ledge (at some water levels) in this next short, straight stretch before Manitou Falls. There is a great campsite right above the big ledge. It is about 20 m off the portage trail to the right.
	354384	Rapids	**Riffles with a Class 2 ledge.** The high sandstone cliffs continue all the way to Manitou Falls, which is closer than you think. Looking ahead after you leave the last portage, you can see the cliffs where

fond du lac river

187

MAP NO	GRID REF	FEATURE	DESCRIPTION
			the river turns to the right. That's the corner just above where the falls start. There are shallows and riffles to be negotiated first, and in the narrowest spot before the island there is a Class 2 ledge that can be run on RL. The portage for Manitou is also on RL, and starts across from the tiny, mid-river island (355388, above the "F" in FALLS). The top section of the falls drops around this tiny island. Be cautious on this approach, especially at high water.
	355388	Manitou Falls Campsite	The **portage (125 m)** is on RL and starts on large, flat rocks across from the small island. It ends in a sandy cove below the falls in the fast water. A fine campsite is to the left of the head of the portage trail, just behind the Inukshuk. Be sure to sign the guest book, which was started in the early '80s. It is located in a cairn that can be found up on a rock ridge behind the campsite. The ridge starts at a funky overhang, and extends to where it overlooks the sandstone gorge you just descended. Remove the top rock of the cairn and find the old, rusty can. It's fun to read the notebooks, but be sure to put everything back as you found it for the next group to enjoy.
	353393 346394	Riffles	The river narrows after the falls, making for several small rapids and sections of fast water.
	343393	Rapids	**Class 1** where the river narrows.
	342391 340390	Rapids	**Class 1+**, waves and rock dodging for 150 m.
	337393 337395	Rapids	**Class 1**. An S-turn after a large bay on the left where the river narrows.
	337397 336399	Rapids	**Class 1+**, starting with a riffle and becoming a rock dodge.
74 P/1	334405 330409	Riffles	There are a series of riffles and fast-water sections as the river narrows again after the confluence of the unnamed river or creek coming in from Moosonees Lake.
	321414	Riffles	The sandstone cliffs start again at 323411, and in this gorge there are a couple of riffles at the narrows as the river bends right.
	320416	Rapids	**Class 2**. A hidden ledge, marked as a tiny mid-river island on the map, can be run on far, far RR. The gorge ends at 320420.
	320420 315425	Rapids	**Riffles and Class 1**. After the gorge, where the river starts to bend in a U-shape, there are riffles followed by rocky, shallow rapids. There are islands on RL here that are not marked on the map.
	289417	Riffle	Where the river narrows again.
74 P/2	261408	Campsite	On RL, a jack pine bench on the point after the braided island section.
	236415	Campsite	On RL, a jack pine bench before a big bay. Easy access.
	235418	Rapids	**Class 1**. Sandstone cliffs begin again after the big bay on RL, and a small rapid follows. There is a burn on RL, and it continues until just before the Pilot's Lodge.

MAP NO	GRID REF	FEATURE	DESCRIPTION
	233430	Eagle nest	On a rock outcropping cliff on RL, about 6 m up.
	220437	Camp	The Pilot's Lodge is on RR. There are cabins, boats and sheds.
	210440	Campsite	On the right side of a small island in mid-river. Nice!
	210441	Campsite	Across from the island camp on RR, with flat rock and open forest. There is fast water out in front of both camps and potential fishing.
	185446 174443	Brink Rapids	**Class 2+ and Class 2**. These long rapids start with Class 2+ ledges above the island. One extends almost all the way across the river. We scouted from RL and ran far RR, stopping on the left side of the island to scout the next section. The second set of ledges are **Class 2** and again span almost the entire channel. We ran far RR, as close around the left shore of the island as we could. After the island, shallow Class 2 rapids continue on into a boulder run that has a very shallow apron at the end. The whole rapid is about 1,200 m long and ends at the last small island marked on the map where the river widens again.
	146441	Rapids	**Class 1**, just above Brassy Rapids.
	145442 137437	Brassy Rapids	**Class 2/2+**. The south channel of Brassy starts with shallow Class 2 rock dodging. Then the rapids become a big, wavy, fast chute. You can see the bottom from this steep chute. The rapids turn to the left a bit near the bottom, and then drop steeply over a tight boulder apron that is Class 2+ at lower water levels. Caution is required here; this is a wrap rapid. Catch an eddy and look for the deep water. Lining and wading may be required to descend safely.
	129433	Campsite	On RR, up on the shoulder of the sand escarpment, there is an open bench for camping. There were stairs fashioned when we were there. It's a good place to dry off if Brassy bounced you around!
	127431	Fast water	In the narrows after the campsite.
	065412	Campsite	On RL, facing west, with a sunset supreme. This is primo camping. There's a sand beach to park and play on with a flat bench to sleep on.
	024411 023411	Rapids	**Riffles and Class 1+**. In the south or left channel around a big mid-river island there is a riffle around the smaller island, which turns into a Class 1+ shelf rapid.
	019411 017411	Rapids	**Class 1**, an S-turn rapid, 400 m downstream from the shelf described above.
	994413	Riffles	Where the channels converge after the big island there is fast water and riffles.
74 P/3	994413	Campsite	On RR the great beach-and-bench combo strikes again.
	982414 977414	Hawkrock Rapids	**Class 1+**. An unmarked chute is followed by a straightforward S-turn, which is represented on the map by two bars. A bit of a letdown!
	931411	Campsite	On RR a sandy jack pine bench with birch trees. A nice spot, with views up and down the river, and good moose watching.

MAP NO	GRID REF	FEATURE	DESCRIPTION
	900425 903435	**North Rapids Campsite**	**Class 2 and Class 1.** These rapids are long and shallow at the end. There are two ledges to be avoided in the first section before the shallows and the mid-river island. The first ledge is the largest and can be run on RR. The second, smaller ledge is just above the point on RR and can be run on far RR, then the rapids are very shallow around the island. Two small ledges on RR follow the island. Just after the first ledge and before the second is a tiny cove on RR. Eddy out here to camp up top at Table Rock (903433). It's a bit of a scramble up, but you have the best view in town. Surfing on the first little ledge can be fun. Fishing is good here, too.
	944469	**Campsite**	I know. How does one choose? Here is another beach-and-bench combo on RL with a view on both sides of the point. Some birch around makes it pretty too.
	953476	**Campsite**	This is a great area for camping. More beach-and-bench on RL with a view times two.
74 P/2	016497	**Campsite**	A prime spot, very sheltered, facing southwest on RL.
	050498	**Campsite**	Your last chance for prime camping for 12 km. In a protected bay on RR with great swimming with a lovely bench for camping. Burn and swamp coming up.
	085526 091533	**Perch Rapids**	**Class 2+ and Class 1.** There are two Class 2+ ledges at the beginning of these rapids. They can both be run on far, far RL. The first is at the very top of the rapids and the second about 150 m later. Shallow Class 1 rapids follow for a long stretch.
	103545 103547	**Rapids**	**Class 2.** Where the dashes are marked on the map is a ledge, which is difficult to see at some water levels. The ledge is after you turn the corner to the right. We ran it on far, far RL while viewing a moose eating in the shallows! After the ledge there are Class 2 rapids for 150 m.
	105554 110562	**Rapids**	**Class 2, Class 1, and riffles.** This is a section of fairly continuous rapids. After the sweeping turn back to the right where the dashes are marked on the map is another tricky Class 2 ledge. It can again be run on far, far RL. Following the ledges are Class 1 rapids and riffles until the river widens into a big bay. In this big bay to the left is another bay full of lily pads. Many northern pike live here. For walleye, fish below the next rapids.
	117575	**Rapids Fishing hole**	**Class 2,** an unmarked chute. Walleye fishing is fantastic when you fish the eddy lines on either side of the chute. Also try the point on RR below the rapids.
	126579	**Campsite**	On RR is a beauty of a spot. Beach-and-bench and a nice walk up the shore to view the confluence of the Porcupine and the Fond du Lac.
	123602	**Campsite**	I call this spot Camping for Millions; esker camping at its largest and best. You can hike around here to your heart's content. You may want to reserve a spot if you are coming down the Porcupine any time soon. I did in 2001, when I paddled the Fond du Lac in July and the Porcupine in August. There is very little for camping from here until after Burr Falls because of the burn in the mid-'90s.

| --- | --- | --- | --- |
	019585 013590	Burr Falls	The simplest way to **portage** this two-channel falls is to carry about **1 km** on RR. The trail begins 300 m above where the fast water begins, as the portage cuts off the point of land. The trail is fairly good after you get through the low spot at the beginning, although there may be some deadfall due to the burn. But lots of people use this trail, so there won't be much. To view most of the falls and catch a glimpse of Black Lake way down the gorge you can cautiously land on the head of Burr Island, and then bushwhack through the burn to view the top of both falls. The RR channel is more impressive, but if you want to stretch your legs, check out the lesser-known Burr Falls in the RL channel. Walleye fishing below the falls is really good if you fish the eddy lines. The points on RL after the falls where there is current can be good too.
	001593	Campsite	On RL there is bench camping just before the outlet to Black Lake. This site is more sheltered than the one on the south shore of Black Lake if you need protection from bad weather.
	002597	Campsite Take-out	A lovely beach-and-bench on Black Lake on the right side of the river outlet facing northwest. Go to the big beach to make your pilot happy.

fond du lac river

191

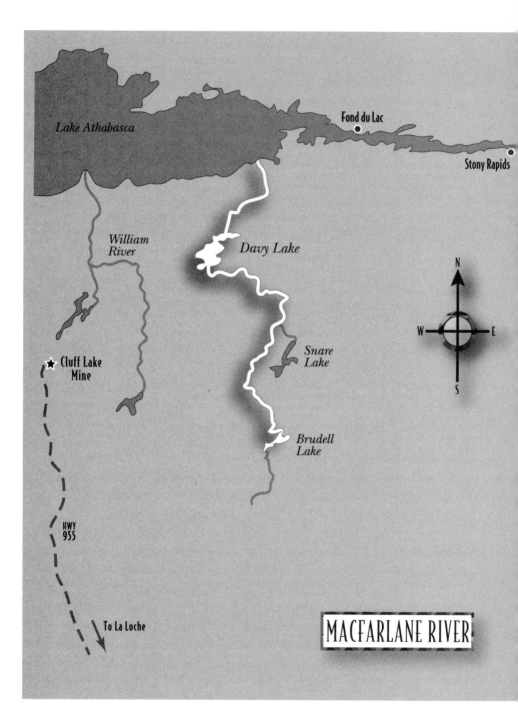

MacFarlane River

The MacFarlane River gets top marks when it comes to wilderness rivers in Saskatchewan's Far North, and that's saying quite a bit. It has stunning waterfalls, 15-m-deep canyons, and sand dunes. The river is a whitewater bonanza, with excellent camping and lots of wildlife. Plus, you are surrounded by hundreds of square kilometres of wilderness, travelled only by the First Nations people and trappers until very recently. A set of rock paintings adds to the ancient feeling of the land.

But be warned, it is also home to one of the worst portages in the province. Luckily the gold-and-orange vertical cliffs and the cascades of multiple falls of Second Canyon are truly spectacular, so spectacular they almost make the extremely long bushwhack portage bearable!

The added bonus of the trip is that the MacFarlane takes you to the eastern tip of the Athabasca Sand Dunes Wilderness Park. Here, the flowing dunes will become your camera's focus. At a small lake 6 km up the river from Lake Athabasca you will find fishing heaven and a place to camp and hike the dunes. You can observe a northern desert engulfing a living forest.

If you choose to carry on down the river to the largest lake in northern Saskatchewan, Lake Athabasca, you will be rewarded with a view of the remnants of a gigantic glacial lake, vast and untouched, in a class of its own. You can also fish for lake trout at the mouth of the MacFarlane. This river is a challenge, but it has it all.

Length

The trip described here is approximately 210 km. It starts at the northernmost tip of Brudell Lake and ends at the small island by Dead Cree Point, east of the MacFarlane's mouth on Lake Athabasca.

If you do not want to portage the canyons or do not feel you have the skill to attempt the lower MacFarlane, you can take out at Davy Lake. This shortens the route to 145 km, and it is a much easier trip. If you want to shorten the trip and do the MacFarlane's canyons you can put in at Snare Lake, paddling the Snare River to its confluence with the MacFarlane. Paddling to the optional pick-up spot on a small, unnamed lake on the MacFarlane about 6 km upstream of Lake Athabasca shortens the trip described in the notes by 13 km.

To extend the trip, you can put in on the southern end of Brudell Lake or Lazenby Lake upstream from there. If you choose to put in at Lazenby, that will add approximately 80 km. Another option for extending the trip is to paddle along the south shore of Lake Athabasca to Fond du Lac or even Stony Rapids or Black Lake. The thing to remember with these options is that they involve exposed paddling on Lake Athabasca, where wind will always be a factor. You may be windbound for one or more days, so you must build extra days into your trip plan.

For the entire trip described in the Trip Notes, from Brudell Lake to Dead Cree Point on Lake Athabasca, you should give yourself two weeks. Don't cheat the dunes; you'll want to spend at least one day hiking. Plus, those canyon portages involve rugged terrain and a lot of time. You also may become windbound on Lake Athabasca.

Brudell Lake to Davy Lake*	145 km
Snare Lake via Snare River to the small lake on the MacFarlane	154 km
Brudell Lake to the small lake on the MacFarlane*	197 km
Brudell Lake to Lake Athabasca island pickup*	210 km
Brudell Lake to community of Fond du Lac	250 km
Lazenby Lake to Lake Athabasca island pickup	290 km

* These trips are described in detail in the Trip Notes section.

Topographic Maps

I recommend 1:50,000 maps 74J/4, 74J/5, 74K/8, 74J/12, 74J/13, 74J/16, 74K/16, 74N/1 and 74O/4. These maps suffice for choosing from the options noted in the previous section, except that for the Snare Lake route you don't need 74J/4. When paddling the south shore of Lake Athabasca to Fond du Lac you will also need 74O/5 and 74O/6. I suggest you purchase these maps in advance and use the map coordinates in the Trip Notes section to mark in the large number of rapids and falls missing from the originals. Many of the rapids on the MacFarlane River are not marked. I strongly recommend you study the notes on the canyons carefully, and pencil in the details for portaging them on your maps.

Getting There and Away

Getting to and from the MacFarlane is an expensive undertaking. This trip is remote, and you must fly in. Most groups fly into Brudell Lake. However, as I outlined earlier, there are a number of other options should you want to shorten or extend your trip. In a low-water year Brudell is probably the best put-in, as the river has some volume at that point.

The two easiest ways to get you and your canoes to the MacFarlane put-ins involve chartering a floatplane from the south. You can drive to Buffalo Narrows; La Loche; or Fort McMurray, Alberta; and charter a floatplane to your put-in of choice. Or you can drive to Points North and fly direct from there with Points North Air. Pick the place that has the size of plane you need for where you want to take out. The cost depends on how many there are in your party and where you are coming from. You can rent canoes from Air Mikisew in La Loche, from CRCO at Points North, and from Voyage Air in Buffalo Narrows or Fort McMurray.

The problem with paddling in the Far North right now is that there is no longer a scheduled DC 3 flight to ship canoes back and forth from Stony Rapids or Fond du Lac to Points North. The simplest solution, if you choose to catch a scheduled flight to Stony Rapids to begin your trip, is to rent canoes from Cliff Blackmur at Athabasca Fishing Lodges. You can also freight your own canoes up by air or drive the all-weather road and charter out of Stony. If you paddle all the way back to Stony and then drive back south, that would probably be the cheapest, but most time-consuming option.

Transwest has scheduled, daily flights from Regina, Saskatoon, Prince Albert, La Ronge and Points North to Stony Rapids. They also have floatplanes for charter at Stony, including a Twin Otter. Northern Dene Air provides floatplane charters, and you can also charter Athabasca Fishing Lodges' Single Otter floatplane from Stony Rapids to your put-in. Pick a company that has the plane that suits the number in your party and can take you out from where you want to end. The rates from Stony are going to be very similar.

There are two common alternatives for flying out from the take-outs. Many canoeists choose to arrange for pickup at the small, unnamed lake on the MacFarlane about 6 km upstream from the mouth at Lake Athabasca. However, some Otter pilots won't want to land there, as the lake is small. You may have to fly out with a Beaver. Make sure you discuss with the air services where you want to take out, before booking a charter.

The other common option is to paddle to the mouth of the river and then another 7 km on Lake Athabasca to a small island near Dead Cree Point. Here, any size of floatplane can pick you up. The south side of the island is used by Athabasca Fishing Lodges as a pick-up and drop-off point for their customers, who fish for lake trout at the mouth of the MacFarlane. You may be able to arrange to meet in the morning when they bring out a group with their Otter from Otherside Lodge and fly back with them — a cost-saving backhaul.

However, if you choose to paddle to the island take-out to catch an Otter or a Twin Otter, the wind can be a problem. The south side of the island, where you will be picked up, is often sheltered. But you have to get there, and there is little shelter at the mouth of the MacFarlane. Be sure to add one or more days into your itinerary in case it is too rough for the plane to pick you up as scheduled. Let me remind you that if you do not want to deal with the canyons and the portages, or do not have the skill to, flying out of Davy Lake after the first section of the river is the best take-out option.

Paddling east along the south shore of Lake Athabasca to Fond du Lac or Stony Rapids will get you to an airstrip, and there are scheduled flights by Transwest during the week from those communities. This is your cheapest option if you don't have canoes to haul back. But you must be prepared to be windbound for one or more days trying to navigate the south shore of the lake. And be cautious: it is potentially dangerous to paddle such a distance of open water.

When to Go

June to August. There is lots of water in the river in May, but the ice may still be on Brudell Lake, and Lake Athabasca will still be full of ice. If you go too late in the season, this moderate-volume river may become difficult to navigate. But if you are a group of advanced and exceptional canoeists and the water levels are moderately low, you may be interested in running some parts of the second canyon. Water levels are highest in May and June, so you may want to wait for the lower-end flow in late July, August or early September, depending on the local precipitation that year.

One of the two water-gauging stations on the MacFarlane, the one at Davy Lake, is still in operation. You can get current water-level information by calling SaskWater. The MacFarlane peaks in May, with average flows for the month running around 80 cu m/sec. At Davy Lake, normal flows for June, July, August and September are 68, 55, 50 and 54 cu m/sec respectively.

There is a point at which the river would be a drag, so to speak. I wouldn't want to run the MacFarlane any lower than 35 cu m/sec — you would be wading and dragging. Yet the optimum water level for running some of Second Canyon is around 45 cu m/sec, so it's a fine line. I wouldn't want to run the MacFarlane in flood, as lining would become very tough. Running the rapids before Second Canyon and in the lower section of Second Canyon would be very difficult, if not downright dangerous. If you are taking a trip at high water be prepared to portage more of the canyons, and intermediates should take out at Davy Lake. Choose your water level carefully.

To check current conditions in the area, try contacting Cliff Blackmur of Athabasca Eco Expeditions / Athabasca Fishing Lodges, or the SERM field office in Stony Rapids. Contact information may be found in the Directory of Services.

Difficulty of the River **¹/₂ and ***¹/₂

The first part of the MacFarlane, from Brudell Lake to Davy Lake, gets two-and-one-half stars for difficulty. The average rapids are Class 2 and highly runnable, and there are no really large lake crossings or large portages. However, this is a very remote area with no chance of easy or fast rescue in an emergency situation. It is definitely not a trip for learning to paddle whitewater. The rapids are on average 250 m long, and generally some combination of shallow, rocky rapids, boulder gardens and ledges.

After Davy Lake, you are confronted with a much more difficult expedition. The second part of the MacFarlane gets three-and-one-half stars, requiring much higher-end paddling and portaging skills. It is no place for beginners, at any water level. From Davy Lake to the end of First Canyon is appropriate to intermediate and more advanced paddlers, but there is a 1.2 km portage of the upper part of First Canyon, no matter what your skill level. Then Second Canyon will take everything you've got to move through it — whether on land or water! Most canoeists will portage the upper section of Second Canyon. Everyone must portage the three mid-canyon falls. Then some will choose to paddle the lower canyon rapids, which are continuous and reach Class 3 in many places. In high water, only advanced or exceptional paddlers should consider running this section.

Along the length of the MacFarlane, there are at least three mandatory portages, two of which are around the falls in the canyons and are very strenuous. In total, you could be carrying your gear for about 9 km, depending on water levels and your skill. The portages are good around all the major rapids upriver of Second Canyon. However, there isn't one around Second Canyon — unless someone has cut one since I last heard. Regardless, this portage is simply an awfully long trek, and may still be a bushwhack on top of it. If you can't run the lower rapids in Second Canyon, either because you are lacking the skill required or the water is too high, you are going to have an even longer haul. If you try to run Second Canyon's lower rapids and have an accident, it is a very dangerous situation and there is no help. Simply put, the MacFarlane is one of the worst rivers I can think of to find out that you have overrated your paddling skills. Rescue from the canyons can only be done by helicopter.

I wouldn't make the MacFarlane your first Far North trip if you are a beginner looking to paddle an Athabasca Basin river. Try the Cree or the Waterfound, or take a trip with experienced whitewater paddlers down the Fond du Lac first. Solid intermediate paddlers that really like to sweat on portages and are willing to lose a little skin in the process will be challenged by this river! But joking aside, the canyon portages are not fun and require high physical fitness and stamina. If you have little whitewater experience and are not physically fit, you should not be taking a trip on the MacFarlane.

The gradient of the river is 1.14 m/km (6.03 ft/mi). This is very steep for a Saskatchewan river. A fair chunk of this drop is a result of the two canyons near the end of the MacFarlane. There are three falls in the middle of Second Canyon. See the Trip Notes section for more detail on the canyons.

Character of the River and Region

The MacFarlane runs from northwest of Cree Lake to Lake Athabasca, and while the river widens a number of times, there is really only one lake of any size, Davy, and it is small for northern Saskatchewan. The MacFarlane starts out skinny and rock-choked, but steadily increases to a relatively continuous moderate-flowing river. The river eventually averages a flow of 100 cu m/sec where it flows into Lake Athabasca. The riverbed is a mixture of sand and erosion-rounded rocks, ranging from bread-loaf to cow-sized. Anywhere the river has eroded the sand deposits to the underlying Precambrian rock, there are smooth sandstone ledges and rock gardens. This is the nature of the majority of the rapids.

The MacFarlane lies completely within the Boreal Shield ecozone, and also entirely within the Athabasca Plain ecoregion. The landscape is less rugged than the Churchill Uplands region below it, and lakes and wetlands are less numerous. Young, open stands of jack pine predominate along most of the river. Pine and spruce forest are found in the drumlin areas, and black spruce and white birch occur on the lower slopes of the dunes. White spruce can be found along the south shore of Lake Athabasca.

The landscape is one of sandy glacial till, and the entire area around the river is an aquifer, which is one of the major reasons for its ecological uniqueness. The Precambrian rock is mostly covered by drift, except in the riverbed where the Precambrian sandstone ledge formations are prominent. This Precambrian sandstone is the result of the erosion of the Earth's first mountains and these were the first sedimentary rocks ever formed. You will not find any fossils in the sandstone. The rock is older than life on this planet. The erosion of the Precambrian sandstone also created the sand that is such a predominant feature of the Athabasca Plain.

The river was formed as a meltwater channel and spillway that carried water north from the melting glacier to Glacial Lake Athabasca. Water drained from Glacial Cree Lake along the Snare spillway to the MacFarlane to the inflow at Davy Lake, where a small delta was built. The MacFarlane still carries sediment to Lake Athabasca at a rate of 11,000 tonnes/day.

At Brudell Lake, the river flows between large kames, steep rounded hills of glacial debris providing endless vistas at each turn of the river. These hills are left behind as the river nears Davy Lake, where the river pools at the end of a wide, relatively level plain. But many long, low eskers are still in evidence. Davy Lake is shallow and sandy, and the waves can kick up fast.

The eskers that start around Davy Lake keep you company until the MacFarlane plunges through two sandstone canyons on its final descent to Lake Athabasca. The two canyons are amazing sandstone formations, and there are steep, vertical walls up to 18 m high. You simply can't believe you are in Saskatchewan, which is usually a very flat land! The many-coloured walls of the canyons have huge crevices where the rock has broken away, as well as slabs of rock perched precariously over others. The many ledges and waterfalls of the canyons are simply gorgeous.

Almost at the end of the river, you can access the most easterly and third-largest of the sand dune fields (49 sq km) — the Yakow Dunes, which are in the Athabasca Sand Dunes Provincial Wilderness Park. There are guidelines all visitors should follow to preserve the fragile nature of the area. Camping and campfires are restricted to certain areas, and you should not walk on the desert pavement or disturb or collect plants, artifacts or ventifacts. All garbage should be carried out. There is an information booklet on the park put out by SERM containing a complete list of the park use guidelines. You can order one by contacting the Stony Rapids field office listed in the Directory of Services.

The MacFarlane ends on the sandy south shore of Lake Athabasca. The mouth of the MacFarlane is low-lying land and does not have the massive delta found at the mouth of the William. The riverbank from the small lake 6 km upstream of Lake Athabasca is low and willow-lined to the mouth of the river.

For an excellent source of information on the geological and botanical details of the Athabasca Sand Dunes, and for some fantastic photographs to give you a feel for the landscape, consult *Northern Sandscapes*, by Arlene and Robin Karpan. This book describes the formation of the sand dunes and the unique plants that have adapted to this terrain and grow nowhere else in the world. It is a must-read to really appreciate the dunes. Peter Jonker and Stan Rowe's book on the sand dunes, and volume seven of the Environment Canada report on the Mackenzie River Basin, edited by Z. Abougnuendia, are also excellent sources of information on the area around MacFarlane River.

Another great resource for learning about the geology of the area is the publication *Geological History of Saskatchewan*, by Dr. John Storer of the Saskatchewan Museum of Natural History. It gives a detailed yet plain-language description of the Precambrian era events and subsequent glaciation that shaped the Athabasca area.

Local History ✳✳✳

The MacFarlane was known by a number of names in the past, and played a role in the local Lake Athabasca Dene peoples' oral history. Numerous archaeological sites have been found at the small unnamed lake on MacFarlane, on both the western and eastern banks of the river below it, and on the beaches of the south shore of Lake Athabasca. The artifacts found date from 7,000 to 8,000 years ago. See the chapter on the Carswell/William Rivers trip for more on the prehistory of the Lake Athabasca region.

According to HBC surveyor Philip Turnor, who explored the region in 1791, the local Dene called the MacFarlane the Great Beaver or Giant Beaver River. He wrote that the Dene had a legend about a giant beaver that turned up all the sand, and giant Indians, who killed the beaver and also became extinct.

Turnor's assistant, Peter Fidler, who spent the following year with the Dene of the Lake Athabasca region, said they called it the Black River, and that it was part of a travel route between Lake Athabasca and Ile-à-la-Crosse on the Churchill River. He said it was not for heavily loaded freighter canoes, but was a very short way to travel between those places. The Dene elders from the communities around Lake Athabasca remember long journeys and all the portages they had to make to travel the MacFarlane. Erik Munsterhjelm also refers to it in *The Wind and the Caribou*, his account of trapping in the Black Lake region.

According to the 1981 *Report on the Mackenzie River Basin*, the main route (coming from the north) took travellers upstream on the MacFarlane to MacFarlane Lake. From there, a portage of 25 km to the headwaters of the Virgin River was made. They went down the Virgin River and through Careen Lake, continuing on to the Clearwater River. Once on the Clearwater they could paddle downstream to the Methy and portage into the Churchill watershed and carry on through to Ile-à-la-Crosse. An alternative route was to ascend the William River to its headwaters and then through a series of creeks and portages and via Carter, Patterson and Preston Lakes to reach Lloyd Lake to descend the Clearwater to the Churchill. Four pictograph sites on the upper Clearwater above the Virgin confluence are signs of the importance of this route for First Nations people moving north to south.

There is a pictograph site with three rock paintings along the river after Brudell Lake, between two rapids and below an overhanging rock face. They were first documented in 1991. The site indicates the importance of the MacFarlane as a travel route for the Cree at some time, as well as the Dene. There is some evidence that at the time the fur traders arrived, Cree territory extended up to the southwest shore of Lake Athabasca. And it is generally agreed that the Cree were the authors of all the pictographs in northern Saskatchewan, except for perhaps one exception on the Clearwater. The MacFarlane pictographs are now the most northwesterly of all the known rock-painting sites. From the MacFarlane, travellers could also access Cree Lake via the Karras River. From there it was a relatively simple matter to reach the Churchill via the Mudjatik.

The river was named in 1867 by Father Emile Petitot, an Oblate missionary from France who lived among the Dene and Inuit from 1863 to 1883. Petitot named the river in honour of Roderick MacFarlane, a long-time factor with HBC who explored the area in 1860 when he was in charge of the Athabasca district. In 1892, while exploring the Athabasca and Churchill River regions for the Geological Survey of Canada, J. B. Tyrrell's surveying partner, Mr. Dowling, noted that the MacFarlane was called the Beaver or Grand Rapids River by the Dene. Hmm, grand rapids. It must have been the canyons. Imagine the upstream portages the people of the First Nations made to ascend the MacFarlane on their long journey to Ile-à-la-Crosse. Just to get around the two canyons of the MacFarlane is at least 10 km, and then there is the 25-km portage to Careen Lake. Whew!

Brudell Lake was named for a trapper, Martin Brudell, who used to trap along the river during the '30s. Many geographical features of northern Saskatchewan around Cree Lake and to the north were named after the trappers that were working in the area when they flew the first aerial surveys in the late '30s.

In the 20th century, local people used to boat across from the north shore to the south shore of Lake Athabasca, and there used to be hunting and fishing cabins, but most have disappeared by now. The only signs of habitation, past and present, right on the MacFarlane River that I know of are the remnants of Brudell's old trapper's cabin on Brudell Lake (of course!) and hunting camps and trapper cabins along the river, especially around the outlet of Davy Lake. The Athabasca Sand Dunes Provincial Wilderness Park, of which the MacFarlane is the eastern boundary, was created in 1992.

For some reading about the MacFarlane area and Lake Athabasca in general, there is the Karpan's book, *Northern Sandscapes*, as I mentioned earlier. Erik Munsterhjelm's *The Wind and the Caribou* is about trapping in the Far North in the '40s, and gives the reader a good idea of the landscape, though his views on cultures not his own are dated, to say the least. "Down to the Kingdom of Sand," a story by Dave Bober in *Canada's Best Canoe Routes* is very good, as is an online article in *Che-mun*, "Goin' Dune the MacFarlane," by Doug McKown. *Water and Sky: Reflections of a Northern Year* is about a canoe trip that takes place in Lake Athabasca, and is good reading. See the References section for more resource material on the Lake Athabasca region.

Level of Solitude ✳✳✳

The MacFarlane is a great trip for wilderness solitude. There are no communities along the river, or anywhere near it, and it is difficult to get to. The river above the canyons is not hunted or fished by any outfitters. There are a few trapping cabins en route, and you will probably only encounter other visitors to the dunes at the small unnamed lake upstream of Lake Athabasca. There also may be a fishing party there or at the Lake Athabasca island take-out. Most of the tourists boat across Lake Athabasca and up the MacFarlane or they are flown into the small lake.

The river is much more popular with recreational canoeists now than it was even a few years ago. In fact, the river was supposedly only run for the first time by recreational canoeists in 1991. Now it is becoming one of the prime destinations in northern Saskatchewan for wilderness canoe trippers with lots of experience. But because it is so remote and expensive to get to, you will probably only see one other party of canoeists, if any, along the river in the high season — mid-June to August.

Wildlife ✳✳✳

The Athabasca Plain is not as rich an ecoregion for wildlife as the Churchill Uplands. However, as travel is so difficult in this remote country and there is less pressure on the populations from hunting, wildlife sightings are very likely. The MacFarlane is one of your best bets for moose, black bears, timber wolves and otters. There is also a small woodland caribou population on the south shore of Lake Athabasca, with some caribou frequenting Carswell Lake and another herd at Davy Lake along the MacFarlane River. It is possible, but unlikely, to see caribou on the river. Just about everyone I know that has paddled the MacFarlane has seen at least one moose and one bear on the trip.

Now speaking of bears, there are lots of blueberries on the river at the end of July and beginning of August, and that means lots of black bears in prime camping areas. Bears on the MacFarlane are not afraid of people because they don't encounter them very often. They may consider you part of the furniture, which means you should pack up and leave your campsite. These bears will not behave like black bears that are used to people. Don't be the reason this changes. Don't act aggressively unless you have no other options for staying safe, and do not leave any garbage on the river. Throw your fish guts and carcasses into deep water with current.

The nature of the MacFarlane River also provides for many large and small fish-eating birds, such as golden and bald eagles, osprey, kestrels, merlins, pelicans, loons and kingfishers. In the canyons you will see amazing aerial displays by ospreys and cliff swallows. At the small take-out lake you will be highly entertained by eagles and osprey diving and swooping for fish. As I mentioned, the fishing there is incredible.

Fishing ✳✳

Fishing on the MacFarlane can be fun, but there is no resident walleye population until the end. However, the usual species of fish found in far northern rivers are in residence — grayling, northern pike, whitefish and suckers. Except for grayling, which you are more likely to find in the upper MacFarlane, fish become more plentiful the farther north you go. As with most of the rivers in the North, the northern pike are just huge! You must debarb your hooks and practise good catch-and-release techniques if you fish for the biggies.

The fishing at the take-out lake upstream from the mouth of the river on Lake Athabasca couldn't be better. All the pools at the base of the many little rapids spreading into the lake are home to walleye coming up from Lake Athabasca, and gigantic northern sharks are lurking along the shores. An added bonus for those paddling all the way to Lake Athabasca, or those diehards like me who would paddle about 13 km or so round trip just to fish: there is good lake trout fishing at the mouth of the MacFarlane.

Not to worry about lots of different tackle for the trip. I've caught walleye, northerns and trout on the same hook, a red-and-yellow five-of-diamonds spoon! Seriously, I normally only carry jigs for walleye and northerns, spoons for trout and northerns (with leaders) and tiny spinners for grayling (and rainbow and brook trout if they are around) on my trips. You will need a heavier spoon if you want to troll for trout. Brad's always been a good Evinrude....

Special Equipment

The best choice of canoe is a Royalex-hull tripping canoe with Kevlar skid plates to protect it from the inevitable hard knocks. A Royalex canoe is ideal for this kind of shallow back-country river — it is a slippery toboggan when you run out of water and if you do happen to wrap it around one of the countless big rocks, it will quite often regain its shape again if you can get off the rock, so you can carry on down the river. The worst choice of material for a canoe for this river is aluminum. It will stick to every rock you touch and it is impossible to slide over rocks and ledges in the shallows. You could paddle a Kevlar or fibreglass canoe. Either will skid over rocks but both are vulnerable to crushing if pinned hard on a boulder. Kevlar is the best choice for the canyon portages because it is so light, but it's not as likely to survive a crash in the rapids as plastic.

The one thing you should bring if you are considering paddling some part of the second canyon is good climbing rope for hauling your boat and gear out of the canyons at strategic spots. You will need at least one length of 25 m.

Bring insect repellent and a bug hat and or jacket. The MacFarlane is not the worst river for blackflies or mosquitoes, but they will be there. You can count on it.

Advanced and exceptional paddlers may consider bringing along a spray skirt if you are considering running the lower section of Second Canyon. You don't need it in lower water, but it sure might help in higher water. Finally, a good axe would be of great help if you felt inclined to put in a little work on that Second Canyon portage.

Trip Notes

MAP NO	GRID REF	FEATURE	DESCRIPTION
74 J/4	380497	Put-in	At a point on RR (or east shore) at the north end of Brudell Lake, 1 km from the river outlet.
	380512	Rapids	**Class 2**. A boulder run, 400 m long with a constricted channel. It's technical but not really fast-moving. It can be scouted from RL, but this is tough — the bush is thick, and the rapid twists around.
74 J/5	342602	Rapids	**Class 2**, a boulder run, 750 m of winding and somewhat tricky rapids ending in a shallow boulder fan.
	348611	Campsite	On RR in mature jack pine forest. The camp is tucked in a little curve of a lake-like widening in the river, directly northwest of the outlet of the rapid above. It's a good place for sunsets and fishing. On RL is a recent burn area.
	335622	Rapids	**Class 2**. This 200-m-long rapid splits around an island at the start. The left channel has greater flow.
	332622	Rapids	**Class 2**, 150 m, straightforward.
	331627	Rapids	**Class 2**, 300 m, winding and quite busy.
	323633	Campsite	On RR, a nice jack pine bench.
	302638	Rapids	**Class 2**, about 150 m long with many boulders.

MAP NO	GRID REF	FEATURE	DESCRIPTION
	265702	Rapids	**Class 1**.
	265705	Rapids	**Class 1**.
	263706	Rapids	**Class 2**, 250 m and very shallow.
	259771	Rapids	**Class 1 to 2**. A fast chute starting at an island, with more fast water at the narrows 300 m downstream. There is a final fast section 400 m farther downstream, where the river narrows and turns sharply left towards the north.
	267774	Campsite	On RL, just after the end of the above rapid. The ground is somewhat undulating and rocky, and you have to push through thick shore willows to the site. Only a moderately good camp for the MacFarlane.
	268814	Rapids	**Class 1+**.
	276827	Campsite	On RL in jack pine at the base of steep kames. A good hike for a view.
	277827	Rapids	**Class 1+**, becoming a rocky **Class 2** after 500 m.
	313839	Falls	A **5 m falls**. The **portage (150 m)** is on RR and in good condition, over some open rock with large "steps." The portage ends at **Class 2** rapids with waves still to navigate.
74 J/12	342879	Rapids	**Class 2**, a boulder run. It's fairly straight for 300 m.
	353894	Rapids	**Class 2**, marked with three bars on the map. The rapid is 200 m long and straightforward.
	358899	Rapids	**Class 1 riffles** around islands.
	353903 351915	Rapids	**Class 2+/3**, marked as a single bar on the map. This is the start of a fairly continuous section of rapids. The top drop may be challenging, depending on water levels. Stop to scout on RR from the rock outcrop. The rest of the rapids are **Class 1 and 2**.
	353936	Rapids	**Class 3, with Class 1+ at the start**. Scout these marked rapids before descending; there are large holes and curling waves, especially at higher water levels. RR has a good rock outcrop for a clear view of the entire rapid. A **portage (125 m)** is on RR.
	355965	Rapids	**Class 1**, a fast section for the next 1.5 km.
	378977	Rapids	**Class 1**, a fast section for the next 500 m.
	388983	Rapids	**Class 1**, a fast section for the next 500 m.
	396987	Confluence	The Snare joins the MacFarlane.
	406993 398021	Rapids	**Class 1**, numerous riffles and fastwater sections at each narrows on the map for the next 3.2 km.
	399022	Campsite	On RR. A good site on a flat, open, jack pine bench.
	397034	Rapids	**Class 1+**. Easy.
	386112 377111	Rapids	**Class 2**, this marked rapid starts out moderately difficult and increases in difficulty as you go along.

MAP NO	GRID REF	FEATURE	DESCRIPTION
	367107	Rapids	**Class 4 and Class 2+.** The rapids go around an island. There is a marked **Class 4 ledge** on the RR side of the island. There is a **Class 2+** technical run through the RL channel, which is rocky and winds a bit. The run is definitely down the RL channel, as the ledge is really a small falls.

Note: From this point on, expect to find the river moving a little faster, often forming minor riffles at narrows, with some long sections of Class 1 water too numerous and frequent to detail here.

MAP NO	GRID REF	FEATURE	DESCRIPTION
	336118	Campsite	In a fast water section, 500 m after a gentle curve left, on RR. A low rock-shelf landing spot with large birch trees, good for bathing, with level tenting back in the trees. A nice site.
74 J/13	284160	Rapids	**Class 1+.** After the fast water at a bend to the right is a short drop indicated by the marked bar. It's followed by fast water and **Class 1** rapids in the narrows and at the bend to the left.
	280174 276177	Rapids	**Class 2**, rocky, with waves for 250 m indicated by two marked bars, followed by **Class 1**.
	273179 266182	Riffles	Fast water and riffles in the narrows.
74 K/16	702207	Rapids	**Class 2+**, this marked rapid is a boulder run. Good manoeuvres are required.
	687204	Rapids	**Class 1+**, improperly marked on the map as a falls. This very easy rapid is a float with no ledge of any kind!
	602181	Campsite	On the upstream or eastern face of the midstream island, with fast water around it on either side. Open, mature, jack pine forest with an old hunting camp.
	569227	Campsite Take-out	On an island with a small, sandy beach facing northwest, great for swimming and sunsets. There's room for at least two tents on the low, vegetation-covered bench on the next level up from open sand. It's a very nice place to wait for your plane if you want to pass on the canyons.

Note: Davy Lake could easily be renamed Wavy Lake. It is open and shallow, and gets choppy very quickly. If the weather is getting too challenging, there are lots of great campsites and interesting sand dunes along the east side, so quit and hike or read a book if it gets white!

MAP NO	GRID REF	FEATURE	DESCRIPTION
	624360	Campsite	On RR or east shore is an OK camp in mature jack pine forest.
	617362	Cabin	On RR is an old, dilapidated trapping cabin.
	626393	Osprey nest	On the second of two small islands in the right-hand channel of the river. Take the main flow channel (RL) so you don't un-necessarily disturb the nesting birds.
	625396	First Canyon	**Class 2 rapids at the start for about 225 m, quickly becoming Class 4 to 5**, with several big ledges/falls and high cliffs. The **portage (1,200 m)** on RR is difficult to find and is located about 20 m above the first ledge, which you really can't see until you're

MAP NO	GRID REF	FEATURE	DESCRIPTION
			very close. To be safe, run the rapids near the RR shore for about 150 m, and look for a landing spot in the thick shore bush. Tie up your canoe and walk down to find the trail. If desired, you can start your carry early. There is a rough, relatively undefined trail 50 m before the main trail. The portage is good to excellent for the first 1 km, then peters out somewhat. At the 1-km mark, leave the trail and walk towards the river. Search for a notch in the cliff that can be scrambled down. A side creek/branch of the river runs through bushes here, separating an island from the shore on the point where the river turns right, GR 624404, about where the last marked rapids appear on the map. The rapids actually continue for another 800 m from this point, but they downshift from **Class 3 (and higher upstream) to Class 2+** at this point. Walk to the far side of the island to scout. You can decide to either put in here or continue the portage another 800 m to the end of the "trail." Or you can find a spot a little earlier to scramble down the bank to where you feel comfortable putting back in. The rapids are fairly wide, filled with scattered boulders and some large holes at the above corner, becoming shallower and slower towards the end.

Note: You will encounter some fast-water sections and small riffles where the channel narrows between First Canyon and the rapids preceding Second Canyon (at GR 347544 as described below).

MAP NO	GRID REF	FEATURE	DESCRIPTION
74 N/1	708507	Campsite	On RR in an ancient jack pine forest with some birch. It's very open, with lots of space for tents.
74O/4	347544	Rapids	**Class 2+ to 3**. These rapids are not marked on the map. They're narrow and fast, becoming wide, rocky and ledgy. Some very wide (and 1-m-high) ledges in the lower section can make this a difficult run. The rapids are also right before the canyon, requiring extra caution.
	346548	Second Canyon Campsite	The midstream island at this grid reference point marks the entrance to the second and final canyon on the MacFarlane. At this point, you will have to commit yourself to one of two plans of action. You must either portage the entire upper canyon, or run through it for approximately 2 km to the top of the set of three major falls. If you want to scout the rapids of the upper canyon, work right before the island to land behind it on RR at a steep, open, sandy bank (346549). There is a nice high sandy bench campsite here. **Land on the RL shore if you are carrying around the upper section.**

The Second Canyon

During its final plunge towards Lake Athabasca, the MacFarlane River drops through an 8-km-long canyon. Over this distance, there is an elevation change of over nine contour intervals, or just less than 100 m! The gradient changes at differing rates, such that the canyon has three distinct sections. The first 2 km drops over 30 m, with most of the loss of elevation concentrated in three large ledges, each a true falls at over 2 m in height. The canyon here is wide, flat-bottomed and vertical-sided, with few or no available shore eddies next to sheer sandstone cliffs. The second section of 1 km contains three large falls. Here the river squeezes between high, steep sand and rock cliffs, plummeting another 30 m in three giant steps. Below the third falls is the lower canyon. Here there is some river-level shore, with canyon cliffs interspersed. This section is 5 km long, and the final 30 m of elevation are lost much more gradually, with the gradient gradually lessening towards the end.

Rapids and Ledges of the Upper Canyon
Overall rating: Class 4, with three Class 5 ledges
If you are seriously considering running the rapids between the ledges in this section, you will need to scout the entire 2 km of it. The best shore to do this from is the RR or east side. Three ledges of over 2 m each in height stretch from shore to shore, at GR 343555, 343558 and 342560. They are steep and straight, each with killer holes at various points along their weir-like lengths, but they can be pulled over at certain water levels.

From the landing point in the bay behind the island on RR, it is possible to walk the thickly bushed, scratchy 2 km along the rim to where the first of the three large waterfalls occurs. Expect to spend at least two hours looking at the rapids and fighting your way through the new-growth jack pine. Use extreme caution along the cliff edges, where the rock is heavily weathered and treacherous — it breaks right under your feet! However, it's a great view, and even if you decide it's crazy to run it (which it is), you will have seen one of the most beautiful canyons in Saskatchewan, with its towering orange-and-gold, multi-layered Precambrian sandstone cliffs.

Portage around the Upper Canyon — Nightmare Bushwhack!
Portaging the upper section of Second Canyon should be done on RL, landing at about **344548** and scrambling up the steep slope. A fixed rope will help with packs and canoes. The distance on land from the start of Second Canyon, near the island to the first big waterfall, is about 1.8 km. This entire area experienced a major forest fire in about 1985. Since that time, a dense new growth of jack pine has come up along the sides of the canyon. These trees are now 1–2.5 m tall, and average about 15 cm apart! What isn't solid new growth is a maze of deadfall and loose rock, with the occasional patch of unburned forest. Walking through on either side of the river ranges from extremely difficult to impossible. To date, no trail has been cut. Game trails appear and disappear randomly, but basically it's pretty solid bush. Knowing this, you would be wise to take along a folding handsaw or a line-cutting axe. By taking turns carrying and cutting trail, a group could make their way along the RL or west shore, but it would be slow. In earlier years, this carry was done without trail cutting, but the trees are now just too thick to just push through. Expect to spend some time here.

Mandatory Portage around the Three Mid-Canyon Falls
Eventually you will reach the start of the semi-trail that bypasses the three major falls at **340566**, which is also a pretty good natural **campsite**, though getting water is tricky — the sloping sand bank is extremely steep. From this point on a high, sandy area that was not burned in the fire you can find faint bits of game trails that appear and disappear as you work your way north. Stay on the high ground, well back from the shore for about 1 km. At this point turn right towards the river, descend the steep bank, and make your way over flats through thick sections of bush towards the shore. You should come out about 150 m to 200 m downstream from the outflow of the third waterfall, at 337574, directly across from where the river splits around a long, narrow midstream island. Expect to get lost at least once!

The Lower Canyon
Overall Rating: Class 3, becoming Class 2, extremely long
At this point the river is Class 3 and very fast, with numerous large holes and boulders. It is as much like mountain paddling as a Saskatchewan river ever gets. The current roars along, with the main flow constantly swinging back and forth at each curve. To avoid being swamped by large, closely set standing waves and to keep out of main current obstacles like large holes and rocks, paddlers should stern set. Use this manoeuvre to keep to the inside of each turn with the stern pointed towards the

inside of the corner. Then while back ferrying in the large waves, cross over the main flow to set into the inside of the next corner. Ideally, you will be back ferrying/stern setting through this whole section — about 5 km of it! Your canoe will stay dry, but your triceps may never forgive you! Fortunately, it gradually lessens in intensity, becoming braided Class 2 for the final kilometre, just before it spills out into a small, quiet lake at 333620. Great whitewater, and a fantastic read-as-you-run challenge for highly skilled paddlers. The cautious who wish to avoid the upper Class 3 section can **portage along an excellent riverside game trail on RL** until things look a little more reasonable.

MAP NO	GRID REF	FEATURE	DESCRIPTION
74 O/4	325631	Campsite	This is a lovely spot — a high, jack pine sand hill with a wonderful view of the small lake below the canyon, which is surrounded by dunes. A sandy landing spot leads up a short trail to the top. While it has some "furniture," it is clean and well maintained.
	324628	Campsite	Try this wooded island campsite if the other is full or doesn't suit your tastes.
	335618	Fishing hole	This area of the lake has pretty amazing northern pike angling. Try fishing the eddies below the falls for walleye. Note the numerous bald eagles and ospreys in this area! There are a lot of fish here.

Note: You are now in the dunes at the east end of the Athabasca Sand Dunes Wilderness Park. Access for hiking is easiest on the west or RL shore, downstream from the above lake. Be sure to abide by the park use guidelines.

	338621	Take-out	Your pilot will be happy if you have your gear and canoes waiting at this low, sandy island. There are no rocks around to hit.
	368689	Take-out	You can reach the island take-out on Lake Athabasca by continuing approximately 7 km down the MacFarlane through the lowlands to the shore of the lake. From there, head to the small island near Dead Cree Point. The south side of the island is used as the pick-up/drop-off point. Camping is possible all along the shore of the lake or on the island if you have to wait.

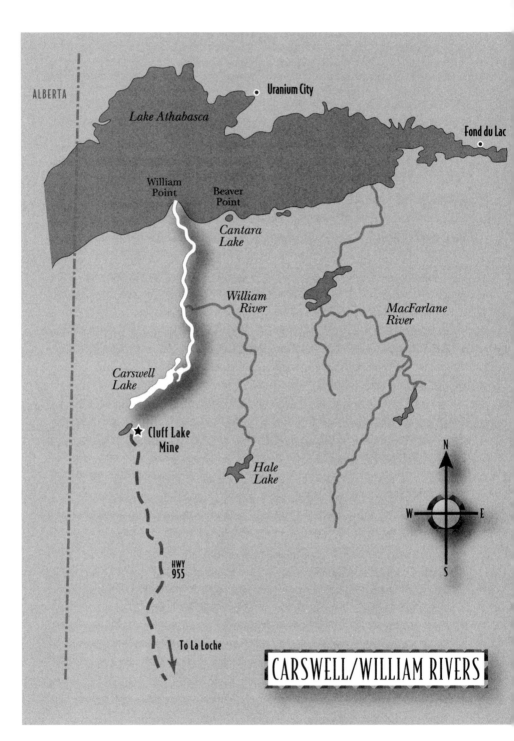

ALBERTA

Lake Athabasca

Uranium City

Fond du Lac

William
Point

Beaver
Point

Cantara
Lake

William
River

MacFarlane
River

Carswell
Lake

Cluff Lake
Mine

Hale
Lake

HWY
955

N

W — E

S

To La Loche

CARSWELL/WILLIAM RIVERS

CARSWELL AND WILLIAM RIVERS

The forest-eating northern desert scenery of the lower William River wins hands down in the magically weird landscape category. This is the river to paddle if you want to really explore the Athabasca Sand Dunes, the most northerly active sand dunes in the world. It just doesn't look like the world as we know it in northern Saskatchewan!

The Carswell River, a shallow, quick-flowing stream, is your quickest route to the lower William and the largest dune field in the Athabasca Sand Dunes Provincial Wilderness Park. Once on the William you will be greeted around the corner by a large sand dune, one side covered with forest and the other with bare sand — exactly half and half. Then you are in the land of sand. The reflection of the orange-and-red light of the dunes on the sky at sunset is the stuff of poetry. Photographers will need an extra Duluth pack just to portage their film around.

For the geologist and the botanist the William is a treasure. The work of the glaciers and the sand has created a landscape of drumlins, desert "pavement," and ventifacts. The exotic plant life of the dunes cannot be found anywhere else in the world.

The rivers will be most enjoyed by those canoeists who like technical, small-volume paddling, but the experience of the William is simply being there. Hiking in the dunes is otherworldly. It can be so quiet it seems like you are on another planet, with no sound (not even insects), no wind, just blue sky and golden sand. A few hours later in the night the wind could come up, and the sand will storm around your tent, hissing. The bedraggled trees with their roots exposed like skeletal feet attest to the power of the wind.

Finally, the river brings you to the largest lake in Saskatchewan — Lake Athabasca, a lake seemingly devoid of islands and five times more vast than the desert you left behind.

Length

The trip is approximately 100 km, with around 80 km of paddling on rivers and almost 20 on the big lake. It starts at the northeast end of Carswell Lake and ends at Cantara Lake just a short portage up from Beaver Point on Lake Athabasca, and takes you to the best of the dunes and the south shore of Lake Athabasca. You can put in at Tuma Lake to miss the couple of short portages from Carswell Lake, but you'll miss the best fishing too!

Shortening this trip is not really an option. Rough conditions on Lake Athabasca make for a difficult pickup at the mouth of the William, where there is a massive delta. Additionally, there are no good places to put in below Carswell Lake. To extend the trip you can paddle another 80 km down the south shore to a small lake 6 km up the MacFarlane River or a small island just west of the mouth of the MacFarlane near Dead Cree Point. You could also put in upstream on the William at Hale Lake, adding approximately 100 km to the trip.

The thing to remember with all the trip options is that wind will be a factor. You may be windbound for one or more days, whether you are waiting for a plane or to paddle down the shore of the lake to your pick-up spot. You must calculate windbound days into all of the options. For the trip described in the notes — the Carswell Lake to Cantara Lake trip — count on taking at least eight days. Don't cheat the dunes; put aside a day to hike. And remember, the rivers require some wading, and wading takes time.

Carswell Lake to Beaver Point/Cantara Lake*	100 km
Tuma Lake to Beaver Point/Cantara Lake	106 km
Carswell Lake to MacFarlane River pick-up	187 km
Hale Lake to Beaver Point/Cantara Lake	200 km
Hale Lake to MacFarlane River pick-up	267 km

*This is the trip described in detail in the Trip Notes section.

Topographic Maps

You will want 1:50,000 scale maps in order to have the level of detail required to figure out where you are on the twisty rivers and in the dunes. For the trip described in detail (and for the Tuma Lake put-in) you will need 74K/11, 74K/14, 74N/3 and 74N/2. I suggest you purchase these maps in advance and use the map coordinates in the Trip Notes section to mark in the large number of rapids and falls missing from the originals. Nearly all of the rapids on the Carswell and William Rivers are not marked, and none of the falls.

If you choose to put in at Hale Lake, you will need maps 74K/7 and 74K/10. If you choose to paddle the south shore to the MacFarlane River, you will need 74N/1 and 74O/4.

Getting There and Away

Getting to and from the William can be a fairly expensive undertaking. This trip is very far north, remote, and most parties fly in and fly out, though there is a drive-in option if you make arrangements with the outfitter on Carswell Lake.

The easiest and quickest way to get to the put-in is to charter a floatplane out of Buffalo Narrows; La Loche; or Fort McMurray, Alberta; and fly direct to Carswell or Hale Lake. Mikisew Air has a couple of nesting Royalex canoes to rent at their La Loche waterbase, as does Voyage Air in Buffalo Narrows.

Another simple option is driving your vehicle or flying on a scheduled flight to Points North and chartering a floatplane with Points North Air to Carswell or Hale Lake. Churchill River Canoe Outfitters has canoes for rent at Points North.

You can also fly on a scheduled Transwest flight to Stony Rapids and charter from there or any larger centre down south. Transwest has scheduled daily flights from Regina, Saskatoon, Prince Albert and La Ronge to Stony Rapids, and from La Ronge to Fond du Lac and Uranium City, and they also operate floatplane charters to Hale or Carswell Lake out of their waterbase at Stony Rapids. Northern Dene Air charters floatplanes from there as well, and Athabasca Fishing Lodges' Single Otter can also be chartered from Stony Rapids. You can rent canoes from Athabasca Fishing Lodges, saving you the expense and trouble of getting your canoes up there.

Finally, if you would rather drive all the way to Stony Rapids, there is now an all-season road extending past Points North. You must have a four-wheel-drive vehicle with two spare tires and jerry cans of gas. Gas stations are very few and far in between, and there isn't anywhere to buy gas after Points North. It is a rough, rough road. Expect the drive from La Ronge to take at least twelve hours, depending on conditions. Then you would charter your floatplane to Hale or Carswell Lake from Stony and paddle or fly back to your vehicle.

Finally, there is a drive-in and fly-out option if you make a business arrangement with Lone Wolf Camps, based in Buffalo Narrows. You can access the south end of Carswell Lake via their camp by driving to the end of the Semchuk Trail (gravel Highway 955), which extends past the Cluff Lake mine. Camp clients have permission to pass through the mine site, and the outfitter has cabins and canoes for rent at Carswell. You would arrange for a floatplane pick up as outlined in the options above. The cheapest flight back to Carswell Lake would be a charter from Uranium City, via Northern Dene Air.

Keep in mind that some Otter pilots will land and take off in places that others will not. Be sure that when you are booking your charter that you are clear about where you want to be picked up. The small, unnamed lake on the MacFarlane isn't very big; neither is Cantara. However, any size of plane can pick you up at the small island by Dead Cree Point. Athabasca Fishing Lodges drops off daytrip fishing parties there, so you may be able to arrange for a cost-saving backhaul. Flight and canoe rental arrangements may be made through the businesses listed in the Directory of Services.

When to Go

June to early July. Go when the water levels are up. The William peaks in May, but if you go too early in the season the ice may still be on Lake Athabasca, and you won't get to your take-out! If you go too late in July this low-volume river running through fast-draining sandy country may be very difficult to navigate. See the monthly and yearly mean discharge charts that include the William on the Canoe Saskatchewan website at www.lights.com/water-ways/local/various.htm.

Unfortunately, the William water-gauging station was closed in 1995, so you can't call SaskWater to get current water-level information. One way to check the current conditions on the William is by contacting Cliff Blackmur of Athabasca Eco Expeditions / Athabasca Fishing Lodges or Churchill River Canoe Outfitters. You could also try the SERM field office in Stony Rapids.

We paddled the river in the third week of June in a moderately low-water year, and it was probably running at around 15 to 17 cu m/sec at the confluence of the Carswell and William Rivers. I wouldn't want to paddle it at a lower water level, as it's too difficult to navigate the very shallow rapids. The Carswell River is particularly shallow, so the Tuma or Hale Lake put-ins may be your best option in a lower-water year.

Difficulty of the River ✳✳✳

The Carswell/William trip gets three stars because of its isolation and its long, winding, shallow rapids, where even the best read-as-you-run paddlers will be challenged. The rapids average is Class 2, but they are very long — 750 m on average. They usually open out into wide boulder fans at the end, where the water is so shallow that navigation becomes a real challenge. At low water levels many rapids will have to be waded, even by highly skilled paddlers. At high water levels the large number of rocks, combined with steep gradients, result in demanding rapids where there is little room for mistakes. These are wrap-o-matic type rapids.

Scouting isn't easy, except where the dunes are. There are no portages around any of the rapids or falls on this river, so paddlers will have to choose between wading, lining or bushwhacking, which, except where there are dunes, is very difficult. This trip requires physical stamina. Recognize that you will be wading in moving water on a rocky, stony riverbed, and the potential for ankle and knee injury is high. A helicopter is the only way to evacuate an injured person.

The gradient of the trip from Carswell Lake to Lake Athabasca is 1.42 m/km (7.48 ft/mi). This trip has the steepest gradient of all the trips in this book, and the William is a very steep river for northern Saskatchewan. It's a whitewater bonanza, as there are no really large drops, nor any lakes. The shallow, windy rapids and swift current entirely account for the gradient.

Character of the River and Region

The volume of the William River increases after the Carswell River junction, but it continues to be a shallow river to the end. The riverbed is a mixture of sand and erosion-rounded rocks, ranging from small, egg-shaped rocks to large, Volkswagen-sized boulders. There are occasional ledge formations where the river flows over exposed shelves of Precambrian sandstone. The William, like the MacFarlane River, was a meltwater channel and spillway that carried water north from the melting glacier to Glacial Lake Athabasca.

The Carswell and William Rivers lie completely within the Boreal Shield ecozone, and also entirely within the Athabasca Plain ecoregion. The rivers drain the Carswell Plain, an upland area of dolomite outcrops and cliffs that is believed to be the site of a meteorite impact event. The landscape is less rugged than the Churchill Upland region below it, and lakes and wetlands are less numerous. Exposed 600-million-year-old Precambrian sandstone can be seen, but sandy glacial deposits cover most of the area. Young, open stands of jack pine predominate. Pine and spruce forests are found in the drumlin areas, and black spruce and white birch occur on the lower slopes of the dunes. White spruce can be found on the south shore of Lake Athabasca.

The sand dunes of the region are best visited by paddling the William. It is the only river you can paddle between two dune fields. On the river left is the West William field and on the river right is the Thomson field. The largest dunes reach up to 30 to 35 m in height, and are home to plants found only in this northern "desert." (It's not really a desert, technically.) The area contains a diversity of soils, landforms and vegetation, some of which are unique to Saskatchewan and Canada. Ironically, the sand is actually engulfing the forest. The William itself pours 3,000 tonnes of sediment into Lake Athabasca every day.

Where the river flows into the lake at William Point, a massive delta has formed and is home to huge numbers of shorebirds. Lake Athabasca is the largest lake in Saskatchewan at 7,936 sq km, and is the fourth-largest lake found entirely in Canada.

The Athabasca Sand Dunes Provincial Wilderness Park was created in 1992, and there are guidelines all visitors should follow in order to preserve the nature of the area. Camping and campfires are restricted in certain areas, and you should not walk on the desert pavement or disturb or collect plants, artifacts or ventifacts. All garbage should be carried out. SERM has an information booklet for the park containing a complete list of the park regulations. You can order one by contacting the Stony Rapids field office at 306-439-2062 or by faxing them at 306-439-2036.

For an excellent source of information on the geological and botanical details of the William, consult *Northern Sandscapes*, by Arlene and Robin Karpan. This book describes the formation of the Athabasca Sand Dunes and the unique plants that have adapted to this terrain and grow nowhere else in the world. It is a must-read in order to really appreciate the dunes. *The Sand Dunes of Lake Athabasca*, by Peter Jonker and Stan Rowe, is another good book on the area. For further reading on the Lake Athabasca area, look in the References section.

Local History **

Archeological evidence points to the Lake Athabasca region having been inhabited for at least 8,000 years. Until about 2,500 years ago, climatic fluctuations were so significant that the traditional patterns of the inhabitants constantly changed. Then, at the end of the last Ice Age, when the treeline again moved farther north as the climate warmed, the ancestors of the Dene moved into the northern and eastern area of the Lake Athabasca region. They were probably following the herds of migrating barren ground caribou. The material evidence suggests that the early residents at either end of Lake Athabasca may have come from different cultures. On the east end of the lake, the Dene, a caribou-hunting people, occupied the land. On the west side of the lake, in what is now Alberta, the presence of bison and woodlands meant that people accustomed to the northern plains cultures could subsist on what the land had to offer.

Barren ground caribou are not found at the western end of Lake Athabasca. However, according to the Mackenzie River Basin Report of 1981, there have been numerous artifacts and prehistoric sites found near the mouth of the William and along the beaches near the mouth. The First Nations people probably camped in these spots seasonally and when they travelled the William as an alternate canoe route to the MacFarlane/Virgin/Clearwater River route to Ile-à-la-Crosse. Travellers ascended the William River to its headwaters, and then moved through a series of creeks and portages and via Carter, Patterson and Preston Lakes to reach Lloyd Lake. From there they descended the Clearwater to the Churchill via the Methy Portage. The four pictograph sites on the upper Clearwater above the Virgin River confluence are signs of the importance of this route for First Nations people travelling north to south. The Mackenzie report also notes that the William has probably changed course and flow over the years, as the sand is continually encroaching on it. People could take their boats up the William a few kilometres 30 or 40 years ago, and they can't now.

There are two Dene Nations inhabiting the northern and eastern areas of the Lake Athabasca region today: the Fond du Lac Denesuline Nation on the north shore of Lake Athabasca at the mouth of the Fond du lac River, and the Black Lake Denesuline Nation on Black Lake, found upstream or east on the Fond du Lac River. They still hunt caribou, but no longer rely on it as they once did, moving seasonally with the migrations.

European fur traders first came to the Athabasca Basin in the late 1700s, following Peter Pond, but there is no written record or evidence that the early explorers or fur traders used the William River. It is not surprising, as the William is just too remote to have been of importance as a highway for shipping furs or trade goods, and there are no safe anchorages at the mouth of the river. The first trading posts were established at the southwest end of Lake Athabasca, near the Athabasca River. Fort Chipewyan eventually became the main HBC post, but the NWC had a trading post called Fond du Lac at the site of the present-day community. So did the HBC much later after the amalgamation.

Turnor wrote briefly about the dunes in a journal of his and Fidler's 1791 expedition to explore Lake Athabasca. The name William River first appeared on Father Emile Petitot's map in 1833. He was an Oblate missionary from France, and travelled with and lived among the Dene and Inuit for twenty years. Apparently the name Gaudet River was also proposed at some point by some official, but William River was chosen because Petitot had referred to the river by that name in his writings at a much earlier date.

Turnor and Fidler's exploration journals are interesting reading if you want to know more about the Lake Athabasca region's history. You can find Tyrrell's edited versions online at the University of Toronto's Barrenlands website. Parker's *Emporium of the North* about Fort Chipewyan is a good read. *The Wind and the Caribou*, by Erik Munsterhjelm, a trapper in the area during the '40s, is interesting reading while travelling on any river in the region, though his views on cultures other than his own are rather dated. There is an article online on the William by Rolf Kraiker called "Doin the Dunes: What it's Like and Why it's Possible to Paddle in a Northern Desert" at http://www.canoe.ca/Adventure/story-dunes.html. Cliff Speers has a piece about the William in *Canada's Best Canoe Routes*, and *Water and Sky: Reflections on a Northern Year* is a good read about a couple's year-long northern adventure that includes a canoe trip across Lake Athabasca from west to east.

Level of Solitude ✳✳✳✳

The William is a great trip for wilderness solitude. There are no communities along it or even near it, and it is difficult to get to. The river is not popular with hunters or fishing parties. Some evidence of past trapping use exists, but the extremely sandy environment does not support a rich resource base.

Visitors boating across Lake Athabasca to the sand dunes usually go to the dune field east of the William at Thomson Bay or up the MacFarlane River. However, the William is much more popular with recreational canoeists now than it was even a few years ago, and you may see one or two other parties of canoeists along the river in high season.

Wildlife ✳✳✳

Since travel is difficult in this remote country, wildlife is relatively plentiful, even though sand is not the best habitat. There is little pressure on the animal populations, so moose, timber wolves, black bears, and otters and other smaller boreal forest mammals are commonly sighted on this river. There is also a small woodland caribou population on the south shore of Lake Athabasca, with some caribou frequenting Carswell Lake and another herd at Davy Lake along the MacFarlane River. It would be very rare to see a woodland caribou, however.

The nature of the William River also provides for small raptors, like the merlin, marsh hawk, kestrel and goshawk. The sand dunes and cliffs along the lower part of the route are home to large colonies of cliff swallows.

Fishing **

The fishing on the William isn't that good; sand does not provide a rich environment for fish either. However, Carswell Lake is an exception. There is a good population of walleye and northern pike. But don't expect to catch walleye after Carswell, as there are no resident populations in the William. Tuma Lake also has walleye, if you decide to start there. Some walleye do come up the mouth from Lake Athabasca at certain times of the year to feed, however, so you may get lucky and catch a couple lower down on the William.

According to SERM, if you put in at Hale Lake instead of Carswell you can catch Arctic grayling. They reside in the southern reaches of the river before the dune field. Once the sand kicks in, northern pike, burbot and suckers are the river's main residents, becoming more plentiful the closer you get to Lake Athabasca. You can probably count on catching pike in the deeper pools below small falls because it is the North, and slough sharks live just about anywhere here! It won't matter much what kind of lure you use either. They do like shiny things, though.

Lake Athabasca is famous for its lake trout, and if you stay and spend some time on the south shore you can always fish for them. Lakers come up in the spring and fall, but are deep in the summer. There are usually some smaller ones hanging around rock points and reefs, and they will bite spoons trolled behind the canoe.

Special Equipment

The best choice for a canoe is a Royalex-hull tripping canoe with Kevlar skid plates to protect it from the inevitable hard knocks. A Royalex canoe is ideal for this kind of shallow back-country river — it is a slippery toboggan when you run out of water, and if you do happen to wrap it around one of the countless big rocks, it will quite often regain its shape again if you can get of off the rock, so you can carry on down the river. The worst choice of material for a canoe for this river is aluminum. It will stick to every rock you touch and is impossible to slide over rocks and ledges in the shallows, which you will encounter many kilometres of. You could paddle a Kevlar or fibreglass canoe; either will skid over rocks, but both are vulnerable to crushing if pinned hard on a boulder. It's a long walk out.

The other piece of equipment you may want to bring is a GPS. You can punch in way stations for the places you would like to hike to in the dune fields. A compass is essential for any large lake paddling, even if you are following the shore, and you'll want it for your hikes.

You might want to bring along your sail if you are going all the way to either of the MacFarlane take-outs. You can always rig up a small tarp, of course. You may want that small tarp around the kitchen anyway. Camping in sand, you need places to put things as you are cooking, to avoid large dentist bills!

Bring insect repellent, and a bug shirt if you have one. It can double as a sun shirt. The William is not the worst river for blackflies or mosquitoes, but they will be there, and in June you can count on the blackflies making their presence well known.

Trip Notes

Map No	Grid Ref	Feature	Description
74/K11	045055	**Fly-in point**	At the northeast end of Carswell Lake, near the short portage into the Carswell River.
	045049	**Campsite Cabin**	An island site in the centre of a bay at the northeast end of Carswell Lake. It's on the south tip of the island, with a southeast-facing landing at a steep sand bank, and is high and flat with a cabin.
	053054	**Portage**	A carry-over **(10 m)** on a narrow strip of land separating Carswell Lake from a small unnamed lake en route to the Carswell River. It starts at an opening in the shore vegetation.
	057057	**Portage**	A carry-over **(10 m)** on a narrow strip of land separating the unnamed lake from the Carswell River. Starts near a large, old, dead tree and goes through willow.
	073067	**Rapids**	Shallow and unnavigable — you'll be wading and dragging.
	073067 073068	**Rapids**	**Class 2**, very low volume, fast and steep. Rocks are hidden in the largest waves, and there's a boulder fan at the bottom.
	073075	**Campsite**	On RL is a nice jack pine bench.
	074078 075080	**Rapids**	**Class 2**, about 150 m long. Very low volume with many boulders. The main flow on RL is the clearest route.
	074082	**Rapids**	**Class 2**, very low volume.
	073082	**Campsite**	On RL, on a jack pine bench just at the bottom of the rapids.
	074086	**Rapids**	Shallow and unnavigable, running around islands. The main flow is in the RL channel — count on wading and dragging.
	074086 073087	**Rapids**	**Class 2**. These rapids can be run in some sections, but about half of them are too shallow to paddle. They require wading and dragging.
	057104	**Rapids**	**Class 1**, a shallow, slow-moving riffle.
	047119 047122	**Rapids**	**Class 1**. Shallow and rather long (400 m), and may require getting out to wade in spots.
	044124 042125	**Rapids**	**Class 2**, about 250 m long, and wider than the last set. They go around a bend to the left and may require wading.
74K/14	040136 042137	**Rapids**	**Class 1**. A riffle, 200 m long.
	025161 028166	**Rapids**	A 750-m-long stretch, so boulder-choked that nearly all of it must be waded.
	022182 024187	**Rapids**	**Class 2+ where navigable**. Very steep and pushy where deepest, with many boulders. This set requires a combination of wading, lining and running.
	022191	**Campsite Confluence**	On the upstream side of the island at the base of the confluence of the William and Carswell Rivers. A nice site in jack pine and reindeer moss.

MAP NO	GRID REF	FEATURE	DESCRIPTION
	019207 018208	Rapids	**Class 1+.** About 150 m long and 60 cm deep. There's a rock bottom and regular waves, with very few rocks to hit.
	018228	Rapids	**Class 2** and very rocky. The current swings from right to left and back to right.
	031265 026277	Rapids	**Class 2** and straightforward, with some rocks. These rapids are shallow, quite long (1.5 km) and fairly continuous, ending with a boulder "ledge" where the current piles up on RL. There's a good channel for wading down left of centre.
	023328 026332	Rapids	**Class 2**, rocky and shallow. About 500 m long with some moderate holes created by groups of boulders.
	018342 018347	Falls/Rapids	This section starts with a **Class 3** ledge, rated this high partly because of the falls 250 m downstream. They can be scouted from a dune on RL. There is a small notch right of centre that skilled canoeists can descend through. Move to the left shore through light rapids to take out on RL on a prominent rock ledge projecting from the bank. Carry past the small **falls** (1.5 m) which occur here. About 200 m downstream is **another falls** (1.2 m), which is much more difficult to get around. Approach on RL to avoid a large and dangerous hole on RR. At lower water levels, a combination of lining and wading will get paddlers down the edge of this boulder ledge. High water would make a carry on shore necessary. **CAUTION:** This drop is one of the most hazardous parts of this section. If in doubt, take an overland route through the bush, as lining and wading powerful drops is very dangerous. From this point, canoeists can get back in and paddle through another 400 m of shallow, rocky **Class 2** rapids.
	019351	Rapids	**Fast water.**
	020357	Rapids	**Fast water.**
	037385 038393	Rapids	**A long Class 2 and 3** section with two ledges just past the halfway mark, which can be portaged on RL over sand. The rapids start as shallow **Class 2 to 2+** rapids, which paddlers should work down to finish on RL in a shallow eddy just above the first ledge. The **portage (60 m)** is relatively easy. More shallow **Class 2 and 2+** rapids follow, ending very wide and rocky.
	044397	Rapids	**Class 1 fast water.**
	052406	Rapids	**Class 1 fast water.**
	055408 056412	Rapids	**Class 2,** with numerous low shelves, some nearly shore to shore. They require a scout.
74N/3	053423 049431	Rapids/Falls	**APPROACH WITH CAUTION:** This section begins with **two falls,** each around 1.5 m, followed 300 m downstream by a 1-m ledge. Take out on RL at the obvious low spot in open sand about 50 m from the top of the falls. **Portage (750 m)** across open sand, angling away from the river at first and ending at a steep notch in the sand just downstream from a large cluster of birch. At this point a small part of the river splits left in a narrow channel

the trips

MAP NO	GRID REF	FEATURE	DESCRIPTION
			marked as a line at 052426. This is actually fairly navigable, and definitely a better option than the shallow and wide main channel. This RL channel is **Class 2**, and about 75-percent paddling and 25-percent wading in shallows.
048432 047435	Rapids		**Class 2**. Relatively easy, with shelves and holes. The obstructions are widely spaced and you have route options.
048442	Campsite		On RL, on the inside of a wide bend to the left where a sand dune extends down a long, low arm to the river's edge. This site provides excellent access to the dune field, and is the best area to stop for day hikes west.
046443 036459	Rapids/Falls		**Class 2, 4, 2+/3, 4, 2**. A long and challenging final section of rapids and big drops. It starts with about 450 m of Class 2 rapids leading up to a 1-m ledge that can be carried around on RL. Following are more rapids, increasing in speed and difficulty as the channel narrows (Class 2+), becoming nearly Class 3 just before a broken ledge (Class 4). This can be avoided by staying out of the powerful main current, which is moving to the outside on RL, and working to RR above the ledge and carrying over the ledge's exposed, large, flat rock outcrop on the right shore. Below are more Class 2 rapids going around a big curve to the left, and then ending in gradually widening shallows.
036459	Braided channel		From the last rapids onward, the William flows through sandbars, slowing and widening, with the main flow splitting and rejoining constantly. Finding water deep enough to paddle is a challenge.
985552 002568	Creek		Very hard to spot, opening in trees on the RR shore. This is the escape route for canoeists to avoid becoming mired in the river delta's near-quicksand shallows. Fast and clear, with no obstructions, and fairly narrow, with the chance of surprising a moose. Don't laugh. It has happened here, and is a dangerous situation, so make sure they can hear you coming. Camping is easy once you reach the south shore of the lake. Look for tent spots up in the trees behind the beaches, that aren't so exposed to wind.
170560 176555	Portage Cantara Lake Take-out Campsites		On the south shore of Lake Athabasca, 16 km as the crow flies from the William's massive delta across Thomson Bay. The **portage** trail **(600 m)** into Cantara Lake is about 750 m west of Beaver Point. You can see the blazed trail going up the hill from the water. It soon becomes an obvious game trail and leads east to Cantara. You can camp right at the beach under the hill, or on the peninsula where the plane will pick you up.

PORCUPINE RIVER

NORTHWEST TERRITORIES

Selwyn Lake

Detour Lake

East Porcupine River

Herbert Lake

Grove Lake

Fond du Lac River

Black Lake

Black Lake

Stony Rapids

All-season road to Stony Rapids

Points North

N
W E
S

PORCUPINE RIVER

The Porcupine is the most northerly trip in this guidebook and one of the most remote. It's a clear, wild river, rushing south from Selwyn Lake on the border of the Northwest Territories to join the Fond du Lac just before it cascades into Black Lake. Large falls and rapids drop through black gorges over large granite boulders and smooth gray gneiss. Called "Dead Man's River" by the Dene for its rugged lower canyon, the trip is arduous. The falls are breathtaking, both to view and to portage. The scenery and the wildness of the river more than balance the effort and cost of doing this trip.

The Porcupine is one of the best trips for photography, from exciting whitewater shots of canoes crashing through large drops to severe and fantastic landscapes unlike any other river in this book. At times I've looked around at the high, craggy cliffs and hills of this river and felt as though I was on the Nahanni. It's as close to a mountain setting as you're going to get in Saskatchewan.

This "Land of Little Sticks" will always surprise you around the next corner, whether it be with a perfect crescent beach, a massive rockslide, or the quintessential taiga. Time seems to have stood still here; it is a world apart from all that we are used to.

Length

The trip highlighted in the Trip Notes section is approximately 150 km. It starts at a small island in Porcupine Bay on Selwyn Lake and ends at a beach near the outlet of the Fond du Lac on Black Lake. I wouldn't want to do this trip in less than ten days — the country is too rugged and awesome to rush through.

To shorten the trip, you can fly in to Detour or Grove Lake. You could also save a day by taking out at the confluence of the Porcupine and the Fond du Lac. Though it is only a distance of 12 km, you don't have to portage Burr Falls — a 1-km carry. I highly recommend you do the whole trip, though. It's one of my favourites.

To extend the trip, you could start at another point on Selwyn Lake, taking advantage of the amazing lake trout fishing. Selwyn Lake Lodge is located on Common Island, and you may want to arrange to use their dock. You may also decide to paddle the 35-km distance across Black Lake to the community of Black Lake. Keep in mind that this is very exposed, open-water paddling, and you may become windbound for one or more days.

Grove Lake to Black Lake*	70 km
Detour Lake to Black Lake*	105 km
Porcupine Bay to Fond du Lac confluence*	138 km
Porcupine Bay to Black Lake**	150 km
Common Island to Black Lake**	162 km
Porcupine Bay to the community of Black Lake	185 km
Common Island to the community of Black Lake	197 km

* These are the trips described in detail in the Trip Notes section.
** The Fond du Lac section of the trip is covered in the Fond du Lac River Trip Notes.

Topographic Maps

You will want 1:50,000 scale maps for the Porcupine trip, at least to the confluence of the Fond du Lac. Only this scale has enough detail to really help you navigate the complexities of the river and its terrain. For the highlighted trip you will need 74 P/16, 74 P/9, 74 P/8, 74 P/7 and 74 P/2. To extend the trip to the community of Black Lake you may opt to purchase 74 P instead of 74 P/3 and P/4.

You will want to purchase the maps ahead of time, and using the Trip Notes, mark in all the rapids that are missing from the original maps. As well, you may want to indicate the falls that are incorrectly marked as rapids. You will also probably want to pencil in where the portages are located. I suggest planning your paddling days ahead of time, noting the possible campsites. There are significant areas of burn on the Porcupine, and you can't rush the end of the trip. The last 40 km of the river could take you three whole days. There are at least three long, mandatory portages and some large, tricky rapids. If it's raining, you will find portaging on the slippery rock slopes very trying. The potential for injury is high. Consult the Trip Notes carefully in order to reasonably assess the distance you can make in a day, and then leave room for the unexpected.

When to Go

June to early September. If you go too early in June, the ice will still be on Selwyn Lake. If you go too late in the season, cold and snow will be a factor. You won't normally have to worry about water levels, though. It would be extremely rare for the larger-than-moderate-volume Porcupine to be too low to navigate. I've paddled the entire river in August twice and been fishing on it in early September. Even in a low-water year I have never had to wade a rapid. The first couple of rapids can be really bony, but that's pretty well it for overly shallow stretches.

The river flow peaks in June. According to historical data for the Porcupine's outflow at Grove Lake (only halfway down the river), June flows average around 118 cu m/sec. In July and August flows average 94 and 70 cu m/sec respectively. In September the river is normally still flowing at around 70 cu m/sec. I can't say I would recommend a particular water level at which to run the river — the pluses and minuses of low versus moderately high water seem to balance themselves out on the Porcupine. Flood conditions are always more difficult and potentially dangerous, however.

The water-gauging station on the Porcupine is no longer in operation. However, you can check the level of the Fond du Lac at its outflow at Black Lake. Call SaskWater for a reading, and then compare the cu m/sec figure you get to the average monthly and yearly mean charts on the Canoe Saskatchewan site. The comparison will generally tell you whether the northeast corner of the province is currently experiencing low, high or average water levels. You can also call the Stony Rapids SERM office or the outfitter on Selwyn Lake about current water levels.

Getting There and Away

As usual for a Far North trip, you have easy, expensive options for getting to and from the river and longer, more tiresome ones that are somewhat cheaper. You cannot get to the put-in for the Porcupine by road, unless you drive to Stony and paddle across Lake Athabasca and do the Chipman Portages route (details in SERM Canoe Trip number 26 booklet) into Selwyn Lake. But most people will fly into Selwyn on a floatplane charter. The closest place to hire a floatplane is Stony Rapids. This is a case where you may want to drive the all-season road to Stony, given that you have a very reliable four-by-four vehicle and want to take your own canoe. It's about a thirteen-hour drive one way from La Ronge on a very poor gravel road, and you can't buy gas after Points North.

Once you get to Stony Rapids, you can leave your vehicle at the air service and fly into Selwyn. At Stony you have three options for chartering: Transwest, Northern Dene Air and Athabasca Lodge's Otter. To return to Stony, you can fly from the south shore of Black Lake or paddle back to the community of Black Lake and hire a half-ton "taxi" to drive you the short distance to Stony. You can also paddle right back to your vehicle at Stony Rapids by continuing up the Fond du Lac, another 35 km and some very long portages away.

Another option is to take a scheduled flight with Transwest to and from Stony from Regina, Saskatoon, Prince Albert or La Ronge. You can either ship your canoes or rent canoes from Athabasca Fishing Lodges or Selwyn Lake Lodge. This saves you the awful drive, but it is an expensive option.

You can also fly to and from the Porcupine from Points North Landing with Points North Air. There's good parking, and the drive to Points is half the drive to Stony Rapids on a much better road. (Yes, the first half is very good compared to the next section to Stony, if you can believe it!) With this option you can rent canoes from Churchill River Canoe Outfitters right at Points North. You could also take a scheduled flight to Points North, and then charter a floatplane to Selwyn Lake from there, renting canoes from CRCO. Then you could paddle to Black Lake or Stony and fly back on a scheduled flight south without having to wait for your canoes to catch up to you or having to drive to Points North at all.

As I've said before about Far North canoe trip shuttles, pick the option that suits your schedule, size of group, and budget. The best one is the one that works for you. See the Directory of Services for contact information.

Difficulty of the River ✷✷✷

The Porcupine is a tough river, but not at all as tough as the Wathaman. It is so different from the other Far North rivers in the book, it's hard to compare. Like the MacFarlane and the William, the trip is very remote. But the country the Porcupine runs through is more consistently rugged and severe. The average difficulty of the rapids is 2+/3-, higher than most rivers in this book, except for the Wathaman. The rapids are not overly long, but they are steep, and the larger volume makes swamping an issue. Like the Churchill River, the Porcupine's rapids are often drops with large chutes, with boulders, stoppers and irregular waves to avoid. Current hydraulics are also a factor as the river gains in volume. Some eddies become whirlpools, which must be punched through to avoid capsizing.

The portages around some of these rapids are in poor condition or non-existent. There are at least six mandatory portages, the majority of which are arduous and not in good condition. Depending on the route you choose, there are lake crossings where wind can be an issue.

I don't recommend this trip for beginners. Guided intermediates looking to make a step up will enjoy the challenge of the Porcupine's rapids and portages. Advanced and exceptional paddlers will have a hoot running the Class 3 and 4 rapids of the Porcupine — take a spray skirt!

The gradient of the river from Selwyn Lake to Black Lake is 0.76 m/km (3.99 ft/mi). But this doesn't really give you a good picture of how challenging the rapids of the Porcupine can be. There are many smaller lakes and stretches of flatwater between the rapids, as it is a Taiga Shield drop-pool type of river.

Character of the River and Region

The riverbed is generally made up of rocks and boulders, football to bus-sized. The boulders are chunky! Boulder ledges and pour-overs are common. Smooth rock ledges and riverbanks also can be found along the river. At times the riverbank is all rocks or trees right to the water's edge, making lining difficult or impossible. There are few sand banks, except as you come out of the lower canyon to the confluence with the Fond du Lac. Moose food and mucky bottoms are found in the wider, slower channels.

The Porcupine is a river that typifies the Selwyn Lake Upland ecoregion of the Taiga Shield, though the far eastern and southern reaches of the Fond du Lac also exhibit some of its characteristics. The Taiga Shield is the transitional area of stunted trees and innumerable lakes between the tundra and the boreal forest. Its rolling terrain, lichen woodland and rock lichen reflect its unique subarctic nature. The taiga extends from Labrador to Alaska.

Precambrian basement rocks, which were once mountains like the Himalayas, have been eroded to a peneplain. The erosion is reflected in a series of broad, smooth uplands and intervening lowlands, with very irregular local relief. Elevations range from 350 m to nearly 600 m, with steep ridges of bedrock dominating. The gray and black lichen-covered rock walls of the Porcupine are impossible to forget. In some places, glacial till masks the bedrock, adding eskers, kames and drumlins to the mix of soaring granite cliffs and rugged outcroppings.

The gorges and canyons of the Porcupine were formed where the glacier preferentially eroded low-lying areas that were mostly softer rock (schistose, for example) or fault zones. The ice polished the resistant bedrock to smooth knobs. Notice the whaleback rock on the river left as you enter the last canyon.

Unlike the Athabasca Plain of the Far North, the taiga's predominant forest is open spruce with a yellow and white lichen understory. Jack pine is found in the drier areas, and birch can be found in old burns and scattered among the old-growth forests. Lowlands are often wooded with stunted black spruce or tamarack. Sphagnum moss peatlands and fens are common as well.

The river starts low in the black spruce, and then gets sandy with jack pine tree starting to dominate. The granite outcropping starts after Offset Lake. You get a nice mix of bench, esker and rock camping in the middle section of the river from Offset to the beginning of the rock gorges after Grove Lake. Then every once in a while the sand appears again, but it really takes over when you come out of the last canyon and approach the confluence of the Fond du Lac.

For more information about the Taiga Shield and the Selwyn Lake Upland, consult *The Ecoregions of Saskatchewan*. For good reading about the geological processes that formed the amazing landscape of the Porcupine, take a look at the *Geological History of Saskatchewan*.

Local History **

Selwyn and Black Lakes are the territory of the descendants of a group of Dene once referred to as the "Caribou Eaters." They carried on a traditional way of life during the fur trade, following the barren ground caribou throughout the year as their ancestors had. Most went north in the summer, migrating with the herds to the Northwest Territories. When the caribou moved south in the fall to northern Saskatchewan, the Dene followed, most often wintering in the Selwyn and Black Lake area.

Pierre Robillard is a Dene elder from Black Lake whom Brad and I met in 1995 when he was moose hunting on Grove Lake. He told us the Dene didn't travel the rough sections of the Porcupine, but that they had always reaped the resources of the river via lake routes. An old canoe route to Selwyn Lake (called Big Lake in Dene before the Tyrrell brothers decided to name it after Alfred R. C. Selwyn, director of the Canadian Geological Survey) from Black Lake started by ascending the Fond du Lac River to Lake Athabasca. From there, one ascended the Chipman (Wolverine) River and travelled a series of lakes to Selwyn.

The Dene came and went from the upper Porcupine through Herbert, Detour and Grove Lakes using numerous other lakes. The lower section of the Porcupine, ending in the canyon that they called Dead Man's River, was too difficult to navigate, so another route was used to go around it to the flatwater above the confluence of the Fond du Lac. These alternative routes allowed the Dene to fish, hunt and trap in the Porcupine area, but avoid the gorges and canyon of the river.

The Forks was an important crossroads for the Dene in winter and summer. Here the McIntyre River (Grease-lip) and the East Porcupine River (Nest) join the Porcupine. Up the McIntyre a short ways was a traditional Dene caribou hunting camp until a flu epidemic struck one year and the Dene fled, according to Munsterhjelm. He describes the Forks as being in the middle of a route between Selwyn Lake and Black Lake. He did the canoe route that Pierre told us about that avoids the lower Porcupine. From Grove Lake, he and his partner travelled up the McIntyre and then portaged into Jervois (Sandy) Creek. This creek feeds into the Porcupine just above the confluence of the Porcupine and the Fond du Lac.

Freddie Throassie, a canoe-trip leader from Black Lake whom I met with the group I paddled the Porcupine with in 2001, showed us this Jervois Creek route and the traditional lake route via Herbert Lake on my maps. He also introduced us to Isaac, an elder of Black Lake and a relative of his. Isaac told us there used to be lots of porcupines in the region until a fire swept through in the '40s. When asked what the Porcupine River is called in his language, he said the river is called the Porcupine in Dene too! That got a good laugh.

Bill Jeffrey, another long-time paddler in the North, told me there might have been some error made in the translation of the river's name. On a trip they did in the area together, Freddie told him the word porcupine in Dene is much like the word canoe. It could really have been called the Canoe River by the Dene.

Munsterhjelm, in his book *The Wind and the Caribou*, is always referring to all the porcupines he and his partner saw or ate on the Porcupine River. One was 12 lbs! They are a delicacy enjoyed very much by the Dene and the Cree, who boil and roast them. All in all, it's hard for me not to associate the river with porcupines now!

There are a couple of books you can consult for more information about the Porcupine and area. Sheila Minni's published thesis on the prehistory of the Dene of the Black Lake area is very interesting. *The Wind and the Caribou* is Erik Munsterhjelm's account of trapping on the Porcupine and around the Lake Athabasca region. And although his perspective on cultures other than his own is dated, the details of trapping life and of the region are very interesting. Maybe you will want to check out his and Karl's cabin site a few kilometres up the East Porcupine when you reach the Forks.

Solitude ✱✱✱

There are few signs of human presence on the river. There is the fishing lodge on Selwyn Lake and Camp Grayling on Black Lake. On Grove and Detour Lakes and the Fond du Lac there is evidence of hunting and trapping activity, with some cabins and kill sites along their shores. It is at Burr Falls that you are most likely to bump into people. They will be fishing or on their way to do some hunting.

Seeing other canoeists along the river is a very remote possibility. I would be surprised if more than three or four parties paddled the Porcupine in a season.

Wildlife ✱✱✱

The barren ground caribou sometimes come this far south in winter, but you won't see them during the paddling season! Moose and black bears are your most likely prospects for large-mammal sightings. There is little hunting pressure in the inaccessible areas of the river. Moose like old burn, and there are large areas of that since the forest fires in the middle of the '90s.

Overall there are fewer species and lower populations than in the southern ecoregions, reflecting the harsh climate and lack of diversity in the vegetation. However, golden eagles are a typical bird, and this is unique to the rivers in this book. You will also see lots of bald eagles and a number of osprey. An old osprey nest sits on top of a huge boulder between the second and third rapids of the river.

Brad and I didn't see a single moose or bear the first time we paddled the river in 1995, just after the fires. Nor did we see any large animals when we were at Selwyn Lake in 1997. But in August of 2001, when I paddled with another group, things really started to happen in the wildlife department! We saw four moose, including a cow and a calf. A big black bear dog-paddled across the river in front of us. We also think we saw a marten swimming across the river just downstream of Selwyn Lake. It was too big for a mink. But never, ever have I ever seen a porcupine — on any river!

Bill Jeffrey, who spends lots of time in the Far North, once saw a porcupine on the shore of Selwyn Lake. Tyrrell explains that porcupines are only plentiful where human beings rarely go, "For they are easily killed, and the Indians are very fond of a nice roasted porcupine." No one travelled the lower section, and there were once many porcupines. It all adds up to an apt name for the river.

Fishing ✳✳✳

Selwyn Lake is a trout hotspot, and not to be missed if you love fishing. More trout can be found in Grove and Herbert Lakes. On the river there are lots of dinner-size northern pike around. Grayling are also plentiful in the shallows of the upper rapids. The walleye action begins at the confluence with the Fond du Lac. Try by the large boulder in the channel on the other side of the weedy island across from the esker — the spot better known as Camping for Millions. There are big ones. Plus, if you stop at good old CFM for a rest day, you can paddle a few kilometres up the Fond du Lac to fish its last drop before the confluence. And of course there is always Burr Falls. If you fish the eddy lines below the falls just in front of the little rock island, you'll be sure to catch some pretties. At Black Lake you're back to lake trout and some big northern pike!

Special Equipment

As I've said many times, if you are going on a remote river trip known for its whitewater you should be paddling a Royalex-hull tripping canoe. The Porcupine is unforgiving. You might even want to beef up your repair kit. We found a lost throw bag below one rapid — an ominous sign. Advanced and exceptional paddlers may want to take a spray skirt for running some of the big drops.

The area you will be travelling in is cooler than any other in northern Saskatchewan. Bring warmer clothes than you would if you were going on a trip to the south or west. The weather is affected by Hudson Bay, and the area gets the majority of its yearly precipitation for the year from rain in July, so bring your wet-weather gear and a tarp. Don't forget your bug jacket and or hat, either. The blackflies are voracious, even in early August.

Trip Notes

MAP NO	GRID REF	FEATURE	DESCRIPTION
74 P/16	356445	Selwyn Lake Lodge	On the northwest side of Common Island.
	442377	Put-in	On a small, triangular island in Porcupine Bay, on the southeast side on a small sand beach. A possible campsite.
	445378	Old camp	An old hunting or firefighting camp with a decrepit dock. On the west side of an island. It's a possible campsite.
	457396	Rapids	**Class 2**. The left channel is Class 2, very shallow and rocky with some boulders. The right channel looks unnavigable at moderate water levels, and is very steep and rocky. The **portage (250 m)** is on the RL shore of the RL channel. There's good grayling fishing here. I wouldn't camp on the portage — the bears may come to see what the fishing party from the lodge left them to eat!
	466403	Rapids	**Class 2+**, shallow, and sweeping to the right. There's a mid-channel boulder to miss near the end. The **portage (225 m)** is on RL. There are boats here for fishing; try for more grayling!

MAP NO	GRID REF	FEATURE	DESCRIPTION
	485402	Osprey nest	On top of a big boulder is a very old osprey nest, no longer in use and falling apart in 2001.
	486382	Rapids	**Class 1** chute.
	485378	Rapids	**Class 2/2+.** A large chute with boulders and stoppers, and an S-turn of sorts. A boulder makes a big wave or stopper at the bottom, depending on the water level.
	484367	Rapids Campsite	**Class 2+/3- and Class 1+.** There are two parts to this rapid, with a campsite in between. The first drop is before the bend to the left and is fairly steep with big boulders to be avoided. Just after the bay on RR is a flat rock campsite. It is on the point on RR, with grayling fishing out front of the kitchen! The next part of the rapid carries on through some winding Class 1+ rapids for another 225 m or so. The bar marked on the map is the last of the rapids in this section, though the fast water continues until the next large rapid, which is indicated by the next marked bar.
	485357	Rapids	**Class 2+/3.** Another steep boulder run with bigger waves. The rapid is marked on the map at the narrows, but it continues until the river widens again. There's a nice high rock outcrop on RL to scramble up for a view or to take photos.
	479352	Rapids	**Class 1.** An unmarked chute in the narrows.
	477344	Rapids	**Class 2**, with a stopper to avoid on RR.
	477336	Campsite	On RL, on an elevated open bench.
	477335	Rapids	**Class 2**, with a big rock at the top of the channel. This becomes a hole in higher water.
	478328	Campsite	On RL in a bay. A nice sand beach with a small bench in behind.
	480314	Campsite	On the north side of the island; beach with a bench in behind.
	484312	Campsite	Open bench on RL.
	494309 497302	Rapids	**Class 2.** There are waves throughout and a few stoppers at the bottom in the middle.
	504304	Camping	A beautiful sand beach with an esker behind. Pick your spot along RL, the south shore of a small, unnamed lake.
	496301	Rapids	**Class 1**, a straightforward chute.
	495297	Eagle nest	In a dead tree on RR. Maybe home to golden eagles!
	493290	Riffle	At the narrows where the river bends to the left.
	491276	Rapids	**Class 1** for 200 m.
	492274	Riffle	Around the island.
	490253	Campsite	On RL, a small beach with a bench behind.
	487254	Campsite	On RL, on the point. A nice high spot for people who prefer rock camping.
	481246	Campsite	On RL, in trees with moss and rock.

MAP NO	GRID REF	FEATURE	DESCRIPTION
74 P/9	473235 475232	Camping	On RR in a big bay are some nice beach and-bench spots.
	504196	Rapids	**Class 2+**, rocky and sweeping around to the right with some waves. A portage is possible on RR.
	505189	Campsite	On RL, on a point on McHarg Lake. In jack pine with a rock landing.
	498187	Majestic Falls	The **portage (430 m)** starts on RL at the head of the falls, and the trail is through the 1996 burn. It starts at an exposed bedrock ridge leading up and away from the river. Don't go low until you can see the tiny bay of the put-in.
	492176 490173	Fast water	Through a series of narrows — a nice channel.
	490171 489168	Camping	A couple of spots on a sandy bench on RL.
	480155	Nest	In a lovely, high, rock channel, a cliff nest perches above the river.
	479156 477156	Fast water	After the nest is a series of fast water sections before next marked rapids.
	476156	Rapids	**Class 2**, straightforward.
	475155	Fast water	In narrows.
	472155 467153	Rapids	**Class 1, 1+, 2, 2+, and 3.** This 500-m rapid should be approached with caution; it's a wrap rapid. Almost every 100 m, the difficulty level increases as the rapids get steeper and more boulder-choked. By the time you are passing the island you are in Class 2+. The boulder apron below the island approaches Class 3. The RL channel is dry in lower water, but easier to navigate if you have high water. You can eddy scout this set. Lining is a good idea for the more cautious and less skilled.
	464152	Rapids	**Class 2, 1+ and 1.** The rapids into Detour Lake get easier as you descend, starting with Class 2 boulder dodging and ending with simple rock avoidance.
	453154	Cabins Put-in	At a beach there are two hunting cabins with evidence of recent winter caribou hunting.
	459133	Campsite	An okay site on the west side of a high island.
	455113	Campsite	An okay site on RR in a little bay at a sand beach.
	459110 461110	Switch Rapids	**Class 2 and 4.** The outlet rapid from Detour Lake is indicated by three bars. An easy, rocky chute (Class 2) above a large boulder ledge and waves (Class 4). The **portage (400 m)** is on RL through muskeg. The trail starts on RL in a little bay and ends in a rocky cove below the big waves.
	463107	Rapids	**Class 1**, marked with dashes on the map.
	464107 465100	Rapids Campsite	**Class 1+**, in the narrows, and unmarked. On the second little wooded island on the north side. A bench makes for good tent sites.

MAP NO	GRID REF	FEATURE	DESCRIPTION
	467087	Fast water	Fast water through the narrows. On RR is a modern pictograph of a fish and an arrow pointing down — as in "fish here." I've tried, believe me, but there are no fish there. I'm thinking maybe it's a joke!
	468077	Rapids	**Class 1+**, a long chute with rocks at the bottom.
	465072 465070	Riffles	
	466055	Campsite	On RL, a nice beach-and-bench combo.
	459050	Rapids	**Class 1**, in the narrows at a sharp bend to the left.
	452045 451045	Rapids	**Class 2**. Marked with two bars, this is a straightforward run with a boulder ledge on RL at the bottom.
	449045	Rapids	**Class 1+**. Straightforward.
	446044	Rapids	**Class 1**. Straightforward.
	444042	Rapids	**Class 1**. Straightforward.
	443042	Campsite	On RR, on a point just before a little, narrow bay is a nice, sandy jack pine bench.
	436037 434037	Camping	Two nice esker camps on either side of the bay on RR.
	434030	Campsite	On an esker point on RL.
	425025	Campsite	At a beach on RL is another esker camp.
	408007	Viewpoint	On a high sand hill after you make the turn into the burn. On RL.
	453000	Fast water	In the narrows at the bend to the left.
	465001	Fast water	In the narrows.
	470977	Rapids	**Class 1**. Straightforward.
	467970	The Forks	The flow really picks up here at the confluence of the East Porcupine. Watch for strong hydraulics in the downstream rapids.
	457967	Rapids	**Class 3+**. A large chute with a ledge and big waves. There's a **portage (350 m)** on RR. It's a good trail, and there are two possible starting places. One is above the first large eddy on RR, the other is directly below the first possible takeout in the next eddy. The rapids can be lined at some water levels.
	453960	Campsite	On RL on an open bench.
74 P/8	417930	Campsite	A beautiful beach-and-bench special on the northeast end of Grove Lake.
	409924	Put-in	A huge beach in a burned bay, with evidence of caribou hunting in behind. The cabins indicated on the map were on the other side of the point until they burned in 1996.
	391911	Campsite	Another nice beach on RL. It's in the burn, but still a really good camp.

porcupine river

MAP NO	GRID REF	FEATURE	DESCRIPTION
	364898	Water survey station	A non-operational water-survey station. A tin hut on RR, 400 m above the rapids.
	363895	Rapids	**Class 2**. There are waves here.
	362885	Campsite	On RL is another good beach camp, regardless of the burn.
	355871 355868	Baptism Rapids	**Class 3 and Class 2**. A long, rocky chute drops over a ledge that almost spans the entire river, and big waves follow. You can portage or line on RR until you feel comfortable putting back in. The rapids continue for another 200 m to just past the corner to the right.
	355861 355859	Rapids	**Class 2+ and 1+**. The top section of the rapid is represented on the map by the first bar. There are lots of boulders, and it's steep. The second bar marks a gentler drop to follow.
	354852	Eat Your Heart Out Rapid	**Class 4**. There's a small ledge on top, then a bigger ledge, then the biggest ledge. There are big waves and stoppers in between the ledges and at the end. You can pull over on the rock point on RR, line the bay, and then pull over on RR again.
	352853	Campsite	A small beach camp can be made in the bay on RR below "Eat Your Heart Out."
	327834	Nest	A raven's nest high on a cliff on LL.
	303814	Fast water	Around the islands.
	301811	Fast water	In the narrows.
	293804	Camping	On RL are pebble beaches with bench. Pick your spot.
	289801		
	287805	Campsite	On RR, not so burned. It's another pebble beach with a bench.
74 P/7	281798	Eye Cave	Towering "very Porcupineish" cliffs. Home to the amazing Eye Cave. Look way up.
	279800	Campsite	Camp here on the island to catch the cliffs and cave at the best light. There's a tiny beach and rock camp spot out of the burn.
	275795	Campsite	On RL, the good old beach-and-bench special.
	266792	Campsite	On RR, a nice beach to camp on.
	272777	Falls	The falls drop around a mid-channel island. The **portage (150 m)** is on RL in the second cove right above the drop. The trail starts on bare rock. Find the way by the mossy areas that have seen wear. It ends in a cove of boulders.
	277771	Rapids	**Class 2**, a straightforward chute.
	273762	Rapids	**Class 2**, a long (850 m), bouldery rapid.
	265747	Fast water	
	254737 254735	Rapids	**Class 2+ and 1**. The first bar indicates a Class 2+ drop with big waves and current hydraulics. The second bar is a straightforward Class 1. A portage is possible on RR.

MAP NO	GRID REF	FEATURE	DESCRIPTION
	249731	EYHO Rapid 2	**Class 4**. A big drop with a large ledge and large waves. In high water you could line the overflow channel on RL. The **portage (150 m)** is on RL and starts and ends at the overflow channel. Be cautious when putting in again; the current is strong and requires a good move to get out into the main flow again.
	245727 244725	**Camping**	On RR, pick your favourite rock point in this lovely channel.
	239724	**Campsite**	A sheltered cove on RR with a tiny beach at the end and a high bench in the trees. Climb up the ridge for a good view of the small lake and high hills.
	242722	**Riffle**	
	228714	**Campsite**	A nice beach-and-bench just down the small lake to the right.
	240714	**Rapids**	**Class 3**, with irregular waves and turbulent water. You could line the top of this set until you felt comfortable jumping in the boat again.
	245712 246711	**Rapids**	**Class 1+** waves around the bend to the right. Stay RL as you are approaching the falls. But don't panic. There is a big slow-water pool before the waterfall.
	247710 248709	**Falls**	The **portage (255 m)** is on RL up a steep rock ridge through trees and then down a very steep cliff path. We belayed the canoes down the sheer part of the cliff rather than pulling them over the path or trying to carry them.
	248705 246706	**Rapids**	**Class 2+**. The rapids start at the bar, but are 400 m long. A straight-forward boulder dodge.
	246703 233688	**Fast water**	Fast water sections through a valley-like section for about 3 km.
74 P/2	248665 247663	**Camping**	On RL are two sand beaches with bench in behind. Very nice.
	236657 234655	**Canyon Falls**	The **portage (450 m)** of this double falls (which is incorrectly marked on the map as a rapid by six bars), can be made on RR or RL. I have done both. The whaleback on RL is best to walk on, but the put-in is better on RR. Plus, if you can't shoot the ledge that follows the falls because of current water levels, you've got a tricky ferry to make to the RR shore to portage it. Neither option is easy, and both are over bare rock that can be treacherous in wet conditions. Both portages start just upstream of the head of the first drop.
	233655	**Rapids**	**Class 3**. This ledge chute right after the portage of the falls is a tricky one at certain water levels. There are big hydraulics at work and you can get flipped in the eddy swirls and whirlpools in a second. You don't want to blow this one. Have a rescue boat to pick up your canoe and gear before the next rapid, as there are many big drops ahead.
	232654	**Rapids**	**Class 2**, just waves, but be cautious. Eventually you will want to be on RR to catch the portage for the next big drop.

MAP NO	GRID REF	FEATURE	DESCRIPTION
230652 227649	Rapids Campsite	**Class 4 and Class 5**. A 500-m-long rapid is indicated on the map by a bunch of dashes. There are two parts to it. The first is a big chute with big waves and a few boulders to avoid. The bottom set is nasty and very steep, with turbulent water flowing over big boulders. The **portage (500 m)** bypasses both parts, and is very difficult at the beginning — like going up a rock cliff. The trail is over bare rock until you reach the end of the first set of rapids, and then it follows a less-steep rock ridge through the trees. Camping is possible on the lower rock ridge, and the flat rocks by the little sand beach make a nice kitchen area.
226645	Fast water	In the narrows.
222642	Fast water	In the narrows.
218640	Rapids	**Class 4 or Class 2+**. The rapids go around an island. The RR channel is the easiest. It is a ledge chute and then a boulder-and-rock dodge for 100 m. It is possible to lift over the ledge and line on RR. A Class 4 ledge rapid is in the RL channel.
216638	Fast water	Around the next islands.
214634 211633	Rapids	**Class 3+ or Class 4 ledges followed by Class 2+ and 2**. This is a gorgeous set of rapids and a beautiful spot. Hike the hill on RR to truly enjoy it. To portage the Class 3+ ledges on RR, carry over the rocks on RR. You can line from there to where you feel comfortable getting back into the boat. The rest of the rapid is a boulder-and-rock dodge, becoming easier as you approach the sharp bend to the right.
211633	Rapids Campsite	**Class 2**. Another rapid with a couple of small ledges to avoid, and rock dodging as well. Just before the first ledge is a great rock-camping spot high on the rocks on RL. Eddy out before the rapid at the blueberry patch preceding the high outcrop.
207631	Rapids	**Class 1+/2**. The last rapid on the Porcupine, with chutes and rocks. Dodge your way through the narrows.
199621	Campsite	A well-used beauty on RL. The beach-and-bench special. Now you are again in the land of sand until the granite of Burr Falls starts to outcrop on the Fond du Lac. Check out Jervois (Sandy) Creek, the traditional way to descend the last canyon of the Porcupine.
146606	Cabin	A trapping and hunting cabin on RL.
122600	Campsite	Good old "Camping for Millions," the esker camp of the universe. You haven't camped in the Far North until you've camped here. People have for a long time. There's good fishing out in front, swimming, hiking, and a view of the Fond du Lac and the sky. This place has it all!

Note: If you are carrying on to Burr Falls and Black Lake see the Fond du Lac Trip Notes.

DIRECTORY OF SERVICES

Note: Phone numbers and e-mail addresses change and businesses change hands, so eventually some of this information will be outdated. However, the government departments listed or telephone directory assistance should be able to give you current contact information in most cases. I do know that the Saskatchewan e-mail addresses with @sk.sympatico.ca in them will be changing to @sasktel.net in the next year or so.

Contact information for fishing lodges and outfitters along the rivers that I have not included here can most often be found in the current *Saskatchewan Hunting and Fishing Guide* or *Vacation Guide*. You can obtain these publications by calling SERM at 306-787-2700.

AVIATION SERVICES

Air Mikisew: 780-743-8218 (Fort McMurray) and 306-822-2022 (La Loche) or 1-888-268-7112

Athabasca Eco Expeditions/Athabasca Fishing Lodges: 306-653-5490 or 1-800-667-5490 (US only), www.athabascalake.com/

Ile-à-la-Crosse Airways: 306-833-2151

Lawrence Bay Lodge and Airways: Reindeer Lake, 306-758-2060 (summer) and 701-262-4560 (Oct.1–May 25), lblodge@stellarnet.com

Osprey Wings: Missinipe on Otter Lake, 306-635-2112

Northern Dene Air: 306-439-4990 (floatplane base — summer only), 306-439-2020 (Stony Rapids), 306-686-2151 (Fond du Lac) and 306-498-2130 (Uranium City)

Points North Landing and Air Services: 306-633-2137, www.pointsnorthair.com

Ross Air Services: Sandy Bay, 306-754-2026

Transwest: 1-800-667-9356 (reservations), 306-425-2382 (La Ronge charters) and 306-439-2040 (Stony Rapids charters), www.transwestair.com

Voyage Air: 306-235-4664 (Buffalo Narrows) and 780-743-0255 (Fort McMurray), www.voyageair.com

GOVERNMENT LISTINGS

Information Services Corporation of Saskatchewan
Map and Photo Distribution, 200-10 Research Drive, Regina, SK   S4P 3V7, Canada
Tel: 306-787-2799 Fax: 306-787-3335
saskmaps@isc-online.ca, www.isc-online.ca

Athabasca Sand Dunes Wilderness Provincial Park: 306-439-2062

Clearwater River Wilderness Provincial Park: 306-235-1740

Canoe Saskatchewan website: www.lights.com/waterways/

Highways (northern division): 306-953-3500

RCMP: **Emergencies** — 310-7267 in northern Saskatchewan only
Detachments: Creighton 306-688-8888, Ile-à-la-Crosse 306-833-6300,
La Loche 306-822-2010, La Ronge 306-425-6730, Pinehouse 306-884-2400,
Stanley Mission 306-635-2390, Stony Rapids 306-439-2185, Wollaston Lake 306-633-1200

Saskatchewan Government website: www.gov.sk.ca

Saskatchewan Parks: 1-877-237-2273 operator 21PV

SaskWater: 306-694-3966, (fax) 306-694-3944, www.saskwater.com

SERM: 306-787-2700, www.serm.gov.sk.ca

Tourism Saskatchewan: 1-877-237-2273 operator 21VG or 306-787-2300, www.sasktourism.com

NORTHERN SASKATCHEWAN CANOE OUTFITTERS/CANOE RENTALS

Air Mikisew: Canoe rentals (see Aviation Services)

Athabasca Eco Expeditions/Athabasca Fishing Lodges: Canoe rentals (see Aviation Services)

Canadian Voyageur Canoe Adventures: Fully outfitted and guided voyageur canoe trips, 250-545-9400, www.canadianvoyageur.com

CanoeSki Discovery Company: Canoe instruction and fully outfitted and guided trips on various rivers, 306-653-5693, www.canoeski.com

Churchill River Canoe Outfitters: Canoe and equipment rentals, guides, canoe instruction, shuttles and fully outfitted and guided trips, 306-635-4420, 780-471-1273 or 1-877-511-2726, www.churchillrivercanoe.com

Lone Wolf Camps: Canoe rentals, access to Carswell Lake, 306-235-4247, lone.wolf.camps@sasktel.net

Pawistik Lodge: Canoe and equipment rentals, shuttles, 403-263-6881 or 1-800-526-4177, www.pawistiklodge.com

Rainbow Ridge B&B and Canoe Outfitters: Fully outfitted and guided trips, 306-833-2590, www.bbcanada.com/3586.html

Selwyn Lake Lodge: Canoe rentals, 306-664-3373, 1-800-667-9556, www.selwynlakelodge.com

Voyage Air: Canoe rentals (see Aviation Services)

ORGANIZATIONS OF INTEREST

Canadian Heritage River System: Parks Canada Agency, Ottawa, ON, K1A 0M5, www.chrs.ca

Canadian Recreational Canoe Association: Box 398 Main St. West, Merrickville, ON, K0G 1N0, 613-269-2910, 1-888-252-6292, www.paddlingcanada.com

Friends of the Churchill: c/o 364 Morland Rd., Comox, BC, V9M 3W2

Keewatin Career Development Corporation: www.kcdc.sk.ca (website lists communities and services in northern Saskatchewan)

Wilderness Canoe Association: Box 48022, Davisville Postal Outlet, 1881 Yonge St. Toronto, ON, M4S 3C6, http://wildernesscanoe.ca

STURGEON-WEIR RIVER

Canadian Voyageur Canoe Adventures (see Canoe Outfitters)

Pawistik Lodge, Maligne Lake: 403-263-6881, 1-800-526-4177, www.pawistiklodge.com

SERM: Creighton, 306-688-8812 and Pelican Narrows, 306-632-5517

Sturgeon Landing Outfitters: Cabins, store, shuttle service, 306-688-4410, sturgeonoutfitters@sk.sympatico.ca

Northern Gateway Museum: Denare Beach, 306-362-2141 (summer only)

MONTREAL RIVER

Mac's Taxi, La Ronge: 306-425-5445

Northland Taxi, La Ronge: 306-425-2222

SERM, La Ronge: 306-425-4234

CHURCHILL RIVER

Aurele's Taxi, Ile-à-la-Crosse: 306-833-2095

Churchill River Canoe Outfitters (see Canoe Outfitters/Rentals)

Jeff's Taxi, Ile-à-la-Crosse: 306-833-2253

Osprey Wings (see Aviation Services)

Kitchi-Miskanow Outfitters, Culture Camp on Iskwatam Lake: 306-632-2054

Rainbow Ridge B&B and Canoe Outfitters, Ile-à-la-Crosse (see Canoe Outfitters)

Ross Air Services (see Aviation Services)

SERM: La Ronge 306-425-4234. Ile-à-la-Crosse 306-833-3220, Pinehouse 306-884-2060

Smith's Taxi, Pinehouse Lake: 306-884-2367 (phone to book in advance)

Transwest Air (see Aviation Services)

Voyage Air (see Aviation Service and Canoe Rentals)

PAULL RIVER

Churchill River Canoe Outfitters (see Canoe Outfitters/Canoe Rentals)

Osprey Wings (see Aviation Services)

Transwest Air (see Aviation Services)

FOSTER RIVER

Osprey Wings (see Aviation Services)

Transwest Air (see Aviation Services)

HAULTAIN RIVER

Smith's Taxi, Pinehouse Lake: 306-884-2367 (phone to book in advance)

Mawdsley Lake Lodge: 403-328-9528 or Key Lake Mobile YR3-2023, www.mawdsleylakefishinglodge.com (only open end of May to mid-June)

SERM, Pinehouse: 306-884-2060

CLEARWATER RIVER

Air Mikisew (see Aviation Services and Canoe Rentals)

Careen Lake Lodge: 306-948-3890

Environment Alberta: (for current flows) 780-427-2046, www3.gov.ab.ca/env/ water/overview.html

SERM, La Loche: 306-822-1700

Voyage Air (see Aviation Services and Canoe Rentals)

WATHAMAN RIVER

Churchill River Canoe Outfitters (see Canoe Outfitters/Rentals)

Lawrence Bay Lodge and Airways (see Aviation Services)

Osprey Wings (see Aviation Services)

SERM, Southend: 306-758-6258

GEIKIE RIVER

Churchill River Canoe Outfitters (see Canoe Outfitting/Rentals)

Osprey Wings (see Aviation Services)

Points North (see Aviation Services)

SERM, Wollaston Lake: 306-633-2112

Transwest Air (see Aviation Services)

CREE RIVER

Churchill River Canoe Outfitters (see Canoe Outfitting/Rentals)

Cree Lake Lodge: 780-853-4911

Cree River Lodge on Wapata Lake: 306-874-5786 or 1-866-707-3726, cree.river.lodge@sasktel.net

Points North (see Aviation Services)

WATERFOUND RIVER

Churchill River Canoe Outfitters (see Canoe Outfitters/Rentals)

Points North (see Aviation Services)

SERM, Wollaston Lake: 306-633-2112

Transwest Air (see Aviation Services)

FOND DU LAC RIVER

Churchill River Canoe Outfitters (see Canoe Outfitters/Rentals)

Points North (see Aviation Services)

SERM, Wollaston Lake: 306-633-2112

Transwest Air (see Aviation Services)

MACFARLANE RIVER

Air Mikisew (see Aviation Services and Canoe Rentals)

Athabasca Eco Expeditions/Athabasca Fishing Lodges (see Aviation Services and Canoe Rentals)

Churchill River Canoe Outfitters (see Canoe Outfitters/Rentals)

Northern Dene Air (see Aviation Services)

Points North (see Aviation Services)

SERM, Stony Rapids: 306-439-2062

Transwest Air (see Aviation Services)

Voyage Air (see Aviation Services and Canoe Rentals)

CARSWELL AND WILLIAM RIVERS

Air Mikisew (see Aviation Services and Canoe Rentals)

Athabasca Eco Expeditions/Athabasca Fishing Lodges (see Aviation Services and Canoe Rentals)

Churchill River Canoe Outfitters (see Canoe Outfitter/Canoe Rentals)

Lone Wolf Camps (see Canoe Rentals)

Northern Dene Air (see Aviation Services)

Points North (see Aviation Services)

SERM, Stony Rapids: 306-439-2062

Transwest Air (see Aviation Services)

Voyage Air (see Aviation Services and Canoe Rentals)

PORCUPINE RIVER

Athabasca Eco Expeditions/Athabasca Fishing Lodges (see Aviation Services and Canoe Rentals)

Churchill River Canoe Outfitters (see Canoe Outfitters/Rentals)

Northern Dene Air (see Aviation Services)

Points North (see Aviation Services)

Selwyn Lake Lodge (see Canoe Rentals)

SERM, Stony Rapids: 306-439-2062

Transwest Air (see Aviation Services)

REFERENCES AND SUGGESTED READINGS

Abouguendia, Z. M., ed. *Athabasca Sand Dunes in Saskatchewan*. Mackenzie River Basin Study Report: Supplement 7. Regina: Environment Canada, 1981.

Acton, D. F., et al. *The Ecoregions of Saskatchewan*. Regina: Canadian Plains Research Centre/Saskatchewan Environment and Resource Management, 1998.

A Land of Many Rivers: Trapping in the Poorfish River Country: http://deep- river.jkcc.com /many.html

Alberta Legislative Assembly Library Online: www.assembly.ab.ca/lao/library/premiers/ haultain.htm

Archer, Sheila. William River trip notes, 1999.

———. MacFarlane River trip notes, 1999.

———. Clearwater River trip notes, 1993.

Arrowsmith, William, A. "Northern Saskatchewan and the Fur Trade." Masters thesis, University of Saskatchewan, 1964.

Atlas of Saskatchewan. 2nd ed. Saskatoon, SK: University of Saskatchewan, 1999.

Barry, Bill. *People Places: Saskatchewan and its Names*. Regina: Canadian Plains Research Centre, 1997.

Beak Associates Consulting Ltd. Canadian Heritage River System, Heritage Resource Background Report on the Churchill River, Volumes I, II and III, for Department of Parks and Renewable Resources and Parks Canada, 1986.

Bober, Dave. "Down to the Kingdom of Sand" in *Canada's Best Canoe Routes*. Ed. Alister Thomas. Erin, ON: Boston Mills, 2000.

———. "Doin the Dunes: Northern Saskatchewan's MacFarlane River." *Kanawa*, Fall, 1994.

———. "The Porcupine River: Where the Cliffs Meet the Sky." *Kanawa*, Nov./Dec., 1996.

———. "The Cool Clearwater River." *Saskatchewan Naturally Magazine*. Vol I, No. 2.

———. "Churchill River." *Nastawagan*. Autumn, 1991.

Brumach, Hetty Jo, Jarvenpa, R, and C. Buell. "An Ethnoarchaeological Approach to Chipewyan Adaptations in the Late Fur Trade Period." *Arctic Anthropology* 19 (1), 1982.

Bryce, George. *The Remarkable History of the Hudson's Bay Company: Including that of the French Traders of North-western Canada and the North-West, XY, and Astor Fur Companies*. Toronto: W. Briggs, 1900.

Buchanan, Angus. *Wild Life in Canada*. Toronto: McClelland, 1920.

Canadian Heritage River System. 1993. Nomination document for the Churchill.

Canadian Heritage River System. 1986. Nomination document for the Clearwater.

Canadian Institute For Historical Microreproductions. Early Canadiana online: www.canadiana.org/

Canadian Recreational Canoe Association. *Canoeists Code of Ethics*, (n.d.).

Coues, Elliot, ed. *New Light on the Early History of the Greater Northwest: The Manuscript Journals of Alexander Henry, Fur Trader of the Northwest Company, and David Thompson, Official Geographer and Explorer of the Same Company, 1799-1814*. 3 Volumes. Minneapolis: Ross and Haines, 1965.

Curtis, Rick. *The Backpacker's Field Manual: A Comprehensive Guide to Mastering Backcountry Skills*. New York: Three Rivers Press, 1998.

Davis, Richard, C. ed. *Sir John Franklin's Journals and Correspondence: The First Arctic Land Expedition, 1819–1822*. Toronto: Champlain Society, 1995.

de Laforest, Marcel. "The Views of the Historic Trails Canoe Club" in *The Churchill: A Heritage River*. Proceedings of the conference held March 8–10, 1995. Saskatoon, SK: University Extension Press, University of Saskatchewan, 1995.

"Ecoregions of Saskatchewan." Map. Compiled by Padbury, G. A. and D. F Acton. Saskatchewan Property Management Corporation. 1994 ed.

Engstrom, E. *Clearwater Winter*. Edmonton: Lone Pine, 1984.

Gillespie, Beryl C. "Territorial Expansion of the Chipewyan in the 18th Century." In *Proceedings of Northern Athapaskan Conference*, 1971, Volume 2. A. McFayden Clark, ed. Canadian Ethnology Service Paper 27, Mercury Series. Ottawa: National Museum of Man, 1975.

———. "Territorial Groups Before 1821: Athapaskans of the Shield and the Mackenzie Drainage" in *Handbook of North American Indians: Subarctic*, Volume 6. June Helm, ed. Washington: Smithsonian Institution, 1981.

Glover, Richard, ed. *David Thompson's Narrative (1784–1812)*. Toronto: Champlain Society, 1962.

Goldstick, Miles. *Wollaston: People Resisting Genocide*. Montreal, QC: Black Rose Books, 1987.

Goode, Peter, Amudson, Leslie and Joan Champ. *The Montreal Lake Region: Its History and Geography*. Saskatoon: Sentar Consultants, 1996.

Henry, Alexander [the Elder]. *Travels and Adventures in Canada and the Indian Territories between the Years 1760 and 1776*. Edmonton: Hurtig Publishers, 1969.

Herrero, Stephen. *Bear Attacks: Their Causes and Avoidance*. Edmonton: Hurtig Publishers, 1985.

Hodgins, Bruce. W and Gwyneth Hoyle. *Canoeing North into the Unknown: A Record of River Travel: 1874 to 1974*. Toronto, ON: Natural Heritage, 1994.

Huck, Barbara. *The Fur Trade Routes of North America: Explore the Highways that Opened a Continent*. Garden City, KA: Sandhill Books, 2000.

Innis, Harold. *The Fur Trade in Canada: An Introduction to Canadian Economic History*. Toronto: University of Toronto Press, 1962.

———. *Peter Pond, Fur Trader and Adventurer*. Toronto: Irwin and Gordon, 1930.

Jarvenpa, R. and Hetty Jo Brumbach. "The Microeconomics of Southern Chipewyan Fur Trade History" in *The Subarctic Fur Trade: Native Social and Economic Adaptations*. S. Krech III, ed. Vancouver: University of British Columbia Press, 1984.

Johnson, Derek et al. *Plants of the Western Boreal Forest and Aspen Parkland*. Edmonton: Lone Pine, 1995.

Johnson, R. and B. Weichel. Churchill River Reach Saskatchewan Analysis of Canadian Heritage River and Wilderness Park Potential, Sandfly Lake to Otter Rapids Reach, for Parks Canada and Saskatchewan Parks and Renewable Resources, 1982.

Johnson, Ron and Lynn Noel. "River Relicts" in *Voyages: Canada's Heritage Rivers*. Lynn Noel, ed. St. John's, NF: Breakwater, 1995.

Jones, T. E. *The Aboriginal Rock Paintings of the Churchill River*. Anthropological Series No. 4. Regina: Saskatchewan Museum of Natural History, 1981.

Jonker, Peter, and Rowe, Stan. *The Sand Dunes of Lake Athabasca*. Saskatoon: University of Saskatchewan Extension Press, 2001.

Karpan, Robin and Arlene Karpan. *Northern Sandscapes: Exploring Saskatchewan's Athabasca Sand Dunes*. Saskatoon: Parkland Press, 1998.

Karras, A. L. *North to Cree Lake*. Toronto: Paper Jacks/Simon & Schuster, 1970. http://deep-river.jkcc.com/north.html

———. *Face the North Wind*. Don Mills, ON: Burns & MacEachern, 1975. http://deep-river.jkcc.com/face.html

Keighley, S. A. *Trader, Tripper, Trapper: The Life of a Bay Man*. Winnipeg, MB: Watson & Dwyer, 1989.

Kemp, H.S.M. *Northern Trader*. Toronto: Ryerson, 1956.

Kesselheim, A. *Water and Sky: Reflections of a Northern Year*. Golden, CO: Fulcrum, 1989.

Kitsaki Career Development Corporation website:
www.kcdc.sk.ca/comm/Montreal Lake.php

Kraiker, Rolf. "Doin the Dunes: What it's Like and Why it's Possible to Paddle in a Northern Desert" in *Che-mun*, 2000. http://www.canoe.ca/Adventure/story- dunes.html

Krech, Shepard III, ed. *The Subarctic Fur Trade: Native Social and Economic Adaptations.* Vancouver: University of British Columbia Press, 1984.

Kupsch, W. D. "A Valley View in Verdant Prose: The Clearwater Valley From Portage La Loche." *Musk-Ox*, No. 20, 1977.

Kupsch, W. D. "The Churchill-Reindeer Area: Evolution of its Landscape." www.lights.com/waterways/geology/kupsch.htm

Mackenzie, Alexander. *Voyages from Montreal on the River St. Laurence Through the Continent of North America to the Frozen and Pacific Oceans In the Years 1789 and 1793. With a Preliminary Account of the Rise, Progress and Present State of the Fur Trade of that Country*, London, 1801. Reprint. Edmonton, AB: M.G. Hurtig, 1971.

MacLennan, Hugh. *The Rivers of Canada*. Toronto: Macmillan of Canada, 1974.

McGuffin, Gary and Joannie McGuffin. *Where Rivers Run: A 6,000 Mile Exploration of Canada by Canoe.* Erin, ON: Boston Mills Press, 1988.

McKown, Doug. "Goin' Dune the MacFarlane." *Che-mun*: www.canoe.ca/chemun/macfarlane.html

Meyer, David. "People Before Kelsey: An Overview of Cultural Developments" in *Three Hundred Prairie Years: Henry Kelsey's "Inland Country of Good Report,"* edited by H. Epp. Regina: Canadian Plains Research Centre, 1993.

Meyer, D. and S. Smailes. "Archaeology" *Churchill River Study*, Final Report 19. J. Mitchell, ed. Regina: Saskatchewan Tourism and Renewable Resources; Saskatchewan Museum of Natural History, 1975.

Minni, Sheila. *The Prehistoric Occupation of Black Lake, Northern Saskatchewan.* Mercury Series Paper No. 53, Archaeological Survey of Canada. Ottawa: National Museum of Man, 1976.

Morse, Eric, W. *Fur Trade Routes: Then and Now.* Ottawa: Queen's Printer, 1969.

Munsterhjelm, Erik. *The Wind and the Caribou.* Toronto: MacMillan, 1953.

Nagle, Ted and Jordon Zinovich. *The Prospector: North of Sixty.* Edmonton: Lone Pine, 1989.

Newman, Peter C. *Company of Adventurers.* Toronto: Viking, 1985.

———. *Caesars of the Wilderness.* Company of Adventurers, Volume 2. Markham, ON: Penguin Books, 1988.

Nute, Grace, L. *The Voyageurs.* St. Paul: Minnesota Historical Society, 1955.

Olson, Sigurd. *The Lonely Land.* Toronto: McClelland & Stewart, 1961.

———. *Runes of the North.* New York: Alfred A. Knopf, 1963.

Parker, James. *Emporium of the North: Fort Chipewyan and the Fur Trade to 1835.* Regina: Canadian Plains Research Centre/Alberta Culture and Multi-culturalism, 1987.

Parks Canada. *Wild Rivers: Saskatchewan.* Parks Canada, Department of Indian and Northern Affairs. Ottawa: Queen's Printer, [n.d.].

Pecher, Kamil. *Lonely Voyage.* Saskatoon: Western Producer Prairie Books, 1978.

Ray, Arthur, J. *Indians in the Fur Trade: Their Role of Trappers, Hunters, and Middlemen in the Lands Southwest of Hudson Bay, 1660-1870.* Toronto: University of Toronto Press, 1974.

Robinson, Sid. "Selected Early Historic Sites on the Churchill River" in *The Churchill: A Heritage River.* Proceedings from the conference held March 8–10, 1995. Saskatoon, SK: Extension Division Press, University of Saskatchewan, 1995.

Robinson, Sid and Greg Marchildon. *Canoeing the Churchill: A Practical Guide to the Historic Voyageur Highway.* Regina: Canadian Plains Research Centre, 2002.

Russell, Dale R. *Eighteenth-Century Western Cree and their Neighbours*. Ottawa: Canadian Museum of Civilization, 1991.

Saskatchewan Environment and Resource Management. Canoe Trip 26: Chipman River

Saskatchewan Environment and Resource Management. Canoe Trip 1: Churchill

Saskatchewan Environment and Resource Management. Canoe Trip 29: Churchill

Saskatchewan Environment and Resource Management. Canoe Trip 40: Clearwater

Saskatchewan Environment and Resource Management. Canoe Trip 58: Clearwater

Saskatchewan Environment and Resource Management. Canoe Trip 57: Foster

Saskatchewan Environment and Resource Management. Canoe Trip 38: Geikie

Saskatchewan Environment and Resource Management. Canoe Trip 36: Paull

Saskatchewan Environment and Resource Management. Canoe Trip 14: Sturgeon-weir

Saskatchewan Environment and Resource Management. Canoe Trip 44: Sturgeon-weir

Saskatchewan Environment and Resource Management in cooperation with the Historic Trails Canoe Club. *Saskatchewan's Voyageur Highway: A Canoe Trip*, 1991.

Sheldon, Ian and Tamara Eder. *Animal Tracks of Saskatchewan*. Edmonton: Lone Pine, 2000.

Smith, Alan. *Saskatchewan Birds*. Edmonton: Lone Pine, 2001.

Smith, James, G. E. "Chipewyan" in *Handbook of North American Indians: Subarctic, Volume 6*. June Helm, ed. Washington: Smithsonian Institution, 1981.

———. "Western Woods Cree" in *Handbook of North American Indians: Subarctic, Volume 6*. June Helm, ed. Washington: Smithsonian Institution, 1981.

Snook, Micheal. 1995. "First Light" in *Voyages: Canada's Heritage Rivers*. Lynn Noel, ed. St. John's, NF: Breakwater, 1995.

Speers, Cliff. "River of Golden Sands, River Beyond Dreams" in *Canada's Best Canoe Routes*. Alister Thomas, ed. Erin, ON: Boston Mills Press, 2000. 116–120.

Storer, Dr. John. *Geological History of Saskatchewan*. Regina: Saskatchewan Museum of Natural History/Government of Saskatchewan, 1989.

Theriau, Ed and Patricia Armstrong. *Lost Land of the Caribou*. Saskatoon, SK: Modern Press, 1978. http://deep-river.jkcc.com/lost.html

Tyrrell, J. B. and D. B. Dowling. Summary Report on the country between Athabasca Lake and Churchill River. Ottawa: S.E. Dawson, 1895.

———. *Report on the Country between Athabasca Lake and Churchill River, with Notes from Two Routes traveled between the Churchill and Saskatchewan Rivers*. Ottawa: S.E. Dawson, 1896.

Tyrrell, Joseph Burr. *Early Explorations of the Churchill River*. New York: American Geographical Society, 1917.

———. *Recent Explorations in Canada, 1890–1896*. Ottawa: Ottawa Naturalist, 1897.

Tyrrell, Joseph Burr, ed. *The Journals of Samuel Hearne and Phillip Turnor Between the years 1774 and 1792*. Toronto: Champlain Society, 1934.

Tyrrell on the web: http://digital.library.utoronto.ca/Tyrrell (includes notebooks)

Van Kirk, Sylvia. *"Many Tender Ties": Women in Fur-Trade Society in Western Canada, 1670–1870*. Winnipeg, MB: Watson & Dwyer Publishing, 1981.

Vesilind, Priit, J. "David Thompson: The Man Who Measured Canada," *National Geographic*, May 1996.

Walbridge, Charles and Wayne Sundmacher Sr. *Whitewater Rescue Manual: New Techniques for Canoeists, Kayakers and Rafters*. Camden, Maine: Ragged Mountain Press, 1995.

Woodcock, George. *The Hudson's Bay Company*. Toronto: Collier-Macmillan Canada, 1970.

Wright, James. *The Prehistory of Lake Athabasca: An Initial Statement*. Mercury Series Archaeological Survey Paper No. 29. Ottawa: National Museum of Man, 1975.

INTERNATIONAL SCALE OF RAPID CLASSIFICATION

The scale I use is based on a number of variations of a rating system endorsed by the International Canoe Federation, and is as follows:

Class 1   Moving water where riffles or small, regular waves may be present. Passages have few or no obstructions and are wide, open and easy to see. The risk of injury to swimmers is slight. Read-as-you-run, and navigable by beginner paddlers.

Class 2   Straightforward rapids with obvious, wide, and unobstructed passages. Features such as rocks, small boulders, small ledges, and sweepers, or artificial obstructions such as bridges or piers can be avoided with simple manoeuvring. The risk of injury is low. Intermediate and advanced paddlers will read and run.

Class 3   Rapids with moderate or irregular waves, or both, which could swamp an open canoe. Waves, rocks, holes, boulders, logs or other obstacles may be present in the passages, and the passages can be narrow. Considerable manoeuvring is required, with risk of injury. Scouting from shore is advisable for advanced paddlers and required for intermediate paddlers.

Class 4   Rapids with high and irregular waves, boiling eddies, steep drops or abrupt bends. Skillful, precise manoeuvring is required within convoluted passages containing irregular features, big hydraulics and or vertical drops. There is a risk of injury and a possible risk to your life. Scouting from shore is required to find safe routes. For advanced and exceptional paddlers only.

Class 5   Rapids with irregular, unpredictable and violent features, with large-scale vertical drops, unpredictable waves, and holes in extremely tight, obstructed and convoluted passages. A series of complex, linked manoeuvres is required. The rapids are dangerous, with risk of serious injury and definite risk to your life. Scouting from the shore is mandatory to determine safe routes. This should only be attempted by exceptional paddlers.

Class 6   Difficulties of Class 5 are carried to the extreme in Class 6. Extremely violent and unpredictable rapids with vertical drops and very large features, and high risk to the boater's life.

Note: All rapids classifications can be bumped up to indicate that a particular rapid is slightly more difficult. For example, in the guidebook I rate a tough Class 3 rapid as a 3+. Using a minus sign indicates that the rapid shares more similarities with the higher difficulty classification than the lower. For example a rapid that is not quite a Class 4, but more difficult than a 3+, would be rated a Class 4-. Some rapid classification systems also make the distinction between technical and non-technical rapids. I have chosen to describe the features of the rivers' rapids in the Trip Notes in order to make that distinction, rather than use a more elaborate classification system.

NO-TRACE CAMPING AND WILDERNESS ETHICS

Leave-no-trace travelling and camping is an attitude, and includes the following general principles that apply to trips in any ecosystem. These principles are based on the Canadian Recreational Canoe Association's guidelines and the leave-no-trace guidelines from *The Backpacker's Field Manual*.

Plan ahead and prepare.
Know what you need and bring what you need with you so your impact is as slight as possible. Do not rely on the environment to supply you. Do not use natural materials for shelters, except in emergency situations.

Concentrate the impact in high-use areas.
You will have the least impact on the wilderness if you continue to use that highly impacted campsite or trail. Do not overstay.

Spread the use and impact in pristine areas.
You should avoid going into pristine areas unless you have to and are committed to and can properly implement leave-no-trace techniques. If the area is pristine, showing little or no impact, then spread yourself out so that you don't create new bald-spot campsites, worn trails, and so on, that would encourage other people to also use the site and increase the impact to damaging levels. If you have to create a portage trail, study the implications upon the environment before blazing new trails.

Avoid places where impact is just beginning.
If a site is showing the beginning signs of impact, leave it alone and let it recover to its natural state.

Pack it in, pack it out.
Whatever you bring in with you, you need to bring out. This means garbage, tampons, etc. that cannot be burned with a careful, small fire that leaves no impact on a campsite. Pick up any litter you find and dispose of it properly.

Properly dispose of what you can't pack out.
If you can't pack it out (waste water from washing or cooking, human waste), dispose of it properly for the ecosystem you are in. In the case of northern Saskatchewan, it is common practice to use small amounts of biodegradable soap and shampoo to wash dishes and people, and to throw cooking water and fish guts and carcasses into the river where they will not contaminate drinking water supplies or be washed up on shore. Human waste is buried carefully in catholes in the moss or groundcover and far away from sources of water. Burn all toilet paper, otherwise use single-ply white toilet paper and bury it completely. If there are outhouses, use them.

Don't change the environment.
Don't alter the environment to suit you or to bring back souvenirs. Doesn't the person behind you want to see as much of the natural world? Minimize any campsite alterations. Don't cut trenches around tents or tarps or build fire rings, shelters or tables. Avoid damaging live trees and plants, especially the moss groundcover often found in the North; it took years and years to grow there. Don't hammer nails in trees for hangers, cut wood from live trees, or damage branches when tying up tarps. Finally, leaving rock cairns by the portage trail may seem like a grand and even helpful idea, but maybe the people behind you want to feel as if they can find their way in the wilderness the way you did, without help.

Leave what you find.
It is illegal in Saskatchewan to disturb or remove artifacts. If you find caribou antlers and other natural objects, why not leave them there for the next person to be able to experience the excitement of finding them, and the next person, and the next person.

Use fire responsibly.
Campfires can start forest fires. Even small campfires scar the land. Carefully evaluate both the need for a fire and your ability to create one that leaves no impact. For instance, use an environmental stove or simply use a gas stove for all your cooking. If you do have a fire at an established campfire ring, let it burn to ash, and make sure it is completely out by dousing it with water. Clean out any bits of unburned garbage from the ash and pack them out.

Group size.
A large group of people in one camping spot can have a significant impact. Keep your group as small as possible and pick high-use campsites that can handle the number of people you have with you, or travel in smaller units. Never take a large group on a river infrequently travelled.

Ecosystem and season.
Learn all you can about the northern Saskatchewan ecosystem(s) and the season you'll be travelling in to determine how best to deal with waste products.

Camping regulations.
Know the specific camping regulations of the area, like the Clearwater and Athabasca Sand Dunes Wilderness Parks. Check with SERM field offices about local conditions. There may be a fire ban due to dry conditions.

PLACE INDEX

239

index